London Review of Books

of Books

An Anthology

Edited by Jane Hindle

VERSO

London • New York

First published by Verso 1996

Verso
UK: 6 Meard Street, London W1F 0EG
US: 20 Jay Street, Suite 1010, Brooklyn, NY 11201
www.versobooks.com

Verso is the imprint of New Left Books

ISBN 1–85984–860–5
ISBN 1–85984–121–X (pbk)

British Library Cataloguing in Publication Data
A catalogue record for this book is available from the British Library

Library of Congress Cataloging-in-Publication Data
A catalog record for this book is available from the Library of Congress

Typeset by M Rules
Printed in the US

Contents

ARTS

IDEAS

DIARIES

Acknowledgements

Thanks are due to Lucy Heller, Brian McKenna and Tom Mertes for help in preparing this volume; and to the staff of the *London Review of Books* for their patience in dealing with so many queries about back issues during their working time. Responsibility for the contents of the book is Verso's alone.

J.H.

Foreword

Alan Bennett

I have written for the *London Review of Books* on and off since it first appeared in 1979; occasional book reviews and, more regularly, a diary.

In many ways it isn't a particularly English paper; it's not gossipy, cosy or cliquey; nor, unlike the *New York Review of Books*, with which it shares some of its contributors, is it snobbish, saved by a welcome streak of silliness, which surfaces in the Letters column and the occasional editorial comment. (Nothing could be less silly than the letters to the *NYRB*.)

Nor does the *LRB* feel that it has to be breathlessly up to date in the manner of the serious Sundays, though it must be gratifying that other newspapers regularly see fit to pick up its controversies and reprint its contributions.

Some of its most valuable contributions, though, remain firmly unpicked up as, ever since its inception, the *LRB* has maintained a consistently radical stance on politics and social affairs. It's one of the few publications that hasn't got shallower or gone deliberately downmarket over the years, its only concession to reader-friendliness Peter Campbell's delightful covers.

There's no similar journal on the right, unless one thinks of the *Spectator* (which I try not to do). In contrast to the un-fevered tones of the *LRB* the *Spectator* seems to be written by the kind of candidates who often used to win scholarships at Oxford and Cambridge: provocative, flashy, determined at all costs to shock and so catch the examiner's eye. The *LRB* is made of sterner stuff.

Of course, writing for it I would say all this, wouldn't I? I do have the odd beef. It's fond of football, which is a pity. I wish the Diary was more of a genuine diary and so a bit chattier; I wish the political stuff made more concessions to dizzy blonds like me; it could 'lighten up' as they say nowadays, the writers allow themselves the odd joke. Still, I know that every fortnight when I see it lying on the mat I cheer up and am grateful for it.

July 1996

Reader's Note

Perry Anderson

On occasion, the *London Review of Books* advertises itself as 'arguably the best literary magazine in the world'. This collection provides some materials for arguing about the claim – though no book-length selection of articles from a publication appearing every fortnight could hope to be adequately representative of it. Inevitably, much that is most distinctive of the *LRB* is absent here. There are no Letters, of the sort Alan Bennett rightly takes to be central to the character of the paper. There are no articles by members of its editorial staff, at their own request. There are no poems, and none of the longer pieces, in various genres, that appear from time to time. The selection is taken from the last decade only. Even within these limits, omissions that any publisher would regret outnumber inclusions.

Generalizations about any significant publication that produces around a million words a year are always liable to go somewhat wide of the mark. For any assertion (or speculation) that can be made, exceptions or contra-indications are all too likely to be found. This is especially true of a journal that relishes the unpredictable. The mysterious elegance of the *LRB* resists easy capture. Little pretence of explaining it will be made here. But some comparative remarks may help to situate the paper; although a publisher's reader (even, or perhaps especially, if an occasional contributor, from the far left of its spectrum) can only express a personal view, no better than that of any other of the paper's readers, who – if its correspondence columns are any evidence – would have different and equally decided opinions about the matter.

The *London Review* belongs to a small class of periodicals, broadsheets based on critical book reviews for a general readership, which originated in England on the eve of the Great War. The first appearance of the *Times Literary Supplement* as a separate weekly dates from 1914. The form was consolidated in the inter-war period, when the *TLS* – however suspect of complaisance in the eyes of Leavis – was by continental standards a journal of notably independent judgement. After the war, under a series of gifted editors who gave it wider ambitions, the *TLS* came to occupy a unique position as a journal of critical record, probably reaching a peak of influence somewhere in the Sixties. It was not until 1966 that the form spread to France, with the appearance of *La Quinzaine Littéraire*, and 1984 that it arrived in Italy, with the launching of *L'Indice*. But although increasingly emulated in Europe (a Hungarian version dates from the Nineties), it still remains preeminently an Anglophone phenomenon. Continental European versions tend to be less outspoken – their function on occasion coming closer to publicity than scrutiny – and less central to the local cultures.

The development beyond the classical English model came from America, when a prolonged strike at the *New York Times* in 1963, temporarily suppressing its book section, cleared a space for the launching of the *New York Review of Books*. Three innovations marked the *NYRB* from the outset. A fortnightly rather than a weekly, it allowed for substantially longer articles than the *TLS* has ever afforded; while retaining the ostensible format of a reviewing periodical, it carried essays unconnected to any books published; and it displayed an overt political profile, picked out by the signatures of its authors. The success of this formula, with its much more sharply focused and topical identity, was immediate. By the early Seventies the *NYRB* was clearly dominant, setting the terms for the field with a circulation far larger than that of the *TLS*, which now adopted the signed contribution and free-standing article within its own, otherwise still largely traditional format, bound to duties of literary record.

At the end of the decade, the scenario in New York was repeated in London, when a lengthy lock-out at the *Times* – prior to Murdoch's purchase of it – took the *Literary Supplement* off the streets for several months in 1979. The opportunity of its absence created the *London Review of Books*, launched as an offshoot of the *New York Review of Books*, and initially distributed as a local insertion folded within the latter's pages. Within a year, when the new venture was still a financial liability, the *NYRB* shed responsibility for the *London Review*. But the common origins of the two papers, and their close original connexion, make comparisons between them more or less unavoidable for readers on either side of the Atlantic today – notwithstanding the obvious discrepancies of scale and style, as of liner to clipper, between them.

The contrasts between the two papers are in part a natural function of their objective settings. The American market, five times the size of the British, supports a much larger and richer journal, endowed with ample revenues from a publishing industry accustomed to spending heavily on promotion to reach a continental readership. Flanked by thicker columns of advertisements, average articles are longer and issues more copious in the New York than in the London periodical. Besides such differences in the structure of the market, the relationship of culture to power is also quite distinct in the two societies. Since the Kennedy era no American administration has been without a substantial penumbra of intellectuals serving or aspiring to serve at the highest levels of government – advisers in office, or advisers in waiting, according to the incumbency in the White House.

The relationship of journalists and academics to government is consequently much closer than in Britain, where the UK state has never brigaded intellectuals on the same scale. Although the Thatcher years did see the first signs of a Downing Street entourage, the parliamentary system in Britain leaves less space for this phenomenon than a presidential one. The difference of working environment is visible in the two Reviews. Articles in the *NYRB* tend to have a 'policy' tone, implying potential counsel to officialdom, that is generally absent from the *LRB*, which remains much more detached from the worlds of Whitehall and Westminster.

There is also, of course, a subjective opposition between the journals. At the time the *New York Review* was launched, the war in Vietnam and ghetto riots in the US had created a radical opposition to the bipartisan establishment in America which found lively expression in its pages. But once the war in South-East Asia was over, and domestic politics had reverted to normal routines, the *NYRB* gradually settled down to the role of a critical mentor of liberal opinion in the States – acutely conscious of social problems within America and hostile to the excesses of Reaganism, but supportive of the general direction of US diplomacy in the last years of the Cold War. Today, under a Democratic presidency, the result is a highly polished but increasingly predictable formula, in which besides the illustrious writers and scholars (many from this side of the Atlantic) on which the journal has traditionally relied, semi-authorized voices of various kinds – former envoys, aides to the First Lady, bureau chiefs and the like – occupy more space than in the past.

Politically, the *London Review* started out from a position quite close to that of its progenitor. In the closing years of the Carter administration, the British equivalent was sympathy for the newly minted Social-Democratic Party. But the *LRB* soon moved in the other direction – towards a more radical stance – with the result that today the politics of the two periodicals have moved quite far apart. It would not be difficult to construct an index of the issues on which they have taken opposite sides. Some of them are reflected in this collection. Simplifying greatly, it could be said that the principal contrast lies in the unspoken aversion of the one to legacies of the Cold War largely accepted by the other. This has not been just a matter of the battle against Communism, but also of the role of the United States in ancillary theatres of conflict around the world.

Victor Kiernan's contribution to this volume, touching on the USSR, is an indication of the width of the gap on the first. Paul Foot and Edward Said on two Middle Eastern issues – the Gulf War and the Palestinian peace agreement – suggest the degree of contrast in attitudes to the second. Similarly, Tom Nairn's reflections on nationalism give short shrift to ordinary judgements in Washington or New York about the Balkans. Above all, perhaps, Christopher Hitchens's indelible portrait of Clinton is a commentary on the circumspection of the *NYRB*.[1] In ways like these, the London journal stands well to the left of its counterpart in New York. It would be an error, however, to take an instinct for a system. The contrariness prized by the *LRB* can go the other way. Progressive pieties are rarely spared, as R.W. Johnson's caustic survey of the new South Africa makes clear. Occasionally, there can even be a cross-over of transatlantic roles. The *LRB*'s gifted correspondent in Russia upheld Yeltsin's brutish rule long after the *NYRB* developed qualms about it: coverage of Chechnya has been entirely to the credit of the American rather than the British paper.

If this case is unusual, it is still a reminder that the *London Review* can never be taken for granted. This holds true even of domestic politics, where the pattern of its interventions has been most consistent. The *LRB* was born under Thatcher, and has passed all seventeen years of its life so far under a Conservative regime in Britain. Very early on, it was a courageous opponent of the Falklands War that entrenched the hegemony of the New Right, and went on to become a savage critic of Thatcherism as a nostrum for national recovery. In fact, no other journal in the country published such lethal attacks on the callousness, futility and corruption of the Conservative system of power, and the ruins of British justice under it. The collection here, alas, gives little hint of this outstanding record.[2]

---

1. For a tremulous example, compare Gary Wills, 'The Clinton Scandals', in the *New York Review*, 18 April 1996: 'Whitewater has been a scandal, but the clearest proved wrong-doing has been by politicians, journalists and (well-paid) Clinton critics . . . Clinton seems by comparison a paragon of virtue': etc.
2. See, *inter alia*, Ross McKibbin, 'Stormy and Prolonged Applause transforming itself into a Standing Ovation', 5 December 1992; Conor Gearty, 'The Party in Government' and 'Our Flexible Friends', 9 March 1995 and 18 April 1996; Ronan Bennett, 'Criminal Justice', 24 June 1993.

The *LRB*'s attitude to the Opposition, on the other hand, has always been less sharply defined. The paper lost patience with the SDP early on, and never showed much interest in either the leadership of the Labour Party, or its left. Kinnock was viewed with brusque disdain, but given the remoteness of the Opposition from office, its vicissitudes never received much attention. With New Labour now finally approaching government, however, a quite different political landscape lies ahead. The *London Review* has always shown resistance to *bien-pensant* outlooks of any kind: no paper could be further from a bandwagon mentality. It is unthinkable that it would become an ornament of the incoming regime. On the other hand, radical readers of the *LRB* would be unwise to assume they can forecast its attitude towards it.

The one article on Britain in this collection, by Ross McKibbin, is an example of the paper's ability to disconcert expectations on the Left. There are not many Labourists – let alone socialists – willing to express nostalgia for the era of Wilson and Callaghan; just as there are few civil libertarians who would dissent from Charter 88's call for a Bill of Rights – firmly rejected, however, by the paper's most regular contributor from the judiciary.[3] In different ways, texts such as these upset a certain consensus. Do they give comfort to another one? Perhaps the fact that Tony Blair, when he was still an obscure back-bencher, first laid out his political wares in the *LRB*, is no more than a historical curiosity.[4] The first direct analysis in the paper of Blair's imprint as leader of his party has been scathing.[5] But the election of a Labour government will change the atmosphere in which the *London Review* has worked, and it is doubtful if anyone outside the journal can be sure quite how it will react to the new dispensation.

There is a reason for such incalculability. The *LRB*, unlike the *New York Review*, is not an ideologically driven paper. Essentially, its freshness of judgement comes from that. Even the main political contrast between the two journals suggests this asymmetry. Positive commitment to the broad lines on which the Cold War was fought to victory is a programme. Negative avoidance of them is not. The sources of the sensibility behind the *LRB*'s escape from the hypocrisies of the 'international community' are not easy to pin down. It seems probable that they include a generational element. The *NYRB*, based in the centre of the New World Order, is some two decades older than the *LRB*. Its

3. Stephen Sedley, 'Free Speech for Rupert Murdoch', 19 December 1991.
4. Tony Blair, 'Diary', 29 October 1987.
5. Seumas Milne, 'My Millbank', 18 April 1996.

principal writers were typically formed at the height of containment. In the last couple of years, the average age of its most frequent contributors (three or more articles) has been over sixty-five. For a younger age group, in what is now a minor power, the passions of that period matter less. The background of the present editor may be relevant too. The *LRB* may be the leading journal in the West edited by a woman; with a deputy of the same sex. Politically incorrect to a fault, there has never been any feminist insistence in its pages, though the situation of women is often addressed in them. But it is reasonable to surmise that a certain indifference to the themes of the Free World may be connected to more contemporary concerns, related to gender. Whether, in the case of Mary-Kay Wilmers, Russian origins or Continental schooling have anything to do with the matter, is less obvious.

What is clear, however, is that the most significant divergence between the way the two papers are run is not a question of personnel but of editorial conception. Articles in both journals will be commissioned on a mixture of grounds, that include the reputation of the author, the urgency of the topic, the direction of the argument. But whereas for the *New York Review* the public salience of an issue is typically an imperative, in the *London Review* the style of a writer tends to come before the importance of a subject, or the affinity of a position. The latter enter into the editorial alchemy, but not at the expense of the former. The result is that the *LRB* is written to a much higher standard, in a wider range of individual idioms – some of great brilliance – than its counterpart in New York, whose prose is often at best workmanlike; but it covers a narrower and more capricious range of current affairs. The *NYRB* – to some extent, this is also true of the *TLS* today, in the capable hands of Ferdinand Mount – is much more sensitive to the scale of issues, and will always publish something moderately informative about the topics of the day, rarely failing to provide its readers with a substantial feature on any major development round the world. By contrast, the *London Review* will ignore any country or a crisis if it cannot find a writer it likes about it. On occasion, it will be a question of means – payment is modest by American standards – that draws the blank; sometimes, no doubt, of knowledge; but much more often of taste.

The greater pleasures of reading the *LRB* are thus paid for in patchier coverage. The Far East is the most striking gap. Suggestively, perhaps, the only text in this collection on Asia – the larger part of humanity – deals with a European missionary in India. Though the idea would be greeted by its staff with hilarity, to outside eyes an unconscious outline, like a faint watermark, of the Commonwealth can be traced in the distribution of the paper's attention. South Africa commands more space than all of Latin America combined. Australia has been generously represented in pages that scarcely register the existence of Japan. The Middle East features strongly; the Maghreb not at all. Even in Western Europe, the only country that can be counted on to figure in the *LRB* is Ireland: the steeples of Fermanagh and Tyrone are rarely out of sight, while the Continent more often than not remains fog-bound.

In these respects, Manhattan is a superior vantage point to Bloomsbury. The global reach of the American Empire leaves no part of the world beyond potential scrutiny, and the *New York Review*'s coverage reflects a sense of this responsibility. But talent is indeed not spread so evenly, and the products of a dutiful journalism that is invariably *à la page* risk being dull and conventional in a way that the *LRB* never is. Nor are its own interests merely wayward. If Ireland looms so much larger than Germany or France, the reason lies in a war that most of England prefers to forget. The *London Review*'s record of publication, on this least popular of all topics, puts to shame many journals to the left of it. No paper can discuss everything; where it picks an issue, it will often excel at it.

No particular line, other than abhorrence of official cant, unites the various Irish writers the *LRB* has published, of whom Colm Tóibín offers an example here. This touches on a more general feature of the paper which distinguishes it from its American counterpart. Writers are never subject to editorial direction in the *London Review*. Texts can be rejected, but once they are accepted, firm punctilio over syntax or phrase is combined with all but complete liberty of political opinion, however quixotic. No contributor here will ever find their conclusions rewritten. This lack of pressure, as an operating principle, may have some relation to the inner metabolism of the journal. Karl Miller and Mary-Kay Wilmers have been two remarkable editors of the *LRB*. But no disproportionate will sets its stamp on every page, and different members of staff – editorial, design and business – themselves write for the paper they help to produce.[6] Anyone who has worked on a

6. For examples of contributions excluded from this volume, see Peter Campbell on Tiepolo, 12 January 1995; Jeremy Harding on Zaire, 8 June 1995; Paul Laity on Murdoch's *Sun*, 20 June 1996; John Lanchester on Auden, 16 November 1995; Jean McNicol on mental health-care, 9 February 1995; Andrew O'Hagan on begging, 18 November 1993; Sarah Rigby on the Yeats sisters, 15 June 1996; John Sturrock on Camus, 8 September 1994; Mary-Kay Wilmers on meeting General Sudoplatov, 4 August 1994.

periodical will know how unlike the dynamics of this kind of office are from a more conventional hierarchy.

Such considerations particularly affect treatment of political issues, of course. The *LRB*, however, is first and foremost – as it describes itself – a literary magazine. The sharpness of its political identity comes, in fact, largely from the absence of ideological reflexes customary in the world of politics, less urgent in that of letters. But the paper is also literary in the more obvious sense that most of it is concerned with what is traditionally described as life and letters. Its approach to these is very much its own. The arts proper are dominated, as one would expect, by fiction and poetry, but not to any great degree. Painting and music have occasioned some of the journal's finest pieces: characteristic here is Nicholas Spice's beautiful reverie on muzak.[7] It is puzzling that the cinema should remain so relatively marginal – films confined to satellite fare. In this volume, the heads of the Marx Brothers stare out like some incongruous ancestral totem. Architecture features, at best, now and then. Geographically the focus is essentially Anglo-American, with the traditional side-glance at France. Chronologically, the framework is principally Late Modern, with the occasional shanghai of classic works along contemporary lines, as in the famous sapphic reading of Jane Austen by Terry Castle included here. But forays, often vivid, into earlier or less familiar terrain – say, Malory or Chamfort – form part of the balance. The mixture is less cosmopolitan than in New York, but livelier.

Ideas trace a somewhat similar pattern. Philosophy and history are better represented than natural science, where the comparison is decidedly in favour of America – the paper has never been able to attract regular contributors of the calibre of Stephen Jay Gould or Richard Lewontin. The social sciences get more of an airing, but the most striking feature of the *LRB*'s interests is a reversal of national stereotypes. Psychoanalysis enjoys much greater salience, and playful respect, in its pages than those of the *New York Review*, which has given ample space to brusque dismissals of it. The contrast of attitudes raises a wider issue. Without question politically radical, how far is the *London Review* culturally so?

That there is no necessary join between the two planes is a familiar fact of intellectual life in general. In Britain, the *New Statesman* of

---

7. By the same author, publisher of the paper, see also 'How to Play the Piano' (on Glenn Gould and Alfred Brendel) and 'Music Lessons' (Mozart), 26 March 1992 and 14 December 1995.

Kingsley Martin's time was famous for the conflict between its front and back halves – vehemently socialist politics attached to blandly conservative letters. *Scrutiny* could be said to represent the opposite combination: literary attack with political regression. These examples are not ungermane. Karl Miller, the founder of the *London Review*, was trained by Leavis at Cambridge and became literary editor of the *New Statesman*, before taking over *The Listener*. But it is just such precedents that indicate the extent to which the *LRB* departs from this pattern. From the beginning, comparable impulses have been visible in the political and literary sides of the journal, which has never segregated them in any particular order – opening (or closing) articles representing either, according to occasion.

Coverage of fiction has thus never been conventional. An established name is no guarantee of notice in the *LRB*, which regularly ignores novels by fashionable authors whose review is *de rigueur* elsewhere. On the other hand, a still unknown writer may have higher chances of attention than anywhere else in the press. Among its 'discoveries' was Salman Rushdie, whose *Midnight's Children* received its only solus review when it first appeared in the *LRB*; more recently Roddy Doyle or James Buchan. Less orthodox forms – Georges Pérec or Christine Brooke-Rose – gain equal hearing. A sense of the new, or overlooked, has from the outset been a noticeable thread in the journal. Unrepresented in this collection, contributors under the age of forty could well make up another one. Here the contrast with the *NYRB* is at its sharpest.

Nevertheless, it is fair to say that the quotient of iconoclasm in the *LRB*'s coverage of cultural life is less than in its commentary on public affairs. By the standards of the *New York Review*, the paper can look firebrand. But in a wider perspective, this is not an irreverent journal. More articles about contemporary authors sustain than question existing reputations. This is a question of a ratio, not a rule. Contrary examples are not hard to find. A famous critical piece on Brodsky would be a case in point:[8] here, however, the target is off-shore – toes closer to home are perhaps more rarely trodden on. There the subjects for demolition are more likely to be found in minor rather than major genres: as it were, P.D. James rather than V.S. Naipaul. There are a number of good reasons for this. A distaste for facile derision is understandable. It is also true that the most difficult form of criticism

8. See Christopher Reid, 'Great American Disaster', 8 December 1988.

is affirmative, and this the *London Review* at its best accomplishes extra-ordinarily well, as a glance at essays it has published on, let us say, Bishop or Nabokov reveals.[9]

Still, there remains a difference between the ways in which common editorial instincts work themselves out in the two fields principally covered by the paper. It is not altogether clear why this should be so. It might be thought that it has something to do with the necessarily closer proximity to the world of publishing than of politics of any literary review, in a metropolitan setting in the UK. This is a scene which has been transformed in the past fifteen years, as processes of concentration have enormously increased the levels of investment that publishers make in leading writers, from far larger advances to huge budgets for publicity, with promotional tours for selling books now an automatic accompaniment of literary success. The saturation of the field by big money has occurred during the period in which the *LRB* has risen – a time when the first lyric poet was to be transported by helicopter to public readings – and has changed the environment of letters, with deeply ambiguous effects for writers themselves, in ways that have yet to be fully understood.

It cannot be said the paper has so far done much to discuss them. But the reasons for its relatively pacific coexistence with this constellation do not lie in any institutional entanglement. The small grant it receives from the Arts Council regularly excites the indignation of pundits on the Right, just because the *LRB* has not conformed to established expectations – the *Sunday Times* recently calling for it to be taken away, since the journal did so little to support British writers. Far from participating in a literary scene agog with vogue and hyperbole, the *LRB* has kept what is widely perceived as a mandarin aloofness from it. Complicity with the institutions of literature, whether patrons or advertisers, is scarcely a charge that can be made against the paper.

An alternative explanation would look to the readers rather than sponsors of the paper. Common observation suggests that the average book-buyer – not, of course, the same as *LRB* subscriber – combines habitual cynicism about politicians, of any kind, with casual credence in literary reputations, however gained. It is enough to think of the relative faith accorded parliamentary debates and literary contests. It is *bon ton* to be caustic about Major or Blair, less so about Barnes or Brookner. The automatic sales of prize-winning novels speak for themselves. Are

9. See Helen Vendler, 'The Numinous Moose', 11 March 1993; John Lanchester, 'Unspeakability', 6 October 1994.

there any traces of this sensibility – which can, after all, appeal to the common-sense view that politics is always a realm of rhetorical deception, literature of imaginary truths – to be found in more sophisticated form in the paper itself?

On the face of it, it might seem there is some connexion between a stratum with this traditional outlook and the *LRB*. The journal aims at what might be called a 'common reader' in an updated Woolfian sense; that is, neither academic nor avant-garde. Although many of its contributors come from universities, and its correspondence columns include frequent jousts of high-spirited erudition, the paper tends to avoid anything that smacks of the chair. Symptomatically, footnotes – a normal and useful feature of the *New York Review* – are banished from the *LRB*, as the corns of pedantry. Likewise, while experimental writing finds a place in the journal's interests, avant-garde forms in the other arts – where they are stronger – on the whole lie beyond its range. One would be as surprised to find a consideration of Godard or Beuys in the *London Review* as a recension of Parsons (though it can always upset expectations). In ways like these the journal keeps close to the ideal of a cultivated lay readership, immune to the tics of common room or coterie.

But this rapport does not depend on any indulgence to passing consumer taste. If the *London Review* on the whole affronts received literary opinion less than political wisdom, a better guess at the reason might be the inverse weight tacitly given each. The key to the contrast seems to lie in its respective strategy of rebuke. If the paper dislikes a literary work, it will typically ignore it – whereas if it takes exception to a political process, it will roundly attack it. For many writers, of course, silence is the worst of punishments. But what the difference of treatment perhaps suggests is a conviction that inferior – indeed even fraudulent – art, however deplorable, is not a major public nuisance. Care with words is a passion of the paper – in one sense, its *raison d'être*. But in the balance of things, it might be deduced, the meretricious or pretentious matters less than the cruel and unjust. The belief that the moral welfare – and *a fortiori* political health – of a nation is ultimately in the keeping of its literature has a long history in English intellectual tradition, and has not gone away. This is the assumption that the practice of the *LRB* denies. Forgetting himself, in a gesture perhaps of over-compensation, its star political writer recently spoke of 'the transmutation of the base into gold that is the raw stuff of literature – our slight and sardonic hope'.[10] No

---

10. Christopher Hitchens, 'After-Time', 19 October 1995 – the note is quite uncharacteristic.

flourish could be further from the tenor of the paper. What distinguishes it is a discreet sense of proportion.

This could also be described as a sort of realism. The term, however, has a deflationary ring at variance with a journal whose note is anything but down-beat. It might be better to speak of its idiosyncratic form of worldliness. As editors, the peculiar genius of Karl Miller and of Mary-Kay Wilmers has been to find a tone that combines the values of the smart and the unpretentious. Smartness always risks vicinity to snobbery, what is exclusive: 'distinction' in Bourdieu's sense. Characteristically, the *LRB* averts this danger by making of style a kind of informal elegance attached to the most ordinary subjects or appurtenances of life. The kinds of writing that really mark out the journal are actually neither political nor literary-critical, but ones which reflect this ethos best. They include the curiosity about chequered individual lives, on display in this collection. Another genre, not represented below, are documentary reports from nether-worlds of social breakdown, in Orwellian vein, which have no counterpart in the *NYRB*. Last and perhaps most significant – *pace* Bennett – is the transformation by the *LRB* of the traditionally humdrum journalistic form of the Diary into a vehicle of astonishing variety, for many of the most memorable pieces the paper has published. The selection here is, if anything, drawn from the lighter contributions.

A wonderful range of writing is offered in these and other forms. Stylistically, there are unspoken limits. The delphic or serpentine are not part of the repertoire. No fear could be more foreign to the journal than 'the mischief of premature clarification', against which Fredric Jameson – whose arrival in its pages is a welcome departure from consistency – once warned. The too vehement is likewise at some discount, suspect of 'rant'. Perhaps the best way of conveying the overall climate would be to say that the paper resists any trace of *l'esprit de sérieux*, in the Sartrean sense: that is, of the portentous, high-minded, hypocritical. Against all these, its playfulness finds expression on the largest as well as smallest of topics. Emblematic in this collection are the saturnine tones of Edward Luttwak, as a 'heavy-weight' contributor.[11] It is enough to glance at the pronouncements of President Havel in the *New York Review* to see their antithesis.

---

11. See, by the same author, 'Screw You' (on Italian corruption), 19 August 1993; 'Programmed to Fail' (US Presidency), 22 December 1994; 'Does the Russian Mafia Deserve the Nobel Prize for Economics?', 3 August 1995; 'Buchanan has it Right', 9 May 1996.

The visual images of each periodical may have the final word. Among the many successful features of the *NYRB*, David Levine's drawings stand out in public impact, like some serial logo endlessly fertile in reproducing the identity of the paper. These are illustrations which play off against the text. Where the prose can be solemn or sententious, the pictures are knowing and cynical. Heroines and villains alike become so many faintly reptilian marionettes, twitching on the ends of derision. The watercolours that adorn the front of the *London Review* work in the opposite way, vivifying rather than mortifying the sense of the writing. The nonchalant wit and beauty of Peter Campbell's typewriters and wash basins, tousled bedspreads and tropical frondage, offer a *promesse de bonheur* of what lies within. Even if, in the nature of things, it is not invariably kept, the covers say more of this periodical than any other in the world.

July 1996

POLITICS

Why Fascism is the Wave of the Future

Edward Luttwak

That capitalism unobstructed by public regulations, cartels, mono-polies, oligopolies, effective trade unions, cultural inhibitions or kinship obligations is the ultimate engine of economic growth is an old-hat truth now disputed only by a few cryogenically-preserved Gosplan enthusiasts and a fair number of poorly-paid Anglo-Saxon academics. That the capitalist engine achieves growth as well as it does because its relentless competition destroys old structures and methods, thus allow-ing more efficient structures and methods to rise in their place, is the most famous bit of Schumpeteriana, even better-known than the amorous escapades of the former University of Czernowitz professor. And, finally, that structural change can inflict more disruption on work-ing lives, firms, entire industries and their localities than individuals can absorb, or the connective tissue of friendships, families, clans, elective groupings, neighbourhoods, villages, towns, cities or even nations can withstand, is another old-hat truth more easily recognised than *Gemeinschaft* and *Gesellschaft* can be spelled.

What is new-hat about the present situation is only a matter of degree, a mere acceleration in the pace of the structural changes that accompany economic growth, whatever its rate. But that, as it turns out, is quite enough to make all the difference in the world. Structural change, with all its personal upheavals and social disruptions, is now quite rapid even when there is zero growth, becoming that much faster when economies do grow. The engine turns, grinding lives and grind-ing down established human relationships, even when the car is stopped; and reaches Ferrari-like rpms at the most modest steamroller speeds.

One obvious cause of the increased destructiveness of the capitalist process is the worldwide retreat of public ownership, central planning, administrative direction and regulatory control, with all their rigidities inimical to innovation, structural change, economic growth, individual dislocation and social disruption alike. From Argentina to Zambia, with the entire Communist world in between, state ownership of economic enterprises was once accepted as the guarantor of the public interest: it is now seen as the guarantee of bureaucratic idleness, technical stagnation and outright thievery. Central planning, once honoured as the arithmetic highway to assured prosperity, is now known to be impossible simply because no group of mere humans can pre-determine next year's demand for every one of hundreds of different polymers, not to mention two to three million other items, from tower cranes to toothpicks. Administrative direction, once gloriously successful in Japan, Korea and Taiwan, at least helpful in France, a famous failure in George Brown's Britain, and ineffective or corrupt, or ineffective and corrupt, almost everywhere else, is now being abandoned (slowly) even in Japan, having been abandoned long ago almost everywhere else.

As for regulatory controls, they do not cease to increase in number, because even if steam locomotives need no longer be prevented by speed limits from causing cows to abort, many rather more recent technical novelties entail regulation, and some positively demand it – for example, to allocate frequencies. Other reasons for regulation are legion, but commercial (e.g. airline) as opposed to health and safety and environmental regulation has definitely retreated, and continues to do so. With that, efficiency increases, once-secure enterprises face the perils of the market, and employees once equally secure no longer are so.

Another partly related and equally obvious cause of accelerated structural change is the much-celebrated unification of the puddles, ponds, lakes and seas of village, provincial, regional and national economies into a single global economic ocean, and thus the increasing exposure of those same puddles, ponds, lakes and seas to the tidal waves of change in the global economic ocean, owing to the removal of import barriers, capital-export prohibitions, investment controls and licensing restrictions on the sale of transnational services; the advent and rapid geographic spread of reliable, cheap and instant telecommunications that ease the formation of new commercial relationships both materially and psychologically; the diminishing significance of transport costs due to the waning material content of commerce, as well as to the cheapening of transport with the improvement of air services, harbours and roads – notably rural roads in Asia and Latin America if not Africa; the diffusion of up-to-date technologies for the production of export goods or components, even within otherwise backward local economies; and the hammering-down of once diverse consumer preferences into uniformity by transnational mass-media imagery and advertising.

The overall effect of 'globalisation' is that any production anywhere can expand enormously, far beyond the limits of the domestic market, insofar as it is competitive – and of course that any production any-where, and the related employment, can be displaced at any time by cheaper production from someplace else in the world. Life in the global economy is full of exciting surprises – and catastrophic downfalls.

Still another cause of disproportionately rapid structural change is the rather sudden arrival of the long-awaited, very long-delayed, big increases in administrative and clerical efficiency that machines for electronic computation, data storage, reproduction and internal com-munication were supposed to ensure long ago. Partly because with generational change even senior managers can now themselves work those machines if they want to, thereby allowing them to understand their uses, abuses and non-uses; partly because more junior managers are increasingly compelled to use those machines in place of clerical help and clerical companionship; and partly because computer net-works allow managers at the next level up literally to oversee, right on their own screens, the work that their underlings are doing or not doing, thereby giving it the same transparency as assembly-line work, with the same immediate visibility of inefficient procedures, inefficient habits and inefficient employees – for all these reasons the long-awaited, long-delayed increase in the efficiency of office-work has finally arrived, exposing hitherto more secure white-collar workers to the work-place dislocations, mass firings or at least diminishing employment prospects that have long been the lot of blue-collar industrial workers in mature economies.

At the present time, for example, even though the US economy is in full recovery, white-collar job reductions by the thousand are being announced by one famous corporation after another. They call it 'restructuring' or, more fancifully, 're-engineering the corporation', and duly decorate the proceedings with the most recently fashionable management-consultant verbiage, those catchy, suggestive yet pro-foundly shallow slogans coined by the authors of the latest business-book bestsellers, who proclaim them expensively and with evangelical insistence on the corporate lecture circuit, with the result that they are then repeated with great solemnity to audiences of def-erential, bewildered employees in corporate briefings, 'workshops' and 'retreats'. But the real economies that Wall Street anticipates by bid-ding up the shares – thereby hugely rewarding mass-firing top executives who have stock options – come not from the background music of the management-consultant verbiage but rather from the displacement of telephone-answering secretaries by voice-mail systems, the displacement of letter-writing secretaries by computer word-processing and faxboards, the displacement of filing secretaries by electronic memories, and the consequent displacement of clerical supervisors; as well as from the displacement of junior administrators by automated paperflow processing and the consequent displacement of their administrative supervisors; as well as from the displacement of all the middle managers who are no longer needed to supervise the doings and undoings of both clerical and administrative employees. That is why corporations whose sales are increasing are nevertheless not adding white-collar positions; corporations whose sales are level are eliminating some white-collar positions; and corporations in decline are eliminating very many tens of thousands in the case of the sick giants IBM and GM.

Economists have long deplored the disappointing productivity gains of the administrative superstructure in advanced economies, in spite of the proliferation of office electronics. This was numerically irritating to the fraternity, because the goods-producing sector, whose productivity did keep increasing very nicely, has long been of diminishing significance, so that the productivity lag of administrative activities was lowering the numbers for the economy as a whole. Those particular economists need fret no longer: office-work productivity is finally increasing at a fast pace, allowing employers to rid themselves of employees just as fast.

There may be additional explanations for the acceleration of structural economic change. What counts, however, is the result: Schumpeter's 'creative destruction' – the displacement of old skills, trades and entire industries with their dependent localities, by more efficient new skills, trades and entire industries – is now apt to span years, often very few years, rather than generations. And that is quite enough to make the colossal difference aforementioned. The same rate of structural change that favours global prosperity, that benefits many nations and regions, and that many other nations and regions can at least cope with, now brutally exceeds the adaptive limits of individuals, families and communities. When the sons and daughters of US steelworkers, British miners or German welders must become software-writers, teachers, lawyers or for that matter shop attendants, because the respective paternal industries offer less and less employment, few of them have reason to complain. But when the same mechanisms of change work so fast that steelworkers, coalminers or welders must themselves abandon lifetime proclivities, self-images and workplace companions to acquire demanding new skills – on penalty of chronic unemployment or unskilled low-wage labour – failure and frustration are the likely results. To be sure, nothing could be more old-hat than to worry about the travails of steelworkers, miners or welders, obsolete leftovers of the hopelessly passé white/male industrial working class. So the big news is the dislocation of white-collar employment as well.

I have no statistics that measure the decline in *security* of employment. But statistics do show very clearly the impact of a weakening demand for white-collar labour in the decline of white-collar earnings. Back in the early Eighties, when trade-union officials and incurable proletariophiliacs were bitterly complaining that American workers were being extruded from well-paid industrial employment into minimum-wage 'hamburger-flipping' jobs, the lusty defenders of the infallibility of free-market economics silenced them in *Wall Street Journal* editorials by pointing to the rapid increase in 'money-flipping' jobs in banking, insurance and financial services, as well as in then-booming real-estate offices. That is where the debate ended – prematurely. By the end of 1992 more than 6.8 million Americans were duly employed in the financial sector (banking, insurance, finance and real-estate offices). One might assume, as the *Wall Street Journal* certainly presumed, that these people were a well-paid lot: but the average earnings of the 4.9 million non-supervisory employees among them were only $10.14 per hour, as compared to $10.98 for production workers in manufacturing. The 1.1 million clerks, tellers and other rank-and-file employees of banks earned much less than the sector's average at $8.19 per hour, while 48,500 of their counterparts in stock and commodity brokerages – at the very heart of 'money-flipping' – duly earned much more at $13.53 per hour. Still, if any disemployed industrial workers did equip themselves with the obligatory broad red suspenders to seek their fortunes on Wall Street, they would have found the rewards surprisingly modest.

At a time when it was forever being explained that it was silly to worry about the decline of manufacturing jobs in the age of 'services', the much larger story is that service employees throughout the US economy are actually paid much less than their counterparts still holding manufacturing jobs. Moreover the average hourly earnings of service employees have been going down for years in real dollars net of inflation. In the entire retail trade, for example, from department stores to street-corner news-stands, the 17.7 million 'non-supervisory' employees earned an average of $6.88 per hour in November 1990. In fact, their hourly average went down from a peak of $6.20 in 1978 to

$5.04 in 1990 in constant 1982 dollars. To be sure, the retail trade is full of teenagers still in school who work only on weekends and holidays, and married women who work only part-time. That can be expected to depress earnings, and it does. Besides, many retail employees get commissions that are not reported to the collectors of labour statistics. But neither part-timers with modest demands nor commissions are to be found in transportation and public utilities (including railroads, local bus services, mass transit, trucking, courier services, river barges, airlines, telephone companies etc). Nevertheless, the 4.9 million non-supervisory employees in that entire sector had average hourly earnings of $13.07 in November 1990 – substantially more, $2.09 more as it happens, than their counterparts in manufacturing, but still substantially less than those same employees had earned in the Seventies in real money. In fact their earnings peaked in 1978 at $11.18 per hour in constant 1982 dollars – as opposed to $9.58 at the end of 1990 in those same dollars.

In the varied mass of service employees as a whole, there are predictable highs, e.g. the 135,400 non-supervisors in film-making who earned $18.87 per hour, and the rank-and-file employees of computer and data-processing services at $15.29 per hour, who numbered only 87,700 in 1972, but reached the impressive total of 637,700 by the end of 1990. The lows are just as predictable. The 1.3 million in hotel/motel non-supervisory jobs were paid only $7.14 per hour on average – though quite a few also receive tips, no doubt. But nobody tips the 436,900 line employees of detective, armoured-car and security agencies who earned only $6.35 per hour on average. From advertising to zoo-keeping many service jobs paid better than that, of course, but the average earnings of *all* non-farm, non-government employees were less, at $10.17 per hour, than those of manufacturing workers at $10.98 – so the brave new service economy obviously pays less than old-fashioned industry. Even that is only half the story, because the higher volatility of services makes those jobs less and less secure. In other words, the relative impoverishment of those working lives is accompanied by even more dislocation.

Even bigger news is the dislocation of managerial lives. That is the latest trend in the always progressive United States – and it is most definitely a structural trend, rather than merely cyclical. Now that the dull-safe 'satisficing' corporation (moderate dividends, moderate salaries, steady, slow growth) is almost extinct, top managers as a class earn very much more than before, rank-and-file managers who can keep their jobs earn rather less, and it is very difficult for those managers who are forced out to find any comparable jobs elsewhere. Few are destined to grace the pages of business journals as entrepreneurial wonders, not born but made by unemployment. Some adjust undramatically if painfully, by accepting whatever middle-class jobs they can get, normally with reduced pay. Others are much worse off. The 50–55 year old male, white, college-educated former exemplar of the American Dream, still perhaps living in his lavishly-equipped suburban house, with two or three cars in the driveway, one or two children in $20,000 per annum higher education (tuition, board and lodging – all extras are extra) and an ex-job 're-engineered' out of existence, who now exists on savings, second and third mortgages and scant earnings as a self-described 'consultant', has become a familiar figure in the contemporary United States. They still send out résumés by the dozen. They still 'network' (i.e. beg for jobs from whomever they know). They still put on their business suits to commute to 'business' lunches with the genuine article or to visit employment agencies, but at a time when more than 10 per cent of the Harvard graduates of the class of 1958 are unemployed, lesser souls in the same position have little to hope for.

Just in case the sentimental anecdotage is unpersuasive, or seems absurdly disproportionate as compared to the plight of, say, indebted Indian peasants, there are now statistics that quantify the downward slide of the entire population from which the class of middle managers is drawn. The median earnings of *all* males in the 45–54 age bracket with four years of higher education – some two million Americans, all but 150,000 of them white – actually peaked in 1972 at some $55,000 in 1992 dollars; they stagnated through three downward economic cycles until 1989, before sharply declining to $41,898 by 1992. From other evidence we know that those numbers average out two phenomena that are equally unprecedented in the American experience: in that same population, the combined total income of the top 1 per cent of all earners increased sensationally, and the combined total of the bottom 80 per cent declined sharply. Again, that implies in one way or another a more-than-proportionate quantum of dislocation. Needless to say, individual working lives cannot be dislocated without damaging families, elective affiliations and communities – the entire moss of human relations which can only grow over the stones of economic stability. Finally, it is entirely certain that what has already happened in the United States is happening or will happen in every other advanced economy, because all of them are exposed to the same forces.

In this situation, what does the moderate Right – mainstream US Republicans, British Tories and all their counterparts elsewhere – have to offer? Only more free trade and globalisation, more deregulation and structural change, thus more dislocation of lives and social relations. It is only mildly amusing that nowadays the standard Republican/Tory after-dinner speech is a two-part affair, in which part one celebrates the virtues of unimpeded competition and dynamic structural change, while part two mourns the decline of the family and community 'values' that were eroded precisely by the forces commended in part one. Thus at the present time the core of Republican/Tory beliefs is a perfect non-sequitur. And what does the moderate Left have to offer? Only more redistribution, more public assistance, and particularist concern for particular groups that can claim victim status, from the sublime peak of elderly, handicapped, black lesbians down to the merely poor.

Thus neither the moderate Right nor the moderate Left even recognises, let alone offers any solution for, the central problem of our days: the completely unprecedented personal economic insecurity of working people, from industrial workers and white-collar clerks to medium-high managers. None of them are poor and they therefore cannot benefit from the more generous welfare payments that the moderate Left is inclined to offer. Nor are they particularly envious of the rich, and they therefore tend to be uninterested in redistribution. Few of them are actually unemployed, and they are therefore unmoved by Republican/Tory promises of more growth and more jobs through the magic of the unfettered market: what they want is security in the jobs they already have – i.e. precisely what unfettered markets threaten.

A vast political space is thus left vacant by the Republican/Tory non-sequitur, on the one hand, and moderate Left particularism and assistentialism, on the other. That was the space briefly occupied in the USA by the 1992 election-year caprices of Ross Perot, and which Zhirinovsky's bizarre excesses are now occupying in the peculiar conditions of Russia, where personal economic insecurity is the only problem that counts for most people (former professors of Marxism-Leninism residing in Latvia who have simultaneously lost their jobs, professions and nationalities may be rare, but *most* Russians still working now face at least the imminent loss of their jobs). And that is the space that remains wide open for a product-improved Fascist party, dedicated to the enhancement of the personal economic security of the broad masses of (mainly) white-collar working people. Such a party could even be as free of racism as Mussolini's original was until the alliance with Hitler, because its real stock in trade would be corporativist restraints on corporate Darwinism, and delaying if not blocking barriers against globalisation. It is not necessary to know how to spell *Gemeinschaft* and *Gesellschaft* to recognise the Fascist predisposition engendered by today's turbo-charged capitalism.

7 April 1994

A Hard Dog to Keep on the Porch

Christopher Hitchens on Bill Clinton

Oxford 1968–9. In the evenings, after dinner in hall, groups would take shape informally in the quad. There was Richard Cobb's lot, making for the buttery and another round of worldly banter. There was this or that sodality, taking a cigarette break or killing time before revision. There was my own cohort, usually divided between the opposing tasks of selling the factional newspaper, or distributing the latest leaflet, or procuring another drink. And there were the Americans. I remember James Fenton noticing how they would cluster a little closer together and talk in a fashion slightly more intense. Mainly Rhodes or Fulbright scholars, they had come from every state of the union with what amounted to a free pass. The Yanks of Oxford were accustomed to going home and taking up a lot of available space in the American academy, in the American media and in American politics or diplomacy. Yet for this contingent, the whole experience had become deeply and abruptly fraught. They were far from home and they were deeply patriotic. You could tell that they had been told by their selection committees, before embarking on the Atlantic crossing, that they should comport themselves as ambassadors and emissaries. But those local lawyers and Rotarians and Chambers of Commerce had not prepared them to hurry up, finish their studies and take ship to Vietnam.

It's often been said since that these young men would not have been bothered by the war if it were not for their own impending draft notices, and that they were quite prepared to let the underclass be conscripted in their stead. This is quite simply a slander. The arguments and conversations of those years disclosed a group of very serious and principled people. They did not like to criticise their own country while overseas, but they could not bear to see it befouled by warmongers and racists. All of them could see the self-evident connection between the rise of the war party in Washington and the defeat of civil rights and the 'Great Society'. Many of them came from families where military service was a proud axiom. All of them felt guilty and indebted for their luck. At 46 Leckford Road, in a scruffy house where many of them hung out, there were debates of a high quality. (There were also biscuits and brownies made out of marijuana, which meant that you didn't have to inhale if you didn't desire.) Frank Aller, the brilliant scholar of China who was one of the chief ornaments of that address, later took his despair and disillusion to the length of self-slaughter. Most were more sanguine. I don't especially remember Bill Clinton, perhaps because he was one of the more moderate and conciliatory types. But I remember several of his girlfriends and I remember being impressed at a house that boasted its own duplicator for the production of Vietnam Moratorium leaflets. And now I live in Washington and I see the old Rhodes Class of those years going about its business: Robert Reich running the Labour Department and Strobe Talbott managing US-Russian relations from Foggy Bottom and Ira Magaziner trying to recover from his moment as person-in-charge of Bill and Hillary's health care 'reform'.

When I want to recall those Leckford Road days, I can turn up a letter that William Jefferson Clinton wrote, on 3 December 1969, to a certain Colonel Holmes of the University of Arkansas Reserve Officers Training Corps. Clinton wanted to clarify his attitude to the military draft:

> Let me try to explain. As you know, I worked for two years in a very minor position on the Senate Foreign Relations Committee. I did it for the experience and the salary but also for the opportunity, however small, of working every day against a war I opposed and despised with a depth of feeling I had reserved solely for racism in America before Vietnam . . . Because of my opposition to the draft and the war, I am in great sympathy with those who are not willing to fight, kill and maybe die for their country (i.e. the particular policy of a particular government) right or wrong.

(My friend Todd Gitlin, author of the best book on this period, points out the ranking of 'fight, kill and maybe die' as the correct order in which anti-war people listed their objections.) But towards the close of this telling letter, Clinton explains to Holmes why it is that, after all, he does not propose to become a full-blown refusenik:

> The decision not to be a resister and related subsequent decisions were the most difficult of my life. I decided to accept the draft in spite of my beliefs for one reason: *to maintain my political viability within the system*. For years I have worked to prepare myself for a political life characterised by both practical political ability and concern for rapid social progress. (Emphasis mine.)

Since Clinton went on both to dodge the actual draft *and to* be something of an anti-war activist, this missive from an old head on young shoulders has been adduced as the early indication of a desire, if not a need, to have everything both ways. In the 1992 Presidential elections the letter surfaced, not as the confirmation of an early stand on principle, but as proof of an ingrained tendency towards excuse-making and evasion. And it set people remembering. When *had* they first noticed Clinton's talent for being all things to all men? Even as Cecil Rhodes's legatees were taking the liner across to Southampton in October 1968, and viewing their own destiny with a high seriousness and purity, they found themselves sharing a ship with Bobby Baker. Mr Baker, who was Lyndon Johnson's bag-man and fixer within the Democratic Party and throughout the capital city, had been convicted in a sensational trial of tax fraud and conspiracy. His attorney, the no less legendary Edward Bennett Williams (known as 'the man to see'), was in effect sending him off on a cruise while he played out the appeals procedure. Confronted with this gargoyle of the old gang, many of the Rhodes boys kept a fastidious distance. 'But Clinton was there,' in one account, 'standing at Baker's side, soaking in tales of power and intrigue . . . It was while watching his performance with Bobby Baker that Strobe Talbott said he first understood Clinton's "raw political talent".'

New Hampshire, January 1992. Before a single vote has been cast, the prestige press has announced that the Democrats have their 'front runner'. This is Bill Clinton, 'New Democrat' and Governor of Arkansas. In the two invisible primaries, which are the press primary and the fund-raising or 'money' primary, he has passed every test with aplomb. Tough on welfare and crime, 'flexible' on defence and foreign policy, solid for Israel, reputedly 'good' with black people, he is moreover young and once shook hands with John F. Kennedy. At the bar of the Sheraton Wayfarer in Manchester, the HQ of the travelling press corps, most correspondents report that their editors only want good news about the new consensus candidate. And, generally, that's what they have been getting and transmitting. A flap has, however, broken out. A classic blonde troublemaker named Gennifer Flowers has gone public. Damage control is in progress, but things look a touch wobbly. (This is the best-rendered chapter in *Primary Colors.*)

Outside a stricken factory somewhere downstate, Clinton is confronted by a host of questions about his Little Rock love-nest. He looks like a dog being washed. Since I don't care about Flowers, I attempt to change the subject – never an easy thing to do at a pack-job press conference. I want to know about the execution of Ricky Ray Rector. Rector was a black cop-killer in Arkansas, lobotomised by a gunshot wound. He no longer knew his own name, and met most of the standard conditions for clemency. But Clinton left New Hampshire specifically to return to Arkansas and have him put to death. He did so in order to demonstrate, or 'signal', that he was not soft on crime. Rector's condition was such that, as he left his cell for the last time, he saved the dessert from his last meal 'for later'. Strapped to a trolley for a lethal injection, he actually assisted the executioners in their hour-long search for a viable vein in which to place the lethal catheter. (He thought they were doctors trying to cure him.)

This, coupled with Clinton's ostentatious membership of an all-white golf-club, strikes me as a more pressing issue of morals and 'character' than *l'affaire* Flowers. But Clinton, who at first looks as if he welcomes a change of subject, doesn't care for this one. He turns his back and marches away. Later on television, his flack says that everything else is a diversion from the Governor's real programme, which is 'a tax cut for the middle class'. Rector is never mentioned again in the entire course of the campaign. There is a brief subsequent flap, when a few questions are asked about land-deals in Arkansas, and a bankrupt savings-and-loan concern, and the role played in both by a law firm associated with Hillary Clinton. There's also something about a shady airport in Arkansas, said to have been used for murky transactions with Central America. But since these questions come from the *Nation* magazine, and from Ralph Nader and Jerry Brown, they can be, and are, easily shrugged off as 'marginal'. Understandably, the Republicans display little relish for dragging up the savings-and-loan scandal, or for raising the question of campaign donations, or for investigating property speculation. And as for reopening the Iran-Contra scandal . . . forget it. A sort of Mutual Assured Destruction guarantees that neither party will breach protocol on these questions. Instead, the Bush campaign concentrates on the old 'draft-dodging' issue, and enlists the help of John Major's mediocre Central Office in rummaging through old passport files. They fail to gauge the extent to which the New Democrat has left all that behind him. Now, what would have happened if Bush or Reagan had executed a retarded black man in order to win a primary? Consensus politics has an interior logic of its very own.

Washington DC, January 1993. On the Mall, there is what they call 'A People's Inaugural'. Before a huge, informal and mainly young crowd, Aretha Franklin sings 'Respect' and Bob Dylan makes a surprise appearance to perform 'Chimes of Freedom'. Clinton and his young family appear to sing along with both. There is much heady talk about the end of the Eighties, that decade of greed and self-delusion and secret government. But if the atmosphere on the Mall is populist, the tone of the real Inaugural is anything but. Pamela Harriman gives a welcome-to-Washington party in Georgetown, which features wall-to-wall lobbyists and power-brokers of the most traditional stripe. Campaign contributors are received and rewarded in proportion to the timeliness, and the size, of their subscriptions. The first harvest of cabinet appointments shows Georgetown beating the Mall every time. Lloyd Bentsen, the prince of Capitol influence-peddlers, gets the Treasury. Alan Greenspan, the reactionary fan of Ayn Rand who has roosted at the Federal Reserve these many years, is beseeched to 'stay on'. Winston Lord, an old Kissinger hand, gets the Asia desk at State. Les Aspin, a plaything of the military contractors, is awarded to the Pentagon. And so it goes. Within a very few months, according to Bob Woodward's book *The Agenda*, Clinton is exploding with rage at the way that Washington is running him, rather than the other way about. He has been told that the bond market will not permit some marginal adjustment on which he had staked 'credibility'. This means, he advises his team, that they are all 'Eisenhower Republicans' now. Have a care, Mr President. Eisenhower was quite an activist chief executive. He built the interstate highway system and warned about the growth of the 'military-industrial complex'. It may be rash to invite such bold comparisons.

The jokes about Clinton are always the same joke. 'When he comes to a fork in the road,' writes Paul Greenberg of the *Arkansas Democrat-Gazette*, 'he takes it.' He wants to have his dozen Big Macs and eat them too. And so forth. (I myself have contributed a one-liner: 'Why did Bill Clinton cross the road? Because he wanted to get to the middle.') In earnest sessions with interviewers, the most overtly therapeutic of which was given to *Good Housekeeping*, Clinton himself has mused aloud about his dysfunctional childhood and his hunger and thirst for approval. Is there a connection between the essence of Clinton and the essence of Clintonism? Does either of them possess an essence?

The answer is yes, if you make the simple assumption that Clinton's consistent aim has been a national shift to the centre-right. This of course is the very assumption that the consensus press and the Republican opposition are incapable of making. It is also an assumption that the liberal mainstream – and its Clintonoid centrepiece – is reluctant to see spelled out too starkly. But if it is sound, it explains Clinton's past and present, and also clarifies his strategy for gaining a second term. As I write, the President has the GOP more or less punching air. Instead of worrying about being an Eisenhower or Rockefeller

Republican, he has embraced the idea. He has even hired a Republican political strategist, Dick Morris, to guide his campaign. And Mr Morris has been sharing poll data with Robert Dole, who was until recently Clinton's complicit partner in the management of the Hill. Only the other week, speaking in Delaware, Dole repeated his call: 'One reason to elect me in November '96 is to keep the promises President Clinton made to you in 1992.' The gap between New Democrat and Moderate Republican could not be narrower, and probably never has been. So all those jokes, about Bill being adamant for drift, are to some extent at the expense of those who make them. When it came to a choice – between Sixties idealism and Bobby Baker; between Ricky Ray Rector and the opinion polls; between the crowd on the Mall and the crowd in Georgetown – Clinton was never anything but swift and decisive.

The origins of his protean and malleable politics can be traced partly to his upbringing, and partly to the morphology of his home state. Arkansas is a bizarre polity which on a single night in 1968 cast its vote like this: Winthrop Rockefeller for governor, William Fulbright for senator and George Wallace for President. It has correctly been described as one of the richest little poor states in the union. Today's Little Rock has a skyline of modern corporatism, housing numerous local monopolies such as Tyson Foods, the Worthen Bank, the Stephens Corporation and Wal-Mart. In the Quapaw district of town, the Flaming Arrow Club is the meeting point for lobbyists and legislators. (Gennifer Flowers used to be a lounge-singer at this joint, but more to the point is its role as the site of Governor Clinton's off-the-record 'budget breakfast' meetings.) Go south into the Delta, however, and you are in what H.L. Mencken once termed 'the hookworm and incest belt'. Here, sharecropper poverty and indebtedness are endemic, and the racial pattern is almost cartoonish. Prison farms are policed by armed men on horseback. Arkansas is a 'right-to-work' state, which means union-busting and a Third World minimum wage. It is also the only state of the union without a civil rights statute. Elected by the lower-income voters, Clinton soon became the favourite son of the high-rolling stakeholders. The contradiction is best expressed by the white lie he often tells about coming from 'a little place called Hope'. No politician could reasonably be expected to pass up such a line, but though Clinton was technically born in the dull hamlet of Hope, Arkansas, he properly hails from the town of Hot Springs. And if Hope is a place of tin-roof piety and stagnation, Hot Springs is a wide-boy's town full of hustlers and whores and easy money. I once went to a Labour Day rally there; Bill and Hillary both spoke. The future First

Lady was breathless with enthusiasm. 'When Bill first brought me here, I said to him: "Just look at all these *small businesses*."' Yes indeedy, ma'am. Ready cash preferred. Bill's mother, Virginia Kelley, was a doyenne of the beauty-parlours, bars and race-tracks of this open city. His father, William Jefferson Blyth, was a smaller-time player in the travelling salesman line. Before his death in a roadside drainage ditch, he put flesh on the bones of every Dogpatch cliché about the region. ('You know you're from Arkansas if you find that you attend family reunions in search of a date.') He formed sexual alliances with two sisters of the same family at the same time, while married to yet another woman, and fathered progeny with unusual casualness. His death left Virginia at the mercy of an alcoholic wife-beating successor.

They say that in the boyhood of Judas, Jesus was betrayed. The saying itself shows the treacherous ground on which psycho-history is based. But in the closing days of his campaign for the Presidency, Clinton began to tell the story of how he stood up to the brutal step-father. Which makes it the odder that he then went to the registry and asked to take this man's surname. If you read the Clinton family profile 'in neutral', so to speak, you would imagine yourself studying a problem kid from a ghetto, where it is a wise child who knows his own father. Yet Clinton's great contribution to American domestic politics has been his stress on the deplorable lack of moral continence among the underclass. His mantra, as a leader of the conservative Democratic Leadership Council, was 'to end welfare as we know it'. In pursuit of this goal, he has advanced a spending bill which removes perhaps some millions of American children from the welfare rolls. Even Senator Daniel Patrick Moynihan, who first opened the argument about the cultural pathology of poverty when he was working for the Nixon Administration, has professed himself appalled at the callousness and want of discrimination which characterise the new dispensation. Marion Wright Edelman, one of Washington's best-loved advocates of civil rights, chairs the Children's Defence Fund. Hillary Clinton used to be the honorary president of this organisation, and drew on the experience for her sentimental book *It Takes a Village, And Other Lessons Children Teach Us.* (This book, inter alia, recommends abstinence from sex until those troubled teen years are behind us.) Now, Ms Edelman complains that she cannot get her phone-calls to the White House returned. It is important, therefore, to bear in mind that the Clintons do not seek *everybody's* approval. Below a certain threshold of power and income, they can be quite choosey.

It seems to me that they acquired this principle of selectivity while operating in Arkansas. There are, currently, three Clintonoid scandals still in play from that period. The first, which goes under the generic title of 'Whitewater', has to do with real-estate speculation. The second, which is vulgarly called 'Troopergate', has to do with Clinton's sexual appetite as recalled by his former bodyguards. The third concerns Mena airport. Taking these in random order, we find that no member of the Clinton entourage doubts the essence of the trooper testimony. The Governor was, in the words of a local saying, a hard dog to keep on the porch. This would scarcely be worth mentioning if the leaders of official American feminism had not rallied to his defence and rallied, furthermore, by pointing to the relative trashiness of some of the women who have complained. Excuse me, but it is surely uneducated and impressionable girls like Paula Jones – vulnerable to predatory superiors and working on short-term contracts – for whose protection the sexual harassment laws were specifically designed. As ever, it is the class element in this dismal narrative that bears watching.

On Whitewater, it has become quite the liberal fashion to say that no laws were broken and that the investigation has been allowed to draw out its length for an unconscionable period of time. It may be too early to say that no laws were broken, but it's not by any means too early to say that this defence has a Reagan-era ring to it. And so do some of the business deals involved. 'If Reaganomics works at all,' wrote Hillary Rodham in a 1981 letter to the ill-starred speculator Jim McDougal, 'Whitewater could become the Western hemisphere's Mecca.' The proven record of the Whitewater partnerships is one of revolving doors, influence-brokering and greasy palms; that all this is legal in American politics is itself the scandal. As for the protraction of the hearings, these could have been wound up in a matter of weeks if it were not for skilful lawyering by the White House, and the seemingly endless outbreaks of amnesia that overcame its normally needle-sharp witnesses. The fact that the case has become an adventure-playground for right-wing paranoids is not conclusive in itself, as some fastidious commentators effect to believe. Several senior White House Arkansans have already had to make hasty departures from politics, some of them clutching Go To Jail cards, and I would not expect these to be the last. Moreover, people with spin skills like the Clintons do not act as if there is something to hide if there is actually nothing to hide. Mrs Clinton in one private missive expressed alarm that an investigation might involve the disclosure of ten years' worth of campaign financing in Arkansas. That's probably the thing to keep your eye on. In Little Rock and its gamey Hot Springs counterpart, the Clintons learned the dirty rudiments of retail politics – and how to wholesale them. And it seems pretty obvious that they brought these talents, and these operators, to Washington. For an example of how the small-time connects to the big-time, one need look no further than a recently-leaked memo, the disclosure of which moved the Oval Office to a paroxysm of fury and mole-hunting.

At the 'anti-terrorism' summit in Cairo last March, Clinton had a private meeting with Boris Yeltsin. An undertaking was given to provide American support for Mr Yeltsin's re-election, and to accept his repeatedly-broken word that the filthy war in Chechnya was being brought to a close. This aspect of business concluded, Clinton raised another outstanding matter. Russia had been threatening to prohibit imports of frozen poultry. 'This is a big issue,' says Clinton according to the notes of the meeting, 'especially since 40 per cent of US poultry is produced in Arkansas.' When Tyson Foods first bankrolled a governor's depleted campaign chest, the company can barely have hoped for representation at this level: chickens for Chechens as you might say. (The whole finger-lickin' subject died within a few days, since Don Tyson is also a major benefactor of Bob Dole's. Mr Tyson's executive suite is an exact scale-model of the Oval Office, except that the door handles are sculpted in the shape of hens' eggs. Recall what I wrote earlier about Mutual Assured Destruction.)

The third and most suggestive delayed-reaction charge from Arkansas receives the least attention. It also gives the right-wing paranoids the most trouble, since it is in essence a tale of depredation by right-wing paranoids. Reduced to its rudiments, the allegation is this. During the scoundrel time of the Central American war, an off-the-record airport in the Ouachita mountains of Arkansas was used to fly illegal weapons to the Nicaraguan Contras. The returning planes were stuffed with cocaine, partly to finance the gun-running and partly to pay off (and also to implicate and silence) those who took part in it. The least you can say for this story is that there is a lot to be said for it. I have myself interviewed Trooper L.D. Brown of Governor Clinton's police *équipe*, who claims to have been on more than one of the flights. He was able to show me documents given to him in Clinton's own handwriting, and to substantiate a good deal of what he alleged in other ways. And it is a fact that Clinton allowed the Arkansas National Guard to be sent to Central America at a time when other Democratic governors, such as Michael Dukakis of Massachusetts, were refusing the poisoned chalice. Indeed, it was Clinton's flexibility in the matter of this criminal and covert war (not unlike his subsequent haste to change sides and be on the winning side in the Gulf conflict) that won him the good opinion of several 'responsible' Establishment institutions, of the sort which never give up in the search for a trustworthy Democrat.

There are micro as well as macro elements in the Mena scandal, since one of the narcotics dealers involved was a man named Dan Lasater, a bond-dealer of the sort often described as 'colourful'. Lasater, too, was a major Clinton fund-raiser and (until his imprisonment) a supplier of controlled substances to the President's chaotic brother Roger. As in the case of his disordered family and courtship background, so with his amateur experience on the drug scene: once in Washington Bill Clinton proselytises for 'family values' and 'the war on drugs' with the zeal of a convert. Not since Nixon has the so-called drug war been prosecuted so sternly. Clinton all but fired his own Surgeon-General merely for re-commending a debate on decriminalisation, and has now delegated narcotics 'interdiction' to a senior member of the military. Bills on drugs and 'terrorism' have stripped protection from citizens and defendants in a way that would never have been countenanced if the Democrats and liberals were in opposition. In his first re-election cam-paign video, Clinton announced himself the candidate of law and order and capital punishment.

Make no mistake, it is this version of 'realism' that animates the Clintons. Rather than be attacked from the right, they will invariably move to occupy the conservative ground. This has been as true of the little things, like prayer in public schools, as it has been of the larger issues like the demolition of the welfare state. In foreign policy matters, and on questions relating to the Pentagon or the CIA, Clinton has done rather more than demonstrate an impeccable orthodoxy. He has actually given the defence chiefs a larger budget than they asked for, and has kept in being some lavish 'military Keynesian' projects (like the B-1 bomber and the Seawolf submarine) which the strategists have declared obsolete. During his campaign against Bush, Clinton ran against him from the right on two important matters – namely, Cuba and Israel. On Cuba, the Bush Administration opposed a Congress-ional amendment which extended the American boycott to third countries and foreign companies trading with Havana. Clinton flew to Miami and – once again in return for a handsome campaign contribu-tion – adopted the position of the more *farouche* exile leaders. Similarly, Bush and James Baker were anxious to see Yitzhak Shamir's regime of petrified intransigence give way to Rabin and Peres. They therefore declined to make an unconditional loan guarantee to Israel, and as a result found themselves in a rugged domestic squabble with 'the lobby' in Washington. Clinton took the earliest possible opportunity of saying that he was for giving the loan guarantee without strings. Again, perhaps, the psycho-historian could posit, in Clinton's strenuous eagerness on matters hawkish, an element of over-compensation for his 'draft-dodging' past. Certainly the organised gay vote, which came out decisively for Clinton in 1992 because of his pledge to end discrimination in the Armed Forces, was to find out speedily that, when confronted with anything like uniformed opposition, the supposed Commander-in-Chief would start to cry loudly before he had even been hurt.

But political hypotheses may be more trustworthy than psychological ones. At Georgetown University, Clinton's mentor was one Professor Carroll Quigley, known to us old Special Relationship hands as the author of arcane but original works on the Anglo-American ruling class. (Some of his books now have a half-life in those wobbly Pat Robertson circles which affect a belief in 'international banking' as the engine of history. He was also a great expert on the power and ramification of the Rhodes Scholarship system.) In the course of his 1992 nomination speech, Clinton cited Quigley as a great influence. Could he have been thinking of Quigley's immense *Tragedy and Hope*, a book which argued for the domination of parties by business interests? As Quigley phrased it, perhaps a little too bluntly for some tastes:

> The argument that the two parties should represent opposed ideals and policies . . . is a foolish idea. Instead, the two parties should be almost identical, so that the American people could throw the rascals out at any election without leading to any profound or extensive shifts in policy. The policies that are vital and necessary for America are no longer subjects of significant disagreement, but, are disputable only in detail, procedure, priority or method.

Quigley was alluding principally to the durable consensus on grand strategy, military alliance and trade, but his argument applies with equal force to the home front. Here, the Clintons only ever made one challenge to the status quo. Inspired by the obvious popularity and also the electoral potential of the idea, they proposed a system of universal health care. Now it may be true (as I think) that nothing could have saved George Bush in 1992. But the change in the political tempo began with a remarkable Democratic triumph in Pennsylvania, orchestrated by James Carville and based like all good campaigns on the ceaseless iteration of a single note. There were forty million Americans without health insurance. No comparable society except South Africa lacked a health system. (Or, as Carville put it with a clever appeal to a different kind of populism: 'If a criminal has the legal right to a lawyer, working Americans should have the legal right to a doctor.')

Of course, the cry of 'socialised medicine' is one of the hoariest slogans of the American Right, so it had to be expected that there would be a political confrontation. But for once, the all-important opinion polls were aligned solidly and consistently with reform. There was expertise to spare among specialists on the subject. One group in particular, based at the Harvard Medical School, proposed the equivalent of a Canadian 'single payer' or National Health plan, combining a wide repertory of benefits with a range of choice between different physicians. The Congressional Budget Office furthermore certified such a plan as the most cost-effective, not least because it would end the fantastically wasteful duplication and competition spawned by America's insurance racket. At an early White House meeting between the Harvard group and Hillary Clinton, the case for a straightforward National Health Bill was put by Dr David Himmelstein. As he recalls the exchange:

> It was evident Hillary was thinking a lot about politics. Can you realistically tell me, she asked, that there are any big powers that support 'single payer' and that can take on the insurance industry's lobbying and advertising budget? I said: 'About 70 per cent of the people in the US favour something like a single-payer system. With Presidential leadership, that can be an overwhelming force.' She said: 'David, tell me something interesting.'

So at the very beginning of the argument, the only possible winning hand was thrown into the discard. The end of the argument – the utter humiliation of the Clinton Administration on Capitol Hill and the relegation of health care to the bottom of the political heap – could not, even in pragmatic terms, have been worse than a stand on principle would have been. Except that to contrast pragmatism with principle in this old-fashioned manner might be a mistake. What if the collapse in the face of the insurance racket *is* the principle? In order to try and construct a more centrist consensus of their own, the Clintons coined the phrase 'managed competition' to describe the highly bureaucratised free market in health care that they proposed. (Something like Milton Friedman's famous allusion to 'socialism for the rich and free enterprise for the poor'.) That term might well do duty for the whole menu of Clintonian rule, from the free-trade agreements with Mexico and Japan, to the care and feeding of the war economy, the distribution of favours for clients like Yeltsin and the quid pro quo relationship between tax exemptions and corporate campaign contributions.

There almost certainly is a relation between Clinton the man and Clintonism as politics, though it may not be as obvious as it seems. If one had to nominate a hinge moment, it would probably be the last days of the George McGovern campaign, in Texas, in 1972. Clinton was sent down to the Lone Star state, along with his friend Taylor Branch, at a moment when the Nixon forces seemed almost unstoppable. (A subsequent post-Watergate myth has depicted the press as anti-Nixon during this period. In point of fact, the general refusal of the media to discuss Nixon's illegal use of state power was one of the most striking features of the election.) Taylor Branch, later the outstanding biographer of Martin Luther King, remembers the dying days of McGovernism very clearly. The Texas Democratic Party was riven with faction, and generally uninterested in the pro-civil rights and anti-war position taken by the young volunteers from up North. More time was spent in hand-holding, log-rolling and back-scratching than on 'the issues'. But as Branch suddenly noticed, his friend Bill was very good indeed at the back-slapping and palm-greasing bit. As the vote drew near, senior Texas Democrats like Lloyd Bentsen and John Connally either deserted the McGovern campaign or joined the front organisation calling itself 'Democrats for Nixon'. It was from this sort of timber that Clinton and others were later to carpenter the Democratic Leadership Council. He evidently decided, for whatever mixture of private and public reasons, never to be on the losing side again.

In other words, Clinton's ambition became the same thing as his politics, and his approval rating from the powers-that-be became the same thing as his electability. From then on, the only test of courage was the ability – which had to be repeatedly demonstrated – to treat his own former principles and core supporters with distance and even contempt. He showed himself to be a swift learner. In many ways, then, his finest hour and his most maturing moment was his throaty speech at Richard Nixon's graveside. Robert Dole cried. Governor Pete Wilson of California also cried. Clinton masked his tears but observed huskily that Nixon was a small-town self-made American who should be judged on his 'whole record' and not just on one regrettable episode. (As I said to Mrs Clinton on the one occasion I was able to mention this, I couldn't agree more. Breaking off from a discussion of how unkind the New Right was being to her, the First of all Ladies exclaimed: 'Oh, you noticed that did you?' I did not know where to look.)

In November 1981, David Stockman gave a long interview. He was then Ronald Reagan's director of the Office of Management and Budget, and had become the herald of the supply-side and trickle-down counter-revolution. Perhaps tempted by hubris, he bragged that the Reaganauts had put politics into a black box. By running up the deficit to a vertiginous level, and by promising deep cuts in taxation as well as a hugely-swollen military-industrial budget, the new Republicans had ensured that no Democratic Congress, and no future Democratic Presidency, could spend a dime more on anything without cutting at least a dime from somewhere else. Thus at last would come the long-delayed revenge on the New Deal and the civil rights movement. To get an impression of the sheer crookery of this, you have to recall that Stockman and Reagan predicted a zero deficit by 1984 and a $28 billion surplus by 1986. Thanks to a compliant media, the test of Democratic 'realism' became that of a willingness to pretend that this was true. (The old Democratic saurians of the Hill, the Bentsens and Foleys and Rostenkowskis, all voted for the Reagan illusion before expiring in the Gingrich flood they had unknowingly beckoned on.) It was Clinton's unsentimental readiness to enter this auction of tax and spending cuts – while protecting the most 'vulnerable', like the wealthy risk-taking donors and the recipients of company welfare – that demonstrated his readiness to govern. It also demonstrated his willingness to accept the 'limits' of government, while hypocritically referring to these as some mysterious 'gridlock'. When he needed a new Director of Communications after a spasm of local White House PR difficulty, he turned to the former Nixon-Reagan hack David Gergen – the very man who had 'sold' the Stockman programme to a credulous Washington élite. The resulting 'managed insolvency', which might neutrally be termed the doctrine of limits, and is neutrally termed by the élite in that way, does not by definition extend to that élite itself. Meanwhile, the United States deficit has become a real peril to societies and economies other than its own.

And now I take another look out over my home town. The Democratic primary has just been held. Amid the pitted streets and gutted schools and rotting clinics, with a ratted-out city nominally run by a corrupt black demagogue, and actually run by a group of indifferent white Congressmen, one can see the sordid end of the idea of 'participation'. It was actually proposed that the primary be cancelled, in order to save money for a bankrupt neo-colonial municipality. But that was thought too brutal and candid, so (even though the two party machines had long ago emitted their white smoke and announced *habemus candidatum)* the vote duly took place. Eleven thousand people turned out in the nation's capital; a total so shameful that it was barely reported. It is probably less than the statistical 'margin of error' by which the opinion poll industry claims the status of a pseudo-science. Is this what the

1968 Rhodes generation intended when it set out with its easy talk of 'grass-roots' and 'empowerment'? Perhaps not, but it is what it has wrought. Politics as a spectator sport, staged by fixers in a parallel universe and determined – in point of 'issues' and 'candidates' – before a single real elector has been invited to comment. Extreme public squalor and tribalism, coexisting with a triumph of special interests not seen since the Gilded Age. Everything More Separate, More Unequal and more rancorous. And everything accepted as somehow beyond the reach of political action.

Post-Modern politics has dinned into us the concept of the 'lesser evil'. One must, in other words, always be ready to accept Clinton (or Blair, or Mitterrand) lest worse befall. At one level, this is what is called a zero-sum game. If true, that is to say, it must be true all the time, and true in the same way as a theorem. How odd; that those who speak of a limitless offering of free will and free choice should be so insistent that one of the main items of decision involves no choice or alternative at all. The rise of Bill Clinton shows that there are indeed rewards for those who can learn to think this way. But those rewards are – shall we say? – unevenly distributed, and they involve a certain amnesia about the choices that were avoided, or repressed, or not made at all. By stressing the idea of 'no alternative', the non-ideological have redefined politics as a question of management, and eviscerated the idea that 'the art of the possible' is indeed an art of possibility. But they may have outsmarted themselves, and their professional apparatus of consultants and pollsters and spinmeisters. The declining landscape of possibility – whether it is the prison-state for young African-Americans, or the return of indentured labour in California, or the erosion of the First Amendment, or the collapse of environmental supervision, or the 'deregulated' airline and food industries, or the free market in judges and legislators – now becomes *their* responsibility. The plea of a lesser evil will not displace it onto other shoulders. In their cleverness, the new class of the privileged have been slow to understand this. I hope to live long enough to see the day, not when they find it out, but when it is found out by the patient and the swindled – and the trusting.

6 June 1996

'Bye Bye Baghdad'

Paul Foot on the Media's Gulf War

The Sun (15 January) announces on its front page: THE SUN SPEAKS FOR EVERY MAN, WOMAN AND CHILD IN BRITAIN. This would normally be a joke, a fantastic flight of fancy to prove that editor Kelvin Mackenzie had at last gone mad. But when, the next morning, the *Sun* devotes its entire front page to the Union Jack with a good old British Tommy in its centre, and the rubric up above SUPPORT OUR BOYS AND PUT THIS FLAG IN YOUR WINDOW, thousands of people do so! The *Sun* has its best morning for years. The *Star*, the ailing tabloid from the Express group, has a good time too, starting with its headline (16 January): GO GET HIM BOYS over a picture of a Tornado jet skimming across the desert 'to blast the evil dictator Saddam Hussein out of his bunker'. 'War is seldom bad for business,' says a leader in the *Times* Business and Finance Section, which goes on to hope that a war in the Gulf will 'pull Britain out of the recession'. Such optimism seems deranged. But as the circulation figures rise, and as the 'key targets' in Baghdad fall victim to allied air power, so caution is thrown to the winds and the papers stoke up the war fever they helped to create in the first place.

What is most remarkable about the press coverage of the Gulf crisis is its unanimity. Those who run the *Sun* and the *Star* will always support a fight, especially if it can be waged under a Union Jack. The *Sun*'s obsession with nuclear weapons (LET'S NUKE 'EM. GET READY TO PUSH THE BUTTON, BUSH TOLD – headline, 8 January) is of long standing. No doubt the *Daily Telegraph*'s enthusiastic support for the war was predictable. That paper's former editor, William Deedes, an archetypal buffer who once dealt expertly with press relations for the Tory government under Sir Alec Douglas Home, tells his readers on deadline day that for every yellow-bellied *Guardian* reader 'a score will find their pulses quicken, when, as Kipling put it in his poem, "the drums begin to roll."' The drums of death and mass destruction do something for the pulses of such people, and always have. Yet if the enthusiasm for the war were confined to the *Sun, Star, Telegraph, Mail* and *Express*, there might at least be an argument. It is the spread of that enthusiasm into the 'middle ground' – the *Independent*, the

Observer, the *Times* and *Sunday Times*, the *Mirror* and its associate news-papers – which gives to the war party its precious unanimity. Even the *Guardian*, which appeared to be against the war before it started, threw up its hands at the first sound of gunfire, and declared that the 'cause' of the war party was 'just'. Like the politicians against the war, the writers against the war – Edward Pearce in the *Guardian*, John Diamond in the *Mirror*, John Pilger wherever anyone prints what he writes – have to be winkled out from the chauvinist mass.

How to explain the mood which swept otherwise independent-minded journalists and editors into the stampede for war? The answer is that the intervention in the Gulf appears to many in the centre as an example of the world order for which they have craved since 1945. Here at last is the United Nations in action, bringing together, under the umbrella of internationally-agreed resolutions, all the forces of the world to defeat the aggressor and the bully. People who hated the Cold War now hail a new era when Russians, Chinese and Americans can fight together against a common enemy who, everyone agrees, has broken the rules. If the allied forces in the Gulf successfully discipline Iraq, so the argument goes, the world can look forward to an age of peace and order which, at long last, can be enforced.

To such people the standard arguments against the war are worse than useless. It is argued, for instance, that the post-war world has been full of dictators, some of them worse than Saddam Hussein, and many of them put in power or sustained there by the very forces which are now calling down death and destruction on the Butcher of Baghdad. Who put Pinochet in power? Who made it possible for Pol Pot to set about mass murder in Kampuchea? Who organised armed resistance to overthrow an elected government in Nicaragua and replace it with something like the dictatorship of Somoza? On any monster-count, these gentlemen, all creatures of American foreign policy, are as bad if not worse than Saddam. So why go to war against Saddam while propping up dictatorships in so many other places? This argument is met by our enlightened warmongers with the riposte: 'five, six or even twenty wrongs don't make a right. The United States may have supported dictatorships in the past, but in this case they are ranged against a dictator. Surely on this occasion they should be supported?'

The same answer greets the other standard anti-war argument – that aggression has been one of the constant features of the post-war world, and has never been checked by the American Government (which is often carrying out the aggression). What happened in Grenada and Panama unless it was naked aggression by a vast military power against a small defenceless state? Why was no armed force sent to throw the Israelis out of the territories they occupied by force in 1967; or into Cyprus to eject the Turkish invader in 1974; or into East Timor to evict the murderous Indonesian aggressor in 1975? In all three of these cases unanimous Security Council Resolutions were passed opposing the invasions, all of which were plainly illegal under what is laughably known as international law. No one could argue that Saddam's invasion of Kuwait was any more brutal in its execution or disastrous in its consequences than these other three invasions. If aggression should bring instant and huge retribution on the aggressor, why was not a man, not a gun sent to deal with the aggressors in the occupied territories of the Middle East, Cyprus or East Timor?

Our middle-of-the-road warmonger waves all this aside. International force was not used in the past, he agrees. It should have been. The United Nations lost face because it could not enforce its Resolutions. Now, thanks to the end of the Cold War, it is able to walk tall and enforce what it resolves. Roll on the war – or, as the *Sun* so tastefully put it, 'Bye Bye Baghdad.'

The grand old tradition of British empiricism, which hates to see patterns in politics and shuns as Marxist claptrap any attempt to discover an economic motive for the foreign policy of great powers, has, through these arguments, reached its logical climax. It has led middle-of-the-road politicians and journalists into outright support for what is, after all, the crudest and probably the nastiest of all modern imperialist wars.

For what is the common denominator which explains the twists and turns of US foreign policy and UN U-turns? Commercial interest – which in the Middle East can be reduced to a single word: oil. There is (and was at the time of the invasions) no oil in the Israeli-occupied territories, no oil in East Timor, no oil in Cyprus. No commercial interest in the US or Russia or any other great power was threatened by any of these invasions. Indeed, all three greatly assisted the commercial and strategic interest of the US, tied as it is so closely to Israel, Turkey and Indonesia. The toppling of Somoza in Nicaragua in 1979 threatened the hegemony of United States capital there, as did the democratic government of Chile from 1970 to 1973, the left-wing government of Grenada in 1982, and the dictatorship in Panama last year. In these cases, US business interests did just as well if not better as a result of old-fashioned aggression, and therefore old-fashioned aggression prospered. None of this had anything to do with the Cold War. All three UN Resolutions calling on the withdrawal of Israel from Gaza and the West

Bank, Turkey from Cyprus and Indonesia from East Timor were passed unanimously in the Security Council. The US, Britain, France, Russia and China supported them all to the hilt – provided, of course, that no one was expected to do anything to enforce them.

Commercial interest and oil provide the only coherent explanation of US policy over Iraq. After the Iranian revolution of 1979, Iran appeared as the main threat to 'stability' (cheap oil) in the region. Thus Iraq was encouraged by the United States (and by Kuwait and by Saudi Arabia) to invade Iran and start a war for a strip of territory which was eventually conceded. During this war, in which a million people were killed or maimed, Iraq, the aggressor, was supported by the US and Britain. When complaints were made about Saddam's genocidal attacks on the Kurdish people in north Iraq, critical UN Resolutions were watered down by the US, and formal British government protests were suitably muted. When an Iraqi missile accidentally hit an American warship killing 38 people, the US Government immediately sympathised with Saddam: 'these things happen in time of war,' they said. After the war, for a brief moment, Saddam became a hero in the Western world. Arms-traders queued up to sell him the weapons he now uses against his former benefactors. British Cabinet Ministers flocked to Baghdad to tie the knot of friendship with the dictator. During the visit of Tony Newton, now Secretary of State for Social Services, Saddam pronounced Britain a 'most favoured nation'. All this stopped only when Saddam, weakened by war and threatened from within, threw his huge army into Kuwait to increase the price of oil. Suddenly the champion of stability in the region (cheap oil) became its enemy. Suddenly, 'poor little Kuwait' (a greedy little dictatorship which exploits its migrant labour as horribly as anywhere else on earth) became a symbol of liberty and independence, and the Government of the United States of America moved to obliterate the monster it had created and had armed.

There is no other credible conclusion but that the war in the Gulf is a war for oil, a war to maintain the central strategy of British and American foreign policy in that region for half a century – ensuring that the Arab people do not get control of the oil produced in their countries. It was for this purpose (as has coincidentally just been clarified by the release of government papers) that Britain offered Kuwait military aid in 1961 to protect it from an Iraqi invasion.

If this is the thrust behind the war effort, the real purpose of the UN Resolutions, then where does that leave our Modern Empiricists, our Peter Jenkinses and Hugo Youngs, our Edward Mortimers and Gerald Kaufmans and Paddy Ashdowns? Their 'practical approach', their faith in the 'cock-up theory of history', their insistence that political events must be judged as they come, each by each, without pattern or precedent and most particularly without any economic drive or thrust to them, leads them to a mealy-mouthed support for 'a military initiative' which is likely (at best) to kill tens of thousands of people, most of them, as always, poor, defenceless and civilian.

If this is, as seems plain to me, a war to ensure that Britain and the United States keep tight hold of the world's richest and cheapest oil supply, then what will be the result of an allied victory over Saddam? Will it really lead to more influence for the United Nations, a better world order, a bleaker prospect for dictators? Or will it simply mean that the most powerful state on earth becomes more powerful, and the dictatorships which it supports in its own commercial interests all over the world will become more secure? Will it mean that the UN, instead of exercising more influence over its member states, will become even more grovelling a satellite of the great powers which control the Security Council: that the Cold War will be replaced by a new condominium of the United States Government, invaders of Panama and Grenada (and Iraq), the Russian Government, invader of Afghanistan and Lithuania (who knows where else?), and the Chinese Government, oppressors of Tiananmen Square? Will it not prove, after all, that the biggest Might is the biggest Right, and that the only way to dispose of a small world bully is by calling in a much bigger and more aggressive world bully whose victory will lead to the further throttling of the voices and aspirations of ordinary people everywhere?

I write this, half-watching early-morning television, on 17 January 1991. A BBC nincompoop in battledress, safe in his bunker in Riyadh, is reading out jingoistic nonsense from *Henry V*, and now Margaret Thatcher regales us with the horrors of Saddam's attack on Iran, an attack she supported. The air is thick with chauvinist drivel. When the dead are stretched out, and the hideous cost of this crazy war is counted, the blame must not be allowed to stop at the *Sun*, the Prime Minister and his exultant predecessor. The Modern Empiricists, the 'practical politicians', the 'sensible' journalists are every bit as responsible.

7 February 1991

The Morning After

Edward Said on the Israel-PLO Agreement

Now that some of the euphoria has lifted, it is possible to re-examine the Israeli-PLO agreement with the required common sense. What emerges from such scrutiny is a deal that is more flawed and, for most of the Palestinian people, more unfavourably weighted than many had first supposed. The fashion-show vulgarities of the White House ceremony, the degrading spectacle of Yasser Arafat thanking everyone for the suspension of most of his people's rights, and the fatuous solemnity of Bill Clinton's performance, like a 20th-century Roman emperor shepherding two vassal kings through rituals of reconciliation and obeisance: all these only temporarily obscure the truly astonishing proportions of the Palestinian capitulation.

So first of all let us call the agreement by its real name: an instrument of Palestinian surrender, a Palestinian Versailles. What makes it worse is that for at least the past fifteen years the PLO could have negotiated a better arrangement than this modified Allon Plan, one not requiring so many unilateral concessions to Israel. For reasons best known to the leadership it refused all previous overtures. To take one example of which I have personal knowledge: in the late Seventies, Secretary of State Cyrus Vance asked me to persuade Arafat to accept Resolution 242 with a reservation (accepted by the US) to be added by the PLO which would insist on the national rights of the Palestinian people as well as Palestinian self-determination. Vance said that the US would immediately recognise the PLO and inaugurate negotiations between it and Israel. Arafat categorically turned the offer down, as he did similar offers. Then the Gulf War occurred, and because of the disastrous positions it took then, the PLO lost even more ground. The gains of the intifada were squandered, and today advocates of the new document say: 'We had no alternative.' The correct way of phrasing that is: 'We had no alternative because we either lost or threw away a lot of others, leaving us only this one.'

In order to advance towards Palestinian self-determination – which has a meaning only if freedom, sovereignty and equality, rather than perpetual subservience to Israel, are its goal – we need an honest acknowledgment of where we are, now that the interim agreement is about to be negotiated. What is particularly mystifying is how so many Palestinian leaders and their intellectuals can persist in speaking of the agreement as a 'victory'. Nabil Shaath has called it one of 'complete parity' between Israelis and Palestinians. The fact is that Israel has conceded nothing, as former Secretary of State James Baker said in a TV interview, except, blandly, the existence of 'the PLO as the representative of the Palestinian people'. Or as the Israeli 'dove' Amos Oz reportedly put it in the course of a BBC interview, 'this is the second biggest victory in the history of Zionism.'

By contrast Arafat's recognition of Israel's right to exist carries with it a whole series of renunciations: of the PLO Charter; of violence and terrorism; of all relevant UN resolutions, except 242 and 338, which do not have one word in them about the Palestinians, their rights or aspirations. By implication, the PLO set aside numerous other UN resolutions (which, with Israel and the US, it is now apparently undertaking to modify or rescind) that, since 1948, have given Palestinians refugee rights, including either compensation or repatriation. The Palestinians had won numerous international resolutions – passed by, among others, the EC, the non-aligned movement, the Islamic Conference and the Arab League, as well as the UN – which disallowed or censured Israeli settlements, annexations and crimes against the people under occupation.

It would therefore seem that the PLO has ended the intifada, which embodied not terrorism or violence but the Palestinian right to resist, even though Israel remains in occupation of the West Bank and Gaza. The primary consideration in the document is for Israel's security, with none for the Palestinians' security from Israel's incursions. In his 13 September press conference Rabin was straightforward about Israel's continuing control over sovereignty; in addition, he said, Israel would hold the River Jordan, the boundaries with Egypt and Jordan, the sea, the land between Gaza and Jericho, Jerusalem, the settlements and the roads. There is little in the document to suggest that Israel will give up its violence against Palestinians or, as Iraq was required to do after it withdrew from Kuwait, compensate those who have been the victims of its policies over the past 45 years.

Neither Arafat nor any of his Palestinian partners who met the Israelis in Oslo has ever seen an Israeli settlement. There are now over two hundred of them, principally on hills, promontories and strategic points throughout the West Bank and Gaza. Many will probably shrivel and die, but the largest are designed for permanence. An independent system of roads connects them to Israel, and creates a disabling discontinuity between the main centres of Palestinian population. The actual land taken by these settlements, plus the land designated for expropriation, amounts – it is guessed – to over 55 per cent of the total land area of the Occupied Territories. Greater Jerusalem alone, annexed by Israel, comprises a huge tranche of virtually stolen land, at least 25 per cent of the total amount. In Gaza settlements in the north (three), the middle (two) and the south, along the coast from the Egyptian border past Khan Yunis (12), constitute at least 30 per cent of the Strip. In addition, Israel has tapped into every aquifer on the West Bank, and now uses about 80 per cent of the water there for the settlements and for Israel proper. (There are probably similar water installations in Israel's Lebanese 'security zone'.) So the domination (if not the outright theft) of land and water resources is either overlooked, in the case of water, or, in the case of land, postponed by the Oslo accord.

What makes matters worse is that all the information on settlements, land and water is held by Israel, which hasn't shared most of these data with the Palestinians, any more than it has shared the revenues raised by the inordinately high taxes it has imposed on them for 26 years. All sorts of technical committees (in which non-resident Palestinians have participated) have been set up by the PLO in the territories to consider such questions, but there is little evidence that committee findings (if any) were made use of by the Palestinian side in Oslo. So the impression of a huge discrepancy between what Israel got and what the Palestinians conceded or overlooked remains unrectified.

I doubt that there was a single Palestinian who watched the White House ceremony who did not also feel that a century of sacrifice, dispossession and heroic struggle had finally come to nought. Indeed, what was most troubling is that Rabin in effect gave the Palestinian speech while Arafat pronounced words that had all the flair of a rental agreement. So far from being seen as the victims of Zionism, the Palestinians were characterised before the world as its now repentant assailants: as if the thousands killed by Israel's bombing of refugee camps, hospitals and schools in Lebanon; Israel's expulsion of 800,000 people in 1948 (whose descendants now number about three million, many of them stateless); the conquest of their land and property; the destruction of over four hundred Palestinian villages; the invasion of Lebanon; the ravages of 26 years of brutal military occupation – it was as if these sufferings had been reduced to the status of terrorism and violence, to be renounced retrospectively or passed over in silence. Israel has always described Palestinian resistance as terrorism and violence, so even in the matter of wording it received a moral and historical gift.

In return for exactly what? Israel's recognition of the PLO – undoubtedly a significant step forward. Beyond that, by accepting that questions of land and sovereignty are being postponed till 'final status negotiations', the Palestinians have in effect discounted their unilateral and internationally acknowledged claim to the West Bank and Gaza: these have now become 'disputed territories'. Thus with Palestinian assistance Israel has been awarded at least an equal claim to them. The Israeli calculation seems to be that by agreeing to police Gaza – a job which Begin tried to give Sadat fifteen years ago – the PLO would soon fall foul of local competitors, of whom Hamas is only one. Moreover, rather than becoming stronger during the interim period, the Palestinians may grow weaker, come more under the Israeli thumb, and therefore be less able to dispute the Israeli claim when the last set of negotiations begins. But on the matter of how, by what specific mechanism, to get from an interim status to a later one, the document is purposefully silent. Does this mean, ominously, that the interim stage may be the final one?

Israeli commentators have been suggesting that within, say, six months the PLO and Rabin's government will negotiate a new agreement further postponing elections, and thereby allowing the PLO to continue to rule. It is worth mentioning that at least twice during the past summer Arafat said that his experience of government consisted of the ten years during which he 'controlled' Lebanon, hardly a comfort to the many Lebanese and Palestinians who recollect that sorry period. Nor is there at present any concrete way for elections to be held should they even be scheduled. The imposition of rule from above, plus the long legacy of the occupation, have not contributed much to the growth of democratic, grass-roots institutions. There are unconfirmed reports in the Arabic press indicating that the PLO has already appointed ministers from its own inner circle in Tunis, and deputy ministers from among trusted residents of the West Bank and Gaza. Will there ever be truly representative institutions? One cannot be very sanguine, given Arafat's absolute refusal to share or delegate power, to say nothing of the financial assets he alone knows about and controls.

In both internal security and development, Israel and the PLO are now aligned with each other. PLO members or consultants have been meeting with Mossad officials since last October to discuss security problems, including Arafat's own security. And this at the time of the worst Israeli repression of Palestinians under military occupation. The thinking behind the collaboration is that it will deter any Palestinian from demonstrating against the occupation, which will not withdraw, but merely redeploy. Besides, Israeli settlers will remain living, as they always have, under a different jurisdiction. The PLO will thus become Israel's enforcer, an unhappy prospect for most Palestinians. Interestingly, the ANC has consistently refused to supply the South African government with police officials until after power is shared, precisely in order to avoid appearing as the white government's enforcer. It was reported from Amman a few days ago that 170 members of the Palestine Liberation Army, now being trained in Jordan for police work in Gaza, have refused to co-operate for precisely that reason. With about 14,000 Palestinian prisoners in Israeli jails – some of whom Israel says it may release – there is an inherent contradiction, not to say incoherence, to the new security arrangements. Will more room be made in them for Palestinian security?

The one subject on which most Palestinians agree is development, which is being described in the most naïve terms imaginable. The world community will be expected to give the nearly autonomous areas large-scale financial support; the Palestinian diaspora is expected, indeed preparing, to do the same. Yet all development for Palestine must be funnelled through the joint Palestinian-Israeli Economic Co-operation Committee, even though, according to the document, 'both sides will co-operate jointly and unilaterally with regional and international parties to support these aims.' Israel is the dominant economic and political power in the region – and its power is of course enhanced by its alliance with the US. Over 80 per cent of the West Bank and Gaza economy is dependent on Israel, which is likely to control Palestinian exports, manufacturing and labour for the foreseeable future. Aside from the small entrepreneurial and middle class, the vast majority of Palestinians are impoverished and landless, subject to the vagaries of the Israeli manufacturing and commercial community which employs Palestinians as cheap labour. Most Palestinians, economically speaking, will almost certainly remain as they are, although now they are expected to work in private-sector, partly Palestinian-controlled service industries, including resorts, small assembly-plants, farms and the like.

A recent study by the Israeli journalist Asher Davidi quotes Dov Lautman, president of the Israeli Manufacturers Association: 'It's not important whether there will be a Palestinian state, autonomy or a Palestinian-Jordanian state. The economic borders between Israel and the territories must remain open.' With its well developed institutions, close relations with the US and aggressive economy, Israel will in effect incorporate the territories economically, keeping them in a state of permanent dependency. Then Israel will turn to the wider Arab world, using the political benefits of the Palestinian agreement as a springboard to break into Arab markets, which it will also exploit and is likely to dominate.

Framing all this is the US, the only global power, whose idea of the New World Order is based on economic domination by a few giant corporations and pauperisation if necessary for many of the lesser peoples (even those in metropolitan countries). Economic aid for Palestine is being supervised and controlled by the US, bypassing the UN, some of whose agencies like UNRWA and UNDP are far better placed to administer it. Take Nicaragua and Vietnam. Both are former enemies of the US; Vietnam actually defeated the US but is now economically in need of it. A boycott against Vietnam continues and the history books are being written in such a way as to show how the Vietnamese sinned against and 'mistreated' the US for the latter's idealistic gesture of having invaded, bombed and devastated their country. Nicaragua's Sandinista government was attacked by the US-financed Contra movement; the country's harbours were mined, its people ravaged by famine, boycotts and every conceivable type of subversion. After the 1991 elections, which brought a US-supported candidate, Mrs Chamorro, to power, the US promised many millions of dollars in aid, of which only 30 million have actually materialised. In mid-September all aid was cut off. There is now famine and civil war in Nicaragua. No less unfortunate have been the fates of El Salvador and Haiti. To throw oneself, as Arafat has done, on the tender mercies of the US is almost certainly to suffer the fate the US has meted out to rebellious or 'terrorist' peoples it has had to deal with in the Third World *after* they have promised not to resist the US any more.

Hand in hand with the economic and strategic control of Third World countries that happen to be close to, or possess, resources like oil that are necessary to the US, is the media system, whose reach and control over thought is truly astounding. For at least twenty years, Yasser Arafat was taken to be the most unattractive and morally repellent man on earth. Whenever he appeared in the media, or was discussed by them, he was presented as if he had only one thought in his head: killing Jews, especially innocent women and children. Within a matter of days, the 'independent media' had totally rehabilitated Arafat. He was now an accepted, even lovable figure whose courage and realism had bestowed on Israel its rightful due. He had repented, he had become a 'friend', and he and his people were now on 'our' side.

Anyone who opposed or criticised what he had done was either a fundamentalist like the Likud settlers or a terrorist like the members of Hamas. It became nearly impossible to say anything except that the Israeli-Palestinian agreement – mostly unread or unexamined, and in any case unclear, lacking dozens of crucial details – was the first step towards Palestinian independence.

So far as the truly independent critic or analyst is concerned, the problem is how he is to free himself from the ideological system which both the agreement and the media now serve. What is needed are memory and scepticism (if not outright suspicion). Even if it is patently obvious that Palestinian freedom in any real sense has not been achieved, and is clearly designed not to be, beyond the meagre limits imposed by Israel and the US, the famous handshake broadcast all over the world is supposed not only to symbolise a great moment of success but to blot out past as well as present realities.

Given a modicum of honesty the Palestinians should be capable of seeing that the large majority of people the PLO is supposed to represent will not really be served by the agreement, except cosmetically. True, residents of the West Bank and Gaza are rightly glad to see that some Israeli troops will withdraw, and that large amounts of money might start to come in. But it is rank dishonesty not to be alert to what the agreement entails in terms of further occupation, economic control and profound insecurity. Then there is the mammoth problem of the Palestinians who live in Jordan, to say nothing of the thousands of stateless refugees in Lebanon and Syria. 'Friendly' Arab states have always had one law for Palestinians, one for natives. These double standards have already intensified, as witnessed by the appalling scenes of delay and harassment that have occurred on the Allenby Bridge since the agreement was announced.

So what is to be done, if crying over spilt milk is useless? The first thing is to spell out, not only the virtues of being recognised by Israel and accepted at the White House, but also what the truly major disabilities are. Pessimism of the intellect first, then optimism of the will. You can't improve on a bad situation that is largely due to the technical incompetence of the PLO – which negotiated in English, a language that neither Arafat nor his emissary in Oslo knows, with no legal adviser – until on the technical level at least you involve people who can think for themselves and are not mere instruments of what is by now a single Palestinian authority. I find it extraordinarily disheartening that so many Arab and Palestinian intellectuals, who a week earlier had been moaning and groaning about Arafat's dictatorial ways, his single-minded control over the money, the circle of sycophants and courtiers that have surrounded him in Tunis of late, the absence of accountability and reflection, at least since the Gulf War, should suddenly make a 180-degree switch and start applauding his tactical genius, and his latest victory. The march towards self-determination can only be embarked on by a people with democratic aspirations and goals. Otherwise it is not worth the effort.

After all the hoopla celebrating 'the first step towards a Palestinian state', we should remind ourselves that much more important than having a state is the kind of state it is. The history of the post-colonial world is disfigured by one-party tyrannies, rapacious oligarchies, social dislocation caused by Western 'investments', and large-scale pauperisation brought about by famine, civil war or outright robbery. Any more than religious fundamentalism, mere nationalism is not, and can never be, 'the answer' to the problems of new secular societies. Alas one can already see in Palestine's potential statehood the lineaments of a marriage between the chaos of Lebanon and the tyranny of Iraq.

If this isn't to happen, a number of quite specific issues need to be addressed. One is the diaspora Palestinians, who originally brought Arafat and the PLO to power, kept them there, and are now relegated to permanent exile or refugee status. Since they comprise at least half of the total Palestinian population their needs and aspirations are not negligible. A small segment of the exile community is represented by the various political organisations 'hosted' by Syria. A significant number of independents (some of whom, like Shafik al-Hout and Mahmoud Darwish, resigned in protest from the PLO) still have an important role to play, not simply by applauding or condemning from the sidelines, but by advocating specific alterations in the PLO's structure, trying to change the triumphalist ambience of the moment into something more appropriate, mobilising support and building an organisation from within the various Palestinian communities all over the world to continue the march towards self-determination. These communities have been singularly disaffected, leaderless and indifferent since the Madrid process began.

One of the first tasks is a Palestinian census, which has to be regarded not just as a bureaucratic exercise but as the enfranchisement of Palestinians wherever they are. Israel, the US and the Arab states – all of them – have always opposed a census: it would give the Palestinians too high a profile in countries where they are supposed to be invisible, and before the Gulf War, it would have made it clear to various Gulf governments how dependent they are on an inappropriately large, usually exploited 'guest' community. Above all, opposition to the census stemmed from the realisation that, were Palestinians to be counted all together, despite dispersion and dispossession, they would by that very exercise come close to constituting a nation rather than a mere collection of people. Now more than ever the process of holding a census – and perhaps, later, world-wide elections – should be a leading item on the agenda for Palestinians everywhere. It would constitute an act of historical and political self-realisation outside the limitations imposed by the absence of sovereignty. And it would give body to the universal need for democratic participation, now ostensibly curtailed by Israel and the PLO in a premature alliance.

Certainly a census would once again raise the question of return for those Palestinians who are not from the West Bank and Gaza. Although this issue has been compressed into the general 'refugee' formula deferred until the final status talks some time in the future, it needs to be brought up now. The Lebanese government, for instance, has been publicly heating up the rhetoric against citizenship and naturalisation for the 350–400,000 Palestinians in Lebanon, most of whom are stateless, poor, permanently stalled. A similar situation obtains in Jordan and Egypt. These people, who have paid the heaviest price of all Palestinians, can neither be left to rot nor dumped somewhere else against their will. Israel is able to offer the right of return to every Jew in the world: individual Jews can become Israeli citizens and live in Israel at any time. This extraordinary inequity, intolerable to all Palestinians for almost half a century, has to be rectified. It is unthinkable that all the 1948 refugees would either want or be able to return to so small a place as a Palestinian state: on the other hand, it is unacceptable for them all to be told to resettle elsewhere, or drop any ideas they might have about repatriation and compensation.

One of the things the PLO and independent Palestinians should therefore do is raise a question not addressed by the Oslo Accords, thereby pre-empting the final status talks – namely, ask for reparations for Palestinians who have been the victims of this dreadful conflict. Although it is the Israeli Government's wish (expressed quite forcibly by Rabin at his Washington news conference) that the PLO should close 'its so-called embassies', these offices should be kept open selectively so that claims for repatriation or compensation can be pressed.

In sum, we need to move up from the state of supine abjectness in which the Oslo Accords were negotiated ('we will accept anything so long as you recognise us') into one that enables us to prosecute parallel agreements with Israel and the Arabs concerning Palestinian national, as opposed to municipal, aspirations. But this does not exclude resistance against the Israeli occupation, which continues indefinitely. So long as occupation and settlements exist, whether legitimised or not by the PLO, Palestinians and others must speak against them. One of the issues not raised, either by the Oslo Accords, the exchange of PLO-Israeli letters or the Washington speeches, is whether the violence and terrorism renounced by the PLO includes non-violent resistance, civil disobedience etc. These are the inalienable right of any people denied full sovereignty and independence, and must be supported.

Like so many unpopular and undemocratic Arab governments, the PLO has already begun to appropriate authority for itself by calling its opponents 'terrorists' and 'fundamentalists'. This is demagoguery. Hamas and Islamic Jihad are opposed to the Oslo agreement but they have said several times that they will not use violence against other Palestinians. Besides, their combined sway amounts to fewer than a third of the citizens of the West Bank and Gaza. As for the Damascus-based groups, they seem to me to be either paralysed or discredited. But this by no means exhausts the Palestinian opposition, which also includes well-known secularists, people who are committed to a peaceful solution to the Palestinian-Israeli conflict, realists and democrats. I include myself in this group which is, I believe, far bigger than is now supposed.

Central to this opposition's thinking is the desperate need for reform within the PLO, which is now put on notice that reductive claims to 'national unity' are no longer an excuse for incompetence, corruption and autocracy. For the first time in Palestinian history such opposition cannot, except by some preposterous and disingenuous logic, be equated with treason or betrayal. Indeed our claim is that we are opposed to sectarian Palestinianism and blind loyalty to the leadership: we remain committed to the broad democratic and social principles of accountability and performance that triumphalist nationalism has always tried to annul. I believe that a broad-based opposition to the PLO's history of bungling will emerge in the diaspora, but will come to include people and parties in the Occupied Territories.

Lastly there is the confusing matter of relationships between Israelis and Palestinians who believe in self-determination for two peoples, mutually and equally. Celebrations are premature and, for far too many Israeli and non-Israeli Jews, an easy way out of the enormous disparities that remain. Our peoples are already too bound up with each other in conflict and a shared history of persecution for an American-style pow-wow to heal the wounds and open the way forward. There is still a victim and a victimiser. But there can be solidarity in struggling to end the inequities, and for Israelis in pressuring their government to end the occupation, the expropriation and the settlements. The Palestinians, after all, have very little left to give. The common battle against poverty, injustice and militarism must now be joined seriously, and without the ritual demands for psychological security for Israelis – who if they don't have it now, never will. More than anything else, this will show whether the symbolic handshake is going to be a first step towards reconciliation and real peace.

21 October 1993

Enrichissez-Vous!

R.W. Johnson in South Africa

Stung by press comment that South Africa's new government had achieved little in its first hundred days, Deputy President Thabo Mbeki, addressing the Cape Town Press Club, suggested that the problem lay with the press. It had, he said, been 'perfectly correct for the press to criticise the previous government' – the word 'correct' is worth lingering over – but such behaviour was now inappropriate. Instead of looking for crises, he said, the press 'should ask what its role is in building a democracy'. Mr Mbeki, it turned out, had been particularly incensed by an article in the *Financial Mail* accusing him of laziness and unexplained absences from important meetings.

A week later he was outdone by the most powerful regional premier, Tokyo Sexwale, who had come under fire for having hired 65 of his cronies at double the normal rates, for jobs that were not advertised, and – it seems to happen all the time – for not turning up to meetings he was scheduled to address. Mr Sexwale heads the government of the PWV (Pretoria-Witwatersrand-Vereeniging) area, which includes a quarter of the population and generates 60 per cent of the country's wealth – and makes him a leading contender for the succession to President Mandela, along with Mr Mbeki and the ANC party boss, Cyril Ramaphosa. (The French seem already to have decided Sexwale is the man most likely to: President Mitterrand, on his recent visit, bestowed the Legion of Honour on him.) Mr Sexwale, like quite a few of the new ANC men of power, has a somewhat chiefly manner – one newspaper editor referred to him as His Regional Highness. Mr Sexwale told the PWV legislature that 'counter-revolutionaries' were abusing the freedom of the press in order to try to prevent the country's reconstruction. It would not be allowed and language of the kind found in the offending article would not be permitted in the legislature.

Thabo Mbeki capped all this with a paper to the ANC National Executive in which he spoke of the ANC's enemies as including 'bourgeois reformism' and 'sections of the liberal establishment'. In particular, he warned that the 'counter-insurgency forces' had never been dismantled and that they had a huge network of informers and agents in the media, the universities and elsewhere, thus echoing almost exactly P.W. Botha's diatribes of a few years ago about the 'total onslaught'. Once again, it seems, criticism from the press or intelligentsia risks being labelled as treasonable. This hyper-sensitivity stems in part from the fact that the ANC, used to being regarded as a protected species, has found being treated like ordinary politicians deeply disagreeable. But Mr Mbeki is also engaged in a succession struggle and needs to keep his supporters convinced of his radicalism.

Such outbursts are interesting partly because since the election the ANC élite has been basking in President Mandela's overwhelming popularity. In mid-August Mandela was given a 60 per cent approval rating by whites (up from 38 per cent last November), 69 per cent by Indians, 70 per cent by Coloureds and 92 percent by Africans. Mandela's complete lack of bitterness, his generosity, his grave, dignified bearing have made him a national totem, an icon quite beyond criticism. Even the conservative *Citizen* solemnly warns that he is being over-burdened, that the man is too precious to the country for any risks to be taken. In other words, it has now dawned on many whites that Mandela is pretty well indispensable. Although the radicals in the ANC caucus are frustrated by his willingness to strike coalition compromises with the National Party and the Inkatha Freedom Party, Mandela is so loved and admired among the ANC faithful that within the ANC open criticism is simply not possible. At the same time, he enjoys the warm regard of both Chief Buthelezi and F.W. de Klerk although they, too, complain about the thrust of ANC policy and talk of a possible future in opposition. But President Mandela is so genuinely impossible to dislike that they would have a difficult job explaining why they couldn't get on with him. Besides, they must have realised that no successor to Mandela is likely to be as conciliatory. Even Constand Viljoen, the leader of the white Right, gets on famously with the ANC these days and has warm words for Mandela. After all the struggles the country has been through, it longs for peace and reconciliation and Mr Mandela can deliver them like no one else.

The trouble is that no country can really be governed – let alone guided through a process of transformation – simply by having a dear old man with a shining moral character as President. There is, quite unmistakeably, a lack of grip in the way the Government is being run. The fact is that Mandela has no experience of administration and really can't be expected to learn how to run a cabinet now.

Quite visibly, the Cabinet doesn't work. Thus Omar Dullah, the Minister of Justice, made repeated speeches about the Truth Commission he was setting up to judge abuses of human rights under the previous regime – until Deputy President de Klerk pointed out that the matter could not become government policy unless it went through the Cabinet, where he would oppose it. The squabble continues. Dullah also attacked the US over its hostility to Cuba, but the Foreign Ministry, conscious of Clinton's support for the Mandela Government, maintained a glacial silence until eventually Dullah declared that he had never actually made the offending speech. Similarly, Joe Modise, the Minister of Defence, denounced Israel, announced the purchase of corvettes for the Navy, and tried to censor a newspaper, all without Cabinet consent. The Ministry of Administration ceded control of the country's water resources to the provinces without consulting the Ministry of Water Affairs, which then had to put up a furious fight to snatch back control. On issue after issue the Cabinet seems unwilling to reach decisions, especially tough decisions. Partly this is a reflection of the difficulties of coalition government, but it is also the case that ANC ministers are running scared of the ANC caucus in Parliament; and – more significant perhaps – the ANC is simply so opposition-minded that many of its ministers seem almost incapable of taking responsibility for clear-cut executive decisions.

The Cabinet originally announced that it was thinking of saving money by moving Parliament to Pretoria. Immediately the ANC caucus grabbed control of the issue – which then vanished. No one can say whether the question of where the country's capital is to be has been resolved, whether it's been dropped or even if it's being discussed at all. Similarly, the Government proudly declared that in future all decisions would be taken far more democratically than in the past. In economic affairs this would mean that the National Economic Forum would acquire considerable importance. It would, crucially, be involved in the centrepiece of government policy, the Reconstruction and Development Plan (the RDP). But months have gone by with no mention of the Forum and no one knows whether it will even continue to exist. Meanwhile the Minister with responsibility for the RDP, Jay Naidoo, has taken six months to bring out an almost wholly vacuous White Paper. Pious principles are still preferred to any indication of how the Government intends to produce the economic growth without which the RDP will founder. It looks very much as if the economy is going to be allowed to drift into the arms of the IMF, who can then shoulder the blame for the difficult decisions being skirted now. Again, despite the huge jobs-for-the-boys pressure, almost no new South African ambassadors or consuls have been named, so that Mandela everywhere relies on old apartheid-era diplomats. More remarkably still, the former bantustans, though legally abolished, still exist – their civil services continue to occupy offices, levy taxes and spend money. Even the farcical bantustan ambassadors and consuls to South Africa continue in post, carrying out their non-existent functions on behalf of non-existent states.

The sense of drift is quite palpable. Apart from the provision of jobs, housing and education are undoubtedly the two areas dearest to the hearts of the ANC and its electorate, yet there is little sign of movement at either. Joe Slovo, the Minister of Housing, is suffering from bone marrow cancer and has been in hospital three times this month so far. As yet his Ministry has produced no housing plan nor, indeed, built any houses. Tokyo Sexwale, the PWV Premier, has repeatedly insisted that he would build 150,000 houses this year in his region alone. Thus far he has exactly one house to show. Most significant is the failure to produce any scheme for housing finance. At present it is often impossible to collect township rents and building societies are afraid to lend: if a township purchaser defaults on payments it is not uncommon for the repossessed house to be burnt down and its new occupants attacked. Unless Mr Slovo can come up with a scheme which gets round this obstacle there will be no housing policy and probably very few houses. Meanwhile squatter invasions of housing land continue – Mr Slovo's courageous stand against such invasions is merely words in the wind – compromising possible future developments.

Education is an even worse mess. The Minister, Sibusiso Bengu, was no sooner in office than he found himself locked in mortal struggle with the ANC Education Desk. Mr Bengu then had a stroke and has only just returned to the fray. Already Bengu has had to accept that even by 1996 there will still not be a single, integrated education system. The universities continue to be racked by student troubles and in Soweto 40 principals have been driven out of their schools by their pupils. There is a great deal of hand-wringing and some threatening noises about what will happen to the former whites-only schools, but no sense of direction and no action at all. Recently Mr Bengu announced a month-long campaign to 'change the culture of education': the people, he says, must decide what they want – change is up to them. This populist excuse for executive inaction is paralleled by ministers involved with the RDP who harangue mystified audiences, telling them that the Government has done its bit and it is now up to the people to make the RDP a reality. Yet, in the case of education, at least, it is impossible to imagine that things can be improved much without a tough executive crackdown on truant teachers, riotous pupils and corrupt administrators, but such a crackdown would gravely offend the ANC's own populist instincts. Mr Bengu sits squarely in the middle of that contradiction. Chris Hani, the assassinated Communist leader, once said that he wanted to get control of the police, the army and the media but that there was only pain and sorrow to be had out of running a department such as Education. It is clear now how right he was.

One of the reasons Mr Bengu's job is such a bed of nails is that under apartheid each homeland and each racial group had its own education department. In addition, white education was split between several departments. The result is that Bengu has the difficult, long-winded and expensive job of amalgamating 19 different education departments into one. In only slightly lesser versions the same problem is met in most other ministries. The more one gazes at the bureaucratic mess the more one wonders if this government will ever find its way out of it.

For a start, the ANC rather unthinkingly promised all homeland civil servants that they would keep their jobs. Realising that the South African state was about to take over responsibility for their wage bills, the homeland administrations celebrated with an orgy of recruitment in their last year of life, thus further swelling the enormous and inefficient bureaucracy. Second, the ANC is under great pressure to find jobs for its clients in the civil service but it also promised de Klerk that existing white civil servants would keep their jobs. To square the circle the ANC announced an additional 11,000 'affirmative' civil service posts – which drew no less than 1.4 million black applicants. There is, of course, nothing for these recruits to do – the problem is a surplus, not a shortage of civil servants. On top of this, the country has been newly divided up into nine regions and each of these regions also has to amalgamate a whole series of homeland and racial bureaucracies. But the central government is nowhere near ready to start handing power over to the new regional governments, who accordingly sit doing very little on handsome salaries. Yet the Government can only carry out its reforms if the regional governments translate them into action on the ground. At the moment this is impossible and the log-jam will get worse next year when a whole new set of metropolitan authorities is created in the cities and the first ever democratic elections take place there. Inevitably, there will be a further round of jobs for the boys and, probably, bureaucratic chaos as a completely untried new élite takes power in the cities. The first team have been sent to Parliament, the second team to the regional assemblies, and the third team have been recruited as placemen: management of the great urban areas, which will make or break the reform programme, is being handed over to the fourth team.

In some sense this is a fine thing: we will have democracy at every level and large numbers of blacks will acquire jobs previously confined to a narrow Afrikaner élite. But it is also clear that the ANC's ambition to transform and democratise all the structures of the state will dramatically impede its ambition to transform and democratise the structures of society. There is no doubt at all which of these objectives has priority: the determining force is the grab for power and jobs on the part of a small black élite. Ministers repeatedly make speeches saying how much they dislike having white civil servants and that their aim is to change this as quickly as possible. In many cases they have already suspended their top white civil servants (at the cost of enormous redundancy payments or, more often, paying them to do no work) in order to give jobs to clients and cronies who, all too often, are far less able to carry out the work of their department than the men they have displaced.

The most vociferous denunciations come from Winnie Mandela, now a deputy minister (arts, culture, science and technology) and, as always, an unguided missile, making speeches and even appointments she doesn't consult her minister about. (Her arrival in Cape Town has, by the by, plunged the local couturiers into panic, for she has expensive tastes in clothes, a well-publicised record as a poor bill-payer and a reputation which instils real fear.)

In her attacks on her white staff Mrs Mandela is, however, speaking for a larger constituency. Not surprisingly, the morale of white civil servants has plummeted and the Public Servants' Association has warned that most departments are in a state of chaos, with a total breakdown in communications between the political and administrative hierarchies: only two departments, they say, seem to be working properly. The ability of the bureaucracy to implement social change is thus being sacrificed to the career ambitions of a mere handful. White conservatives are horrified by all this, and you could say that that only goes to show how stupid most of them are: if they examined their own interests a little more thoughtfully they would surely be delighted at this self-inflicted paralysis on the part of the Government. But one of the most heartening sides of the new South Africa is the lack of such cynicism: people of all races and persuasions, even the most reactionary, want the new government to work.

Yet the fact is that power in South Africa is merely being transferred to the same bureaucratic bourgeoisie that took power elsewhere in Africa.

To anyone who has read René Dumont's famous *False Start in Africa*, the tell-tale sign is the large salaries of the new élite in what is, after all, merely a medium-income developing country. President Mandela is paid the same as Bill Clinton, both his Vice-Presidents are paid more than Al Gore, and all cabinet ministers are paid considerably more than a British prime minister. The remuneration of MPs is similarly lavish: indeed, some of their privileges are quite startling – for example, a ration of 48 free air-tickets a year, which has not prevented ANC MPs demanding an 80 per cent reduction on air tickets beyond that, free airport parking etc. Thabo Mbeki's irritation with the press may have something to do with the coverage the refurbishment of his two vice-presidential mansions has elicited: rather than use the stairs to go up to his first floor, as ordinary mortals do, he has decided that he must, at vast public expense, install elevators. There is a great deal more of this sort of thing. One of the choicest examples is the Public Service Commission, the body that has the job of supervising civil service recruitment – which, at the moment, just means ignoring all the obvious meritocratic rules. Asked what their salaries were, the members of the Commission tried hard not to divulge them but in the end admitted that they were each taking home more than a British prime minister does.

In opposition the ANC had (rightly) been loud in criticism of the government 'gravy train' operated by the Nationalists, so the sight of ANC MPs and ministers helping themselves to more gravy than the Nationalists ever dared to has naturally provoked a strong reaction, not just in the press but among the ANC's own rank and file, led in this instance by Archbishop Tutu, who declared himself shocked by the greed of the new élite. The result was pure comic opera. The ANC National Executive, which had not met for four months, was summoned to urgent conclave at this threat to its membership of the acquisitive society. The Executive issued a communiqué sternly declaring that 'the ANC is committed to eradicating the gravy train arising from the apartheid era', but went on to caution against 'hasty and uninformed judgments' about high government salaries. The next week ANC MPs rammed through another increase in their salaries and voices were raised suggesting that the press be barred in future from meetings of the Rules Committee (which controls such changes), something not even the Nationalists had thought of. Criticism of their salaries was, they said, 'racist'. This point was put to Archbishop Tutu. 'Have you noticed my complexion?' he asked.

NP and IFP Ministers and MPs are, of course, enjoying the same perks as their ANC colleagues, but since neither party has ever been famous for its egalitarian aims, this has passed with much less comment. The NP, still traumatised by its loss of power, has little to say in any case – the tiny Liberal Democratic Party has been ten times more effective as an opposition. The IFP has been getting on far better with the ANC than most would have anticipated. Chief Buthelezi, the IFP leader, had won good reviews for his stand, at Home Affairs, against illegal immigration and the old censorship legislation, when he ruined everything by blundering into a TV studio and preventing one of his opponents within the Zulu royal family from finishing an interview he was giving. Although Buthelezi later apologised, the sight of the minister in charge of liberalising the censorship laws intervening to stop an opponent speaking against him on air has done him great damage, and a large question mark now hangs over his suitability for high office of any kind. Certainly his tirades against the dangers to liberty posed by the strength of Communist Party representation in government aren't going to carry much weight after this.

This is true despite the fact that Hani's dream has been largely realised – we have Communists in charge of Defence, the police and the SABC. All told, 12 ministers are Communists – or 'close to the SACP', as the saying goes. So are Jakes Gerwel, who runs Mandela's office, and Kathy Kathrada, Mandela's special assistant. The Party seems able to place its people pretty much as it wishes and its instinct for slipping its cadres into key posts is in no way dulled. But, as any Marxist would know, political labels are of slight importance next to the sociological fact of class creation. It is doubtful if any set of laws, let alone moral strictures, can halt this process. Among the new élite there is, indeed, a decided casualness about observing the law. There seems to be little hope, for instance, that the ANC security guards who shot down scores of royalist Zulus in the streets of Johannesburg shortly before the election will be brought to book, the police having been several times prevented by main force from conducting their enquiries. This massacre – almost on the scale of Sharpeville – is simply an embarrassment to the new class and is being swept under the carpet. Another example: the Communist Party has suspended its Natal leader, Harry Gwala, in connection with allegations that he was attempting to murder a number of ANC leaders, but even this is treated as a purely party matter and the police have not been brought in. Similarly, Tokyo Sexwale's office keeps regaling us with stories about drug barons who are threatening his life. Apparently negotiations with various groups of gangsters have taken place – but there is no thought of involving the police. Merchants of all sorts around the country are filing suit against the ANC over its huge chain of bad debts, but they are having little joy. In Durban the local sheriff, ordered by the court to distrain upon the ANC offices for their non-payment of rent, has been forcibly prevented from doing so by armed ANC guards. Exactly how far the writ of law runs often seems quite uncertain.

The prevailing lack of direction does not mean that nothing has been happening. Since the election we have seen three nation-wide strikes, many lesser ones, a deliberate blockading of motorways, the eruption of rioting in Coloured areas of the Reef, marches, littering campaigns, and hostage-taking by students demanding the resignation of their vice-chancellors, and a major regional hospital crisis. Several of the weaker universities are on the point of collapse, wracked by endless student populism ('Pass one, pass all', 'One student, one degree' etc) and financial crisis. So, too, are many hospitals: Mandela's promise in his inaugural speech of free medical care for all children and nursing mothers was given without any provision being made for extra staff or spending. The result has been that many hospitals are simply over-whelmed by a tide of patients, with doctors and nurses fleeing towards the private sector. Social change of every kind is rapid, ubiquitous and uncontrolled. Even a workaholic, ultra-competent government would find it hard to stay on its feet with the ground shifting beneath them, and this is not that kind of government.

The Government's irresolution and the enrichment of the new class go hand in hand, shielded by President Mandela's charisma. The political truce with Inkatha remains in place and while it does, levels of political violence remain lower than before. Foreign visitors and trade delegations come and go, the country's sportsmen tour abroad, South Africa is back in the world. It all feels better; is, indeed, better. The post-election honeymoon continues, despite repeated attempts by journalists to declare it dead. For the moment the public is prepared to overlook a bit of inefficiency here, a bit of corruption there. President Mandela is himself quite incorruptible – he gives away a large chunk of his salary, would never dream of wasting money on elevators for his house, and has the old prison habit of making his own bed when he gets up at dawn. When Archbishop Tutu remarked on the greed of those in power, Mandela said that the excessive salaries of his MPs and ministers should be cut, but the ANC caucus simply brushed this aside and, in fact, demanded more. He then reversed his position, saying first that much of the criticism had been ignorant, and then that Tutu was guilty of 'irresponsibility' in speaking about the matter at all. At which people simply shrug and blame Mandela's speechwriters. Similarly when, responding to the furore over press criticism of the Government, the President called for a 'partnership' between press and government a truly hair-raising idea, if taken seriously nobody got upset because everybody knows he means well.

One is tempted to say that things can't go on like this, except that they probably will. These are early days, of course, and some of the new ministers, at least, will gradually learn how to do their jobs. But the markets haven't failed to notice the Government's tendency to throw money at problems without really dealing with them. Accordingly, long bond rates have drifted up from 12 per cent in January to over 17 per cent now, an effective vote of no confidence, costing the country dear in extra debt interest. Unless the Government can reverse the impression it has made on the markets it could find its reform plans crippled by the higher cost of capital.

Equally, the tension between the *enrichissez-vous* ethics of the new élite and the still worsening poverty of the masses is bound to produce criticism which the new élite will absolutely hate. How secure press freedom will then be is a good question. The three parties making up the Government – the ANC, Inkatha and the Nationalists – have three things in common: a long history of resistance to liberal democracy, an intolerance of criticism, and a willingness to use violence in pursuit of their own political ends. Paradoxically, the collision between them has produced a liberal democratic constitution, but the cause of liberal democracy is still under considerable threat. One safeguard is the Government's dependence on international aid, trade, investment and diffuse institutional support, a dependence which will require at least formal compliance with certain liberal norms. Despite his uncertain grip on affairs, Mr Mandela is the other guarantee: his is a genuinely democratic spirit and while he is at the helm the more hegemonic and authoritarian impulses within his party will be held in check. The really unfortunate thing about Mr Mandela is that he is now in his 77th year. The tragedy of his wasted 28 years in jail grows, rather than diminishes, with time.

20 October 1994

Homage to Wilson and Callaghan

Ross McKibbin

The clamorous whispers of an impending election remind us that the present government must soon devise a plausible electoral campaign. Given the events of the last four years, this will not be easy: on any objective reckoning, almost no government this century will present the electorate with such a record of wilful failure. But, of course, objective reckonings matter little in the outcome of British general elections, and 'failure' has several definitions: even from failure many gain, or think they gain, which is why the political system devised by the Conservatives in the Eighties will long outlive Mrs Thatcher. Nonetheless, there will be some testing moments for Central Office, and their campaign is likely to be dominated by a combination of audacity and reticence.

They will certainly follow international fashion and pretend that what they were a year ago they are not today. Just as many of the neo-Brezhnevites who ran the old Soviet Union have miraculously metamorphosed into radical democrats, Ukranian nationalists, Islamic fundamentalists or Christian mystics, so will the Conservative Party not be the party which almost unanimously supported Mrs Thatcher's legislation (including the poll tax) until at the eleventh hour the normally docile backbenchers realised the electoral consequences of their actions. We can also be certain that the party, and its legion of apologists in both the polite and tabloid press, will assure the electorate (once again) that there is no alternative. In an ideological sense this is now probably a rather tatty argument, since the policies with which 'no alternative' is associated are themselves largely discredited. The Conservative strategy is, therefore, more likely to take a folk-historical turn: that the alternative to any sort of Conservative government is impossible and that this is historically demonstrated by the disasters of the Wilson and Callaghan governments from 1964 on. This is a powerful argument because it has only to be insinuated, not made explicit; it needs merely to reinforce what are already a number of conventional wisdoms. It will be the Conservatives' trump.

What has been constructed is a kind of folk memory of decline and disorder which has been wholly disadvantageous to the Labour Party. Such contrived history is of great political significance since much of the present electorate has in fact little or no actual memory of what happened in the Sixties or Seventies and is largely dependent on this received view for its image of Labour as a governing party. Had such a view simply been created by the Conservative Party's engines of propaganda we might expect time to diminish its force. As a political imperative, however, it is powerful precisely because so many in the Labour Party (both right and left) helped create it or acceded to it. The Labour Party has been peculiarly disabled in the last ten years because so many of its own members have written off its history. Thatcherism was in practice distinctly vulnerable to attack – but not by a party which had denied its own past. How people choose to 'remember' the Wilson and Callaghan governments is consequently something to which the Labour Party should urgently attend: only if they 'remember' them benevolently (or at least not malevolently) can Labour hope to re-establish itself securely as a governing party. Yet there is still no evidence that the Labour leadership wishes to attend: on the contrary – as Mrs Thatcher did with the Heath government – they seem either to pretend that the Wilson and Callaghan governments did not exist or that they were mistakes for which the Party must endlessly atone.

This received view need not go uncontested. In the first place, we have had 12 years of the Conservative 'alternative': the critics of Wilson and Callaghan have had their go and must in turn be judged. In the second, we now have a significant scholarly literature on the Sixties and Seventies. Keith Middlemas, for example, has completed his remarkable study of Britain's post-war political economy (a remarkable study even if the conclusions the reader draws from this mass of material are – as in my case – not always Professor Middlemas's), while Michael Artis and David Cobham have edited a detailed and careful examination of the 1974–1979 governments which replaces all previous accounts.* What conclusions might the reader draw from all this kind of evidence? Negatively, the historical record suggests that, as against the post-1979 Conservative governments, Wilson and Callaghan glow with a particular lustre. It is true, as the pure-school free-marketeers have begun to

---

* Keith Middlemas, *Power, Competition and the State. Volume II: Threats to the Post-War Settlement, Britain, 1961–1974. Volume III: The End of the Post-War Era, Britain since 1974* (Macmillan, 1991); Michael Artis and David Cobham, eds, *Labour's Economic Policies, 1974–1979* (Manchester University Press, 1991).

argue, that Thatcherism was polluted by electoral calculation and a fear of offending vested interests, and to that extent is not the real thing. But it defies sense to believe that a patient who was nearly killed by half a dose would be cured by a whole one. In any case, the real thing has been administered to the Australian and New Zealand economies, and if any free marketeer wishes to see the consequences of that historic 'betrayal'* he should go and look. Furthermore, given how favourable international circumstances were throughout the Eighties (as compared to the Seventies), it makes what has happened to the British economy even more astonishing.

The reasons for observing the Wilson and Callaghan governments benevolently, however, are not simply that their critics have made an even greater mess – true though that is. Both governments, particularly the 1964–70 government, deserve a much more positive evaluation than they have usually received. Indeed, apart from Attlee's, the 1964 government is probably the only post-war British government whose record we can read with some satisfaction. While it would be too much to say that in 1970 the horizon was cloudless – among other things, as Middlemas emphasises, the relationship of the trade unions to society and the Labour Party remained highly problematic – the sky was pretty blue. Unemployment and inflation were low, the balance of payments was in equilibrium, productivity growth was by British standards high, it was a peculiarly good period for British manufacturing industry, infrastructure investment remained high, there were important social and institutional reforms. The Government had a discernible sense of the national interest, of what was possible: but there was also a discernible sense of direction and control – a sense fully shared, as Roy Jenkins's memoirs perhaps surprisingly confirm – by Wilson himself. Within two years – *before* the 1973 oil crisis overwhelmed the Heath government – many of these gains had been thrown away.

The case for the 1974 government is obviously more difficult: for most people (insofar as they remember anything), it represents exclusively what it to some extent undoubtedly was – low growth, poor productivity, high inflation, strikes, 'chaos'. But the 1974 government was left as wretched an inheritance as any modern British government – much worse than that left to Wilson in 1964 – which operated insidiously throughout its whole term. Nor, putting it delicately, was the government much helped either by its enemies or friends. Yet Artis and

---

*The word is that of Tom Fitzgerald, doyen of Australian financial journalists, in *Between Life and Economics* (Sydney, 1991). This book should be read by free marketeers of all parties.

Cobham's argument that institutionally and politically (despite its well-publicised blemishes) it coped surprisingly effectively is difficult to deny. One way of seeing that government is to imagine what might have happened had it won the 1979 Election and remained in office throughout the Eighties. It seems reasonable to suppose that the great majority of the British people would have (at least) the same standard of living as they do today, the health and education systems would be in significantly better shape, there would not have been two grinding recessions, unemployment would be lower while inflation could scarcely have been higher, there would have been fewer beggars in the streets of all our major towns, the government would have exercised some responsible control of our financial system, thousands of our fellow citizens would not now hold mortgage debts on houses that greatly exceed the value of the houses themselves, manufacturing industry would not now be so skeletal, a working relationship between industry and the government (towards which the Callaghan government was slowly moving) might have partly compensated for the deficiencies of our existing capital market, the very rich would have been less rich and the very poor less poor. Not all these things would have happened, perhaps, but it is a fair bet that some would, and even if only one of them had happened we would be better-off than we are.

One conclusion that we can therefore draw is that since 1945 Labour governments have left the country better than when they found it, and Conservative governments worse. Should the Conservatives lose the next election that conclusion, I think, will still hold. But does it matter? It is not a conclusion that the electorate has drawn, or been allowed to draw. The implication of Middlemas's study is that it does not much matter. His is a story of an economically-emancipated 'public' declining to accept the social foundations of the Keynes-Beveridge settlement, and of an increasingly weak state unable to modernise in unfavourable international conditions and capitulating to powerfully-asserted sectarian interests. There are reasons, however, for thinking that it does matter and that we need not read the past quite so pessimistically.

The first is that what appears to be a result of long-term developments is much more historically specific. Contemporaries often see fundamental (sometimes revolutionary) change in events which in hindsight were very much less than that: the French in 1936 after the victory of the Popular Front, or the Americans during the industrial conflicts of 1936–37, are examples. This country in 1978–79 is another: there was a clear tendency to see in trade-union behaviour (particularly that of public-sector trade unions) one of these fundamental changes –

John Goldthorpe argued then that the 'phenomenon of prestige' had 'decomposed' and Middlemas seems to agree. It would be unwise to reject this argument entirely: but we might equally suggest that what happened was almost inevitable in the circumstances, particularly given the Government's decision (which most of its members probably now think to have been a mistake) to hold wage increases to a 5 per cent norm. The 'winter of discontent' ranks high in the demonology of the last Labour government but we should be careful before accepting it.

There is also a moral argument for thinking that it matters, even if it does not carry much weight with the electorate. Many of the policies of the present government – its housing policies, for instance, or the establishment of the Social Fund – have been tantamount to the creation of poverty and deprivation. The transformation, say, of Central London has been one of the most depressing developments of the last ten years. No doubt the Government did not intend this, and homeless teenagers on innumerable doorsteps are not its responsibility alone: but it is hard to know what else it thought would happen when it concocted these policies. The Government's defenders have implied that we can divorce the moral from the social sphere, that even if we all agree to deplore homelessness, there are no social consequences from doing nothing about it. But we cannot make such a distinction: sooner or later, if we continue on this path, society simply falls apart.

Whether Mrs Thatcher did or did not believe that there was no such thing as society, she certainly acted as if social cohesion had nonetheless to be preserved. For one thing property becomes threatened if it is not. Her way of securing this increasingly relied upon patriotism and xenophobia on the one hand, and coercion on the other. It did her no good. While it is clear that much of the present social dislocation is common to all Western societies and probably beyond the reach of their governments, it is also clear that the 'alternative' social cohesion which Mrs Thatcher brought to 'ungovernable' Britain has disastrously failed. The quite conscious attempt to replace one form of social relationship by another (and thus one form of social cohesion by another) has had all too practical consequences: we are now very much more likely to be burgled or mugged. Mr Major, to his credit, appears to understand this but it is hard to see what he, as leader of a party very largely shaped in the Eighties, can do about it.

There are two other reasons why it matters whether the present regime survives or not. The first is that the Conservative Government has enormously increased the force of inertia in British society, and the Conservative Party as it is at present constituted depends for its existence on perpetuating that inertia. The Conservative Party has in the past had its share of movers and shakers, and both Mrs Thatcher and those around her, at least in the first years, wished, or said they wished, to move and shake. In practice, however, that was not their primary concern, and the saturnalia of attempted electoral manipulation which characterised her last years further constricted Britain's social and economic flexibility. A deliberate attempt to purchase social inertia through housing policy, through its encouragement of owner occupation at almost any cost, has also had the effect of making the economy more unstable and more difficult to manage. It might not have been inevitable for the Conservative Party to have gone this way, but by associating herself with its most powerful tendencies, by giving them their head, Mrs Thatcher ensures that the Party now (and Mr Major's government) is Thatcherite in everything but name. The result is that the Conservative Party and much of British society cling to each other in a kind of dying embrace, and the only way to save them both is by uncoupling them.

The second reason is that the state can be restored to its proper place in the British economy only – and perhaps not even then – if the Conservatives are required to leave office. The ideological corollary of structural inertia is the predominance of a narrow and futile orthodoxy of which the Conservative Party is (at the moment) the principal political vehicle. This orthodoxy demands the expulsion of the state from any active part in the country's economic life, despite the transparent foolishness of this aspiration. The orthodoxy has assumed a quasi-religious aspect, as free trade did before 1914.

We now find ourselves in a position analogous to Edwardian Britain, where it was political death to question the wisdom of free trade despite ubiquitous evidence of the destructive consequences of this: but, unlike the Edwardians, we are without a government able to construct a coherent compensating policy. It is thus impermissible to argue that British Aerospace, Rolls-Royce, Rover or Jaguar should not have been privatised, or that one of them should never have been encouraged to buy another. The result of this silence is that a paralysed government stands helplessly by hoping that what is all too likely to happen does not. But in Britain the degree of inertia is now such that the state, for all its past failings, is one of the few dynamic economic agents which remain. By denying this, the present government has abandoned any kind of responsible action: it is one thing to say that the state cannot pick winners, quite another that it should let winners go bankrupt.

Which returns us to Wilson, Callaghan and the Labour Party, since the current orthodoxy is justified almost exclusively by the apparent 'failure' of the state-interventionist policies they practised. If an ideological alternative to the Conservative Government is to be made acceptable to the electorate, both folk memory and the Labour Party will have to change their minds about the 1964 and 1974 governments and the Labour Party will have to do it first. The Labour Party has committed the cardinal rhetorical error of any political party by apologising for its own past: the Conservatives may ignore their own past, but they never apologise for it. Labour has done this partly because of the utopianism of many of its activists – to them the best is always the enemy of the good – and partly because of a certain timid and innocent defensiveness. Labour always plays the game by other people's rules. A measure of this defensiveness is the extent to which the Labour Party is happy to be thought the 'caring' party but is plainly less happy to be thought the 'competent' party, even though there seems no logical reason why it could not be both. It thus apologises for the Wilson and Callaghan governments because the activists said they fell below perfection while those in economic and cultural authority said they failed. But there are entirely adequate justifications for these governments which the Labour leadership should start making. Although it seems scarcely possible, the majority of the electorate still believes that the Conservatives are more 'competent' economic managers than Labour, and this basically means that they think the Tories are more fit to govern. We can be fairly certain that as an election approaches this belief will become more intense – much to Labour's detriment. The Labour leadership must, therefore, assert that the Wilson and Callaghan governments were more 'competent' than their predecessors and successors, which they were, and sound as though they mean that as a compliment, and also recognise that their policies, though indeed imperfect, were better suited to a sluggish, rather uncohesive society than the alternatives. They might then be able to argue that the rather rough-hewn social democracy with which the Labour Party is historically associated has worked very much more in the national interest than anything else we are likely to have. And that we are more likely to have a productive capitalism under Labour than under its principal opponent. A Labour Party which restores itself to its own past might, having perceived its strengths, accept its weaknesses: namely, that under our present institutional and constitutional arrangements its spells in office may be fitful and unrewarding.

24 October 1991

LIVES

Why Calcutta?

Amit Chaudhuri on Mother Teresa*

Among the welter of images and mythologies that constitute the middle-class Bengali's consciousness – P3 and Ganesh underwear, the Communist hammer and sickle, Lenin's face, fish and vegetable chops outside the Academy, wedding and funeral invitation cards, the films of Satyajit Ray, the loud horns of speeding state transport buses, Murshidabadi and Tangail sarees, the daily *Ananda Bazar Patrika*, the songs of Tagore, the destitute outside Grand Hotel, Boroline Antiseptic cream, Madhyamik school examinations (to name just a few of the constituents) – Mother Teresa, too, is present. Not only is she undeniably a part of the contemporary history of Calcutta, but she is, to the ordinary middle-class Bengali, only a segment in a reality that is complex and constantly changing, and is composed impartially of the trivial and the profound. In contrast, to the average middle-class European or American Mother Teresa *is* Calcutta, or certainly its most life-affirming face. The rest of Calcutta is impossibly 'other', romantically destitute and silent; the 'black hole', unsayable. It is interesting that the poor whom Mother Teresa attends never speak. They have no social backgrounds or histories, although it is precisely history and social background, and the shifts within them, that create the poor. Instead of speaking, the poor in the photographs look up at her silently, touch her hand, are fed by a spoon. The 'black hole' of Calcutta, figuring as it does an open, silent mouth, no longer refers to the historical event that took place in the 18th century in which English men, women and children were trapped by Indian soldiers in a small, suffocating cell in the city. It refers to the unsayable that lay, and still often lies, at the heart of the colonial encounter, the breakdown in the Western observer's language when he or she attempts to describe a different culture, the mouth open but the words unable to take form. In Western literature, the unsayable is represented by 'The horror! the horror!' in Conrad's *Heart of Darkness*, and 'ou-boom', the meaningless echo in the Marabar Caves in Forster's *A Passage to India*, the complexity of both

* A response to Christopher Hitchens's *The Missionary Position: Mother Teresa in Theory and Practice* (Verso, 1995).

Africa and India reduced to hushed, disyllabic sounds. In history and the popular imagination, another two syllables, 'black hole', have come to express the idea that, for the Westerner, Calcutta is still beyond perception and language.

Silence is a strange attribute to ascribe to the noisiest and most talkative Indian city. Calcutta, capital of India and second city of the Empire for 138 years, until 1911, was the crucible of Indian nationalist politics, and the home of its chief instrument, the Indian National Congress – and of modern Indian liberal consciousness itself. Nehru thought that if, in a sort of metaphorical laboratory, you were to mix, in a metaphorical beaker, an equal amount of Western rationalism and science on the one hand, and ancient Eastern values (a vague and largely unexamined ingredient in the experiment) on the other, you would produce a new compound that was the modern Indian personality – an idea that was actually prefigured by the beliefs and works of people such as Raja Rammohun Roy in Bengal in the early 19th century and Henry Louis Vivian Derozio, the Anglo-Portuguese poet and lecturer at the Hindu College, Calcutta, and his fervent Bengali followers. The metaphorical laboratory turned out to be the Indian middle classes.

Bengal had the earliest printing presses in India, with sustained output of scholastic and literary material; during the 19th and early 20th centuries more books were produced in Calcutta, the capital, than in almost any other city in the world. This was not surprising given that Bengal was the site of perhaps the most profound response to the colonial encounter, and in the middle of the 19th century began what is sometimes called the Bengal, and sometimes the Indian, Renaissance: an aspect of it being the flowering of one of the richest modern literatures – Bengali – in the world.

Bengal's history has also been one of political unrest and even tragedy. In particular, there were the famines, the last of which, in 1943, was not caused by a real food shortage at all. It was partly created by the unscrupulousness of local traders and by the diversion of staple foods, such as rice, to the British Army; the largest share of the blame must be apportioned to British rule. With the famines came an influx into Calcutta of the rural poor, who arrived in the city to die. Many of the poor to whom Mother Teresa would have ministered when she opened her first slum school in Calcutta on 21 December 1948 (she had been teaching geography in a missionary school in the city from 1929) would have been victims of the famine or their children. The number of poor people in Bengal is always being added to, and in 1948 Mother Teresa would also have encountered a huge insurgence of homeless refugees from East Pakistan, newly-created after the 'stupid' (to use Hitchens's adjective) partitioning of Bengal by the British at the time of Independence. Partition would permanently alter, even disfigure, Bengal (or West Bengal, as it had now become) and its capital. The backbone of Bengal's heavy industry would be broken and a huge homeless, rootless population of East Bengalis would be added to the population of Calcutta. Leave alone the poor, even the middle-class or upper-middle-class Bengali, bereft of ancestral property, have had to struggle to make a home in the city. (One of my mother's closest friends from her childhood in Sylhet, Bangladesh, a retired schoolteacher, still lives with her older sister in North Calcutta in a small rented flat. My father's ancestral house languishes in Bangladesh and is at last, we hear, to be torn down; but he has been luckier than most other 'refugees' – he rose to a high position in the company he worked for, and bought his own flat in Calcutta in his middle age.) After Partition, the constitution and nature of the Bengali middle or *bhadralok* (literally 'civilised person') class changed significantly: once associated with privilege, education and genteel values, it now became increasingly beleaguered, both culturally and economically.

In 1971, millions of refugees – a large number of Muslims among them – began to flee from East Pakistan to Calcutta. The reason for this was a political impasse between East and West Pakistan, resulting in the genocide of the largely Muslim East Bengali population by (West) Pakistani troops, a project backed by American and Chinese diplomacy and arms. India intervened and went to war with Pakistan; East Pakistan was liberated and a new country, Bangladesh, created; but, in Calcutta, the number of the poor and homeless increased substantially. Areas like the Esplanade and Gariahat in central and south Calcutta respectively were to change forever; colourful pavement stalls selling T-shirts, woollens, trousers, kabaab rolls, sprang up in these parts to provide a livelihood for the new jobless and homeless. Families began to live in abandoned bus-stops and under partially constructed bridges; the smell of rice being cooked in a pot would occasionally surprise the passer-by. Add to this the daily migration from villages in Bengal and the neighbouring states of Orissa and Bihar (for Calcutta continues to be the major metropolis in Eastern India), not to speak of the continued migrations from poverty-stricken Bangladesh, and one begins to get some idea of where the destitute that Mother Teresa lifts up from the pavements come from. Two facts should be mentioned in this context. First, there have been no more famines in West Bengal since Independence. Second, in contrast to other, richer cities like

Bombay, and even certain Western cities, Calcutta, despite unique pressures, has been free of Fascist or right-wing politics. The only chauvinist party, *Amra Bangali* – 'We Are Bengalis' – has almost been laughed out of existence. A Marxist government has ruled the state for the last twenty years (which has brought about a special set of problems associated with long-running governments, as well as a constant neglect of the state by central government, where the Congress Party has almost always been in power).

My own mixed feelings about Mother Teresa were born some time in the early Eighties, when I was an undergraduate in London. There was a film about her on television (not Malcolm Muggeridge's *Something Beautiful for God*, which apparently first turned Mother Teresa into an internationally known figure, and about which Hitchens writes extensively in his book); the only things I recall about the film are the large number of affluent, admiring British people in it in close proximity to Mother Teresa, and the latter smiling and saying, more than once to the camera: 'We must sell Love.' Both these memories irritated me for some time, I couldn't see in what way, except the most superficial, these affluent and photogenic Europeans had anything to do with the poor in Calcutta. Nor could I see how 'selling Love' was going to help the poor.

One of the things that has struck me ever since about the publicity concerning Mother Teresa is that it has less to do with the poor than with Mother Teresa. The poor are shown in a timeless, even pastoral, light: Muggeridge even claims that the interior of the Home for the Dying appeared in his film in spite of insufficient light because of a 'miraculous light' that emanated from Mother Teresa. Hitchens and the cameraman Ken Macmillan believe that it was the new improved Kodak film that did it. Whatever really happened, the 'miraculous' light seems to be a metaphor for the ahistorical; it fixes the Bengali destitute in a timeless vacuum; it further uproots from community, background and identity those who have already been uprooted from community, background and identity. In blocking out history, the 'miraculous light' also blocks out one's proper empathy with, and understanding of, the poor. While it may be true that the poor are people like you and me because we were all created by God, it is only through an understanding of a country's history, and the history of the poor, that we can begin to appreciate that, indeed, the poor were people like you and me before something happened to them. Mother Teresa herself, too, is always represented out of context, as an angel of mercy who descended on Calcutta to pick the dying off the streets. If Muggeridge's film made

Mother Teresa a 'star', as Hitchens puts it, in 1971 (the year of the Bangladesh war, of which Muggeridge seemed blissfully unaware), it still leaves unaccounted for the immense stretch of time between 1948 and 1971, during which her Order must have established and entrenched itself in Calcutta. This was a time when there were no Reagans, Clintons, Thatchers, Queen Elizabeths or Duvaliers to give her their largesse or approval. Could she have worked, then, during this most crucial time, without the support of the local people or local government? After all, she was working, not in a desert, but in a major city which provides a context and parameters for everything working within it, including organisations that do social work, among which Mother Teresa's is only one. (For instance, the Ramakrishna Mission and the Bharat Sevasram Sangh are only two of the most active and well-known organisations doing social and charity work here for the poor.) If Mother Teresa worked for the poor in Calcutta, then it goes without saying that this work was made possible in fundamental ways by the support of Bengali people and the West Bengal Government. And in the flood of publicity and photo-opportunities that have followed Mother Teresa's celebrity, in which various world leaders have basked in the reflected light of her virtue (and her gratitude), it would seem that only the people of Calcutta and the West Bengal Government have missed out, even been blanked out, to be represented only by the solitary destitute at the Mother's hand. This is somewhat unfortunate because the Marxist West Bengal Government, whatever its other limitations, has done more work in land reform and land redistribution than almost any other Indian state, immensely benefiting the poor and less privileged in rural areas. The positive aspects of this on the alleviation of poverty would certainly be more profound than the work done even by the most well-intentioned charity.

And yet, whatever reservations one might have about the media projections of Mother Teresa and her work (done with her tacit endorsement or not), however banal her occasional utterances might be (several examples are provided by Hitchens, including her exhortation, 'Forgive, forgive, forgive', after the Union Carbide disaster in Bhopal), not even the stupidest banality can cancel the importance of real action and real work done for the poor. And so far, this much seems to have been undeniable: that Mother Teresa and her Sisters *do* pick up the poor from the pavements of Calcutta, give them shelter, food to eat and, if need be, the possibility of a dignified death.

Hitchens has much to say about this aspect of her work in his book (which is really an extended essay of about 25,000 words), giving information that would be new and even shocking to most readers. If there is a slight Eurocentric quality about *The Missionary Position* this is because Mother Teresa and her reputation in the West, the workings of the Western media, and Mother Teresa the Roman Catholic proponent of anti-abortion dogma are central to Hitchens; Calcutta and its history and people are mentioned sympathetically, intelligently, but briefly, and remain in the background.

Hitchens's Introduction examines, with the acuity of a literary critic, a portfolio of photographs, printed in the middle of the book, each showing Mother Teresa with a dubious character – either with people known to enrich themselves at the cost of others and to terrorise the powerless, like Michèle Duvalier, wife of Jean-Claude Duvalier of Haiti, or big-time crooks like cult leader 'John Roger', 'a fraud of Chaucerian proportions'. These people have donated money, at one time or another, to Mother Teresa's organisation. Indeed, there is something Chaucerian about the world explored in this short book, with its range of tricksters and frauds and their close proximity to the holy and to absolution. Two-thirds of the way through the book, we come across Charles Keating, who is 'now serving a ten-year sentence for his part in the Savings and Loan scandal – undoubtedly one of the greatest frauds in American history'.

> At the height of his success as a thief, Keating made donations (not out of his own pocket, of course) to Mother Teresa in the sum of one and a quarter million dollars. He also granted her the use of his private jet. In return, Mother Teresa allowed Keating to make use of her prestige on several important occasions and gave him a personalised crucifix which he took everywhere with him.

During the course of Keating's trial, Hitchens adds, 'Mother Teresa wrote to the court seeking clemency for Mr Keating.' Her letter elicited a response from a Deputy District Attorney for Los Angeles, Paul Turley, who pointed out that, in all fairness, the stolen money Keating had donated to her Order should be returned to its original owners. Turley has still not heard from Mother Teresa.

For all that, there is no evidence in *The Missionary Position* to suggest that Mother Teresa has used any money from donations for her personal material benefit – in this much, at least, she stands apart from most modern godmen and television evangelists, as well as from Chaucer's Pardoner. Money might have helped her operations in Calcutta to expand into a 'missionary multinational', but conditions in her 'homes' are hardly opulent – indeed, if anything, they are unnecessarily austere. This is precisely Hitchens's point – much of the money she receives remains unspent and unaccounted for. Hitchens's contention is that Mother Teresa's ambitions aren't material at all, in the ordinary sense of that term; her aim is to establish a cult of austerity and suffering. The most disturbing section of the book, the first part of the chapter entitled 'Good Works and Heroic Virtues', does something to support this contention. Among the testimony of others (former nuns, social workers), we are given an account by Robin Fox, editor of the *Lancet*, written after a visit to Mother Teresa's 'operation' in Calcutta. Dr Fox, although favourably disposed towards Mother Teresa's work, found that medical facilities for the ill and the dying were not only woefully inadequate, but even prohibited or deliberately circumscribed beyond a certain point. Sterilised syringes, antibiotics and choloroquine for malaria were unavailable. Blood tests were seldom permitted. According to Fox, 'such systematic approaches are alien to the ethos of the home. Mother Teresa prefers providence to planning; rules are designed to prevent any drift towards materialism.' Moreover, 'how competent are the sisters at managing pain? On a short visit, I could not judge the power of the spiritual approach, but I was disturbed to learn that the formulary includes no strong analgesics.' Hitchens comments:

> Mother Teresa has been working in Calcutta for four and a half decades, and for nearly three of them she has been favoured with immense quantities of money and material. Her 'Home for the Dying', which was part of her dominion visited by Dr Fox, is in no straitened condition. It is as he describes it because that is how Mother Teresa wishes it to be. The neglect of what is commonly understood as proper medicine is not a superficial contradiction. It is the essence of the endeavour, the same essence that is evident in a cheerful sign which has been filmed on the wall of Mother Teresa's morgue. It reads: 'I am going to heaven today.'

The charge of deliberately curtailing medical care, of promulgating 'a cult based on death and suffering and subjection', is a serious and substantiated one, and it cannot be ignored. Surprisingly, although Hitchens gets his information from authoritative sources – such as Dr Fox, among others – the facts about Mother Theresa's neglect of the poor are not widely known: certainly not in Calcutta. Most Bengalis have viewed Mother Teresa's work with admiration (there seems to be little doubt in most people's minds that she *does* do valuable work for the poor), although rumours that her main aim is the conversion of the poor to Christianity have circulated from time to time. Not long ago, she was embroiled in something of a controversy, when the BJP, the Indian right-wing nationalist party, accused her of demanding job reservations for Dalit (low-caste) Christians. It is not unusual for caste-structures to persist among Indian Christians, Sikhs, and even Muslims, bringing all kinds of problems to the already problem-ridden matter of 'quotas' and 'reservations' – for jobs, and places in schools and colleges – kept aside by the government for the 'backward classes'. This time, unusually for her, Mother Teresa decided to answer her detractors. At a press conference at the headquarters on A.J.C. Bose Road, she denied not only the BJP's allegations but also it seems, Hitchens's accusations. According to *The Statesman* of 25 November, 'she said she would like her detractors to come to the Missionaries' home for the sick and dying in Kalighat and see how "the sisters serve the suffering humanity irrespective of their religion, nationality, caste or colour."' Moreover, 'she also admitted that in her mission for the "salvation of the poorest of poor" . . . she would not mind taking charity from "dictators and corrupt people. Everyone should be given the chance to show his compassion – even a beggar on the street," she said.' (It has to be said here that Hitchens's book, which is now being sold and reviewed in India, and from which an extract was published recently in a Calcutta newspaper, seems to have been generally received in this country without rancour and with equanimity.)

In the climate of tremendous political and popular support for Mother Teresa, especially in the West, it is obvious that Hitchens's investigations have been a solitary and courageous endeavour. The book is extremely well-written, with a sanity and sympathy that tempers its irony. In spite of this, Mother Teresa remains an enigma even after we have finished reading it. According to Hitchens, she is 'a religious fundamentalist, a political operative, a primitive sermoniser and an accomplice of worldly, secular powers'. She might be all these, and yet one feels that there is more to the complex personality of the Albanian Agnes Bojaxhiu, who arrived in Calcutta from Yugoslavia one day in 1928. Hitchens's Mother Teresa, at times, is in danger of assuming the one-dimensionality of the Mother Teresa of her admirers. As drawn by him, she becomes something of a wizened but powerful machine of single-minded intentionality. Hitchens quotes Freud towards the beginning of the book, and as a reader of Freud he would know that the genesis of, and reasons for, actions are never clearly revealed to the protagonists themselves, let alone to others.

4 January 1996

At least they paid their taxes

Linda Colley on Nancy Reagan

On the dust-jacket of this book* is a photograph of its author. Kitty
Kelley, formerly of Spokane, one-time Lilac Princess at school, mil-
lionaire biographer of Jacqueline Onassis, Elizabeth Taylor and Frank
Sinatra, looks not all that different from her current subject. There is
the same bright, taut face which a good surgical lift always ensures, the
same immaculately-dyed and coiffeured hair, the same fixed smile
exhibiting the kind of teeth that only an American orthodontist can fix,
the same chunky gold jewellery and expensive clothes overlaying a diet-
starved body, and the same clawed, no longer young hands about which
nothing can be done whatsoever. Here, however, she is able to hide
them behind the thousands of document files that surround her, a
solid wall of research material on which someone has plopped a clearly
reluctant cat.

As those who have ploughed through its five hundred-plus pages, full
of this kind of upfront bitchiness, will already know, this is an indictment of Nancy Reagan composed by the vacuum-cleaner method. Five
years of 'meticulous' research and over a thousand interviews have
been sucked into the Kitty machine so as to give us the accumulated
dirt. The book has been enormously successful, justifying its author's
3.5 million dollar advance by selling almost a million copies in its first
week of publication. The popular American press has quoted its more
salacious anecdotes in lip-smacking fashion. Up-market dailies and
weeklies have shaken their collective heads censoriously, before regaling
their readers with the same prurient stories. And Barbara Bush has
done her bit for the sales by describing the book as Kitty-Litter. Even
now, when the initial publicity surge is well over, it can still be seen in
almost every airport lounge and railway bookstore on both sides of the
Atlantic. It is still a best-seller. It is even reasonably well written. But is
it true, and does it matter?

These questions need to be asked because, as the document files are
intended to demonstrate, this is purportedly a serious work. The

* Kitty Kelley, *Nancy Reagan: The Unauthorised Biography* (Bantam, 1991).

acknowledgements extend for over nine pages, and there are more than forty pages of notes setting out the author's debt to 'Presidential documents, FBI files, financial disclosures, IRS returns, letters, diaries, memoirs, oral histories, film archives, personal recollections, calendars and correspondence'. Relays of research assistants have been employed, and Kelley assures us that knowing 'how it feels to be depicted unfairly and inaccurately', she has striven throughout to be 'fair, accurate and thorough'. She has certainly dug far more deeply into her subject than any relatively impoverished professional historian is likely to be able to do, and until all the personal papers become available in the Ronald Reagan Presidential Library, those interested in post-war American politics and history will have little choice but to consult this book.

And this is where the vacuum-cleaner method becomes a problem. Kelley has sucked up so much, so indiscriminately, that what is important and true gets lost in the mass of rubbish that is neither. She has treated all of her sources, snubbed manicurists, or cast-off lovers, or disappointed Presidential aides, or dismissed cabinet ministers, as if they were of equal worth, and has made no allowances for the axes that were clearly being ground or for ordinary human error. It also appears that not all the people she claims to have interviewed had been approached; and those who were are not always quoted correctly or in full. The end-result is an entertaining, over-detailed and less than reliable mish-mash of a biography which cruelly exposes Nancy Reagan without ever really understanding her, or the power she and her husband were able to exercise.

Yet the basic story line seems clear enough. She was born in 1921 in one of the poorer New York boroughs, the only child of an ambitious but unsuccessful actress and an ineffectual but apparently genial salesman. Her parents separated when she was a toddler, and she was farmed out with an aunt. Only when her mother married again, this time to a right-wing Chicago surgeon called Loyal Davis, was Nancy able to begin the climb out of her unsatisfactory origins. She dropped her real father and got Davis to adopt her. She began to lose her puppy fat. And she enrolled in Smith College – like all the so-called Seven Sisters, something of a finishing school for young ladies from the East Coast's upper middle class. At this point, though, Kelley's thesis (and it is her only one) that Nancy, like her mother, was an all-out social climber begins to falter. For she did not, as might have been expected, use Smith as a gateway to a nice fresh-faced Yalie called, say, Charles ('Chip') Staunton Webster III, with a law opening in Daddy's firm in Boston and a summer place in New Hampshire. Instead, she took up acting, still

W very much a *déclassé* occupation, and decided to go to Hollywood.

She got there, Kelley claims, by sleeping with Benjamin Thau, head of casting for Metro-Goldwyn-Mayer. There followed 11 films, including one that sounds a real gem about God broadcasting by radio to the whole of planet Earth barring the Communist bloc. Nancy was always well-groomed, thoroughly professional and unfailingly hard-working. But she was too short, her legs were too thick, and she was perhaps too brittle and self-conscious to lose herself in a role. Then, on 15 November 1949, bitterly aware that she would never be anything more than 'a crumb on the banquet table of MGM', Nancy Davis wangled a date with Ronald Wilson Reagan.

For more than two years, however, the rest was not history, but still more anxious striving on her part. Reagan had just been dropped by his wife, Jane Wyman, and was doing the rounds of B-movie starlets. It was only when Nancy got pregnant that he married her in 1952, and only after their first child was born that he became a faithful husband (with just one brief lapse thereafter, Kelley assures us). But the transformation that followed was an extraordinary one. They became a devoted and massively successful couple, climbing to the top with the sort of relentless ease which had utterly eluded both of them before their marriage. The immaculate grooming, taut ambition and relentless perfectionism that had killed her performances stone-dead before the camera were channelled into Reagan's political career. And his crooked smile, small-town anti-Communism, and 'gee whiz, golly shucks crap' as Sinatra styled it, which had been such a bore to Hollywood's predominantly liberal aristocracy, made him a highly attractive candidate to rich Californian populists. By 1966 he was the Republican governor, and 'Mommy', as he always called her, was cleaning up the gubernatorial mansion in Sacramento.

There is, understandably, a great deal of interior and body decor detail in this book. We learn how Nancy revamped her husband's office, getting rid of the old burnished leather walls, laying miles of bright red carpet, and installing plenty of beige burlap ('modern, classy'). And we learn what Nancy admired in her best friend and fashion mentor Betsy Bloomingdale: 'Betsy wore cashmere trenchcoats with mink collars and cuffs; her 18-carat-gold belt was decorated with 50 carved emeralds from David Webb, one of the finest jewellers in America; her three-acre garden brimmed with the rarest orchids in Southern California, and her kitchen produced cuisine worthy of connoisseurs. In addition to a Los Angeles mansion in affluent Holmby Hills, the Bloomingdales owned an apartment in New York City and a *pied-à-terre* in Paris.'

And so it goes on . . . To the new three million dollar mansion the Reagans extracted from their Californian friends before leaving it empty and unused when they moved to Washington. To Nancy's pet hairdresser, Julian, who always had to be given a seat on the Presidential jet together with her personal maid. To the 220 sets of china she ordered for the White House at $1000 a set, just when Reagan was cutting welfare. To the $46,000 wardrobe she wore for the Inauguration in 1980, accepted as a gift from couturiers who wanted the cachet of dressing her. Here is a guide to arriviste style and greed: and we are clearly intended to deplore the vulgarity of it all.

Yet to do so would be to miss the real point. Reagan was the Governor of America's richest state, before becoming President of the wealthiest and most powerful nation on earth. Even so, what he and his wife begged, borrowed and spent was mere pin money in comparison with our own Royal Family's rate of expenditure – and at least the Reagans paid their taxes, albeit, as Kelley shows, with considerable reluctance. It was not their extravagance as such, but rather the nature of their extravagance, which was striking, revealing as it did their parvenu origins and ignorance of the customary rules of patrician life. Never rich enough to come close to the Trumps of this world, they were not grand or secure enough not to care. Nancy, in particular, was always worried about money and doing the correct thing. So on one occasion she and her girlfriends spent hours desperately practicing how to curtsey to the Queen, not knowing – as any Daughter of the Revolution would certainly have known – that by tradition Americans never genuflect to monarchs. And then there was the Hollywood entertainment with which Nancy once again hoped to impress the Queen on her state visit in 1983. Kelley mocks the bad taste and invites us to join her. But the wider and historically important point – that the Reagan phenomenon can only be understood in the light of the post-war decline of the old Wasp ruling class, and the shift in power and wealth from the declining industrial East Coast of America to the booming silicon-chip West Coast – is never acknowledged.

This lack of a political, social and above all historical context for her subject means that Kelley never comes to grips with what must be the essential question a biographer of Nancy Reagan has to ask: how much influence was she, as the wife of supposedly the most powerful man on earth, able to exert? It is, admittedly, a difficult question to answer satisfactorily, in part because this kind of indirect female influence has rarely been adequately examined in the past. The majority of political historians have always been male, and as such only occasionally interested in the female contribution to successful masculine careers, while that new generation of historians that concentrates on the experience of women prefers its subjects to be oppressed, or powerful in their own right. And there is a still more intractable problem. Women who manipulate powerful men rarely boast about it or leave written evidence of their influence behind them. To do so would be to abandon that discretion and subterfuge which are their main weapons. The men on whom they practise their persuasion are naturally unlikely to confess their tractability either. In the absence of hard proof, how can we reach an estimate of Nancy's political role? One answer is by looking at previous 20th-century First Ladies. The record suggests that their potential for interference has been growing alongside the increased visibility of their husbands' office and the changing status and expectations of women. In the 19th century, with some exceptions, Presidential wives stayed in the background, sometimes even handing over their duties as White House hostess to a younger, female relation. But since the American Constitution does not prescribe what a First Lady can or cannot do, there was nothing to stop Woodrow Wilson's wife from moving in on his office when he was incapacitated by a stroke from 1919 to 1921. 'I studied every paper sent from the different Secretaries or Senators,' Mrs Wilson, the former Edith Bolling Galt, would write later, 'and tried to digest and present in tabloid form the things that, despite my vigilance, had to go to the President. I, myself, never made a single decision regarding the disposition of public affairs. The only decision that was mine was what was important and what was not, and the very important decision of when to present matters to my husband.' In other words, without being elected or liable to dismissal or impeachment, Edith Wilson was able to take advantage of her husband's frailty and the Constitution's silence to influence the agenda of American government. Subsequent First Ladies have demanded still more autonomy. By the 1930s, Eleanor Roosevelt was holding her own press conferences. Forty years later, Rosalynn Carter was sitting in on Cabinet meetings, carrying out her own missions to foreign governments, and making suggestions that she should be given her own salary and staff.

At one level, then, modern Presidential wives pose the same kind of problem as the wives of Masters of Colleges or the wives of diplomats or the wives of royalty do in this country. With the rise of female expectations, all arrangements of this kind have come under strain, since intelligent women are no longer so content to stay in the background or to lose themselves in their husbands' careers.

On the one hand, traditional Americans still expect the First Lady to play a visible role as helpmate, hostess and cultural icon, to be the model for decent and supportive womankind which her title suggests. On the other, feminist voters now expect that the First Lady will have her own identity and her own cause, and they, too, have to be catered to. So Ladybird Johnson pushed environmental issues. Betty Ford backed the Equal Rights Amendment in defiance of her husband. Mrs Carter took up the cause of the mentally ill, and Mrs Bush associated herself with the literacy campaign. Even if they wanted to, therefore, it would be difficult for these women to hug seclusion to themselves to the degree that their predecessors were able to do in the last century, or that Mrs Major still does today. And of course even if they were able to insist on a strictly private role their position would still allow them extraordinary opportunities. Assuming that they occupy the same beds as their husbands, Presidential wives are guaranteed time alone every day with the most important man in the world, something which no male politician can necessarily expect. Like it or not, they are married to power and have the opportunity of exerting power in their own right. And within the limits of her tense disposition, Nancy Reagan seems to have liked it a great deal.

Even before they made it to Washington, some of her contribution to her husband's success was already clear. No more ambitious and probably no shrewder than he was, she was infinitely more hard-working. She pushed her man when necessary, but she also knew him well enough to acknowledge his weaknesses and work around them. She ensured that his campaign managers knew that he performed better later in the day. She made sure that they allowed him a nap every afternoon, as well as time by the pool to maintain the glowing suntan cherished as part of his outdoor macho image. She rehearsed his speeches with him, and prompted him when necessary – which by the end of his second term as President it frequently was. She also played tough girl to his nice guy. Reagan desperately needed to be liked both by the voters and by those around him – a formidable weakness for a politician. I suspect that at least some of Nancy's rudeness, bullying and nagging campaigns to get rid of people was a case of her doing what Reagan himself could not bear to do, or bother to do. By acting the scheming virago, she allowed him to emerge with clean hands, folksy candour and that bemused, fresh-as-the-prairie smile.

Kelley quotes only one statement by Nancy on her position and it is nicely ambiguous: 'A woman, I would hope, would be a help to her husband no matter what he does. Of course, the more successful he is, the more important her role becomes.' But important in what ways exactly? Until the archives are open, we shall never know. And since so much of what Nancy did must have been conducted over the phone, or in private conversations with her husband, we will never know it all. Former members of the Reagan Administration who have published memoirs have certainly testified to her influence over questions of political personnel. Michael Deaver, the former Deputy Chief of Staff, has claimed that she influenced the sacking of Reagan's campaign chairman, John Sears, in 1980; Larry Speakes has argued that she kept Lyn Nofziger from becoming Press Secretary; while Donald Regan, the former Secretary of the Treasury, has accused her of a host of similar sins, including campaigning for the resignation of William Casey, the CIA Director, when he was terminally ill with cancer. There seems little doubt that she hastened the departure of Donald Regan himself. 'I don't think most people associate me with leeches or how to get them off,' she would say in a speech delivered four days after his exit. 'But I know how to get them off. I'm an expert at it.'

Much more surprising, however, than these accusations (which are, after all, made by bitter and disappointed men) are the suggestions that Nancy was a closet liberal who attempted to guide the direction of domestic and foreign policy as well as patronage decisions. Following Deaver and Regan and others, Kelley tells us that Nancy worked to sabotage the Far Right's influence over her husband on the Star Wars project, on abortion, on aid to the Contras, and on a pardon for Oliver North. Little evidence is given for these claims, and Kelley rather spoils her case by describing Nancy on another page as 'uncommitted to a core of political principles herself'. But was she perhaps not so much a liberal as an instinctively pragmatic and unillusioned woman determined to safeguard her husband from extremists of all sorts? Did she seize on the opportunity afforded by Reagan's mental slippage in his second term as President to deepen her already very strong influence over him? And did she use her astrologers to reinforce that influence, passing on messages from the stars to Reagan which conveniently endorsed her own far more down-to-earth opinions? It all seems quite probable.

What is abundantly clear is that a biography showing that Nancy Reagan isn't a very nice woman is besides the point. She may have been and probably was a bad mother to her children. She may have indulged in lesbian practices at Smith, and been an expert at oral sex in Hollywood. Perhaps she did have a long-running affair with Frank Sinatra. Almost everyone else did. And she almost certainly never was deeply serious about her anti-drug campaign as First Lady. Why should she have been when it was essentially a publicity stunt, just one more example of the kind of soft-edged, human interest cause which a woman in her position is obliged to espouse? What matters in the end is what she did in the Governor's mansion in Sacramento, in the East Wing of the White House, and in her husband's mind. Finding that out will be difficult, but it will be more interesting than Kelley's breathless disclosures.

25 July 1991

Fellow-Travelling

Neal Ascherson on John Reed*

Good journalism often has a guising element in it, in which the voice of the journalist seems to come from an unexpected direction. The best journalism transcends this. But it is still true that many of the great practitioners who have written for the British or American press have been evasive about their native backgrounds and have used their trade to affect or colonise quite different ones. These are personalities who, while not exactly rebels in the out-and-out sense, feel dissatisfied and embarrassed with the social identity into which they were born and in which they were raised, and migrate into new ones – sometimes into several. Most people have come across the crypto-Etonian columnist with the Tyneside accent and the warm loyalty to working-class experience, or the swaggering Texan brute of a newshound, festooned with body-armour and film pouches, who began life as the only child of a Harvard professor of literature.

Why this guising is peculiar to the Anglo-Saxon press world is hard to explain. It is more than just revolt against the confines of a class system, and my guess is that it relates to puritan yearnings for rebirth in a new body with a new soul. But it does produce wonderful reporting. Men with this kink (it's not a common manoeuvre for women journalists) make magnificent interpreters, as they transmigrate into what they fancy are the hearts of strange or inarticulate groups with a story to tell. They usually get those hearts about right, and the force of their empathy projects the story to seize the attention of thousands of reluctant or ignorant readers.

There are emotional penalties to be paid for these gifts of transmigration, however. Any travelling 'fireman' journalist comes to know them. You arrive at the site of some emergency – a lost revolution, a group evicted from their homes, a valiant strike against terrible odds, a burst dam – and within hours you are being tugged into intimacy by people desperate for your help and urgent to have their story told. For a while you transfer, the empathetic guising takes place and that particular group

---

* A response to *The Collected Works of John Reed* (Modern Library, 1995).

of people become your intimate comrades, their cause your cause. Sex, always wildly liberated by catastrophe and insurrection, may well be one of these emotional bonds obscuring the category difference between reporter and reported. But then, as the story dies down or the desk loses interest, the day comes when you must kiss these wonderful friends goodbye. The taxi waits, about to take you through roadblocks and across snipers' alleys to the airport. You have a return ticket, but they do not. And in three or four months' time, you will be appalled to discover that you are beginning to forget their faces, their names, the details of their struggle . . . apart from what you wrote about it.

To go on doing that – constantly to amputate that identification with others and to replace it with the 'next story' and its new cast of moment-arily unforgettable people – is profoundly destructive to any personality, to any journalist. People who live like that cease to be human beings in a fairly short span of time – in my experience, ten years or so. But, of course, there is an alternative. It is the condition dreaded by foreign and feature editors alike. It is the moment when they realise that 'our guy has gone native'. He (or she, because I also know women journalists who have done this) has put his life where his laptop is, and formally enlisted with the people he is supposed to be writing about. Yesterday's bourgeois media correspondent becomes today's revolutionary press officer.

John Reed was not the first or the last journalist to follow this tra-jectory. But he remains the most spectacular. He went to report Russia after the February Revolution in 1917, made straight for the Petrograd Bolsheviks and became a denizen of the seething halls of the Smolny Institute. On 7 November, in the right place at the right time, Reed joined a band of Red Guards who decided to make a rush across Palace Square and – a few moments later – found that he had stormed the Winter Palace. After working for the victorious Bolsheviks for some months, he returned to the United States and in 1919 completed *Ten Days that Shook the World,* to this day far the best-known and most influential eyewitness account of the Bolshevik Revolution. Returning to Russia as a delegate to the Comintern, he died of typhus in Moscow in October 1920, at the age of only 32. Lenin wrote an Introduction to *Ten Days*: 'unreservedly do I recommend it to the workers of the world.' Reed became an immortal, and was buried under the Kremlin wall. Sixty years later, Warren Beatty impersonated him in the movie *Reds*.

He was anything but a callow romantic. In 1917, Reed was already a socialist journalist who had covered revolutionary war in Mexico and had involved himself not only in writing about some of the most brutal industrial struggles in the United States – the Paterson silk-workers' strike and the 1914 Ludlow massacre, when 21 people, mostly women and children, were killed during the Colorado coalminers' strike – but in active support for them. It was his involvement in socialist politics which had brought him into contact with the group of Russian Marxist émigrés in the United States, who returned home in 1917 and later provided Reed with the priceless network of English-speaking contacts which made *Ten Days* possible. And yet, experienced as he was, John Reed found in the Russian Bolsheviks a fresh, final identity into which he entered and in which he died. His grasp of Marxism seems to have been hazy; his socialism was broad, angry, generous, coloured with radical ideas about the New Life. But in the Smolny Institute he found at last 'his' revolution.

He started life in Portland, Oregon. This gave him a certain cachet in New York radical circles; John Dos Passos thought of him as a tall man from the West whose natural Western integrity was a rebuke to the denizens of smoke-filled rooms. This was not an image which Reed discouraged, but in fact he seldom visited Oregon and was far more at home in the East. His father, a Portland businessman, backed the 'Progressive' wing of the Republican Party and put unwise trust in Teddy Roosevelt, but his campaigns against local corruption in Oregon brought him the respect and friendship of Upton Sinclair and Lincoln Steffens, the last giants of the 'Muckraker' generation of American fiction and journalism which was already – by about 1910 – in decline. Steffens, especially, became a sort of literary and political godfather to young Jack Reed when he graduated from Harvard and hit the New York radical scene in 1910, introducing him to old Muckrakers and, equally helpfully, to their editors. 'Big and growing, handsome outside and beautiful inside, when that boy . . . came to New York, it seemed to me that I had never seen anything so close to pure joy,' wrote Steffens (that quotation and the next come from Eric Homberger's shrewd and reliable biography *John Reed*, published by Manchester University Press in 1990). Max Eastman, the socialist editor of the *Masses*, who met his future star correspondent in 1912, was more specific:

> He had a knobby and too filled-out face that reminded me, both in form and colour, of a potato. He was dressed up in a smooth brown suit with round pants legs and a turned-over starched collar, and seemed rather small and rather distracted. He stood up or moved about the room all through his visit, and kept looking in every direction except that in which he was addressing his words.

This volume calls itself *The Collected Works*, but the title is misleading. Here are Reed's three longest works: *Insurgent Mexico*, *The War in Eastern Europe* and *Ten Days that Shook the World*. The first two are in part Reed's own compilations from long feature articles, which makes it all the more of a pity that it was decided to omit all his shorter pieces. 'The Colorado War' (1914), a report on the coal strike, 'Daughter of the Revolution' and 'The Worst Thing in Europe' (these two written from Europe for the *Masses* in 1915), and the two long articles he wrote from wartime Germany for *Metropolitan Magazine*: all are excluded – although those who have read them declare that they belong to his best work, and their inclusion would not have added much to the costs of a collection already nearly a thousand pages long.

It was in 1913 that *Metropolitan Magazine* asked Reed to go to Mexico and report the revolution of Pancho Villa. The outcome of his stay, the articles which were subsequently published in 1914 as *Insurgent Mexico*, is one of the triumphs of reportage literature, a work whose empathy, humour, descriptive talent and sheer verve are not matched by the far more famous *Ten Days*. Reed is not out to report politics or even military news. The only historical background provided in *Insurgent Mexico*, as it stands, is a vague impression of Pancho Villa as the man of the people, of his enemies as a deluded soldiery in the service of the brutal landlord class, and of Villa's commander Carranza as a chilly grandee who would prefer reform to the agrarian revolution for which Villa's men are fighting. The political situation is just the frame, within which Reed paints a tremendous panorama of human struggle as he witnessed and sometimes shared it.

The first words of the book reveal its particular quality. 'Mercado's Federal Army, after its dramatic and terrible retreat four hundred miles across the desert when Chihuahua was abandoned, lay three months at Ojinaga on the Rio Grande.' Here is a young American writer already practised in the literary tricks of his day, devices which Hemingway, among many others, was soon to develop and perfect. Resonance is all: you may never have heard of Mercado or his retreat, or know where Chihuahua is, but you are included by a weatherbeaten somebody who evidently does know – and his offer is too flattering to refuse. On the surface, you might think that the sentence was modelled on the *Gallic Wars*. Under the surface, however, expert showbiz is at work.

There is a ballad quality in the book; and at many moments, journeying in carts or on horseback, marching or resting with Villa's ragged men, Reed inserts their touching and extemporised ballads – sometimes at considerable length. So it is disconcerting to find out (not from this book, but from Homberger's) that Reed went to Mexico speaking almost no Spanish. As the tape-recorder had not been invented and Reed never mentions having an interpreter, the credentials of these songs remain quite a problem. In general, it is unsafe to use *Insurgent Mexico* as a historical source; Reed deliberately mixes up and changes the chronology of his own movements and of the events he describes in order to satisfy his sense of narrative. The dialogue he records throughout is probably almost all invented; sometimes perhaps based on scraps heard and understood, but essentially confected for effect. At this level, Reed's book is a history of Pancho Villa's rebellion like *For Whom the Bell Tolls* is a source-book for the Spanish Civil War.

With all those qualifications, it is a magnificent feat of writing. It is highly personal, about dusty rides, plunges into cool water, the scent of early morning in the barren plains of northern Mexico, the joy of food and a cigar and companionship. It describes Reed's initiation into the experience of battle, in a skirmish at La Cadena: 'I suddenly discovered that I had been hearing shooting for some time. It sounded immensely far away – like nothing so much as a clicking typewriter. Even while it held our attention it grew . . .' Villa's men are driven back. Reed sees some of his friends killed and then runs wildly from the enemy horsemen until he can run no more and falls into a gully hidden by mesquite bushes. This is a tricky, Red-Badge moment in the life of any young American writer, but Reed, recording with terse words the horrors around him, affects no heroics for himself.

The book begins to work towards its climax as Reed joins Pancho Villa's army preparing to advance along the railway to capture the city of Torreón. He gives us the scene at dawn as the steam whistles shriek and the order to move is given; the trains lined up behind one another for miles, their locomotives pouring black smoke into the blue sky, the plain on either side of the tracks covered by the army drawn up on foot or on horseback. Reed himself rides in the cowcatcher of the leading locomotive, with a peasant family which has made its home in the big iron basket. What a young man's fantasy of glory! Only gradually, as the story moves to its finale – the long and horrible battle for the town of Gómez Palacio – does the reader become aware that Reed also has a place in a press boxcar, full of American newspapermen, photographers and film crews and equipped with darkrooms and whiskey.

But long before the advance on Torreón, when Reed ceases to be a loner and becomes a member of a press corps, he has implied his relationship with Villa's men. 'At noon we roped a steer and cut his throat. And because there was no time to light a fire, we ripped the meat from the carcase and ate it raw.' That is a suggestive 'we', unless Reed is seriously saying that he personally helped to rope and slaughter the steer. Guising is taking place as Reed – although he admits that the others teased him and called him 'gringo' or 'Meester' – extracts himself from the position of educated spectator and slides into a new identity which is literary but at the same time subjective and emotional. As Disney's repulsive Monkey King chants: 'I wanna be like You.'

The next book, *The War in Eastern Europe*, is based on Reed's experiences in Serbia and Russia during the First World War. Compared to *Insurgent Mexico*, it is an awkward and often strained bit of work. This time, identification eluded him; there was no side which he cared to join. An earlier journey into wartime Europe, to France, Britain and Germany, had left him miserable; while most of his American friends and employers were already (in 1915) cheering for noble Britain and poor little Belgium in their resistance to fiendish Germany, Reed could see only the triumph of a ruling capitalist class which had deluded the masses into patriotic illusion. In August 1914, Reed had written an anonymous piece for the *Masses* which contained the famous phrase: 'This Is Not Our War.' The almost universal collapse of European socialist parties into war fever appalled him. Reed found it impossible to write what was expected of him by *Metropolitan Magazine*, although he managed some memorable pieces for the *Masses* in which he expressed his revulsion.

Later in 1915, Reed tried again. In France, he had failed to reach the Front, or to escape the stranglehold of army press officers whose job was to keep war correspondents away from the real story. Now he headed for the Balkans and the Eastern Fronts, in the company of the illustrator Boardman Robinson. They reached Salonica, and then travelled slowly north into Serbia, ravaged by two unsuccessful Austrian invasions and a typhus pandemic. At Belgrade, half-ruined, they came under shellfire from the Austrian positions across the Sava; they visited typhus hospitals crowded with the dead and dying, and rode up to the top of the Gucevo massif in northern Serbia to find it still heaped with the rotting dead of the past year's battle. From Serbia, they travelled across the Balkans to the Bukovina and crossed the River Pruth in order to reach the Russian armies fighting in what is now western Ukraine or eastern Poland.

This was Reed's first experience of what was still Imperial Russia. It was nearly his last; after wandering about behind the collapsing front, the two Americans in their Stetson hats and puttees were arrested in Chelm as suspected spies and locked up for several weeks. They would probably both have been shot, if the American Embassy in Petrograd had not – pretty reluctantly – intervened; as it was, they were deported to the capital and, after many bureaucratic battles, expelled to Bucharest.

Here, although he had lost most of his notes, Reed sat down and put his journey into a book. Boardman added his sketches, done in a jaunty caricature style discordant with the sinister subject matter. Not surprisingly, *The War in Eastern Europe* came out as an unsatisfactory mish-mash, wandering from highly conventional travelogue prose about bustling Salonica, city of contrasts, to amateurish generalisations about national character. Admittedly, Reed hit some of his targets: 'with such a stock, with such a history, with the imperialistic impulse growing daily, hourly, in the hearts of her peasant soldiers, into what tremendous conflicts will Serbia's ambition lead her?' he speculated. And it is important to read, even with gritted teeth, Reed's horrified reaction to the sight of the Jewish communities in the small towns and villages of the Pale. He did not conceal his own revulsion, not just from the poverty and filth but from the social habits which those conditions had bred. He writes about 'fetid smells' and 'whines', about 'a pale, stooping inbred race, refined to the point of idiocy', and remarks that the Russians saw a potential traitor in every Jew. But here Reed's robust socialist instinct saves him: of course the Jews would betray the Tsardom, he continued, and why not? What possible reason had they to support it? He records the routine massacres and lootings which Russian troops were encouraged to carry out when they captured a Galician shtetl, and describes Eastern European Jewry as 'a hunted people made hateful by extortion and abuse'.

With hindsight, Reed's first impressions of Russia are suggestive. In some 'Face of Russia' sketches appended to the book, he tries to define his own affection for this people ('Russians . . . are perhaps the most interesting human beings that exist') and for their culture, which he found 'the most comfortable, the most liberal way of life' – meaning, it seems, the genial chaos of daily existence, beset with glasses of tea and nocturnal arguments about life's meaning, indifferent to clocked time or planned routine. His political predictions were good, but no better than those of most foreign observers at the time, for whom revolution was by now a question of when rather than if. 'Is there a powerful and destructive fire working in the bowels of Russia?' he asked rhetorically.

There certainly was. But the overthrow of the Tsardom in early 1917 did not immediately bring John Reed back to Russia. He set out with his bold-hearted partner Louise Bryant in August, and reached a darkened, tense Petrograd in early September. His Russian was almost nonexistent – 'even sketchier than his Spanish', commented the American socialist Bertram Wolfe – and although he eventually reached the stage of being able to make out more or less what a speech was about, his grasp of the language was never up to much.

It is important to remember that when reading *Ten Days*. The late A.J.P. Taylor, in his Introduction to the 1966 Penguin edition, called Reed a 'great writer' but warned that the book was not history; as in *Insurgent Mexico*, Reed was unreliable about the dates and order of events, offered second-hand accounts as first-hand, added imaginative detail and generally heightened the drama. Taylor called 'much of it . . . fiction'. Notoriously, Reed gives a thrilling account of Lenin's appearance at a closed Bolshevik meeting in Smolny on 3 November, allegedly communicated to him outside the door by Volodarsky as the meeting went on. No such meeting took place, and it is not easy to find another one in those days which would fit Reed's account.

But this is simply to say that Reed was a journalist. Most of us in the trade understand what it means to be thrown into a fast-moving foreign crisis without knowing much of the language; we grasp desperately at the foreign correspondents already there and at anyone involved in the crisis who speaks English. Translators are useful only up to a point; every day, we find ourselves synthesising, from a few understood phrases or the offhand comments of some more fluent colleague, a plausible version of what is being said or done. John Reed was no exception. He was very lucky to befriend some first-class British and American journalists who both spoke good Russian and took the Bolsheviks seriously, and to find waiting for him that group of Russian socialist exiles he had known in New York. Between them, they took him straight to the heart of things. He had access to most of the leading Bolsheviks, including Trotsky and, some time after the November Revolution, to Lenin himself.

To read *Ten Days* is to feel immediately: yes, that is how it must have felt. The book lacks the romantic allure, the literary devices, of *Insurgent Mexico*; it opens with an impassive Preface quite unlike anything in the two previous books, and instead of peon ballads Reed inserts the texts of numerous leaflets and proclamations. And yet he is not consciously breaking with his own past; he salutes the Bolshevik Revolution as an 'adventure . . . one of the most marvellous mankind ever embarked on, sweeping into history at the head of the toiling masses, and staking everything on their vast and simple desires . . .' The romantic impulse is still at work, and all his skill goes into constructing a suspense which thickens until the reader is desperate to reach the resolving explosion. There are wonderful accounts of things seen, of human beings intolerably stretched and sleepless, of roaring mass meetings skilfully contrasted – as Homberger notices – with the cold and deserted palaces of the old regime. There are impish details: when Reed first sees Lenin speaking, he is struck by how far too long his trousers are and by his 'little winking eyes'. There is even humour, as when the Commissars for War and the Navy rush to the Front by motor-car and have to borrow pen and paper from their unnamed passenger (Reed himself) to write an order.

Ten Days is a work of commitment, close to a work of propaganda. Reed did not cleave to the Bolsheviks because of some sophisticated analysis about class struggle, but because he felt that the Bolsheviks were the only party in the autumn of 1917 with a coherent programme which corresponded to the 'wishes of the masses'. How did he know what the wishes of the masses were, it can fairly be asked? Right or wrong, he thought he sensed them, and took the plunge. This time, the guising was serious and beyond play-acting. It is significant that Reed does not attempt to include the Bolsheviks in any 'we', as he had done with Pancho Villa's men. 'We' now means simply John Reed and the other journalists, or sometimes Reed and Louise Bryant, but no more.

The road ahead was not the roving correspondent's return to New York and on to the next big story. Instead, it led to his part in the founding of the Communist Party of the United States, to his journey back to Russia as a Comintern delegate, to his death and sanctification. Stalin would probably have murdered him if he had lived that long. But the rumour that he died already disillusioned with Communism has little evidence to support it. John Reed had grown up at last, and in his final disguise became himself.

8 February 1996

An Unfinished Project

Fredric Jameson on Walter Benjamin*

Walter Benjamin was not a letter writer of the order of Lawrence or Flaubert, for whom the medium of the letter seems to fill a need, not for mere self-expression, but for some larger exercise of the personality in exasperation or enthusiasm, in that almost instinctive enlargement of reaction to things which others find in unmotivated physical activity. Benjamin was, on the contrary, a person of the greatest reserve; even where he lets himself go with people he trusts, one has the feeling not of the revelation of some true inner self but merely of the relaxation of that reserve. The extraordinarily stiff manner of a central European bourgeoisie – which sought no doubt to designate a certain class pride by its eschewal of aristocratic nonchalance and easiness, as well as of the barbarism and ignorance of country nobles in general – is appropriated and made part of the personality, like a mask that grows onto the skin of your face. Such a reserve may well also express fear, both of the rituals of a class you detest and devote your life to undermining, and of the artificialities of the artists who secede from it. It is in any case very European, and has no American equivalent, even where writers like Henry James have thought it desirable to produce one.

This peculiar 'death of the subject' may account for some of the fascination Benjamin has had for several generations of left intellectuals, by lending the interests and commitments of the absent subject a kind of monumental objectivity. Even Benjamin's hobbies, such as book collecting, are thereby sacralised in advance, as relics and mementos of a defunct will and desire; nor are his more private notes – the Moscow diary, for example, in which traces of a passionate sentimental agitation are preserved – any more revealing. It is as if language were unable to say any more than this; indeed, many of the letters seem to have been provoked less by a need for expression than by all the painful practical necessities of which Benjamin's life was so full.

* Gershom Scholem and Theodor Adorno, eds, *The Correspondence of Walter Benjamin 1910–1940*, trans. Manfred Jacobson and Evelyn Jacobson (University of Chicago Press, 1994); Henri Lonitz, ed., *T. W. Adorno/Walter Benjamin: Briefwechsel 1928–1940* (Suhrkamp, 1994).

One sometimes wonders whether these practical problems were visited on Benjamin as an innocent from the outside, or whether at least a few of them might not have been the fruit of his own awkwardness, his bad judgments and incapacities, if not his self-indulgence. Just as one wonders, faced with a record of his travels, whether exile and the flight from German boredom and *misère* (even that of the fabled Weimar!) might not have corresponded to some deeper choice fulfilled in its usual grisly and unforeseeable way by History. To have been obliged to spend the Thirties in Paris, for example, does not seem to have been an inconceivable destiny for Benjamin, even in a world without Hitler; nor would the straitened circumstances and appeals for money have been absent from such a world, along with the search for residence permits and the endless negotiations with editors of reviews and the possible intermediaries of possible publishers.

The crucial difference about such a world would have been the existence of a German-language readership. In one of his rare moments of expression, if not of self then at least of its fantasies, Benjamin declares that his life's ambition is to become 'le premier critique de la littérature allemande'. In the long run he became something better than that perhaps; it was in any case the one thing he could not become, when a literate German newspaper-reading public was absolutely sealed off from him. For this was an age when the *feuilleton* still existed, when critics and cultural commentators, writing regularly in the journals, could still claim to form and inflect public taste. Six hundred pages of book reviews by Benjamin exist, in the as yet untranslated third volume of his *Collected Works:* they give a very different picture of his activity from the lonely achievements of the volume we call *Illuminations,* or the immense and fragmentary *Arcades* project.

Like Kafka, Benjamin had to decide early in his life whether he was to be a Jewish writer or a German writer. The reviews show the choices he made, and in the spaces between the lines of this correspondence we can read his attempts to ward off Scholem's over-enthusiastic embraces, even though the final decision not to emigrate to Palestine (see letter to Scholem of 20 January 1930, written in French and translated into English without comment in the present edition) seems to have been as much as anything else the result of laziness (in learning Hebrew), incompetence (in sorting out his divorce) and sheer lack of ideological commitment.

The present edition of the *Correspondence* was co-edited in 1966 by Scholem and Adorno, who keep silent on their own priorities (and who had little in common save their friendship with Benjamin, which was obviously supremely precious to each of them). Their attempts both during his lifetime and after it to wrench Benjamin away from bad influences must necessarily inspire some suspicion about their confidences. Scholem deplored Benjamin's Marxist commitments, and tells us that the essay on Eduard Fuchs was a piece of hackwork, which Max Horkheimer made Benjamin write for the *Zeitschrift*. As for Benjamin's trip to the Soviet Union, Scholem comments acidly that, although Benjamin was unaware of it, he was allowed contact with nobody but Jews. For Adorno the contamination was personified by Brecht, whose influence on Benjamin he tried to undermine like a jealous suitor. 'I held his arms up,' he boasts about this new Moses, whose temptation to sink back into Brechtian vulgar Marxism and militancy clearly demanded eternal vigilance, even beyond the grave. Coming from Adorno, this will not exactly be considered anti-Marxism, except by the most orthodox, yet the reaction has a family likeness to Scholem's (Scholem pointed out that, for his generation, both Zionism and Communism were related and equivalent ways of rebelling against the German-Jewish bourgeois family) while Adorno's concern to defend 'the autonomy of art' may now seem as tiresome as Scholem's lavish insistence on Benjamin's fascination with Jewish mysticism.

Benjamin himself seems to have regarded all this with bemused impersonality: 'Our philosophical debate whose time was long due' – the reference is to Scholem's visit to Paris in 1938 – 'proceeded in due form. If I am not mistaken, it gave him an image of me as something like a man who has made his home in a crocodile's jaws, which he keeps prised open with iron braces.' The letters show a hapless intellectual at odds with life's practicalities, and are biographically distorted insofar as they omit the whole 'middle period', the friendship with Brecht (of which we get some glimpses in Benjamin's diary of his visit to Brecht in Svendborg) and his exploration of Marxism; and insofar as they centre on the friendship with Scholem in the early period (Scholem emigrated to Palestine in 1925) and on the more intellectual exchanges with Adorno (they seem never to have said *du* to each other) in the later one. More complete versions of both correspondences are now available, the Scholem cycle appeared in German in 1980 (after Scholem's originals were miraculously rediscovered), and was translated in a 1989 Schocken edition; and the first volume in a series of Adorno's complete correspondence appeared in German last year. The famous letters (Adorno's rather ostentatious critical responses to various Benjamin texts, and above all to the *Arcades* materials, in which he shows off his own very keen intelligence a little too feverishly) have mostly been printed already, although without the catty personal references to friends and acquaintances which have been made much of in the German press. (Benjamin thought Bloch had plagiarised him, particularly in *Erbschaft dieser Zeit;* Adorno describes Marcuse's great affirmative culture essay as 'the work of a converted although very zealous high school teacher'.)

Yet, as in the elephantine jokes with Scholem, such exchanges can also be seen as a way of confirming what Adorno considered their narrower alliance against the outside world – our 'general line', as he calls it, 'our old method of immanent critique'. But Adorno seems more anxious to seal this alliance than Benjamin, whose replies reflect his confusion and disappointment at the rejection, by Horkheimer and the Frankfurt School, of his first version of the *Arcades.* Adorno's extensive (and quite sensible) critiques and explanations make his responsibility in the matter plain enough to Benjamin, who was probably not aware that Horkheimer had also been responsible for the other great failure of his life, the refusal of his academic thesis on German baroque tragedy: with friends like these . . . The Adorno correspondence is a far more satisfactory volume than the collected letters (about which the American publishers complain, 'we were not permitted' – by the notorious Suhrkamp people – 'to revise the notes or to include any additional comments, prefaces, afterwords etc.'), and is splendidly edited and annotated.

The notion of the public intellectual has been much abused in recent years, and has served as a stick with which to beat academics (whether political or not) and to reinforce a general climate of anti-intellectualism. But any serious discussion of the matter clearly needs to address changes in the media: Régis Debray has charted this transformation in France, where writers have given way to professors, and journalists to television personalities. These are features of the systemic changes in capitalism, along with its technologies and the enlargement of its markets. Culture, and along with it the possibilities of cultural politics, must necessarily adapt to modifications of the larger social system of which it is a part. Did Benjamin wish to be a public intellectual in this sense? Did the other members of the Frankfurt School? Probably they didn't think in these relatively post-modern terms about 'political' and apolitical. In their time, the choice was between Left and Right. Benjamin's numerous reviews for a left journal called *Die Literarische Welt,* which does not seem to have had a very large circulation (not necessarily a gauge of its influence, however), are, I believe, best seen not as an attempt to reach some wider public and to make a political mark so much as to exercise the literary life in all its variety.

Benjamin was fortunate in still being able, in the interwar years, to participate in that unique form of the 'public sphere' which was organised around books and journals and inhabited by literary intellectuals whose domain was print. It was not only for reasons of personal taste that he wrote on novels and cookbooks, antiques, travel books, children's literature, linguistics, social history, dolls, ideological tracts, French literature, dictionaries and encyclopedias, pedagogy, Chaplin, Jews and cities. Everything was grist to his mill and what was not yet a 'text' fairly itched to be turned into one. One assumes, of course, that the 'literary life' of Berlin, emerging from the rawer, late-industrial realities of the Wilhelmine state, was not so promising as that of Vienna (the figure of Karl Kraus haunts these letters), let alone that of Paris, which for these intellectuals – like most other Western ones – remains the Utopian ideal: Benjamin's approach to this centre of destiny (with which only a few foreigners could hope to be intimately associated) was not brought about only by exile.

This, then, is the way to investigate the matter of Benjamin's political commitment, which, like all deep ideological choices, must be grasped on a number of levels at once: Marxism as a form of personal revolt; Communism as a new kind of universalism in which Jews could participate fully; loathing for one's own class and an instinctive identification with people of radically different backgrounds; ideal images of action, no doubt, whose appeal is a function of the peculiar status of the intellectual. Nor is the appeal of justice to be thought of as some figment of misguided Nietzschean altruism for, as Wilde put it, socialism precludes the necessity for people to 'spoil their lives by an unhealthy and exaggerated altruism'. Indeed, it is most often imagined (by those intent on repressing their complicity with the system) that left intellectuals are unhappy in their own (generally bourgeois) class – that they wish to secede from it and to enjoy an imaginary identification with simpler people, industrial or farm workers, underclasses, oppressed minorities, exotic populations in situations of cruel subjection or heroic revolt. Such identifications are certainly to be welcomed, as they enlarge our sympathies and undermine or dissolve the confines of our own class limits.

Yet Benjamin's letters are instructive also in the way in which they show how political commitments are something a bourgeoisie does for itself, for its own good and its psychic well-being. Maimed as well as privileged, it has an interest in lifting the burdens of exploitation it, too, necessarily suffers (and not only, as at the present time, when capitalism devours its own bourgeois children). Benjamin makes the point in his arguments with Scholem. His Communism is not something chosen independently and somehow added onto his writing and intellectual life, capable, as Adorno thought, of deflecting it in wasteful or deplorable directions. The political choice is motivated by the writing itself: 'a victorious party' – the German Bolshevist party – 'might make it possible for me to write differently.' This is the crucial issue: under what conditions might a truly 'literary' life be lived, in what kind of situation might the vocation of the intellectual be most fully realised?

The critique of capitalism is for Benjamin first and foremost a critique of how it affects his own possibilities for writing, the commitment to socialism first and foremost a kind of class interest for the bourgeois intellectual, who suffers under the market and yearns to make fuller use of his intellectual energies. This is why classical right-wing talk about the *ressentiment* of intellectuals is ignorant and misplaced, and the familiar counter-revolutionary analysis of their role in revolutions and their lust for power an ingenious misconception. True intellectuals want to write, and their deeper political reflections turn on the obstacles a given social system places in the way of that vocation. Hence Benjamin's allegiance to Brecht, whose 'essays are the first . . . that I champion as a critic without (public) reservation. This is because part of my development in the last few years came about in confrontation with them, and because they, more rigorously than any others, give an insight into the intellectual context in which the work of people like myself is conducted in this country.'

The impersonality I have attributed to Benjamin – it might better be called by Eliot's term, 'depersonalisation' – also plays its part in the glorious effects of style which achieve their most intense concentration in the great essays but which we can surprise here and there in these letters: 'True criticism does not attack its object: it is like a chemical substance that attacks another only in the sense that, decomposing it, it exposes its inner nature, but does not destroy it. The chemical substance that attacks *spiritual* things in this way (diathetically) is the light. This does not appear in language.' The digression is self-referential to the degree to which it includes a theory of its own necessary impersonality (leading the more fatuous, no doubt, to murmur 'deconstruction'); the two final sentences then prod this formulation upwards into associative leaps that can be grasped either as the intensity of the thinking process or as a dialectical multi-layering (from which, incidentally, alchemy and allegory, the baroque and mystical language theory, are never far away).

Both Adorno and Benjamin wrote important studies of epistolary texts and took the letter seriously as a form. Under a pseudonym, Benjamin edited a beautiful series of classical German bourgeois letters (*Deutsche Menschen*) which, exceptionally, was published under the Nazis. Adorno used his analysis of the Stefan George-Hugo von Hofmannsthal correspondence to analyse the most significant aestheticist currents in the Weimar period. Unsurprisingly, in the present collection, it is often a question of the letter itself, but now as a form in some sense constructed after the fact, by an interested readership (such as ourselves): 'The *exchange* of letters characteristically takes shape in the mind of posterity (whereas the *single* letter, in regard to its author, may lose something of its life).' By this Benjamin means to designate the way in which a single communication fulfils its immediate function, whereas the lengthier, more consecutive form of a correspondence we read in a book is neither available nor relevant to its participants.

These bookish letters, then, will interest only those interested in Benjamin – but ought we not to suppose the same about every correspondence centred on a single author? For them, however, the correspondence will be exciting, offering tantalising and fragmentary testimony on student politics in the prewar period, on Benjamin's early and impenetrable 'theories' of language, on literary history and its problems, on nationality and ethnicity ('for me . . . circumscribed national characteristics were always central: German or French'), on travels and places, sometimes on people, much less on historical events or political positions (at least with these particular correspondents); finally and above all on his own reading and projects. Several immense Kafka letters (a fragment of one was included in *Illuminations*) constitute a more accessible literary criticism of Kafka than the 'official' statement in the great essay, and I have already mentioned the exchange with Adorno about the *Arcades* project (probably, despite its insufferable pretensions, even more important for Adorno's thinking than for Benjamin's): one of the classic moments in contemporary theory. There is also the abortive correspondence with Florens Christian Rang, who stands as Scholem's opposite number and one of the rare non-Jews with whom Benjamin had productive exchanges ('I was indebted to this man . . . for whatever essential elements of German culture I have internalised').

One can, then, read a correspondence like this in a novelistic way, reconstructing the biographical narrative and re-inventing the various characters at varying distances from the enigmatic central figure himself. Or one can ransack it for moments of particular brilliance; for example, Benjamin's way of dealing with Bloch's *Erbschaft dieser Zeit,* which was published as Hitler came to power. Benjamin felt that Bloch had pre-empted him and stolen something of the thunder of the *Arcades* project:

> The severe reproach I must level against the book (even if I will not level it against the author) is that it in no way corresponds to the circumstances under which it has appeared. Instead, it is as out of place as a fine gentleman who, having arrived to inspect an area demolished by an earthquake, has nothing more urgent to do than immediately spread out Persian rugs that his servants had brought along and which were, by the way, already somewhat moth-eaten; set up the gold and silver vessels, which were already somewhat tarnished; have himself wrapped in brocade and damask gowns, which were already somewhat faded.

We must not take it here that Benjamin repudiates Bloch's Utopian doctrine of hope and the future, which he himself shared in far more complex and internally conflictual ways; rather, that (alongside the satisfaction involved in portraying Bloch as a rug merchant) he is calling for a much more sombre characterisation of the Utopian in a situation – capitalism – of which he famously said that 'the catastrophe is that it just goes on like this', and for which his own notion of the Messianic, as the radically unprepared and unexpected, was a rather different kind of solution. (I cannot resist quoting Adorno's complementary characterisation of Bloch, which comes during an appreciation of *The Old Curiosity Shop,* a novel about which he wrote in the early Thirties and which he held to be 'a book of the highest rank – full of secrets compared to which the Blochian variety show themselves up to be the cloacal odours from eternity which they really are'.)

Passing over the visual details ('the gas mask in my small room . . . looks to me like a disconcerting replica of the skulls with which studious monks decorated their cells'), it seems advisable to juxtapose with the earlier statement about literary criticism what can only be Benjamin's version of Frankfurt School 'critical theory' – it is noteworthy that Scholem feels obliged to comment in a rare personal footnote on the 'unmistakably esoteric, if not almost conspiratorial, tone' of this passage:

> The point here is precisely that things whose place is at present in shadow *de part et d'autre* might be cast in a false light when subjected to artificial lighting. I say 'at present' because the current epoch, which makes so many things impossible, most certainly does not preclude this: that the right light should fall on precisely those things in the course of the historical rotation of the sun. I want to take this even

further and say that our works can, for their part, be measuring instruments, which, if they function well, measure the tiniest segments of that unimaginably slow rotation.

We measure, in other words, not the past itself and its realities and energies, but rather the distance separating what is currently in shadow from some fuller natural light. We measure the distortions of our current unknowledge, without attempting to train our own artificial light on the 'thing itself'. These sentences map out a tortuous path around the Uncertainty Principle of historicism proper, in which we ourselves, and our 'current situation', intervene between our own cognitive faculties and even those moments of the past with which we might have been expected to have some special 'elective affinities' – indeed, particularly such moments, for which we think we have been vouchsafed a privileged understanding.

This means that Benjamin's 'esoterical and conspiratorial' relations with the past of Baudelaire and the Paris of Haussmann are relations it is possible we no longer share today. We have none of us succeeded in reconstructing the *Arcades* project to the point at which the whole operation becomes satisfyingly intelligible (like Pascal's fragments or Gramsci's 'prison notebooks', perhaps it was necessary that the pieces not be recontained and domesticated by a successful form). But, at least in the version discussed by Adorno and Benjamin in their correspondence, the emphasis on myth and the archaic no longer seems to resonate in a postmodernity which has abolished those things:

> As for me, I am busy pointing my telescope through the bloody mist at a mirage of the 19th century that I am attempting to reproduce based on the characteristics it will manifest in a future state of the world, liberated from magic. I must naturally first build this telescope myself and, in making this effort, I am the first to have discovered some fundamental principles of materialistic art theory.

Again, the images of telescopy and celestial measurement, but now the content of the investigation is the peculiar co-existence of a mythic archaic and a birth of modernity in the mid-19th century (along with the historicist question of how a society liberated from such magical elements – and very precisely from that 'commodity fetishism' which was Marx's contemporary version of the paradoxical co-existence – might wish to view such a peculiar past and 'inherit' it, to use Bloch's expression of the same year).

And here is Adorno's echoing discussion of 'our central question, that of the identity of modern and archaic':

> It occurred to me that just as the modern is somehow the oldest, so also the archaic is itself a function of the new: in other words historically produced as archaic and to

that degree dialectical – not 'prehistoric' but the exact opposite. That is: no less than the place of everything silenced by history: measurable only by way of the historical rhythm which alone 'produces' it as Ur-history.

Predictably, in this spirit, he goes on to compare his own current work on Wagner to the *Arcades* project, 'along with the Ur-history of the 19th century a foreshadowing of the principal and categorical historicity of the archaic: not as what is historically the oldest but what itself emerges only from the innermost law of time'.

We are here at the very secret of Modernism as such, if not of modernity, of which both Adorno and Benjamin now stand revealed to us as prime embodiments fully as much as analysts and interpreters. For modernity can be distinguished from our own post-modernity as a space of 'unevenness'(the theory of Bloch in *Erbschaft dieser Zeit)*, in which the most modern uneasily co-exists with what it has not yet superseded, cancelled, streamlined and obliterated. Only from the vantage-point of the Post-Modern, in which modernisation is at last complete, can this secret incompleteness of the modernisation process be detected as the source of modernity and Modernism alike.

In which case Benjamin and Adorno are themselves, now and for us, just such incomprehensible objects covered by shadow in the course of the rotation of history, and we must not seek to illuminate them with our artificial light. Their form of intellectual life is perhaps outmoded, even though the Frankfurt School's mission, along with their own narrower and more intense version of it, is, in Habermas's memorable phrase, an unfinished project. They formed a true intellectual avant garde, the formal equivalent of the great artistic or literary movements, about which it is said that in post-modernity they can no longer exist. Yet the rewards of historical commemoration do not always take the form of imitation.

3 August 1995

Secrets

Adam Phillips on Freud and Ferenczi*

There has always been a resistance, at least among psychoanalysts themselves, to thinking of their work as mind-reading or fortune-telling. Despite the fact that most ordinary conversation is exactly this, or perhaps because it is, psychoanalysts have wanted to describe what they do as different, as rational even: dealing with the irrational but not dealing in it. ('On waking,' Ferenczi writes mockingly to Freud, 'one wants on no account to have thought something quite nonsensical or illogical.') It was important to Freud that psychoanalysis should not become a cult of the irrational. The unconscious may be disreputable, but the psychoanalyst must not be. And yet Freud's description of the unconscious was a threat to, and a parody of, the more respectable versions of professional competence. If a psychoanalyst knows what's in the unconscious, or knows how it works, she has a specific expertise. But if the unconscious is what cannot be anticipated, can there then be experts of the unknown? 'The weather,' as Freud puts it here, 'of course never comes from the quarter one has been carefully observing.'

If you locate psychoanalysis somewhere between literature and science it can begin to look like a legitimate and intelligible social practice: not so much a mystery for initiates but a skill that can be learned, with real rules and a body of knowledge. Like the so-called neurotic whose project is to be extremely normal, psychoanalysis has always struggled to distance itself from supposedly discredited things like religion, glamour, mysticism, the paranormal, and all the scapegoated 'alternative' therapies. Psychoanalysis, that is to say, has used its discovery of the unconscious to legitimate itself. This would once have been called an irony. Psychoanalysis as a treatment may be about reclaiming the marginalised parts of oneself, but psychoanalysis as a profession has always been resolutely committed to the mainstream, which at the moment happens to be science and various literary theories of narrative. So it is perhaps not entirely surprising that psychoanalysis has been especially dismissive of – indeed, pathologising of – what was once referred to as

* Eva Brabant, Ernst Falzedar and Patrizia Giampieri-Deutsch, eds, *The Correspondence of Sigmund Freud and Sándor Ferenczi. Vol. I: 1908–14*, trans. Peter Hoffer (Harvard, 1994).

the supernatural. From this extraordinary correspondence, which will radically change the way we read psychoanalysis, it is clear that 'sexuality' and the 'unconscious' were the new, the scientifically prestigious words for the occult: for that which is beyond our capacity for knowledge, for the weird, unaccountable effects people have on each other. In psychoanalysis the supernatural returns as the erotic. And it was Ferenczi, and Jung in a different way, who had to keep reminding Freud of the limits of scientific enquiry; that to rationalise the unconscious was not only an aim, but also a betrayal of psychoanalysis. When Ferenczi wrote to Freud in 1911 that he 'considered the fight against occultism to be premature', he was trying to keep alive something he saw as integral to the psychoanalytic project – something which might be called, say, inexplicable human powers – and that Freud, in his view, was too keen to disavow.

If the aim of a system is to create an outside where you can put the things you don't want, then we have to look at what a system (or a person) disposes of – its rubbish – to understand it; to get a picture of how it sees itself and wants to be seen. Freud had apparently included sex and violence in the science of psychoanalysis, but he baulked at the investigation of occult phenomena. If sexuality was the unacceptable in psychoanalysis, then what kind of sexuality was the occult if it was proscribed by the master of the forbidden himself? (One answer, as we shall see, is homosexuality.) Ferenczi, Freud wrote in a foreword to a collection of his papers, was 'familiar to an extent that few others are, with all the difficulties of psychoanalytic problems'. In these letters it is as though Ferenczi is Freud's repressed unconscious – the prodigal son who keeps coming back for more – wittingly and unwittingly drawing Freud's attention to the implications of psychoanalytic theory that Freud preferred to forget; partly because they were, inevitably, connected to all the difficulties of his own 'problems'. Intimacy between people, like occult phenomena, is fundamentally bewildering. Freud, as Ferenczi knew, was cautious about passion in his private life. If psychoanalysis, for Ferenczi, was a way of dispelling the secrecy between people, it was also a way of having an intimate relationship with Freud (Ferenczi did, of course, have a brief analysis with Freud). But Freud, unlike Ferenczi, was a lover of secrets, and believed that they should not be squandered, or allowed to become some spurious currency of intimacy. 'Don't sacrifice too many of your secrets,' he warns Ferenczi, 'out of an excess of kindness.'

Freud, Ferenczi had written in one of his early papers, 'had succeeded in surprising a process . . . in taking it in the midst of its work, in flagrante, so to speak'. Dreaming was the process in question; Ferenczi clearly liked the idea of Freud as the man who found things out, the transgressor of privacy. But from a Freudian point of view that Ferenczi would never quite accept, human beings were the animals that kept secrets. Ferenczi always wanted to get to the bottom of such things, so to speak; and the secrets of sexuality, that Freud had discovered, were inextricably linked for him with the mysteries of more traditional, folkloric forms of magic. Of course a lot of 'artists and intellectuals', not to mention ordinary people, at the turn of the century were interested in what was then called, to give it scientific credibility, psychical research. Freud himself had been made an honorary member of the Society for Psychical Research in 1911, but he was wary, as this correspondence makes clear, of psychoanalysis being associated with the fringes of science. He preferred to think of psychoanalysis as a medical treatment rather than a séance. But despite Freud's misgivings, Ferenczi went to visit a medium, Frau Seidler, with Freud's full endorsement, after his and Freud's trip to America in 1909. He went 'with the intention', the editors write calmly, 'of investigating parapsychological phenomena', as if we might be suspicious of his real motives (as in, 'he bought pornography with the intention of investigating erotic phenomena'). He enthusiastically reports the outcome to Freud and the intrepid conquistador of the other mysteries is 'shocked'. 'Keep quiet about it for the time being,' Freud counsels. In his next letter, written five days later, Freud has, as it were, changed his mind: 'let us keep absolute silence about it . . . should one now, as a result of this experience commit oneself to occultism? Certainly not; it is only a matter of thought transference.' But what, then, is thought transference, and how does it work? The vocabulary for one mysterious form of exchange merely replaces another. And what has happened to the honesty (a key word in this correspondence), the spirit of open scientific enquiry that Freud and psychoanalysis had prided itself on? The psychoanalyst could protect himself from sexuality, but he might not be able to resist the contamination of the paranormal.

But Ferenczi, who planned a book on thought transference that he never wrote, was beginning to discover something in his clinical work that the peculiar practices of psychics helped him to think about; and that it has taken psychoanalysts virtually until now to appreciate fully (or rather, face). Ferenczi was finding that sometimes his own free-associations to the patient's material seemed to be of a piece with what the patient was saying to him. As though the analyst might be having some of the patient's (repressed) thoughts for him; continuing them, as it were. The analyst therefore became, in a slightly different sense of the word, a medium for the thoughts and feelings the patient could not bear. The patient, that is to say, could evoke in the analyst – as though by thought transference – the disowned parts of himself. In a way that parapsychological phenomena made crudely vivid, there was a kind of hidden exchange of psychic states going on between people, a black market of feelings that was not subject to conscious control. And it was obvious to Ferenczi that if this was true, then it was going to be a two-way traffic: it couldn't only be the patient doing this to the analyst but it must also be the analyst doing it to the patient. This made psycho-analysis a rather more reciprocal venture than Freud's resolutely scientific, quasi-medical model could allow. When two people speak to each other they soon become inextricable. As Freud and Ferenczi went on speaking to each other, and of course to other people, they needed to find theories about what happens when people speak (and listen) to each other, to manage the intensity of the experience. It was as though Freud had invented the psychoanalytic relationship as a refuge from intimacy – a place it could be studied, a relationship about intimacy but not 'really' intimate itself – and that Ferenczi was determinedly show-ing him that there was no talk without intimacy or its refusal.

It is, as it were, no accident that, in the years covered by this corres-pondence, Freud and Ferenczi, as their relationship evolves, begin to write about the connections between homosexuality and paranoia (between sameness and difference). In 1911 Freud published his Schreber case ('I am Schreber, nothing but Schreber', Freud writes to Ferenczi); and Ferenczi published 'On The Part Played by Homo-sexuality in the Pathogenesis of Paranoia', and his remarkable paper, 'The Nosology of Male Homosexuality'. And towards the end of this correspondence Freud published a provisional summation of all this in *Totem and Taboo*, which Ferenczi ingenuously praises as Freud's 'new and outstanding idea of transmission by means of unconscious under-standing' – an idea that Ferenczi had been 'carrying' for Freud for several years, an idea derived from parapsychology. As the editors put it, I hope with unconscious irony, 'Freud and Ferenczi did more work together than has sometimes been acknowledged.' Theory, as psycho-analysis shows, is always first and foremost local emotional politics. 'If psychoanalysis is a paranoia,' Ferenczi writes 'jokingly' to Freud, 'then I have already been successful in overcoming the stage of persecution mania and replacing it with megalomania.'

If psychoanalysis is a paranoia then it is, in the terms of its own theory, a love between men. 'Paranoia,' as Ferenczi wrote, more or less echoing Freud, 'is perhaps nothing else at all but disguised homosexuality.' There is something so unbearable about love for one's own sex that it is turned into hatred, and the hatred is then projected into other people and comes back from outside as persecution. In fact Ferenczi believed that men adored women to protect themselves from their love for men; so the men then hated the women because they weren't men and the women felt inadequate, unable to satisfy their men or themselves. 'I quite seriously believe,' Ferenczi wrote in 'The Nosology of Male Homosexuality', 'that the men of today are obsessively heterosexual as the result of this affective displacement; in order to free themselves from men, they become the slaves of women.' But what is it in men that men are so much on the run from? This was the question that Ferenczi implicitly addressed to Freud, sometimes as theory and sometimes as a direct appeal to Freud for a different, less careful intimacy.

Despite Freud's commitment, in theory, to bisexuality – love, hate and rivalry with *both* parents – it was more or less assumed in psychoanalysis (and still is in some quarters) that if all goes well heterosexuality wins the day. For example, in psychoanalytic theory love for the parent of the opposite sex is referred to as the positive Oedipus complex and love for the parent of the same sex is called the negative Oedipus complex. It is, in other words, quite clear what we are supposed to be doing. But, of course, as Ferenczi intimates in the letters and his 'scientific' papers, heterosexuality is, among other things, a form of self-hatred; after all, what is so distasteful about one's own sex that one has, so exclusively, to desire the opposite one? The interesting link that psychoanalysis had constructed between paranoia and homosexuality revealed something even more disquieting which Freud and Ferenczi could never quite formulate: that in psychoanalysis, at least, heterosexuality was a form of redemption from a profound, perhaps constitutive self-fear. In theory psychoanalysis promoted the value, indeed the necessity, of love for both sexes. Unlike Freud, Ferenczi wanted to try and live out – or 'act out', as psychoanalysts would say disparagingly – the consequences of psychoanalytic theory; and in part, with Freud himself. Or, as the editor says in his sensible Introduction, Ferenczi 'made little clear or defensive distinction between his professional life and his private life'. The unconscious does not have a professional life. Except, that is, in psychoanalysis.

Ferenczi proposed the new term 'ambisexuality' in place of 'bisexuality' to stress what was perhaps the real novelty of the psychoanalytic version of this old, indeed ancient idea. In his view it better described the child's actual predicament, his 'psychical capacity for bestowing his erotism, originally objectless, on either the male or the female sex, or on both'. The translators' word 'bestow' sounds quaint now, but it accurately captures the sense of desire as something conferred. For the child, like the adult, his or her desire is experienced as a gift; we privilege people with our desire for them, though they don't always recognise quite what an honour they are being given. As these letters show, with amazing candour Ferenczi bestowed his child-like capacity for intimacy on Freud, and Freud responded with a wariness and a generosity no less passionate, but, of course, never quite passionate or open enough for Ferenczi. 'You actually do feel best,' Ferenczi writes to Freud, as compliment and reproach, 'when you can be independent of the whole world.' Both of them, inevitably, were confronted, as in a psychoanalysis, with the question of what they wanted from each other; which brought with it the question that was to haunt psychoanalysis: should wants be understood or met? In Freud's view psychoanalysis was defined as a treatment in which wants could be thought about and not pre-empted by being gratified. In Ferenczi's version of psychoanalysis, to frustrate the patient too much was to re-create in the treatment exactly the childhood trauma that had necessitated the treatment in the first place. This issue of whether a want is something that can be satisfied or whether it in and of itself spells the impossibility of satisfaction – the necessary gap between desire and its object – was one of the many contentions that bound Freud and Ferenczi together, and set the terms for the future of psychoanalytic debate. This correspondence, like the theoretical work written during these years – 40 works by Freud and 56 by Ferenczi – is a record of the inspiring turbulence they evoked in each other, in which issues of truth and honesty were bound up with the apparently theoretical question of homosexuality; of the feelings two men might have for each other (in the context of other significant relationships). It is unusual to be able to read such theoretical love letters, a genre traditionally associated with fantasies of truthtelling.

For Ferenczi, 17 years younger than Freud, and more emotionally extravagant, psychoanalysis was useful as a way of thinking about what he called his 'ideal of honesty'. 'Not everything that is infantile should be abhorred,' he writes to Freud in the early years of their relationship, 'for example the child's urge for truth, which is only dammed up by false educational influences . . . I still hold firmly to the conviction that it is not honesty but superfluous secrecy that is abnormal' – one of the things that Ferenczi might be hinting at here is the superfluous secrecy between Freud and himself. In Ferenczi's view the child is an instinctive truth-teller potentially perverted by adult conspiracies. 'Many intelligent children,' he writes in 'Transitory Symptom Constructions During the Analysis' (1912),

> at the stage of repression marked by the latency period, before they have gone through 'the great intimidation', regard adults as dangerous fools, to whom one cannot tell the truth without running the risk of being punished for it: and whose inconsistencies and follies have to be taken into consideration. In this children are not so very wrong.

From the child's point of view parents can be occult phenomena. And children, and the adults they will become, suffer from their parents' inability, or unwillingness, to acknowledge their truth.

For Freud it wasn't that children told the truth, it was that they desired their parents. So is desiring, as Ferenczi implies, a way of telling the truth, or is this belief in truth, at least in a psychoanalytic context, a noble and innocent – noble because innocent – cover story for the forbidden mess of desire? Freud believed that children lived the truth about sex; Ferenczi believed that children spoke the truth about Truth. It was as if Original Virtue was being smuggled back into psychoanalysis, Rousseau returning through the back door. Because if there is a Freudian unconscious what exactly is this truth that the child has an 'urge' for? 'Superfluous secrecy' could just be a way of describing the repressed unconscious of Freudian Man. What Ferenczi never quite spells out is what the child wants from telling the so-called truth; that would be the Freudian question. In so far as childhood, in Ferenczi's version, is a state of submission then the fault lies fairly and squarely with the parents, and the child is virtually robbed of his intrinsically ambivalent and complicated nature.

At its best, of course, Ferenczi is saying something that has come to seem very important: that children grow by being listened to, that adults are frightened of listening to children because of what they might feel as a consequence; that some secrets in the family turn children into sleepwalkers; that adults seem extraordinary to children. But at its worst children are burdened with a quasi-oracular status that they cannot make sense of, or bear the responsibility for. Fantasies of Truth, after all, are adult constructions, something children learn from the adult world. Children are not 'naturally' anything, other than the adult's construction of (their) nature. But these issues, as discussed between Freud and Ferenczi, are part of the origins of the contemporary debate about child sexual abuse. And Ferenczi's 'ideal of honesty', which is a recurrent theme in these letters, alerted psychoanalysts to the senses in which interpretation can be a refusal to listen; and that believing the patient – which means believing in the patient – is both integral to the successful process of analysis and, more importantly, is a fundamental form of kindness. But in what sense does believing what people say entail agreeing with them, and how do I know if I've believed what someone says to me? If I hear something they don't hear in what they say, am I then disbelieving them? Freud's work, in a way that Ferenczi could not always acknowledge, ineluctably complicates these notions of truth and belief. In fact, one of the implications of Freudian theory was that the idea of Truth, as some consensual superordinate idol, as something around which we might all agree, could be a coercive attempt to deny differences. Ferenczi, at various points in this correspondence, suggests that psychoanalysis, with its promise of free speech, might itself be a unifying force.

Freud, however, experiences his younger colleague's ideal of honesty as a more complicated appeal than it in fact was. Characteristically, Freud picked up the demand in Ferenczi's often expressed wish for openness and honesty. 'Just think what it would mean,' Ferenczi wrote to Freud in 1910, 'if ONE COULD TELL EVERYONE THE TRUTH, one's father, teacher, neighbour, and even the king. All fabricated, imposed authority would go to the devil – what is rightful would remain natural.' Ferenczi understood like nobody else, even Freud perhaps, the revolutionary potential of psychoanalysis. He knew that people speaking differently to each other changes the world (it is noticeable, though, that the people he wants to speak the truth to, in so far as they are explicitly gendered, are men). Ferenczi doesn't, however, tell us quite why or how being able to tell everyone the truth – whatever one conceives that to be – would destroy those forms of oppressive authority. But in his reply to this letter of Ferenczi's it is as though Freud has heard this as a wish, which it must also have been, for freer talk between the two of them: Freud was certainly, as Ferenczi was quick to tell him, father, teacher and king to him. 'I feel myself to be a match for anything,' Freud replies cannily, 'and approve of the overcoming of my homosexuality, with the result being greater independence.' For Freud freedom was, at least explicitly, in the overcoming, the silencing of his homosexual self: for Ferenczi independence would be in its free expression. Freud sensed, I think, that Ferenczi's fantasy of honesty, of people saying anything and everything to each other, was also a fantasy of symbiosis, of there being no differences between people – if we tell each other everything it is as though we never leave each other out. Saying whatever comes into one's mind was something Freud believed one should do in analysis; Ferenczi wanted the psychoanalytic relationship to be the paradigm for social relations. But it would have to be a version of psychoanalysis in which the analyst could tell the patient whatever was on his mind as well. Mutual interpretation and mutual free-association. No kings.

What was homosexuality for Freud, we are obliged to wonder now, if he needed to 'overcome' it to sustain his independence? It often seems as though Freud experiences Ferenczi, in these letters, as both the son trying to seduce the father, and as the son trying to turn the father into a mother. Unsubtly, Ferenczi refers in a letter to Jung's wife talking of Freud's 'antipathy toward giving completely of yourself as a friend'. Was Freud anxious about intimacy, as Ferenczi often implies in this correspondence, or was it that Ferenczi couldn't tolerate the differences between them; differences of generation and temperament, different ways of loving? Difference or defensiveness, of course, has always been a dilemma that psychoanalysis has been unable to deal with. Is the patient different from the analyst's description of him, or merely resistant to the analyst's interpretation, and who is in a position to decide? If one way of talking about these perplexing issues, albeit guardedly, was to theorise about homosexuality, the other, significantly less contentious way, was to talk about the women in their lives. Or rather, for the younger men to talk to Freud about the women in their lives. Mrs Freud was another of Freud's secrets.

As in all Freud's correspondences, the men tend to flex their psychoanalytic muscles over the women. The psychoanalytic 'movement' is always an invigoratingly fraught subject around which they can divide and bond; but it is as though they have the women in common, as a problem they can huddle over. Managing the women – Freud, for example, refers in a letter here to Lou Andreas-Salomé as 'a woman of dangerous intelligence' – and the so-called heretics kept Freud's psychoanalytic group together. The drama of Freud and Ferenczi's relationship in this correspondence is fed by the well-known drama of Jung's dissension, and the less notorious drama of Ferenczi's love affair with an older woman, Gizella, his mistress and future wife, and her daughter Elma, who was Ferenczi's, and later Freud's, analysand. Ferenczi was briefly engaged to Elma, who eventually married someone else. Jung, as this correspondence shows, was clearly scapegoated as an occultist and anti-semite; which is not to say that he wasn't both those things, but it is to say something about what the psychoanalytic group used him for. And Ferenczi's professional reputation was to be retrospectively disparaged because of his supposed emotional and erotic instability.

In these letters, the first of three volumes, we see Ferenczi gradually trying to cure himself of Freud, but sustain his relationship with him. Jung, Ferenczi writes to Freud in 1912, 'identifies confession with psychoanalysis and evidently doesn't know that the confession of sins is the lesser task of psychoanalytic theory: the greater one is THE DEMOLITION OF THE FATHER IMAGO, which is completely absent in confession.' Ferenczi realised at the future of psychoanalysis depended on analysts understanding their relationship with – their transference to – Freud himself. Freud, after all, had done a very paradoxical thing; he had invented a form of authority, the science of psychoanalysis, as a treatment that depended on demolishing forms of authority. It was to be a double-bind that drove people mad; either crazily conformist or crazily bizarre. 'I had to observe not without pain,' Ferenczi writes to Freud after their holiday together in 1914, 'that my position with respect to you, specifically, is still not completely natural, and that your presence arouses inhibitions of various kinds in me that influence, and at times almost paralyse, my actions and even my thinking.' It takes two to create this kind of unease.

Ferenczi was showing Freud something very important, making the difficult demands on psychoanalysis and its discoverer that would be the source of its future vitality. How could two people sit in a room together talking and go on believing that one was more authoritative than the other? Why would a person want to understand someone, or even cure them, rather than have sex with them? How could one protect a person's best interests by being unfriendly to them? Psychoanalytic theory made these questions, as Ferenczi knew, unavoidable. Psychoanalytic institutions ruled them out of court.

Psychoanalytic trainings are still paralysed by their excessive regard for the older generations (the average age of the contributors, if they are not actually dead, to the so-called New Psychoanalytic Library must be at least sixty). The legacy of Freud and Ferenczi – the correspondences between them – might lift some flagging spirits in a profession whose moralism and truth claims are rightly under suspicion.

6 October 1994

The Heart's Cause

Michael Wood on the Trillings

Slugging it out with Diana Trilling in the pages of *Commentary*, Robert Lowell remarked: 'Controversy is bad for the mind and worse for the heart.' Mrs Trilling, for all the world like Dorothea Brooke or some other 19th-century heroine of the strenuously examined life, replied: 'I have never thought controversy bad for either the mind or the heart.' She missed the grace and weariness of Lowell's phrase, as well as the sense of genuine damage which lurked in his irony, but she had found a triumphant definition of what she herself was about. She was a controversialist not out of belligerence or righteousness or arrogance, but out of cultural conviction. There are things we don't need to argue about, she would say, but not many. Argument is the visible, sequential life of ideas. Controversy is good for the heart, and indispensable for any but the lazy mind.

This is a stance which leads to stridency, almost entails it. It also tends to literalism, to an underrating of the meanings of silence, or of motivations which are signalled but not fully declared. Mrs Trilling has been belligerent and righteous, and she herself, in her remarkable new book,* speaks of her arrogance ('an intellectual confidence – an arrogance, if you will'), and says, with beautiful understatement, that her mother left her 'a substantial legacy of determination'. Or again: 'The lust for honesty in my family was ravaging and incurable. I am its product.' More tellingly still, evoking her childhood fear of sharing the fate of the crazy lady next door, who died with her clothes off and her furniture all upside down, she writes: 'On emotional tiptoe, daring as I could, dodging as I had to, I approached a first vagrant notion of rape; also, more soundly, an intuition of the fiercer manifestations of insanity. For all of my life, the fear of insanity has blocked the free play of my imagination and made me too intent upon reasonableness.'

There is a poem by R.P. Blackmur which speaks of marrying reason when the heart's cause is lost. But one might also marry reason for the heart's sake; for the heart's peace. Mrs Trilling's sense of herself as too

---

* Diana Trilling, *The Beginning of the Journey: The Marriage of Diana and Lionel Trilling* (Harcourt Brace, 1994).

intent on reasonableness allows us to understand, and shows us that she understands, what many of her most extravagant arguments were about. The controversy with Lowell (and not only with Lowell – Mrs Trilling, in *We Must March, My Darlings*, 1977, speaks of 'a considerable correspondence, most of it hostile to my view') concerned a long essay of hers about the Columbia student uprising of April 1968. Students occupied university buildings, and after a week were forcibly ejected by the police; there was fear of racial riot; flying rhetoric, some vandalism, much dissension among teachers and students and administrators who had previously not known how much room there was for disagreement in their lives. Mrs Trilling has some sympathy for the black demonstrators – she admires their dignity and self-respect, and thinks they have a case against American society – but thinks the white student radicals were just spoilt and ungrateful kids, peeing on the carpet that welcomed them. One of these delinquents, famously photographed during the occupation smoking a cigar, with his feet on the university president's desk, later called to ask why Lionel Trilling was not out there defending the students against the police, as many faculty members were. We may well think that this was some cheek, or some chic, chutzpah well beyond the call of Oedipal protest. But it's not so easy to see why Mrs Trilling should be 'shaken' by the photograph, and her reading of the telephone call is extraordinary. 'This was revolutionary scorekeeping, its own fine intimation of terror; to my ear it spoke all too reverberantly of concentration camps and the knock on the door in the night.'

This is the sort of thing that led Lowell to say that all was twisted in the essay's 'rattled sentences', and that 'no one thought Mrs Trilling heaves into my thoughts lands straight.' But for her the students had not simply taken over a large university, they had stormed the house of reason, desecrated some noble, elective family of the mind. 'I admit a possible bias,' she says. 'One marries into a university much as one once married into one's husband's family: there develops a not insignificant attachment and a perhaps distorting intimacy.' And in *The Beginning of the Journey* she writes of Columbia as if it were self-evidently the centre of the charted intellectual world in the first half of the century. Didn't these fractious children know where they were? 'Still, with all allowance for subjectivity, I find myself unable to locate a sufficient cause of revolution at Columbia – reason for complaint, certainly; reason for protest, yes, especially in the graduate schools . . . but no reason, no reasonable reason, to tear the place to pieces.' This is certainly true – what would be a reasonable reason for tearing any place to pieces? But the trouble with insisting on reasonable reasons, and harshly judging all those who lack them, is that you fail to care about the other kinds of reason, the ones that aren't reasonable and won't speak, or won't measure up. The students were not rioting for nothing, and the proper response to the accusatory telephone call, even on Mrs Trilling's own terms, is either to refuse to answer or to explain one's actions, not to treat the question as if it could only have come from the secret police. There is a remarkable anticipation here of one of the key strategies in the attribution of political correctness. A question is asked, characteristically by someone with very little institutional or political power except that which your conscience concedes them. You are so outraged or scared or worried by the question that you can't ignore it or answer it, you can only wish it hadn't been asked. But it has been asked, so the next best thing is to turn the asker into a Stalinist or a Nazi.

We need to go further, though. If Mrs Trilling's understanding of herself as too intent on reasonableness gives us a context for what seem to be her extravagances, we must remember that she was also saying, all along, some very stern and quite unextravagant things about what we have been doing to our minds and hearts. 'Almost with each passing day,' she wrote in her essay about the Columbia uprising

> it becomes harder for liberalism to claim that it has been adequate to the tasks it undertook. We caution against capitulation to the revolution designed by the New Left, point to its ugly violence . . . But must we not also caution against the comfortable assumption that liberalism has only to shine up its old medals and resurrect its old rhetoric of responsibility . . . ? By confusing quiet with quietism, by buttressing legality with inertia, liberalism has earned at least some part of its present poor reputation on the campus. Yet it will suffer more than disrepute, destruction, if in admitting its deficiencies it either rests with these as its cosy guilt or, in its desire for revitalisation, takes the revolution as its alternative.

We may think that there were in 1968 and ought to be now radical alternatives to liberalism which don't lead straight to the Gulag or the Apocalypse, but the case for liberalism itself could hardly be better put, and there is no mistaking Mrs Trilling for a neo-conservative.

Diana and Lionel Trilling were both born in July 1905; they married in 1929. They came from well-to-do Jewish families who lived, at various times, in Manhattan, Brooklyn and Westchester County. She studied at Radcliffe, he at Columbia. After a year in Wisconsin, he got a job at Columbia, and for the rest of their lives, apart from vacations and stints as visitors at Oxford, they lived in New York – most of the time on Morningside Heights, close to Columbia. Lionel Trilling died in 1975, and the book ends as an elegy, not only for him and their marriage, but for their friends and their world. The tone here is as far from stridency as it could be.

> Seventeen years have now passed since Lionel's death, and hour by hour, minute by minute, I still listen for a clock which no longer ticks . . . I have not found a substitute for his unhurried and unostentatious thoughtfulness. He lived in the world of ideas and he constantly brought me its news. He valued his intellectual endowment all too lightly and I am afraid that I also undervalued it.

She goes on to speak of 'the strange difficult ungenerous unreliable unkind and not always honest people who created the world in which Lionel and I shared', and you understand a lot about them and their time when you realise that all of those apparently negative ascriptions are to be taken as compliments. In similar fashion Lionel Trilling, in full awareness that Whittaker Chambers had betrayed his country and his friends, could nevertheless describe him as 'a man of honour'. Mrs Trilling (twice) says this was 'a careless phrase', and perhaps she's right. Her gloss makes clear, though, the sort of moral evaluation she and Lionel Trilling were after. 'I too felt,' she says of Chambers, 'that while he would perhaps have killed for his cause, he would not lie to destroy a friend.' These distinctions are a way of saying not that we can't make a better world, but that we can't make a world at all with anyone other than the people we've got, reliable and unreliable, kind and unkind, and the rest. It's a Brechtian perception, a recognition that the land is unhappy when it needs heroes, not when it hasn't got them, although both the Trillings would say it was a Freudian perception, an acknowledgment of what they endlessly called the conditioned life. One of the weirdest features of this particular patch of intellectual history – I'm not in a position to dispute it, I only note its strangeness – is that Communism, once flirted with and for ever after abhorred, is seen as a striving for the *unconditioned* life, an escape from social constriction into a vast and enchanted theology. Lionel Trilling, in his 1975 Introduction to a new edition of his novel *The Middle of the Journey* (1947) writes of 'an impassioned longing to believe', and 'an ever more imperious and bitter refusal to consent to the conditioned nature of human existence'. I don't doubt that this is where many American intellectuals found themselves, or that this location represented a real moral danger in American life, but I don't see how they can have got there from Marx. The script has somehow been rewritten by Emerson and Captain Ahab. Or rather – this is clearer in Mrs Trilling's writing – the script has been moralised, aligned exclusively with the individual conscience. What skews the aftermath of this moment, and makes Mrs

Trilling look like the neo-conservative she is not, is the notion of the single colossal error – an error so interesting that everything pales into insignificance beside it. It may also be that people who feel they were wrong only once have an even stiffer and more exalted sense of virtue than those who believe they were never wrong at all. We certainly need to know why people would want to dedicate themselves to a murderous dream of ruthlessness when they didn't have to, but we also need an understanding of all those, Communists and other, in Europe, Africa and Asia, whose only choice was between forms of ruthlessness.

Mrs Trilling's elegy also evokes a critical time and style. 'The New York intellectuals had their moment in history and it has passed. Theirs was uniquely the age of criticism. Their criticism went everywhere. They had no gods, no protectorates or sacred constituencies. They were a small, geographically concentrated group, but if they did nothing else, they kept the general culture in balance.' I'm not sure about the balance, and the age of criticism – the phrase is Randall Jarrell's – was well represented by writers who weren't New York intellectuals at all. We could think of Kenneth Burke, R.P. Blackmur, Allen Tate, many more. But Mrs Trilling's point is important. What hides in the phrase 'general culture' is the belief that literature and culture and politics are connected, that controversy is good *and* bad for the mind and heart, that we can share moral and intellectual ground only if we care enough about the principle of sharing it – or if you like, that only a myth of shared ground will allow us to find whatever ground we share. The work of James Agee, Hannah Arendt, Fred Dupee, Mary McCarthy, Dwight Macdonald, Philip Rahv, Delmore Schwart, Edmund Wilson – these are some of the names Mrs Trilling mentions – gave the myth one of the best runs it has had anywhere. The language of the myth looks a little odd now – people have repeatedly attacked both Trillings' use of the Morningside 'we' – but what is odd is its distinctive hovering between the highly local and the grandly universal.

This is very clearly seen in Lionel Trilling's wonderful (and strange) essay of 1951 on *Anna Karenina*, where he argues that Tolstoy's apparent objectivity is really a deep subjectivity, and that we accept his world as real because it is the world we *want* to be real. Unlike Dostoevsky's world, that is, which is the one we know to be real.

> We so happily give our assent to what Tolstoy shows us and so willingly call it reality because we have something to gain from its being reality. For it is the hope of every decent, reasonably honest person to be judged under the aspect of Tolstoy's representation of human nature. Perhaps, indeed, what Tolstoy has done is to constitute as reality the judgment which every decent, reasonably honest person is likely to make of himself.

This is further than the darkest deconstructionist would go. The practical limits to deconstruction are political and historical – it is the point of deconstruction to show that that is what they are, but the world Lionel Trilling evokes is a universal flung across a void. 'We' are decent and reasonably honest, likely to make certain (rather tame) judgments of ourselves. But what if we don't see ourselves this way? Or if we have quite other notions of what decency and honesty are? Or just can't understand the categories? The world of Tolstoy evaporates, and with it the world we wanted. To say nothing of whoever 'we' are. Yet it is a sign of Trilling's courage that he looks at the void, even as his generalities allow him to look away again, and the rest of his argument is very closely pursued. Believing in Dostoevsky, and the truths of horror and evil, as our century means we must, we are in danger of believing *only* in those truths. This is the great modern orthodoxy, and an overwhelming heresy against the kindness and ordinariness we also know. Since Tolstoy, Trilling says, 'virtually no writer has been able to tell us of pain in terms of life's possible joy.' We see Trilling's own commitment to the orthodoxy in the fact that pain is unqualified and joy is just 'possible', and one of Diana Trilling's purposes in writing her book is to remind us of the 'essentially tragic view of life' which underlay Lionel Trilling's justly famed grace and moderation. This point is very well made, and a glance at *The Liberal Imagination* (1950), for instance, confirms it amply. There the echoing words are 'complex', 'terrible', 'difficulty', 'pain'. 'What marks the artist is his power to shape the material of pain we all have.' This is a doctrine not of pain as the source of art, as in Edmund Wilson's *The Wound and the Bow*, but of pain as one of the crucial grounds of life.

One of the most controversial claims of *The Beginning of the Journey*, flamboyantly offered as such, is Mrs Trilling's assertion that she taught her husband to write:

> Lionel taught me to think; I taught him to write . . . In a society such as ours, where despite the efforts of feminism, women continue to be treated with less generosity than men, I realise of course that whereas my statement that Lionel taught me to think will be received without a murmur, I put myself at risk by saying that I played a role in his literary accomplishment. In fact, I recently tested the response which I might expect to this bald assertion: I tried it on an old friend, the editor of a magazine to which Lionel and I had contributed. He made no attempt to conceal his displeasure. 'How could you teach Lionel to write?' he asked irritably. 'He was a better writer than you are.'

But Mrs Trilling wasn't saying he *wasn't* the better writer, only that she taught him to be the writer he was.

Lionel was a writer of broader vision than mine and of more complex purpose and in the course of time he developed a prose which I could only envy. It was the perfect instrument of his ideas, cadenced yet forceful, precisely elegant, with a curious ability to suggest that space was being saved for what the author had left unsaid.

Mrs Trilling did not usually save such space, and even in this book, with its admirable honesty and vulnerability, she often makes announcements rather than gives clues. 'I knew that I would be vindicated by history,' she says of an old quarrel with Mary McCarthy, forgetting no doubt that Fidel Castro famously used much the same phrase. 'Communism was not the fulfilment of an ideal. It was itself a movement of power, and like all movements of power it was led by ambition and self-interest.' 'It would have been unthinkable for Lionel and his Columbia friends to be moved by ideology in their judgment of literature.' 'British intellectuals are more accomplished than Americans at being rude.' The evidence here is Cyril Connolly's flicking ash into a cream dessert, as compared to Randall Jarrell's deliberately dropping Mrs Trilling's watch on the floor: pretty close thing. But then there are marvellously stealthy phrases here, and some fine musical paragraphs. I wonder if the fact that Mrs Trilling (who is almost blind) had to dictate the book was a help rather than a hindrance here – stylistically, I mean, since it obviously complicated her labour immensely in other ways. She says the world of the Fifties was 'perhaps too complex for our imaginative grasp', and that she 'would not have thought to describe any of Lionel's friends, in college or after college, as sunlit'. Her jokes about her husband manage to be both sharp-edged and amiable, even fond: 'even for a literary man he danced badly'; 'Poor Lionel! As man-about-town he had a long way to go and would never really make the course.' And writing about her father and mother, she comes close to saying the unsayable:

> My father's early life is almost more vivid to me than my own . . . At will, I conjure up the little boy he was then: I see him rising at dawn and treading the worn earth behind his tenement as he goes about the preparation of his long dark day. I see him at *heder*, bright-eyed, timid, shrewd, studying his Talmud, rocking and chanting in unison with the other little scholars, all of them hungry and sleepy and scared, all of them at the mercy of the Reb, that seedy and greedy tyrant over the young . . . There is no Chagall in my father's Jewish boyhood: nothing floats, there is no scent of flowers in the air . . .
>
> On a winter's day, I stood at the window of my father's apartment and looked out at the season's first snowfall. I thought of my mother's body freezing in the cold ground and my heart ached. I sometimes think that my heart has never stopped aching, whether with my masked and injured love for my father or my injured and buried love for my mother.

The Beginning of the Journey has its repetitions, often literal ones; the journey isn't always interesting, and its circles sometimes seem small. Maybe New York isn't really the Big Apple; just a little apple with great expectations. But there are admirable notations of American Jewish life in the early part of the century; shrewd comments on the Depression and on the American response to World War Two; on what it meant to be a woman in an intellectual world assumed to belong to men. There is a powerful description of becoming the mother of a first and only child at 42.

The finest critical insight in the book concerns Lionel Trilling's hesitation between fiction and criticism. He idealised the creative writer as a recklessly liberated figure, trampling on the codes that fetter the rest of us, but he became (mainly) a critic through decency. And yet – this is Mrs Trilling's shrewd suggestion – the whole perspective was mythological, and Lionel Trilling's criticism was always informed by what we usually regard as the novelist's gifts.

Lionel Trilling was often depressed; Diana Trilling endlessly phobic. She was frequently, on her own account, almost impossible to live with. But she creates, seemingly without trying and certainly without boasting, the impression of a woman of great courage – the courage which comes from getting the best of your terrible nerves – and of remarkable generosity. She doesn't forgive her enemies (or her doctors or her analysts), but she recognises the complicated worth of her friends, and she knows there are wonders to be found among imperfections. 'The miracle of marriage,' she says, 'if it works, is that it makes you the most important person in the world for at least one other person.' And this in turn allows you to lose, at least with one person, your craving for importance.

9 February 1995

Heart-Stopping

Ian Hamilton on being a soccer bore

For years – since boyhood, really – I've seen myself as an above-average soccer bore. At my peak, I would happily hold forth for hours about the rugged terrace-time I'd served, at Feethams, White Hart Lane, the Manor Ground. And when it came to the archival stuff, if you could spare the time, well, so could I. 'Name three of the Spurs' double side's *reserves*,' I'd say, or: 'How many of the 1964 West Ham cupwinning team had names beginning with a B?' Or it would be: 'Pick an XI in which every position is taken by a Gary. I will start you off. Gary Bailey in goal. Gary Stevens right back. Now you carry on.'

Yes, truly boring. But in those days soccermania was dark and lonely work. Outside my small circle of co-bores, most people I knew just didn't want to know. From time to time, I'd cut a prole-ish dash in pubs or quell some terrace skinhead with a deft statistic but there were few other social benefits, so far as I could tell. Soccer scholarship cut no ice in the examination halls of Life and it helped not at all with girls. 'I thought you were supposed to be a *poet*,' they would say. 'But soccer,' I'd protest, '*is* poetry – well, at its best, it can be, or it nearly is . . . Take Jimmy Greaves. The Man United game.' And that, usually, was that.

Those were the days. Now everything has changed. Over the past five years or so, soccer has moved to the very centre-circle of our culture. Books, magazines, TV shows have been sprouting on all sides.* Nowadays everybody wants to be a soccer bore. And, what's worse, everybody seems to have found it pretty easy to become one. Trivia I once treasured as peculiarly, eccentrically mine are now revealed to be the dreary stuff of common knowledge. Faced with my archival fire-power, these new young soccer bores don't even blink: 'Who *doesn't* know of Bovington, Boyce, Brabrook, Bond et al,' they say. 'And as for

---

* In particular, here, David Bennie, *Not Playing for Celtic: Another Paradise Lost* (Mainstream, 1995); David Platt, *Achieving the Goal* (Richard Cohen, 1995); Gary McAllister with Graham Clark, *Captain's Log: The Gary McAllister Story* (Mainstream, 1995); John Brown with Derek Watson, *Blue Grit: The John Brown Story* (Mainstream, 1995); Rogan Taylor and Andrew Ward, *Kicking and Screaming: An Oral History of Football in England* (Robson, 1995); Tom Watt, *A Passion for the Game: Real Lives in Football* (Mainstream, 1995).

all those Garys you're so keen on, why not make up *two* teams of them, plus subs? Let's see now: Ablett, Bennett, Brookes . . .'

These past few years, these years of rampant soccer cred, have been a slow torment for the antique soccer bore. In the old days we were friendless and perhaps despised but we enjoyed a steady faith in our own expertise, our strength-in-depth: we knew the lot. The depressing thing about these new-wave chaps is that they know it too, and then some. For instance, quite a few of them were ten-year-olds when England played Brazil in the 1970 World Cup but mention that Jeff Astle miss and they will shed real tears. And they go further back than that. Tell them about the first Wembley Cup Final, the one with the white horse, and they will talk as if they had had a seat in the front row: actually, the horse wasn't white, they'll say, it was dark grey – it just looks white in that over-exposed snapshot you keep showing me.

Where did they get this stuff? From Sky TV, from *Fever Pitch*, from Skinner and Baddiel? Or did they get it from their fathers, old soccer bores with nobody to talk to except their captive kids? 'Once upon a time there was this big white horse.' Another dismaying feature of the new 'soccer-literacy' is that its exponents tend to be Lit-literate as well. They can zap you with fantasy-league teams of big-name authors: Borges and Márquez up front, Kundera in midfield, Sam Beckett 'in the hole'. They like to assure you that Gunter Netzer's hairdo belongs in the same world as Günter Grass's prose. They know all about Nabokov and Camus, and not just because the pair of them kept goal. A recent new-wave soccer-book gives something of the flavour:

> Albert Camus, Algerian goalie and French Existentialist, never took a penalty but it would have been interesting to watch him try (if, say, a penalty shoot-out against a Structuralist XI went all the way to the respective goalkeepers during sudden death). Would Camus have beaten an upright and non-diving Russian Formalist like Vladimir Propp? And if a penalty shoot-out is inherently meaningless and absurd, would Camus have exercised his will effectively by scoring, thereby bringing individual meaning to the experience? Or would he have deliberately ballooned the ball over the crossbar, thereby defining himself through negative action? And what would he have made of that old Romantic bourgeois Hamish McAlpine, the Dundee United keeper who used to take all of his side's penalties whenever one was awarded during regular 90-minute matches? Come to think of it, Camus taking a penalty at Tannadice doesn't bear thinking about. He'd probably have stood over the ball for 30 agonising seconds, before whipping out a revolver and shooting a suspiciously dark supporter in the George Fox Stand (since United fans are known colloquially as 'Arabs').

This muddle of transdisciplinary pretentiousness comes from a book called *Not Playing for Celtic: Another Paradise Lost*, and, yes, the paradise in question is indeed John Milton's – or Big John's (as he is called here):

> Beating Airdrie in this year's final has hardly sent warning shock-waves reverberating around the football giants of Europe, but having witnessed the emotional scenes which followed, it seems appropriate to quote Milton once again:
>
>> Some natural tears they shed, but wiped them soon;
>> The world was all before them, where to choose
>> Their place of rest, and Providence their guide:
>> They hand in hand with wondering steps and slow
>> Through Eden took their solitary way.

A 'lack of pace' might seem to be the problem with this dual strike-force, but happily the author – David Bennie – does not say so.

Nick Hornby cannot be blamed for writing of this kind, although *Fever Pitch* has helped to set the tone. In some ways, Hornby has links with the old school. He knows and cares that there is something 'moronic' about his passion for the game, and about his Arsenal-fixation. Old-style bores used to keep quiet about this aspect of their calling; Hornby has had the nerve to make a book out of it – and a most unmoronic book, at that. A terrace Holden Caulfield, he doesn't even *like* Arsenal, for Chrissake, but he knows that he is stuck with them, just as he is stuck with pop music, junk lit crit, trash TV, just as he is stuck, really, with himself – a self shaped not by action or direct experience but by a kind of bombed-out cultural passivity, a wry/glum putting up with what's on offer, what's served up to him, week in, week out.

Soccer fans are nothing if not passive. The games they go to hardly ever turn out as they would wish, as they have dreamed. Football is nearly always disappointing. Epic confrontations turn out to be tepid stand-offs; celebrity performers are forever going through 'lean spells' or getting injured. If a star actor were to turn in a succession of sub-standard performances – forgetting lines, appearing onstage at wrong moments, tripping over during sword fights – he would soon enough not be a star. With soccer, the spectator is conditioned to expect the second-rate. He gets to like it; he gets even to prefer it. As with Nick Hornby, the new soccer bore's most vivid memories tend to be drawn from adolescence, that stretch of non-life when everything is less than it should be. TV at the moment is obsessed with soccer of the Seventies: the soccer watched with maximum intensity and thwartedness by the now-thirty-somethings who decide what is broadcast on TV. For types like these, supporting, say, Watford is remembered as a kind of pimply rite of passage, like going out with the wrong girl, the only girl who would have them in those days.

To be a new-style soccer bore, then, it is not enough merely to know about the soccer. It is what you muddle the soccer up with that wins marks. For Seventies adolescents, all of life's dramas were enacted to the sound of music, the music that just happened to be there, as Watford – and that girl – just happened to be there. Thus, the new soccer bore is expected to be as knowledgeable about chart-placings as he is about league tables and cup-runs. He has to be able to come on (more or less) as follows:

> Abba's 'Super-Trouper' got to Number One on the Friday before the Luton game. I remember hearing it on someone's tranny on my way to Vicarage Road. I'd just split up with Sue, partly because I'd missed her birthday the week before; it was the same day as Wolves away. That was a crap game, nil-all, but I suppose it served me right. Anyway, Abba at the time were spot-on, so I thought: 'I was sick and tired of everything/When I called you last night.' And I was reading Philip Larkin, where he says about nothing like something happening anywhere. The next Saturday it was West Brom at home.

Puppy love, pop tunes, A-level poetry, crap soccer. This seems to be the recipe. Old soccer bores don't really stand a chance.

Even so, it has to be confessed that soccer-writing is a lot livelier these days than it used to be. Even the lowest forms of soccer-lit – the star player's ghosted 'Life', for instance – have become noticeably more candid and style-conscious. For one thing, not all players choose to hire a ghost. David Platt's *Achieving the Goal* is, we are told, all Platt's own work. Unluckily, in this case, the author seems to have modelled his prose style on soccer books that *have* been ghosted, so not a lot is gained. As a player, David Platt always seems over-anxious to project himself as the 'model professional', and on the page he evinces a simi-lar unease. When in doubt, he falls back on backpage soccer-speak, as if believing this to be a model of correct procedure.

Still, now and then he does come close to speaking his own mind, or so it seems. He admits that the goal he scored against Belgium in the 1990 World Cup changed his status overnight from 'eager-midfield-runner' to 'man-capable-of-magic-moments'. Without that goal, Platt may not have been so lucratively pursued by the Italians. He may not even have lasted in the England team.

Graham Taylor, though, was always a Platt fan, and Platt owes a lot to Taylor. One of the most strenuous sections of Platt's book is devoted to repairing Taylor's reputation: a forlorn task, but rather touching to behold. Taylor, we learn, is 'one of the best observers of people I have ever met', whatever that might mean. Platt never quite praises his old boss as a tactician but he makes no mention of that foul-mouthed video and manfully condones Taylor's notorious substitution of Gary Lineker during the 1992 European Championships: 'I know Graham well, and can state categorically that the substitution was tactical and not vindictive. If we had equalised in that final twenty minutes Gary would have worn his number ten shirt in the semi-final. Quite simply, it wouldn't have been his last game.'

This anodyne generosity of spirit is in evidence throughout. Even Ron Atkinson, who long ago 'released' Platt from Manchester United's youth squad – released him to Crewe Alexandra – comes in for a few words of praise. The only time Platt shows even a flicker of unwholesomeness is when he comes to describe his unhappy season with Juventus. Juventus, he says, never got the best out of him because they played him in the wrong position. One suspects, though, that Platt's experience of the Italian big time was more sharply humbling than he makes it out to be. In Turin, he may well have come to recognise that he was not, and never would be, quite the equal of his reputation. He would never improve on that heart-stopping Belgium goal – but then, who could?

A few years ago, David Platt's book would have been an altogether thinner, shoddier affair – aimed cynically at a fan readership not used to reading books. This is not to say that he does not incline towards the shoddy: 'You can only take people as you find them'; 'confidence is a funny thing'; 'an old cliché says that time flies,' and so on. All the same, Platt does from time to time make a real effort to analyse the mechanics of a footballer's career. He is no good at describing what the soccer itself feels like but on the subject of what the papers call 'personal terms' – cars, contracts, houses, perks – he is enthusiastically informative. For access of this sort, we should be grateful. Platt even reveals that his own Access card was once withdrawn because he had strayed into an offside position. This disclosure – from an England captain – would have been unthinkable in the old days.

Ghosted lives still have a market, though. This season has already brought us Gary McAllister's *Captain's Log* ('with Graham Clark') and *Blue Grit* by Glasgow Rangers' John Brown ('with Peter Watson'). Would Brown reveal some juicy Gazza tales or give us the dirt on Graeme Souness? Not a chance. Gascoigne is not mentioned (perhaps he arrived too late) and as for Souness: 'I haven't got a bad word to say about Graeme. I don't know if he was appreciated the way he should have been in Scotland. He had an arrogant streak, but he knew what he wanted and was a winner.' Would McAllister provide some inside dope on Eric Cantona? No, not a drop. These footballers write about their teammates as if they had never met them, as if – like us – they get their information from the *Sun*. Take McAllister on Cantona: 'But Eric, on and off the pitch, is different, and you have to live with that. His biggest problem is undoubtedly his temperament. We never saw too much of the dark side of that when he was with us, but it has reared up time and time again since he left. I think it must go with the territory of being something of a genius, even if that in no way excuses some of his excesses.' Cantona 'was a great guy any time we went out'; 'he had simple tastes and wasn't at all materialistic'; 'he spoke what is basically a football language and gelled immediately with the rest of the lads'; 'Lee Chapman was particularly pleased to see him.'

For all I know, the real-life Gary McAllister is as boring and pious as this 'log' makes him seem. I doubt it, though. And one day we may find out. Television's current soccer-madness has engendered a fashion for 'oral testimony' and already a few tongues have been loosened – usually the tongues of players who no longer play, but even so. *Kicking and Screaming*, the edited text of BBC TV's recent 'oral history of football in England' has several splendidly unbuttoned sound-bites. The book covers all soccer history's important milestones – the Matthews final, the Hungarians at Wembley, the Munich disaster, the various World Cup campaigns – and offers intelligent close-ups of individual players, clubs and managers. It also covers most of the big soccer 'issues' – the maximum wage, hooliganism, bungs, all-seater stadiums. Altogether, the ideal 'how to' book for the aspiring soccer bore. But there are also rich pickings for the fan who knows it all: *Kicking and Screaming* is particularly good on English soccer in the early post-war years, when star players were paid next to nothing and, on top of that, were treated with crass condescension by the suits and bowler hats at the FA. There are several sardonic contributions here from members of the 1947–8 England team that beat Holland 8–0, Italy 4–0 and Portugal 10–0. For such triumphs the England players got a £10 appearance fee and a third-class train ticket home. And maybe a 'well done'. Just around the corner lay the 1953 defeat by Hungary, and a new epoch for English soccer: more money, higher status, fewer wins. *Kicking and Screaming* is admirably undecided on the matter of which epoch it prefers.

Less useful is Tom Watt's *A Passion for the Game*, which pokes about 'behind the scenes' of week-to-week league soccer, interrogating the game's faceless servants, from club secretaries to groundsmen to tea-ladies. Watt says that his book is modelled on Studs Terkel's *Working* but his tape-recorded informants are less interesting and much less articulate than Terkel's. A ticket-office clerk, a press-box assistant, a programme editor: Watt does his best to heroise these worthy toilers but most of them are deadly dull, and so too are their jobs. Some of Watt's workers are humble volunteers: 'They don't do it for the money. For them, it's Mark Bosnich calling them George or Steve.' Others view their tasks as inherited family traditions: Brentford's chief steward, for example, is the son of a Brentford turnstile operator and already has two daughters selling Brentford programmes. For several, though, the 'soccer industry' is just a job, and involves no special loyalty to the employer. These hard men tend to belong in merchandising or match-day hospitality. Thus, Liverpool's commercial department is staffed by Evertonians, and Manchester United's away strips are the brainchildren of a fugitive from Irving Scholar's Spurs. Hmm. Is that so? How boring. I must take a mental note.

25 January 1996

ARTS

Hubbub

Nicholas Spice on music and Muzak*

Around eleven o'clock on Monday morning, I phone Dell Computers to query an invoice, but the accounts department is engaged, so I get put through instead to the development section of the first movement of the *New World* Symphony. The music I intrude on is intense and self-absorbed. I am like a child in a children's book who has stumbled through a gap in reality and fallen headlong into another world. I pick myself up and follow Dvořák's gangly, adolescent theme as it strides from instrument to instrument and key to key on its way home to the tonic. I think of it as healthy, wide-eyed and affirmative, trumpeting an ingenuous faith in energies which will lead to a new world far braver than any Dvořák might have imagined, the world of Dell Computers in Bracknell, of fax-modems, of the Internet, of telephones capable of pouring Dvořák's impassioned certainties into the ears of office workers on humdrum Monday mornings.

Into my mind drifts the image of Dvořák's head, moustachioed and visionary, gazing, a bit like the MGM lion, out of a locket-shaped gold-embossed medallion in the centre of the box which housed my LP of the *New World* Symphony when I was 12, a record whose brash appearance made me uneasy and slightly embarrassed. Reception interrupts my nostalgia to ask me if I want to go on holding (ah, if only I *could* let go!). When I mumble assent, I am returned to the symphony, where the mood has changed. It is the second movement now, and a cor anglais is singing above muted strings. This tender melody reminds me of a mawkish novel by Josef Škvorecký. The details elude me, but I fancy *Dvořák in Love* to have been a soft-focus, rural idyll, and I fall to imagining a red sun rising behind a field of gently rippling Bohemian corn, and, beyond it, a girl in a dirndl beckoning seductively. 'Good morning, Sales Ledger, this is Martine, how may I help you?' I have been put through.

Phone-hold music is a late, trivial but characteristic effect of the

---

* Michael Chanan, *Repeated Takes: A Short History of Recording and its Effects on Music* (Verso, 1995); Joseph Lanza, *Elevator Music: A Surreal History of Muzak Easy Listening and other Moodsong* (Quartet, 1995).

technical revolution which over the past century has transformed the way we encounter music. Until the development of the radio and the gramophone, people only heard music when they played it themselves or when they heard other people playing it. Music was bound by time and space. Now, music is everywhere, streaming through the interstices between the lumpy materials of life, filling the gaps in the continuum of human activity and contact, silting up in vast unchartable archives. In *Repeated Takes*, Michael Chanan has written a concise history of the technology that has wrought this change and the commercial and creative forces that have shaped it. His account is elegant and impressively well-informed. He ranges across the entire technical field, from Edison's invention of the phonograph in 1877 to the samplers and MIDI technology of the Nineties. He tracks in detail the peristaltic movements of the market, as it ingests and digests each technical innovation and reacts to and directs the whim of the punters and the creativity of musicians. And he has a strong grasp of the way different musical cultures – different 'musics' – from Machaut to Maderna, Tin Pan Alley to dub reggae, have adapted themselves to the revolution they have been caught up in, and been changed by it.

Chanan is an intellectual, and his ruminations on the meaning of his story are always sensible. Joseph Lanza despises intellectuals and has no more interest in being sensible than he has a talent for it. *Elevator Music*, subtitled 'A Surreal History of Muzak Easy Listening and other Moodsong', is a dotty book, a tireless and tiring panegyric to musical trash, a history which is surreal only in the capacity of its author to believe his own relentlessly foolish propaganda. 'Muzak and mood music,' Lanza announces, 'are, in many respects, aesthetically superior to all other musical forms.' He goes on to argue for this with all the acumen and none of the irony of Norman Tebbit arguing for the aesthetic claims of page-three girls (Rubens painted naked women, too). Thus Lanza: 'Judging from their literature, the Greeks were rarely without some kind of perpetual musical soundtrack'; 'Gregorian chants most likely tranquillised monks for hundreds of years'; 'the first church organ recitals . . . pacified worshippers between sermons'; 'much of what today's audiophiles reverently call the "Classics" served as background music for bluebloods.'

Elevator Music is mainly interesting as a work of inadvertent autobiography, the portrait it suggests of a man who really does seem to believe that 'a world without elevator music would be much grimmer than its detractors . . . could ever realise,' a portrait animated as much by anger as by enthusiasm. Lanza the super-nerd, the techno-freak, the fetishist of cultural marginalia, is also the red-neck barricaded inside his obsession, scanning the horizon for the cultural smart-arses, the liberal intellectual spoilsports, the neurasthenic pedants, the sickheads who want to turn off the heavenly choirs for just a bit of morbid peace and quiet.

I scoff at Lanza, but I see myself reflected in his crazy encomia, gesticulating, as it were, on the other side of the mirror. Angry exchanges swim up from the past. I am in some crass restaurant in Holland Park which has been dolled up to look like the outside of a street in Rome – walls artfully distressed to resemble weathered stone, trompe-l'oeil window grilles, a floor of bumpy flagging. A waiter waltzes up to declaim the day's specials. His rococo soliloquy is made unintelligible by being delivered, like a piece of 18th-century melodrama, against the 'Dies Irae' of the Mozart Requiem. By the time I'm eating the main course, the tape has been changed to the *Four Last Songs*. Unable to hold a rational conversation against Strauss's heavy-lidded eschatology, I ask the waiter to turn the music off, but he looks blank and calls the manager, who flatly refuses. We argue. I give up. As I pay the bill I catch the five last words of 'Im Abendrot': 'Ist dies etwa der Tod?' 'You might well ask,' I growl, escaping into the street.

Much as I hate classical music in restaurants, I realise that it cannot be reasonable to argue in principle against background music in places where you are not obliged to suffer it. The case for a ban on public music seems stronger in places where people have no choice but to endure it: in airports and railway stations or in hospital waiting-rooms. But suppose it were to be rigorously demonstrated that certain sorts of public music lowered stress levels, enhanced productivity at work, cut absenteeism and illness and thereby reduced demand on public health resources. If it turned out that most people enjoyed and welcomed it, should we not then embrace piped music as a public good? The American Muzak Corporation would say that we should.

Since it began selling canned music in the Thirties, Muzak's viability as a business, like that of a pharmaceutical company, has always depended on convincing its customers that its products do them good. The customers have mostly been other large corporations, and the benefits Muzak has sold them have been improved productivity and a more compliant workforce. Muzak's corporate literature bristles with the results of scientific and behavioural research to back up its claims. An early boost came from Britain. In 1937, two industrial psychologists, Wyatt and Langdon, published a paper, 'Fatigue and Boredom in Repetitive Work', which showed that young women worked more efficiently and with less resentment when they worked to music. Meanwhile, cows in Mckeesport, Pennsylvania were reported to yield more milk when milked to the 'Blue Danube'. Data accumulated on every side: experiments by the Human Engineering Laboratory of the US Army found that programmed 'functional' music improved vigilance, mental alertness and working efficiency; in 1972 Black & Decker reported a 1.42 per cent gain in productivity once music by Muzak was installed, while, at St Joseph's Hospital in Yonkers, NY, Dr Frank B. Flood, chief of cardiology, saw improved recovery rates in the intensive care unit.

From the start, the two cardinal aims of Muzak's operation have been that its music should not draw attention to itself and that it should work in optimal co-operation with nature, with the laws governing the ebb and flow of biological energy. A technique called 'range of intensity limitation' flattens the music out to make it unnoticeable, 'like wind playing between the leaves of trees' (Joe Coco, Muzak engineer for more than forty years). Meanwhile, 'Stimulus Progression' matches the pace and rhythm of the music to the highs and lows of the working day. A thoroughgoing refinement of these techniques was master-minded by U.V. 'Bing' Muscio, who became Muzak president in 1966. The aptly named Muscio, 'a man of international education and cul-ture . . . a man of forceful candour, concise wit and deft literary allusion' (Muzak corporate blurb), ushered in the era of the 'New Muzak', setting up a Scientific Board of Advisers, psychologists and doctors who worked closely with Muzak 'musicologists' and engineers to re-examine the content and effect of Muzak's programming.

Nowadays, Muzak's programmes are created by a computer which slots tunes (coded for stimulus value) into a 24-hour schedule which is then beamed around the world by a satellite transmitter in North Carolina. The schedule is divided up into 15-minute segments (13.5 minutes, to be exact, with 1.5 minutes of silence in between), each of which plays five or six tunes, arranged in ascending order of stimulus value. The 15-minute segments are themselves arranged in a Muzak stimulus curve, with peaks between 10 and 11 a.m. and 3 and 4 p.m., when workers tend to flag, and troughs after 12 midday and 6 p.m. to 'counteract the excitement at lunchtime and at the end of the day'.

Although the 15-minute programme segments end in silence, it is a fundamental assumption of the Muzak project that people do not like silence. As a Muzak spokesperson has said, 'we maintain that most people are uneasy with an absence of sound. We feel an empty space requires some kind of pleasant sound. Music is one of the more pleasant sounds.' And, of course, Muzak has the data to prove it.

The systematic exploitation of the subliminal effects of music (as narcotic and stimulant) is especially abhorrent to those musicians and listeners who wish to think of music as an art, and who are often most vocal in their opposition to background music of any kind. The grandfather of their cause, its most formidable prosecutor, was Theodor Adorno. Adorno's life (1903–69) was co-extensive with the rise and flourishing of the mass market in music. He watched its phenomenal growth with horror. At the heart of his concerns was an ideal of attention, just as, one might almost say, at the heart of Muzak's concerns is an ideal of inattention. For Adorno, great music is music which demands and repays a full and undivided attention. Undemanding music, music which can accompany another activity (eating, dancing, talking), is, by Adorno's definition, a degraded, worthless kind of music, a music which panders to human laziness, to what he scathingly calls our habit of 'regressive listening'. Proper listening, 'concentrated listening', requires effort, but repays the listener with an experience of alertness and a sense of reaffirmed individuality. By contrast, 'regressive listening', easy listening, turns the listener into an unindividuated consumer, a passive purchaser of commodities. Music which repays 'concentrated listening' is a highly differentiated music. Music for background listening is standardised and one piece sounds much like another.

The political dimension to this analysis is immediately evident. Adorno's concentrated listener, critical faculties fully awakened, is a potential activist, an individual capable of opposing the established order. The regressive listener, drugged by the music of the mass (Stravinsky spoke of such a listener as falling 'into a kind of torpor'), is an acquiescent accomplice of a marauding capitalism.

Part of me returns a powerful echo to Adorno's ideal of concentrated listening. When my attention is held by music, I achieve a state of mental and physical equilibrium which no other experience gives me, except perhaps the experience of silence, and I sometimes think of music as a species of silence. I was recently struck by this relationship of music to silence when I saw the Mark Morris Dance Group perform 'Neue Liebeslieder Walzer' to the music of Brahms. At the end of the work, when the dance has subsided into a circular tableau of figures sleeping in the shadows, at the precise moment when the sound of the last note is about to merge with silence, one of the dancers at the farthest edge of the circle suddenly sits up, a silhouetted figure looking out into the dark, an image of alertness at the edge of a silence as manifold and interesting as the music that has given place to it. If this is music, then muzak, which seeks to fill up silence, must be anti-music. And any music which abuses silence could be thought of as aspiring to the condition of muzak.

In one sense, radio and recording inevitably disturb music's relationship to silence. The breaking of silence by music is at its most beautiful when there is a real rapport between player and listener. A recorded performance hands over the decision to start the music entirely to the listener, so that the onset of recorded music will always have a certain mundanity to it. On the radio, the performer regains control of the start of the music, but this time at the listener's expense. On the other hand, the radio allows the listener randomly to butt in on the music and to leave it again just as abruptly. Chanan, summarising Adorno, expresses this well: 'Music on the radio . . . becomes a potpourri, a continuous atomised medley which leaves the impression of a kind of collage.' In Britain, Classic FM has contrived, perhaps even set out, to exaggerate this effect. It broadcasts music as though it were a piece of fabric to be unrolled, one pattern succeeding another without acknowledgment of the differences between them. On Classic FM the disregard for silence is wilful: music, advertising, features, news, the weather, are spliced together seamlessly so that the music is robbed of its poise, its place within the flow of time.

There is a view, which Chanan does not contradict, that the act of recording music does not just disturb its relationship to silence, but damages it fundamentally, by freeing it from its dependency on the contingencies of a particular time and place and by making it permanent: 'The integrity of the musical work of the past, its intimate unity with the time and place of performance, what Walter Benjamin called its aura, has been destroyed. Music has become literally disembodied.' But, as Chanan points out elsewhere in *Repeated Takes*, when Benjamin spoke of aura he was referring to visual art and the image, not to music and sound. To apply Benjamin's observations about the effects of photography on art to the effects of recording on music is to make a false elision. For in music there are no original objects as there are in art. We cannot refer back to an object identified a Beethoven's *op.* 111 Piano Sonata as we can refer back to Brueghel's *Hunters in the Snow*, and we cannot, therefore, speak of reproductions of the sonata as we can speak of reproductions of the painting. In one sense, our only access to the sonata is through reproductions (performances) of it, and there is no difference in category between the reproduction we create in our heads when we read the score, the one we hear when we listen to someone play the sonata in front of us, and the reproduction we listen to on a recording. In each case, we encounter a version of the sonata, and a version is all that is available to us. The coherence and beauty of any one version will depend on how the performer puts the notes together. Except for the way the music begins and ends (its relationship to the circumambient silence), these tensions and connections are unaffected by the act of recording.

The idea that recording destroys music's aura, derives, in part at least, from a misconception of the nature and role of spontaneity in music. Chanan speaks of the way a record 'robs the performance of its sense of spontaneity', and he quotes Jacques Attali's remark, in *Noise*, that recording removes from a performance the 'unforeseen and the risks'. 'The new aesthetic of performance,' Attali continues, 'excludes error, hesitation.' But error, hesitation and other unwished-for spontaneities have never been part of the felicities of live performance. Classical musicians devote themselves to trying to thwart the uncertainties and hazards of playing live. This is because they have something very specific they wish to get across: their understanding of how the music should go, the interpretation they have worked on for months, perhaps years, prior to the performance. While acknowledging that the special tension and atmosphere of live performance can, at best, create moments of unplanned beauty, classical musicians know that such moments only happen within a rigorously pre-ordained design. This design, even when it appears to unfold spontaneously before our ears, does not get lost when it is fixed on a recording. What does get lost, but then only when the recording is heard for the second time, is the listener's surprise. In this respect, the experience of music is no different from any other aesthetic experience. We can only see the Sistine Chapel for the first time once, and we can never be surprised twice by the outcome of a poem or a novel, the unexpected modulations of a piece of Haydn or the wild ramifications of an improvisation by Coltrane. Only those who did not know the result of the 1995 European Cupwinners' Cup Final, only those who had sat through the unfolding drama of the match over two long hours up to its final thirty seconds, could experience the consternation and wonder wrought by Nayim's unimaginable spontaneity, lobbing the ball from the half-way line clean over David Seaman's head into the net to win the match for Zaragosa. In none of these cases is the beauty of the events lost when we revisit them. Indeed, one could well argue that it is only by revisiting the site of a moment of artistic inspiration that its beauty can properly be understood and enjoyed. Surprise has its disadvantages, and, until the arrival of recording technology, music was particulary handicapped by them.

To borrow a term of Adorno's, I would say that Chanan and others, maybe Adorno himself, 'fetishise' the physical actuality of musical performance. In doing so, they turn our attention away from a truer cause for despondency: the routine deadness of so much classical music performance today, irrespective of whether it is recorded or played live. If it is true that performances of music from the classical canon now rarely invite the sort of concentrated attention Adorno spoke about, then this can only be indirectly attributed to the effects of recording technology. The transformation of music overnight into an art form like literature, with a past available to anyone with the inclination to consult it, cannot have been anything but an advantage to the performing musician. But the concomitant increase in the amount of music a musician could hear (whether or not he, or she, wished to hear it) may have contributed to a gradual undermining of interpretative confidence.

In a world which is drenched in diatonic harmony, giving meaning to diatonic music demands a degree of musical independence and originality far beyond what was demanded of musicians in the pre-recording age. Musicians have responded to this identity crisis by fleeing the responsibilities of authorship (having something of their own to say about the music) for the relative safety of authenticity (mimicking what someone else might once have had to say). As a result, performing music has increasingly become an occasion for visiting historical (or pseudo-historical) objects, rather than for making something fresh happen. A sense of the vital presentness of the music (its aura, if you like) has been forsaken. This loss is there to hear. You need only compare older performances of the classical canon on record with the experience of modern performances live in the concert hall to get the point. Without Rosenthal's performances of Chopin, or Artur Balsam's Mozart, early Menuhin, the Budapest String Quartet, Klemperer conducting Mahler or Furtwängler conducting Brahms, I think our sense of what 'aura' in music might possibly be would be well on the way to extinction.

The problem – if there is one – could be greatly eased, if performers spent more of their energies with the music of their own time rather than with the music of the past. The turning away from contemporary music which has characterised 20th-century culture was underway well before recording technology came on the scene, and the technology cannot be held to have caused the trend, although it was certainly used to accelerate it. As Chanan observes, the technology itself is neutral in this respect. While classical music culture has been busy building its vast musical mausoleum, pop and jazz and folk music have used recording technology as a means to create an endless succession of new works.

When new technologies bring about a shift in the way we relate to each other and to the world, there are always voices warning of decline and loss. The pharaoh who is offered the invention of hieroglyphics by a god, in Plato's story in the *Phaedrus*, refuses it, as John Ray recalled in these pages, 'because it would ruin his subjects' powers of memory and concentration'. Television stands accused of promoting apathy and inertia, pocket calculators of the decay of mental arithmetic. Often technology is blamed for an aspect of human behaviour which it just happens to make conspicuous. Joseph Lanza is so far right when he points out that the aristocrats who listened to new work by Haydn and Mozart were scarcely paragons of concentrated listening.

A favourite object of techno-censure is the walkman, which is held to have encouraged deplorable displays of private anomie in public places (Chanan speaks of the way the walkman 'induces a sense of solipsism . . . by isolating the listener from the world through music'). But it is ludicrous to think that people wearing headsets have somehow retreated from the warm community life of the inner city street or the camaraderie of mass commuting. There's nothing to retreat from, and listening to music is no worse a way of acknowledging this than sitting immersed in a book or lost in a daydream. In any case, who wants to live in a world where behaviour has to be unrelentingly positive and where pleasure is uniformly conflated with edification? Adorno's strictures ignore the range, variability and inconsistency of human needs. There are times for attention and times to relax, times for concentrated listening and times when you just want the music to flow over you or flow on by.

Eighteenth-century concert promoters kept the audience for art music exclusive by setting ticket prices very high and through advertising for listeners of the right social class. Until the 20th century, art music remained the preserve of a relatively small Western cultural élite. The new recording technologies and radio democratised music at a stroke, bringing every kind of it within earshot of a large part of the world's population. At the same time, music was freed from the confinement of the concert hall and the domestic salon. It became as portable as the written word. We can now listen to Bach as we climb into the heavens in a Boeing 747, which is neither more wonderful nor more inappropriate than reading Proust. And we can dip into music as we might dip into a book, to remind ourselves of it without having to sit through it from beginning to end. Adorno hated the way people dealt in what he called musical 'debris' – bits and pieces out of context. But he underestimated our ability to recall the whole from a quick reference to the part. My forty seconds of the *New World* were enough to remind me that I didn't need to hear the symphony complete in a concert hall.

The hugely increased participation of music in the processes of ordinary life, and the sometimes bizarre conjunctions it can lead to (listening to Gibbons while you have your teeth drilled), has undoubtedly altered the sorts of thing music may seem to say to us. Music is naturally promiscuous. It attaches itself to our moods, to the meaning of words, to images and to stories, so that even the most severely inexpressive music can fall into deplorable (to the composer) allegiances. If you played a section of Boulez's *Pli Selon Pli* as the background to a natural-history film about dangerous spiders, it would acquire a menacing, creepy-crawly character. It was a long time before I could rid the slow movement of Schubert's E Flat Piano Trio of the unpleasant emotional atmosphere of Kubrick's *Barry Lyndon*. And, of course, the bonding process works even more powerfully in reverse: music lends its expressiveness to the world. Once you know Britten's setting of Hardy's 'At Day-Close in November' you will never again be able to read the poem innocent of the music's view of it.

Most films would be helpless without music – *Jaws* without the rhythmic thud of approaching doom. Film, TV and even radio now expect us to feel uncomfortable with action or image unaccompanied by music. It's as though we are not to be trusted to react properly without the promptings and guidance of a musical score. Certainly, much good TV and film drama is marred by its soundtrack. The emotional complexity of Jane Campion's *The Piano* had a constant battle with the sentimentality of Michael Nyman's simple-minded music. In the BBC's well-mannered and agreeable dramatisation of *Middlemarch*, it was felt necessary to point up the progress of Dorothea and Ladislaw's love with a plangent oboe.

The presence of music shifts any represented action towards fiction. So there is perhaps good reason to deplore the tendency of news analysis and real crime programmes on television to use music to put us in the proper frame of mind. News bulletins the world over are introduced by music, all of it basically in the *Also Sprach Zarathustra* vein: stirring orchestral gestures to signal urgency, crisis, global portent. *The Big Breakfast*, which punctuates the flow of items in its news updates with volleys of marcato chords, is only a step away from orchestrating the items themselves, though how they'll devise a soundtrack for the trade figures is anyone's guess. Classic FM already plays Baroque music behind the weather forecast, and *Classic Reports*, its news feature programme, attaches a piece of music to each item of analysis: for example, a chunk of Delius's incidental music for Flecker's 'Hassan' to introduce an update on the Middle East peace process.

In real life, this fictionalisation of reality can be deranging. I am intrigued, for instance, by the soundtrack which Gatwick Airport has deemed suitable for the brief ride on the monorail that takes you from the satellite terminal to the main building. If you have just staggered off an intercontinental flight and are already suffering from time slippage, the experience of this little trip is especially disorientating. The doors suck themselves shut and the transit train slips away to the sound of a high electronic humming. A voice-over in the accents of a Pathé Pictorial announcer (the same voice which tells you to 'mind the gyap' at Embankment tube station) welcomes you to Gatwick Airport ('the hub without the hubbub') on behalf of British Airways (sponsors of the shuttle), and goes on to tell you of the delights, awaiting you in the main terminal, of 'Avenue Shopping and Eating', a mall which is apparently the only reason for your visit to Britain. As you try to make head or tail of all this, you become aware of a strangely disquieting music played by a string orchestra, a faintly minatory, darkling piece, which tips the atmosphere towards nightmare and gives you pause to wonder whether you haven't perhaps died in an air crash and are not now in transit across Purgatory.

Provided we are in control, we seem to like to arrange a soundtrack for our lives, perhaps because music makes us feel as though we belong to a more exciting story than the one we mostly seem to take part in. As we swing out onto the open road in our Vauxhall Cavalier, music enhances the pleasure of feeling free, that momentary delusion that we are going somewhere. At the end of an evening with friends, the Miles Davis track 'Mood' can seem to bind the good things together. The sound of a Bach organ prelude thundering up the stairwell on a bright Sunday morning stirs us, as we brush our teeth, with the feeling that life might, after all, be rather grand.

We choose these musical backgrounds to match and enhance the rhythms of our lives, but the most poignant encounters with music are inadvertent and unplanned. Church bells heard across the fields on a Sunday evening, the forlorn plinking and plonking two streets away of an ice-cream van on solitary summer afternoons, someone practising the saxophone in a neighbouring house: such half-heard music sets up momentary perspectives on our situation, touches us with sadness or strikes us with interesting incongruities. It is the literary imagination which is stimulated by music heard by chance, the imagination that enjoys the possibilities suggested by the collision of disparate realities, the imagination that feeds on the ironies which a split attention (not a distracted attention) perceives. The history of music has been a long argument between musicians' music – pure music for a pure attention – and literary music, music which celebrates the relationship of music to narrative, to mind states, and which has sought, especially in song, to depict the ironies of a split perspective. In his great essay 'On the Beautiful in Music' Eduard Hanslick complained about the organ-grinder out in the street who interrupts his conversation, but it is an organ-grinder overheard by the protagonist of *Die Winterreise* who inspires one of Schubert's greatest songs.

Even the most thoughtlessly mechanical abuse of music can provide moments of curious richness. The forty seconds I spent that Monday morning lost in a daydream about Dvořák, about my childhood, about a bad novel I once reviewed, were reclaimed from vacancy and oblivion by the phone-hold music on the Dell switchboard. And my encounter with Martine was transformed: 'her words came, as through bubbling honey' and she spake of VAT.

And what then of the dreaded muzak? What countless scenes of love and anger and indifference have been enacted against the background of its blithe fatuities? How many moments of emptiness and despair has it redeemed through incongruity? You are alone on a sales trip to Holland, staying in a hotel in Rotterdam. It is November and you're up at 7 a.m. The breakfast room is in a windowless basement. Outside, fog hugs the cobblestones and Dutchmen cycle to work. You sit down at a table covered with a carpet. A young waiter just out of catering school brings you a module of Dutch breakfast: two pieces of currant bread, a jug of hot water already too cold to revive the Lipton's tea-bag in the accompanying cup, a boiled egg – white, tepid and undercooked. No one speaks. The waiter moves about discreetly behind the breakfast hatch clinking tea-cups. Only the occasional pop of vacuum seals on miniature jam pots breaks the silence. You take a bite out of the currant bread which is sweet and unappetising, crack the egg and attempt to spoon the slobbery transparent egg white into your mouth, but you do not succeed, so that a strand of protein bounces between your lower lip and the spoon. At this point you feel so sad that you do not know where to put yourself. And then you notice the muzak – 'songs of time-travel into amniotic bliss', perhaps – and the incongruity of it all tips this moment, which, experienced in complete silence, would be unbearable, into absurdity. A gap opens up between you and the music, and into that gap you escape.

6 July 1995

Sister-Sister

Terry Castle reads Jane Austen

It is impossible for the lover of Jane Austen – and lover is the operative word here – to have anything but mixed feelings about Austen's older sister Cassandra. On one hand, we owe to Cassandra the only surviving (if bad) portraits of Austen other than silhouettes: the famous, somewhat lopsided sketch of 1801, in which the novelist's mouth is awkwardly pursed and her eyes, gazing in different directions, look like small, astigmatic raisins; and an equally inept watercolour back-view from 1804, in which nothing of Austen can be seen – Cassandra giving her all to the rendering of the complicated dress and bonnet – except the nape of a neck, the exposed back of one hand, and a tentative, slipper-clad foot. Crude they may be, yet without these sisterly gleanings we would know next to nothing of Austen's face or figure or how she held herself in space: dead at 42 in 1817, she is part of that last, infinitely poignant, generation of human beings who lived and died before photography.

On the other hand, one can only deplore Cassandra's high-handed actions after Austen's death; these included burning great quantities of her sister's letters and censoring others by snipping pieces out of them. The vast majority of these letters were written to Cassandra herself. Though Austen wrote from time to time to other members of the large Austen clan – her three brothers and their wives, various favourite nieces and nephews – Cassandra was the person around whom her life revolved, and she wrote regularly to her whenever they were separated. (Spinsters both, the two Austen sisters lived together all their adult lives – first at Steventon and Bath with their parents, then after their father's death in 1805, with their mother and a female friend at Chawton in Hampshire.) At her own death in 1845, Cassandra bequeathed the scant batch of letters she had saved from the flames to her grand-niece, Lady Knatchbull, whose son, Lord Brabourne, had them published – like precious relics – in 1884. A number of other letters have surfaced since then; the great Austen scholar, R.W. Chapman, issued the first modern edition of the correspondence in 1932. Still, only 161 Austen letters are known to exist today, and many only in Cassandra-mangled form.

Deirdre Le Faye, editor of the excellent new revised Oxford edition of the letters,* defends Cassandra somewhat backhandedly, suggesting that her weeding-out and censorship 'shows itself more in the complete destruction of letters rather than in the excision of individual sentences; the "portions cut out" usually only amount to a very few words, and from the context it would seem that the subject concerned was physical ailment.' Le Faye speculates that Cassandra, not wishing to cause embarrassment or ill-feeling, destroyed letters in which Austen wrote too freely or satirically about other family members. But for the reader of Austen's fiction, hungry for a sense of the author's inner life, Cassandra's depredations can only seem like older-sister arrogance of the most mortifying sort: a jealous winnowing down of her brilliant younger sister's personality in the name of a dubious decorum.

What was their relationship like? In a telling family memoir from 1867, James Edward Austen-Leigh, Austen's nephew, described it thus:

> Their sisterly affection for each other could scarcely be exceeded. Perhaps it began on Jane's side with a feeling of deference natural to a loving child towards a kind elder sister. Something of this feeling always remained; and even in the maturity of her powers, and in the enjoyment of increasing success, she would still speak of Cassandra as of one wiser and better than herself. In childhood, when the elder was sent to the school of a Mrs Latournelle in the Forbury at Reading, the younger went with her, not because she was thought old enough to profit much by the instruction there imparted, but because she would have been miserable without her sister; her mother observing that 'if Cassandra were going to have her head cut off, Jane would insist on sharing her fate.' This attachment was never interrupted or weakened. They lived in the same home, and shared the same bedroom, till separated by death.

Cassandra was 'colder and calmer', wrote Austen-Leigh; the family said that 'Cassandra had the *merit* of having her temper always under her command, but that Jane had the *happiness* of a temper that never required to be commanded.' When *Sense and Sensibility* was published in 1811, some readers thought Austen had modelled the characters of the Dashwood sisters – the sober Elinor and the sprightly Marianne – on her sister and herself. Austen-Leigh demurred, but only in order to pay tribute to the novelist's superior moral insight; 'Cassandra's character might indeed represent the *sense* of Elinor, but Jane's had little in common with the *sensibility* of Marianne. The young woman who,

* Deirdre Le Faye, ed., *Jane Austen's Letters* (Oxford University Press, 1995).

before the age of twenty, could so clearly discern the failings of Marianne Dashwood, could hardly have been subject to them herself.' The entire family seems to have shared his not-so-secret preference for Jane over Cassandra: another Austen nephew, Henry, of whom Austen had been particularly fond in his teens, told a cousin after Austen's death that whenever he visited the house at Chawton – where Cassandra and Mrs Austen lived on for some years – 'he could not help expecting to feel particularly happy . . . and never till he got there, could he fully realise to himself how all its peculiar pleasures were gone.'

Perhaps because of the ambivalence Cassandra inevitably inspires – implicit in everything everyone says about her is the unspoken question, why did Jane have to be the one to die? – biographers and critics have tended to downplay her centrality in Austen's life. Even the sympathetic Chapman sought to depersonalise the sororal relationship: defending the surviving Jane-Cassandra letters against charges of being 'trifling' in subject and style, he asserted that the sisters' purpose in writing to one another was to exchange information not only 'between themselves, but between two branches of a large family. There are indications that these letters and others like them were read by, and to, a number of people. Even if this had not been so, it would not have been consonant with the sisters' temperament, or with their way of life, to exchange letters of sentiment or disquisition.' Le Faye suggests we consider Austen's letters to Cassandra 'the equivalent of telephone calls between the sisters' – 'hasty and elliptical', full of family news, but little more.

It is certainly true that the surviving letters contain their share of trivia. Whole passages can go by as a blur of names and now meaningless events:

> Yesterday I introduced James to Mrs Inman; – in the evening John Bridges returned from Goodnestone – and this morn before we had left the Breakfast Table we had a visit from Mr Whitfield, whose object I imagine was principally to thank my Eldest Brother for his assistance. Poor Man! – he has now a little intermission of his excessive solicitude on his wife's account, as she is rather better. James does duty at Godmersham today. – The Knatchbulls had intended coming here next week, but the Rentday makes it impossible for them to be received & I do not think there will be any spare time afterwards. They return into Somersetshire by way of Sussex & Hants, & are to be at Fareham – & perhaps may be in Southampton, on which possibility I said all I thought right – & if they are in the place, Mrs K. has promised to call in Castle Square; – it will be about the end of July.

Elsewhere we learn more than we want to know, perhaps, about the incessant visits of various collateral family members, the meals eaten and cups of tea drunk, whether fires have been necessary in the sitting-room, the muddy state of nearby roads and similar minutiae.

And yet reading through the correspondence in 1995 – especially in the light of recent historical findings about the psychic complexity of female-female relationships in late 18th and early 19th-century Britain (the recently rediscovered diaries of Austen's lesbian contemporary, Anne Lister, are an example) – one is struck not so much by the letters' hastiness or triviality as by the passionate nature of the sibling bond they commemorate. Sororal or pseudo-sororal attachments are arguably the most immediately gratifying human connections in Austen's imaginative universe. It is a curious yet arresting phenomenon in the novels that so many of the final happy marriages seem designed not so much to bring about a union between hero and heroine as between the heroine and the hero's sister. At the end of *Northanger Abbey*, while the heroine Catherine Morland is clearly delighted to marry the entertaining Henry Tilney, the most intense part of her joy seems to derive from the fact that in doing so she also becomes 'sister' to his sister Eleanor, whose subtle approbation she has sought – and glowingly received – throughout the novel. But even Austen's heroes are often more like sisters than lovers in the conventional sense. The soft-mannered Henry, for example, takes a feminine interest in fabrics, and 'comforts' his female relations with his knowledge of muslins and chintzes; and he is repeatedly contrasted with his father, General Tilney – a far more domineering and stereotypically masculine type.

Reading Austen's letters to Cassandra, one cannot help but sense the primitive adhesiveness – and underlying eros – of the sister-sister bond. The first surviving letter dates from 1796, when Austen was 20 and Cassandra 23. From the start the tone is rhetorical, literary (not like a phone call at all), and one of whimsical yet fierce attachment. Austen wants more than anything to make her older sister laugh. As in her novels, she uses first lines flirtatiously, like comic bait, to catch Cassandra in webs of mock-heroic invention. From 1801: 'Expect a most agreeable letter, for not being overburdened with subject – (having nothing at all to say) – I shall have no check to my Genius from beginning to end.' 'This will be a quick return for yours, my dear Cassandra,' she begins a missive from 1813, 'I doubt its' having much else to recommend it, but there is no saying, it may turn out to be a very long, delightful Letter.' 'Here I am, my dearest Cassandra, seated in the Breakfast, Dining, Sitting room, beginning with all my might.' And again, from 1814: 'Do not be angry with me for beginning another letter to you. I have read the Corsair, mended my petticoat, & have nothing else to do.'

Once Cassandra is ensnared, Austen holds her fast with in-jokes and sisterly games of style, complete with loveable misspellings. For all the family gossip they impart, Austen's letters remain intensely scripted: full of parodic references to shared reading and the cherished (or maligned) books of female adolescence. 'So much for Mrs Piozzi,' Austen concludes after a passage of ludicrous Miss Bates-like ramblings on the salutary effects of the Bath waters, 'I had some thoughts of writing the whole of my letter in her stile, but I beleive I shall not.' She parodies Pope's comic catalogues ('In a few hours You will be transported to Manydown – & then for Candour & Comfort & Coffee & Cribbage'), Johnsonian lapidary pronouncement ('I am looking over Self Control again, & my opinion is confirmed of its' being an excellently meant, elegantly written Work, without anything of Nature or Probability in it'), the effusions of Mrs Radclyffe ('the shades of Evening are descending & I resume my interesting Narrative') and the twee Caledonian jests of Sir Walter Scott ('I do not write for such dull elves!'). Elsewhere she announces: 'I am going to write nothing but short Sentences.' The result – rather more uncannily – is like proto-Gertrude Stein:

> There shall be two full stops in every Line. Layton and Shear's *is* Bedford House. We mean to get there before breakfast if it's possible. For we feel more & more how much we have to do. And how little time. This house looks very nice. It seems like Sloane St moved here. I believe Henry is just rid of Sloane St – Fanny does not come, but I have Edward seated by me beginning a letter, which looks natural.

One can imagine the pleasure-addiction such writing engendered. For the reader, like Cassandra, is seduced by the constant foolery:

> I will not say that your Mulberry trees are dead, but I am afraid they are not alive.

> What dreadful Hot weather we have! – It keeps one in a continual state of Inelegance.

> So much for that subject; I now come to another, of a very different nature, as other subjects are very apt to be.

> Where shall I begin? Which of all my important nothings shall I tell you first?

And what *of* these important nothings? It is frequently said of Austen's letters that they 'illuminate' the world of her fiction. This is certainly the case, though to say so is hardly to say very much. Sometimes, it is true, Austen comments directly on work in progress – in particular, on the earlier novels, *Sense and Sensibility*, *Pride and Prejudice* and *Mansfield*

Park. (In a famous letter written just after the publication of *Pride and Prejudice* in 1813, she tells Cassandra that she is 'vain enough' over her book, but thinks it 'rather too light & bright & sparkling; – it wants shade'.) But what advocates of Austen's correspondence usually mean is that the letters deal in a general way with the same topics explored in the fiction: marriages and family life, parties and balls, domestic entertainments and the now-antiquated courtship rituals of the early 19th-century provincial English gentry.

Yet with Cassandra in mind, one wants to put a finer point on it. Both Austen and Cassandra received marriage proposals at different points in their lives; Cassandra was in fact engaged to be married in 1797, only to have her fiancé die of a fever in the West Indies. Austen received at least two proposals in her youth, both of which she turned down. Biographers have made much of a mysterious 'gentleman' at Lyme Regis in 1804–5 who, according to Austen's niece Caroline (who heard about it from Cassandra), had 'seemed greatly attracted by my Aunt Jane . . . I can only say that the impression left on Aunt Cassandra was that he had fallen in love with her sister, and was quite in earnest. Soon afterwards they heard of his death.' Whatever one makes of the story (and Austen's own part in it goes unrecorded) neither she nor Cassandra showed much real inclination for matrimony later in life. One can't help but feel that both found greater comfort and pleasure – more of that 'heartfelt felicity' that Emma Woodhouse finds with Mr Knightley, or Elizabeth Bennet with the handsome Darcy – in remaining with one another.

The letters from Austen that Cassandra allowed to survive testify to such a primordial bond. Virginia Woolf observed of Austen's fiction that 'it is where the power of the man has to be conveyed that her novels are always at their weakest.' Perhaps this is because men are inevitably inferior to sisters. Even more so than in the fiction, Austen displays a remorseless eye in the letters for male fatuousness. It is as if she were at once trying to reassure Cassandra – no one is good enough for me but you – and inviting her complicitous laughter. Men are fools and imaginists and know nothing of the droll, shared cynicism of intelligent women. Thus of one admitted suitor, gone out of Hampshire to practise law in London, she writes sardonically in 1798:

It will all go on exceedingly well, and decline away in a very reasonable manner. There seems no likelihood of his coming into Hampshire this Christmas, and it is therefore most probable that our indifference will soon be mutual, unless his regard, which appeared to spring from knowing nothing of me at first, is best supported by never seeing me.

'Your unfortunate sister was betrayed last Thursday into a situation of the utmost cruelty,' Austen begins another letter from 1801; 'I arrived at Ashe Park before the Party from Deane, and was shut up in the drawing-room with Mr Holder alone for ten minutes.' A flirtation with the silly, would-be alluring Mr Evelyn is endured for the sake of his shiny new phaeton: 'There is now something like an engagement between us & the Phaeton, which to confess my frailty I have a great desire to go out in; – whether it will come to anything must remain with him. – I really beleive he is very harmless people do not seem afraid of him here, and he gets Groundsel for his birds & all that.' The comically appended 'all that', with its sly echo of an appropriate line from *The Rape of the Lock* ('*Snuff*, or the *Fan*, supply each Pause of Chat, / With singing, laughing, ogling, and all that'), is Popean indeed in its brisk satiric dismissal.

When Austen encounters, rarely, a man who disturbs her sexual self-possession, her protestations of dislike are liable to become spinsterish and strident. The handsome, unfriendly Henry Wigram 'is about 5 or 6 & 20, not ill-looking & not agreeable. – He is certainly no addition. – A sort of cool, gentlemanlike manner, but very silent . . . I cannot imagine how a Man can have the impudence to come into a Family party for three days, where he is quite a stranger, unless he knows himself to be agreeable on undoubted authority.' But for the most part she retains her levity – to the point of joking with Cassandra about various possible (impossible) matches. One James Digweed, she teases her sister, 'must be in love with you, from his anxiety to have you go to the Faversham Balls, & likewise from his supposing that the two Elms fell from their greif at your absence.' 'Was it not a galant idea?' she asks. 'It never occurred to me before, but I dare say it was so.' She imagines herself married to certain literary men of the day. After reading of the death of the poet Crabbe's wife, she writes: 'Poor woman! I will comfort *him* as well as I can, but I do not undertake to be good to her children. She had better not leave any.' And elsewhere, listing some favourite comic fantasies – which include having her portrait painted for the Royal Academy – she announces she will marry 'young Mr D'arblay', the adolescent son of Fanny Burney.

If men are ultimately insignificant, women, by contrast, are a source of unending sisterly preoccupation. Austen's physical descriptions of women – their faces, voices, hair, clothing, comportment at balls and in sitting-rooms – are funny, complex, often poignant, and as exquisitely drawn as any in her fiction. Yet they inevitably reveal, too, what can only be called a kind of homophilic fascination. Unlike men, women have bodies – to be scrutinised and discussed, admired or found wanting. Thus Mrs Powlett, seen at a dance in 1801, 'was at once expensively & nakedly dressed; – we have had the satisfaction of estimating her Lace & her muslin.' Of a Mrs and Miss Holder: 'it is the fashion to think them both very detestable,' but 'their gowns look so white & so nice I cannot utterly abhor them.' '*Miss* looked very handsome,' she says of another plausible young lady, 'but I prefer her little, smiling, flirting Sister Julia.' 'I admire the Sagacity & Taste of Charlotte Williams,' the novelist writes approvingly in 1813; 'those large dark eyes always judge well. I will compliment her, by naming a Heroine after her.'

At times the sexuality of women's bodies elicits oddly visceral effects: 'I looked at Sir Thomas Champneys & thought of poor Rosalie; I looked at his daughter & thought her a queer animal with a white neck.' 'I had the comfort of finding out the other evening who all the fat girls with short noses were that disturbed me at the 1st H. Ball. They all prove to be Miss Atkinsons of Enham.' 'I have a very good eye at an Adultress,' she boasts in 1801, after seeing a well-known demirep at the Pump Room in Bath, 'for tho' repeatedly assured that another in the same party was the *She*, I fixed upon the right one from the first.' Even unseen women can be arousing; witness the peculiarly proprietorial fantasy inspired by the news that an Austen family friend is to marry a Miss Lewis at Clifton. 'I would wish Miss Lewis to be of a silent turn & rather ignorant, but naturally intelligent & wishing to learn; – fond of cold veal pies, green tea in the afternoon, & a green window blind at night.' It is as if Austen were first conjuring the woman up, then projecting herself, shamanistically, into the role of tutor-husband.

Yet two female bodies are even more insistently 'present' in the letters – Austen's and Cassandra's own. The extraordinary number of passages in the letters devoted to clothing, for example – on her trips to London and Bath Austen often bought fabric, pieces of trim and other items to be used in the making or refurbishing of her own or her sister's dresses – bespeak the close terms of physical intimacy on which she and Cassandra lived and the intense psychic 'mirroring' that went on between them. A passage like the following, in which Austen's wish to have Cassandra 'see' a gown being made up for her in Bath – and by implication the body that will wear it – is so fantastically detailed as to border on the compulsive:

> It is to be a round Gown, with a Jacket, & a Frock front, like Cath: Bigg's to open at the sides. – The Jacket is all in one with the body, & comes as far as the pocketholes; –

about a half a quarter of a yard deep I suppose all the way round, cut off straight at the comers, with a broad hem. – No fullness appears either in the Body or the flap; – the back is quite plain, in this form; – ☐ – and the sides equally so. – The front is sloped round to the bosom & drawn in – & there is to be a frill of the same to put on occasionally when all one's handkercheifs are dirty – which frill *must* fall back. – She is to put two breadths & a half in the tail, & no Gores; – Gores not being so much worn as they were; – there is nothing new in the sleeves, – they are to be plain, with a fullness of the same falling down & gathered up underneath, just like some of Marthas – or perhaps a little longer. – Low in the back behind, a belt of the same; – I can think of nothing more – tho' I am afraid of not being particular enough.

Such passages remind us strikingly of how important a role clothes have played in the subliminal fetish-life of women – how much time women spend looking at one another, dressing one another and engaging in elaborate and mutually pleasurable 'grooming behaviour'. Austen and Cassandra were hardly exempt: indeed, the conventions of early 19th-century female sociability and body-intimacy may have provided the necessary screen behind which both women acted out unconscious narcissistic or homoerotic imperatives.

But the desire to be seen and imaginatively embraced – to be held in Cassandra's mind's eye – is everywhere in Austen's letters. 'Own-body' references (to borrow a term from the sociologist Erving Goffmann) are frequent in her correspondence and carry a powerful existential charge. She constantly invites her sister to think about her – about her precise location in space, or about the various physical sensations that either soothe or discomfit her. 'I am in the Yellow room – very literally –,' she tells Cassandra on arriving at their brother's estate in Kent, 'for I am writing in it at this moment.' 'How do you do to day?' reads a somewhat plaintive missive from Bath; 'I hope you improve in sleeping – I think you must, because *I* fall off; – I have been awake ever since 5 & sooner, I fancy I had too much cloathes over my stomach; I thought I *should* by the feel of them before I went to bed, but I had not courage to alter them.' Far from being trifling, such details bring to life the phenomenology of the novelist's emotional life. Cassandra was indeed the person she slept with, we realise with a start, and without her sister's comfortable warmth, slumber itself was altered.

In their own way the letters to Cassandra may ultimately say more of Austen's fiction – the inner sensual content of the works – than other seemingly more relevant or better-known pieces of Austeniana. Besides the Cassandra letters, the new Oxford edition includes two famous shorter correspondences: a series of letters Austen wrote to her novel-writing niece, Anna Austen, in 1814 (Anna had sent some chapters-in-progress to her aunt for criticism) and a set from 1817 to her niece, Fanny Knight, who was debating over several marriage proposals. The former correspondence contains a number of much-quoted pieces of authorial advice ('3 or 4 Families in a Country Village is the very thing to work on') and displays all of Austen's characteristic humour and taste: 'Devereux Forester's being ruined by his Vanity is extremely good; but I wish you would not let him plunge into a "vortex of Dissipation". I do not object to the Thing, but I cannot bear the expression; – it is such thorough novel slang – and so old, that I dare say Adam met with it in the first novel he opened.' Yet the flippancy sometimes borders on condescension and was perhaps not entirely helpful: Anna ended up burning the work in question after developing a painful creative block.

As for the letters to Fanny, though one might expect them to shed light on the novelist's powers of empathy (Fanny's predicament is one that occurs often in Austen's fiction) they make for rather unpleasant reading. Were one wanting to make the vulgar case for Austen's homoeroticism, here would be the place to look: the tone is giddy, sentimental and disturbingly schoolgirlish for a 42-year-old woman. Austen was infatuated with Fanny and slips often into embarrassing coquetries: 'You are inimitable, irresistable. You are the delight of my Life. Such letters, such entertaining letters as you have lately sent! – Such a description of your queer little heart! . . . I shall hate you when your delicious play of Mind is all settled down into conjugal & maternal affections.' As a love adviser she is dithery and contradictory – sometimes fearing the hold Fanny has over men ('Mr J.W. frightens me. – He will have you'), at other times breathlessly suggesting new lovers for her. She is rather like her own Emma Woodhouse, who, in an excess of displaced amorosity in *Emma*, persuades her dim-witted little protégée, Harriet Smith, quite wrongly, that three different men are in love with her – with comically disastrous results.

What one ends up realising is that more than anyone else Cassandra provided the essential ballast in Austen's life – was the caretaker of her mind and body, and guarantor of her imaginative freedom. ('Aunt Cassandra nursed me so beautifully!' Austen wrote to Fanny near the end of her life. 'I have always loved Cassandra, for her fine dark eyes & sweet temper.') It is always surprising to realise that Jane Austen had a mother, who indeed outlived her: when she is mentioned, rarely, in the letters, it is only as a kind of background presence – someone there, but half-forgotten. (The ailing Mrs Austen is recorded as saying to a grandson some years after Austen's death: 'Ah, my dear, you find me just where you left me – on the sofa. I sometimes think that God Almighty must have forgotten me; but I daresay He will come for me in His own good time.') Cassandra, one might say, was her real mother. And to the degree that Austen's fictions are works of depth and beauty and passionate feeling – among the supreme humane inventions of the English language – one suspects in turn it is because she loved and was loved by Cassandra.

Can we forgive Cassandra her jealousy? Reading the last, wrenching letters in the new Oxford collection – those written by Cassandra herself to their nieces after Austen's agonising death from Bright's disease in 1817 – there is nothing for it but to do so. Cassandra sat by her sister's bedside all of the long final evening and night, at one point supporting Austen's dying head, which was 'almost off the bed', in her lap for six hours. 'Fatigue made me then resign my place to Mrs J.A. for two hours & a half when I took it again & in about one hour more she breathed her last.' 'I *have* lost a treasure,' she wrote to Fanny Knight a few days later, 'such a Sister, such a friend as never can have been surpassed. – She was the sun of my life, the gilder of every pleasure, the soother of every sorrow, I had not a thought concealed from her, & it is as if I had lost a part of myself.' She had a ring made up with a lock of Austen's hair set in it – she wore it for the rest of her life – and dreamed of meeting her again: 'I know the time must come when my mind will be less engrossed by her idea, but I do not like to think of it. If I think of her less as on Earth, God grant that I may never cease to reflect on her as inhabiting Heaven & never cease my humble endeavours (when it shall please God) to join her there.' If such prayers are ever answered, one can only hope that she did.

3 August 1995

Nothing goes without saying

Stanley Cavell re-views the Marx Brothers

Movies magnify, so when pictures began talking they magnified words. Somehow, as in the case of opera's magnification of words, this made their words mostly ignorable, like the ground, as if the industrialised human species had been looking for a good excuse to get away from its words, or looking for an explanation of the fact that we do get away, even must. The attractive publication, briefly and informatively introduced, of the scripts of several Marx Brothers films* – *Monkey Business* (1931), *Duck Soup* (1933) and *A Day at the Races* (1937) – is a sublime invitation to stop and think about our swings of convulsiveness and weariness in the face of these films; to sense that it is essential to the Brothers' sublimity that they are thinking about words, to the end of words, in every word – or, in Harpo's emphatic case, in every absence of words.

Marx Brothers films, as unmistakably revealed in these scripts, are extensively explicit about their intentions. Their pun-crammed air, well recognised as a medium of social subversion, also presses a standing demand to reach some understanding – which is incomparably better avoided than faked. Someone is always barking sentiments at the Brothers such as 'Keep out of this loft!' to which Chico once replies, 'Well, it's better to have loft and lost, than never to have loft at all,' upon which Groucho pats him on the shoulder and says, 'Nice work!' (*Monkey Business*). (When is to speak to do something? When is to

---

* *The Marx Brothers: 'A Day at the Races', 'Monkey Business' and 'Duck Soup'*, introduced by Karl French (Faber, 1993). 'Film script' is not an unambiguous designation. In the present edition, on which my remarks here are based, it designates a record of dialogue and action faithful to the finished film (supposing there is a canonical version of that). This is a sound choice and I have no quarrel with it. Other choices would have been to publish the scripts as they stood before filming, but there is apparently no surviving such text for *Duck Soup*, whose script here is therefore wholly reconstituted from the film, and in any case such a collection would serve quite specialised purposes; or to publish original scripts together with their respective reconstitutions as filmed. This dual publication was followed by Viking some twenty years ago for *A Day at the Races* and for *A Night at the Opera*. In obvious ways this is desirable – such documentation underscores the collaboration, or mutual inspiration, of the Brothers with some of the most gifted writers, and teams of writers, of comic observation and plot, of gags, and of songs during the golden period of interchange between Hollywood and Broadway. But the mere credits included in the present scripts should themselves suggest this. Anyway, what is mutual inspiration?

bark to say something?) Groucho's positive evaluation is an instance of the recurrent reflexiveness in the Brothers' craft, letting us know that they know that we may fall to imagining that they do not know what they are doing. A repeated example, as if to wake us from this stupor, is Chico's turning to Groucho with pride, asking: 'Ats-a some joke, eh Boss?' Groucho is complimenting Chico not only on countering a dour threat with a serene wipe-out, but on maintaining his responsiveness to a world deadened with banal and unreasoned prohibitions. (Occasionally, as in *Duck Soup*, Groucho specifically probes to see whether the compliment is warranted, as when he feeds Chico a straight line and says in an aside: 'Let's see you get out of that one.') To me it is a philosophical compliment. So I have been aggrieved to hear Groucho called a cynic. He is merely without illusion, and it is an exact retribution for our time of illusory knowingness that we mistake his clarity for cynicism and sophisticated unfeelingness.

Intention, or the desperate demand for interpretation, is gaudily acknowledged in such turns as Chico's selling Groucho a tip on a horse by selling him a code book, then a master code book to explain the code book, then a guide required by the master code, then a subguide supplementary to the guide – a scrupulous union, or onion, of semantic and monetary exchanges and deferrals to warm the coldest contemporary theorist of signs; or as acted out in Chico's chain of guesses when Harpo, with mounting urgency, charades his message that a woman is going to frame Groucho (both turns in *A Day at the Races*). But Groucho's interpretive powers achieve distinct heights of their own.

The famous packed cabin sequence from *A Night at the Opera* is simultaneously an image of the squalor of immigrant crowding and of the immigrant imagination of luxury. Groucho is outside, as befits him, ordering exhaustively from a steward (getting food is one of the Brothers' standing objectives). After each item is ordered, Chico's voice from within the cabin appends, 'And two hard-boiled eggs', which, after Groucho dutifully repeats it, is punctuated by a honk from within, which Groucho effortlessly responds to by adding, 'Make that three hard-boiled eggs.' That Harpo evidently accedes to Groucho's understanding of his honk is variously interpretable. You can imagine that Groucho has some private knowledge of Harpo's language; or you can see that Harpo's insatiability, or unsocialisation, signals that he has no language (that is, that he is unable to speak in the etymological sense of being in the state of infancy). In the latter case, Harpo trusts Groucho implicitly to know his wants and to have them at heart, a trust well placed. That Harpo is shown to be asleep during Groucho's exchange with the steward suggests that Harpo is honking, wishing, in his dreams, and so with the directness of infants, preceding the detours of human desire, a possibility of dreams separately noted by Freud. Originality in speech is the rediscovery of speech. (It is, by the way, not true, as it is said, that Chico can trick Groucho. Groucho has nothing to lose and is not out to win anything for himself. He follows Chico's elaborate cons out of pure interest, to see, as if to satisfy his professional curiosity about the human situation, how they will come out. One outcome is as interesting as another. Of the other thinkers I know fairly well, I believe only Thoreau is Groucho's equal in this capacity for disinterested interest, or unattachment.)

The familiar, or familial, relation between Groucho and Harpo in the arena of food suggests a relation in their sharing of certain gestures of lechery. If they were really lecherous they would no longer be funny. (Adam Gopnik was making such a point about Woody Allen a couple of months ago in the *New Yorker*.) Being parodies of lechery, they enact claims on the part of each human creature ('All God's chillun' is how they name them in *A Day at the Races*) to be loved, for no reason. Harpo would not know what to do if one of the women he chases stopped running; for him the instincts of hunger, of sex, and of the destruction of whatever can be snipped or chopped, seem equal in imaginary satisfaction. Groucho, the opposite of innocent, is a lover, but one who thinks it just as hilarious as anyone else might think it that he should be found lovable. It does both him and Margaret Dumont an injustice not to see that he wins her love and is a faithful husband to it; he courts her as fervently as, and much more persistently than, he does any other woman – he amuses her, shocks her, tells her the truth, expresses contempt for the boring and brutish flatterers in her second-rate world who would deceive her for their private purposes, and with good spirits survives her doubts about him and her faiths in him. How much can one ask for?

I see no good sense in being reasonable in my admiration for these achievements. Thinking recently about the conditions of opera, as mys-terious and as initially contrived as the conditions of film, I asked myself why it was, when the Marx Brothers' thoughts turned to opera, that they proposed (or inspired others to propose to them), in *A Night at the Opera*, *Il Trovatore* as their example. In their realm, nothing goes without saying. It turns out, in this juxtaposition, that Leonora's initial mistaking, as it were, of her love of one brother for that of the other, becomes a fun-damental issue: it is to the villainous brother, in the early shadows of the drama, that she declares: 'My love'. Perhaps she was not wrong about

152 · STANLEY CAVELL

herself that initial time. Then one remembers that the Marx Brothers are brothers, and declare their family resemblance in one of their greatest turns, in *Duck Soup*, when Groucho and Harpo all but become mirror images of each other; and then one considers that these brothers, famous for their absurdities, may be taking on, as a grand enemy, the famously dark fixations of *Trovatore* that just about anyone regards as exemplary of the supposed absurdities of grand opera; and so consider that their competition with that darkness, absurd only in its terrible lack of necessity, is to use the power of film to achieve the happy ending in which the right tenor gets the part, the film concluding triumphantly with the opera's most famous, ecstatically melancholy duet.

Other speculations about their choices of routine keep finding confirmation – these brothers are dashing way ahead of us. Thinking more or less blankly one time of the ships on which they approach America, quite early in *Monkey Business* and quite late in *A Night at the Opera*, I think further: of course! The films present America as requiring discovery and as providing a home for immigrants. Then not only am I swiftly embarrassed at having forgotten that the elaborate finale of the first half of *Monkey Business* is just about the anxiety of needing a passport to enter upon the American streets of gold, but I am soon rewarded by finding Groucho conclude an exasperatingly contentious exchange with Chico by looking at the camera and declaring: 'There's my argument! Restrict immigration!'; and rewarded again, or piqued, when – in response to Chico's and Harpo's attempt to thwart the woman's plan to frame Groucho (to compromise him in Margaret Dumont's eyes) by hanging, so to speak, new sheets of wallpaper over Groucho and the woman seated cosily on a couch, thus concealing them from the entering suspicious one – Groucho pokes his head out of the sticky sheets to observe, 'I must be a citizen. I've just got my second papers,' that is, the final documents in an alien's naturalisation process (as if any process could naturalise this alien).

Until my father died, seventy years after arriving on America's shores as a young man, and not many fewer than that after naturalisation, he never fully shook the feeling that something might be discovered to be wrong with his 'papers'. Perhaps helped by this knowledge, I go further into the sequence with Chico that leads to Groucho's momentary wish never to have been cast together with him. It opens in the Captain's cabin, where Groucho is so to speak impersonating the Captain.

Groucho: A fine sailor you are.
Chico: You bet I'm a fine sailor . . . My father was-a partners with Columbus.
Groucho: Columbus has been dead for four hundred years.

Chico: Well, they told me it was my father . . .
Groucho: I'll show you a few things you don't know about history. Now look . . .
[*Drawing a circle on a globe.*] Now, there's Columbus.
Chico: That's-a Columbus Circle . . .
Groucho: Now, Columbus sailed from Spain to India looking for a short cut.
Chico: Oh, you mean strawberry short cut.

And it gets still further afield. It is some mimesis of the shattered tiles of facts and interpretations, the urgent implacement of which had to prepare masses of arrivals for citizenship, learning who their new fathers are, the fathers of their new country, and searching to put new and old names to unheard-of objectives. And when Groucho lets it out in disgust, 'do you suppose I could buy back my introduction to you?' I again find myself speculating: the comedy is that of outrage, of exhaustion, of the last straw. And again I feel rewarded. I'll come back to say how in a moment.

The sense of culture as something overheard, and probably as tales or plots of incomprehensible manias, comes out also in those asides of Groucho's that fill the space of responses to impossible situations and incomprehensible demands.

Woman: But I haven't any children.
Groucho: That's just the trouble with this country. You haven't any children, and as for me . . . [*Dramatically*] I'm going back to the closet, where men are empty overcoats.

Or again, also from *Monkey Business*:

Same woman: What brought you here?
Groucho [*Dramatically*]: Ah, 'tis midsummer madness, the music in my temples . . . Kapellmeister, let the violas throb. My regiment leaves at dawn!

Or again:

Same woman: You can't stay in that closet.
Groucho: Oh, I can't, can I? That's what they said to Thomas Edison, mighty inventor, Thomas Lindberg, mighty flyer, and Thomas Shefsky, mighty like a rose. Just remember, my little cabbage, that if there weren't any closets, there wouldn't be any hooks. and if there weren't any hooks, there wouldn't be any fish, and that would suit me fine.

To speak, as I believe is still common, of Groucho's 'one-liners', as if this were his characteristic genre of response, is not helpful, not just because it is so incomplete, even inaccurate, but because what it omits reaches from the closeness to madness, or hysteria, of so much of what he has to say, to the sheer range or reference of his uncontrollable thoughts – from some memory of Russian or Cartesian melancholy about overcoats and empty men, through wisps of operetta, to a string of heroes that the natives seem to name Thomas, for the moment missing a Jefferson but including a figure from the Yiddish theatre otherwise known as Boris Thomashefsky, associated, compulsively if not altogether surprisingly, with some association of Abie's Irish Rose with the teary mother's song 'Mighty Like a Rose', all sometimes addressed to imaginary characters, here one called 'Kapellmeister', later one called 'Your honour'. This delirium is to be compared, not identified, with Harpo's closeness to madness, as when, in his frantic search for the frog who has jumped away from his place in Harpo's hat, Harpo hears a man confess that he has a frog in his throat, grabs the man and prises open his jaws to retrieve his companion. It touches the madness of childhood. And it enacts an unexpected understanding of Wittgenstein's perception, in *Philosophical Investigations*, that Augustine, as characteristic of philosophers, 'describes the learning of language as if the child came into a strange country and did not understand the language of the country; that is as if it already had a language, only not this one'. This is illuminatingly implausible if taken as about the condition of infancy, with no language yet in the picture; but illuminatingly plausible if taken as about an older child, with a certain budget of words, all due for unforeseen futures, hence against an idea or the condition of immigrancy, between languages.

What is this humour? If we take Bergson's theory of comedy as bespeaking a form of madness, of men behaving like machines, and vice versa, then we can say that the Marx Brothers turn this theory on the world, showing themselves to remain improvisatory, original, in a setting of absolutely mechanical reactions to them ('This is an outrage'; 'I've never been so insulted in all my life'; 'Beat it!; 'Oh!'; 'Just what do you mean?'; 'Hey. Hey. Hey.'; 'Are you crazy or something?'). Their madness is a defence against madness, and neither is something over which they claim control; it is a struggle to the finish, in which the question is which side will create the last word, or destroy it.

Let's accordingly go back to the idea of a comedy of the last straw, or rather of a comedy about the last straw, about the sometimes fatal whimsicality with which people announce the judgment that a straw is the last. In *Duck Soup*, Ambassador Trentino (played by the Caesaresque Louis Calhern) says to Margaret Dumont: 'Mrs Teasdale this is the last straw! There's no turning back now. This means war!' – words Groucho may well be imagined somewhere to dispose of in his own person, if perhaps he decides to take an imaginary slight as directed to his entire regiment. When later in *Duck Soup* Groucho uses the words, 'Gentlemen, this is the last straw,' it is in response to picking up a straw boater with its crown flapping, from among the rubble of war. Then what, if anything, do we make of Harpo, in *A Day at the Races*, attacking a mattress with a knife, pulling out the straw, and then feeding it to a horse he discloses in a closet. I would like to take this in conjunction with the line of Groucho's that closes *Monkey Business*, when after events in an old barn in which a wagon wheel becomes an imaginary wheel of fortune, a cow bell becomes a time bell in a brawl, and a watering can and then a buggy lamp are talked into as microphones, Groucho turns to a pile of hay and starts pitching strands into the air. Asked what he's doing he replies: 'I'm looking for a needle in a haystack.' Now some moments earlier we had seen Groucho rise from under this hay and ask: 'Where's all those farmers' daughters I've been hearing about for years?' and then disappear under the hay again. It strikes me that Groucho's self-interpretation of looking for a needle in a haystack undertakes to transfigure the coarse genre of farmer's daughter gags into a search – almost hopeless, with just room for good spirits to operate – for a heart's needle of pleasure somewhere within the dry medium of this world (like the bereft husband in *L'Atalante* diving into the river, eyes open for his vanished love).

For Groucho, throwing last straws to the wind, the world as it stands has placed its last straw, suffered its last judgment, a long time ago; yet the world as it may yet be, attested in any event in which genuine interest is shown – like a Harpo craving, a Chico scam, a young woman in love and trouble, the scandalised, ecstatic devotion of Margaret Dumont – exists beyond counts of straw.

Evidently I take the value of the published scripts of these films not to be solely or primarily that of sending us back to the films (the films themselves must do that), but also that of releasing these words and deeds from a confinement to film, or to what we think of as film, or think of as a Marx Brothers film. Released to themselves, these observations are free to join the observations of, say, Bergson; or Brecht, whose *Three Penny Opera* is no more valid a development of *The Beggar's Opera* than *Duck Soup* is (it needn't be as good as *The Three Penny Opera* still to be very, very good); or Beckett, whose two barrels housing the married pair in *Endgame* make excellent sense, even of the idea of the stowaway, of the four barrels in which the stowaway brothers have set up house below decks at the opening of *Monkey Business*. And then we are free to think about one of Groucho's responses to the recurrent idea that a situation he's created, this time involving his medical practice, is 'absolutely insane'. Groucho: 'Yes, that's what they said about Pasteur.' No doubt the direct reference is to the celebrated Paul Muni film *Pasteur* made the year before *A Day at the Races*; but must one deny that Groucho is claiming his own discovery of a germ theory, this time about the disease of language, about its corruption by communications of a corrupt world? He puts it differently, but not much differently.

I was talking about Groucho's searching for pleasure, another topic about which these films are, if asked, fully explicit. In *Duck Soup*, after Firefly (Groucho), in song, promulgates the laws of his administration as not allowing smoking, telling dirty jokes, whistling, or chewing gum, he sums it up, still singing:

> If any form of pleasure is exhibited
> Report to me and it will be prohibited.

From which it does not follow that the Brothers trust any given form of pleasure, any more than they trust any other fixation, any more than they trust; they test. Nor are their films as films exactly or purely pleasurable, any more than compulsive punning is exactly or simply funny. The unpolished air of the film-making, and Groucho's Brechtian objectivity, are not meant to be winning, any more (if no less) than Groucho's crawling and meowing on a balustrade.

The broad groan in response to a broad pun is a criterion of real, if a little sublimated, pain. 'This is no time for puns,' says Groucho, gasping with them, almost at the end of *Monkey Business*. Had someone the presence of mind to say this to Groucho, he might have answered: 'Yes, that's what they said about Shakespeare.' No time is the time for puns, since puns stop time, stop the forward motion of assertion, peel back the protective self-ignorance of words. Is this the pain of puns? Their pain is that of, let us say, incessant thinking – thinking among the endless things there are to say, which of them we shall have for ever said, and not said, now. Their pleasure is the illusion that nothing is going unsaid.

And what is the cultural economy, say the relation between high and low thinking, in a society whose as it were popular culture has such as the Marx Brothers in store – what is its art, its philosophy, its politics, its entertainment, its seriousness?

Let us before ending linger once more over an invitation into whose depths of implication I cannot deny Groucho perception, and, as always, without presumption, he is nothing if not tactful. It comes as

part of the packed cabin sequence, cited earlier, that royal levee of services, when a woman appears to Groucho with a portable beauty tray
hung before her and asks, 'Do you want a manicure?' Groucho replies:
'No. Come on in.' I take for granted that some will be satisfied to suppose that he means, fixatedly: 'No, but I want something else you could
provide.' Let us suppose, however, that he has the poise with meaning,
whatever command of it accrues from obedience to it, to mean or
imply at least also the following: 'No, but there are lots of others here;
perhaps they want what you suggest'; and 'Nobody really wants a manicure, but if that's all you're offering, I'll take it'; and 'No, but come in
since you're here and we'll see what happens.' All this is quite in character for Groucho. An array of implication, like the disarray of puns, will
threaten anarchy, against a demand for autarchy; but both work to
make what sense is to be made of a world whose sense is stolen, in
which it is to be stolen back. Both show aspects of our victimisation by
words, fools of them, but thereby show that there are, still, ordinary
words, beyond and between us, whose lives we might imagine, which
might share lives we can imagine – not simply signs and signals hovering over a destroyed landscape.

A few years ago, on a walk during a conference break, a French
philosopher and I exchanged friendly regrets that we were not, as it
were, culturally better prepared to do the promise of each other's work
more explicit justice in our own. He reported that American friends of
his had been urging him to read Emerson and Thoreau, which seemed
to both of us an unlikely eventuality. I took the implication quite kindly,
anyway impersonally, that no one would, or could easily, without insult,
urge an American intellectual to read Montaigne and Descartes and
Rousseau and Kant and Hegel . . . Culture is – is it not? – European
culture. Besides, Emerson and Thoreau had read them. Had I then
been fresh from reading the film scripts before me now, I might have
replied – whether hopefully or not is uncertain – that to the extent he
was wondering what was on my mind, hence in that tangle of American
culture, an equally accurate access, and one in a sense more efficiently
acquired, could be had by a few days of immersion in half a dozen
Marx Brothers films. But that would have been, to borrow a self-
description of Thoreau's and of Walt Whitman's, bragging.

6 January 1994

She Who Can Do No Wrong

Jenny Turner on Muriel Spark

At the end of *Curriculum Vitae*,* Muriel Spark has just published her first novel, *The Comforters*. It is 1957 and she is 39 years old. After happening on Spark's novel in proof while working on his own *Gilbert Pinfold*, Evelyn Waugh has decided to write it a glowing testimonial, which he publishes in the *Spectator*: 'It so happens that *The Comforters* came to me just as I had finished a story on a similar theme, and I was struck by how much more ambitious Miss Spark's essay was, and how much better she had accomplished it,' is how this testimonial goes. '"I dare say," drawled Al' – Al being Muriel Spark's publisher, the young Alan Maclean – '"that this is the shape of things to come." It was a risky saying, for many fine first novels are followed by duds. However, I took great heart from what he said, and went on my way rejoicing.'

The years leading up to this occasion for rejoicing have been strange and thrilling ones, a real-life intimation, should Muriel Spark have needed one, that life, when looked at from the long-sighted point of view, sometimes works itself out in mysterious and wonderful ways. In 1951, she wrote her first short story, straight out on foolscap paper. 'The Seraph and the Zambesi' – one of the strangest and most beautiful things she has yet written – won first prize in the *Observer* short-story competition of that year, and caused, Spark says, 'quite a stir'. But Spark still saw herself not as a fiction-writer but as a poet and literary critic, and she was still desperately poor. By 1954 she was overworking frantically, sending out poem after poem, keeping critical projects on T.S. Eliot, Cardinal Newman and possibly the Book of Job all bubbling on the back-burner at the same time. Spark then became anorexic, using dexedrine as a substitute for regular meals. Her breakdown when it came appeared as a visitation from Eliot, whose poetry, Spark convinced herself, was full of secret messages encoded in ancient Greek.

The Eliot book, unsurprisingly, never got done. In 1953, Spark, up until then a half-Jewish agnostic with a Scottish Presbyterian

---

* Muriel Spark, *Curriculum Vitae* (Constable, 1992).

educational background, had converted to Anglicanism; in 1954 she went the whole hog and became a Roman Catholic instead. She recovered from her breakdown with the help of her priest, who helped her find a cottage, and later a Camberwell bedsit, from which to put her life back together and start writing anew. Spark seems to have lost interest in T.S. Eliot from that point on. Her edition of the letters of John Henry Newman, however, went ahead as planned. And her interest in Job and his dreadful afflictions, the capricious God who made him suffer dreadfully for the sake of a wager, and his horrible friends who only made things worse, she displaced, with a mischievous obliqueness that would come to seem typical of all her fiction, onto the title and author-as-God structure of *The Comforters*.

Small wonder, then, that Muriel Spark ends her first volume of memoirs by going on her way rejoicing. But hold it there a minute. For this business about going on one's way rejoicing, as faithful Spark fans may already have recognised, is one of Muriel Spark's favourite catch-phrases, along with such classics of the catch-phrase form as 'crème de la crème', 'pisseur de copie', 'neither good-looking nor bad-looking', 'we must always think about les autres'. *The Comforters*, in fact, itself concluded with a character going on his way rejoicing; *Loitering with Intent* (1981), a story which returns to the threadbare milieu of Spark's own post-war London life, ends in this fashion too. And the latter's first-person heroine, Fleur, surely isn't rejoicing just because she is thinking about 'how wonderful it is to be an artist and a woman in the middle of the 20th century.' For we have already watched her lift the phrase, word for word, from Benvenuto Cellini, whose autobiography, along with Cardinal Newman's *Apologia*, has already put in a cameo appearance as one of the prime movers in that novel's plot. Yes, life when looked at from the long point of view sometimes does work itself out in mysterious and wonderful ways. Especially when you are dealing with an author who enjoys playing tricksy narrative games.

Curriculum Vitae is not one of those autobiographies which works as a piece of literature in and of itself. It is not Newman, it is not – to cite the other great favourite of *Loitering with Intent* – Cellini, it is not a be-all or end-all statement like the autobiograply of, say, Simone de Beauvoir. If you read it expecting anything very frank or deep or sustained, you will find it, as I did to begin with, disappointing. But unlike John Henry Newman, Muriel Spark is not a priest but an artist, and so does not need to apologise to anybody for her life. And unlike, say, Simone de Beauvoir, Muriel Spark doesn't need to write an unusually frank, deep or sustained autobiography in order to assure us of her interest and originality as a person and as a writer.

Muriel Spark is now 74 years old. She is the author of 19 novels, all of which sell pretty well, four of which have been adapted for film or TV, one of which, *The Prime of Miss Jean Brodie* (1961), has become a living legend of literature both Scottish and English. She is the author also of several collections of short stories, of two collections of poetry and half a dozen volumes of literary criticism. She knows fine that journalists and scholars find her of interest. Indeed, as a tetchy commentary in *Curriculum Vitae* shows, she has for years been following the handful of myths and half-truths which pass for fact among such. She knows fine too that she will, at some point, die; as the cheerful morbidity of *Memento Mori* (1959) made plain, Spark has no patience with people who find it difficult to contemplate the likely imminence of death. The purpose of *Curriculum Vitae*, then, is no more and no less than to present the facts of her early life as she sees them, for other people's future reference. It's a debunking job, it's a pre-emptive attack, and it's a fond but highly selective trip down memory lane.

Curriculum Vitae is not the sort of book that encourages you to pry. Though – like Spark's novels – affectionate where affection is due, it is – like the novels – pretty merciless as regards everything else. It dutifully points out people and places that inspired various episodes in her writing: the benevolent Miss Kay who became the monstrous Miss Jean Brodie; the lookalike Edinburgh schoolmate who became the lookalike colonial harpy of 'Bang bang, you're dead'; the jobs at the Foreign Office, at the Poetry Society, at Peter Owen, that became the jobs written about in *Loitering with Intent, A Far Cry From Kensington* (1988) and no doubt others. But it skates over many things about which eager beavers may want to know more: Muriel Camberg's disastrous teenage marriage to Sydney Oswald Spark, whom she dubs 'SOS'; her twenties in Rhodesia as a bored and miserable colonial wife; her son from that marriage, sent off to his grandparents in Edinburgh after the war in order that Spark could seek her fortune in London. But none of this, *Curriculum Vitae* makes plain, is anybody's business but Spark's own. Any further speculation on the reader's part would be viewed very dimly indeed.

I'm afraid that I for one won't be trying to do anything to offend her. For as a Muriel Spark fan of many years' standing, I know exactly what happens to eager beavers and people like them. They get ridiculed, they get mocked, they get shown up as pitifully, hilariously venal. And fair do's really. As all of Spark's stories share a similar moral structure in which She Herself, or her appointed narrative agent, Can Do No

Wrong and everybody else had better watch it, nobody can pretend they weren't warned. But more profoundly, there is really no point in trying to take issue with Muriel Spark's chosen version of herself. For to do so would involve taking issue with every aesthetic, moral and theological attitude Muriel Spark's writing stands for, and thus to move unhelpfully away from getting to grips with whatever it is that this writing is.

In her autobiography as in her fiction, Muriel Spark is not a person but a persona. Just look at the photographs of herself she chooses for her dust-jackets. She is pretty, she is pert, she is immaculately chic; she signifies drop-dead lady wit, a flirt, a charmer, a dandyess and a poseuse. If somebody has put this sort of effort into their self-projection, it's kind of by the way to call them affected or inauthentic, for, unlike, say, Simone de Beauvoir, they have never pretended to be anything else. You just have to decide whether you are impressed by the effect or not, and go on your way accordingly.

Because Muriel Spark is by birth Scottish and a woman, her work frequently attracts response from critics who identify with either or both of these attributes. But whatever else critics may do with a persona, trying to identify with it is unlikely to bring much joy. You start deploring Spark's work, love it as you do, for its unsisterly cruelty and lack of empathy with human motivation; you get all gauche and genu flecting as your own lily-livered agnosticism finds itself in the presence of the great other-worldiness and mysterious ways of Spark's religion. This is dim. Muriel Spark is a tough-minded grown-up woman; Muriel Spark is also obviously some sort of a mistress of irony. She is therefore presumably quite capable of deciding for herself which aspects of her faith need to be kept private, and which might enjoy being let loose in her novels for some worldy fun and games.

There is, of course, no outward conflict in being a serious Roman Catholic of the British convert sort and being also a charmer, a flirt and a poseuse. As the wise grandmother in *The Comforters* says, 'the one certain way for a woman to hold a man is to leave him for religion . . . The man might get another girl, but he can never be happy with anyone else after a girl has left him for religious reasons. *She* secures him for good.' Which is to say: Muriel Spark's novels use their author's religion for many things, but among those things they certainly use it as a source of a peculiarly English sort of Roman Catholic camp. In dowdy old Protestant England in the frumpy Fifties, becoming a Catholic was an excellent way of making manifest one's own felt specialness socially. As a gesture of cultural aspiration and disdain, it signified much the same sort of will to the moral high ground as joining the Communist Party did in France, where to have been a mere Catholic would have caused no sort of a stir at all. Within the British tradition Muriel Spark elected, with her conversion, to hobnob with a small but disproportionately powerful historical clique of Catholic-convert novelists led by Ronald Firbank and Evelyn Waugh, stylistic affectation-mongers, social climbers and inveterate poseurs the both of them. And within the wider Western tradition, she elected to join a tradition of Catholic kitsch and cruelty which included such apostate writers as Antonin Artaud and Georges Bataille, whose blasphemy would have been pointless had they not had the body of Catholic ritual there to egg them on. Catholicism, unlike Protestantism, is a religious tradition that is rich in irony. It's hardly surprising then that after she had joined it, Spark immediately set about making her faith and her fiction fit exquisitely together, immaculately manicured hand in impeccably chic glove.

Once Spark got going on her fiction and her religion, her religion and her fiction, she started, as she says in this book, 'a new life'. Elsewhere she has said that, after her conversion, she found her voice as a writer immediately and with ease. She left Britain for good in the mid-Sixties, on her own admission, to get away from old friends from whom success had estranged her. She has since lived unassailably above the rest of us, in New York, in Rome, in Oliveto, from whence *Curriculum Vitae* is datelined. That she left behind her in England, too, the sort of puritanical morality that looks for usable truths in people's dirty washing is obvious from all her subsequent work.

But camp, and Catholic camp in particular, only works if it is in some way devout and serious, which is why Pedro Almodóvar, after making hilarious, loving and utterly reverent films about junkie nuns and sex-crazed madonna figures, has started going off, and why Madonna with her crucifixes and her mother's graveside is boring and embarrassing as hell. For the big irony on which all other Catholic irony turns is precisely that Catholicism is for its adherents the most rigorous and rational of all possible faiths, and yet the one that offers its flock so many weird and wonderful sacramental activities with which to stimulate their consciences while biding their time in the temporal world. Thus Muriel Spark has made herself a mistress at writing stories which seem to trip blithely and bitchily along life's way until the reader is suddenly pulled up with a shock recognition of death and judgment, heaven and hell, the four last things that have been lurking on the bottom line all the story through: God help me. Life is unbearable, as the heroine of 'The Go-Away Bird' says at the end of her story, which up to that point might have been misrecognised as a mere comedy of one young woman's utterly futile and wasted youth.

'When I am asked about my conversion, why I became a Catholic, I can only say the answer is too easy and too difficult,' says Muriel Spark in *Curriculum Vitae*. 'The simple explanation is that I felt the Roman Catholic faith corresponded to what I had always known and believed; there was no blinding revelation in my case. The more difficult explanation would involve the step by step building up of a conviction; as Newman himself pointed out, when asked about his own conversion, it was not a thing one could propound "between the soup and the fish" at a dinner party.' It is interesting to note how what Muriel Spark expresses as a sort of dialectical movement, whereby everything absolute is known right from the beginning and yet one has to move step by step over a great number of life's pages before this absolute can be recognised, is mimicked in the proleptic structure of her novels, whereby the reader learns about a character's ultimate fate long before their story has been fully played out. But it is also interesting to note the way that, according to the mysterious and wonderful patterning of events in *Curriculum Vitae*, knowledge and conviction, fiction and religion all sparked together at what seems to have been the rock-bottom point of Muriel Spark's own life. In 1957 Spark was 39 years old, not a spring chicken either as artist or woman in the 20th century or any other. Now to approach one's late thirties – one's prime as a woman and as an artist indeed – as a penniless single mother of few marketable skills could not have been much of a joke in the middle of the 20th century. It isn't much of a joke in the late 20th century either. To approach one's prime convinced of one's genius as an artist, but with precious little formal recognition to show for it, must have been at least slightly enervating too. Semi-starvation, dexedrine, psychosis, a life materially collapsed to the point that Muriel Spark had to turn to her priest to help her find a place to live: this is just desperate, desperate stuff.

It is for Muriel Spark to tell us if she chooses in a later volume of memoirs how much her desperate lifestyle as a woman and an artist in the 20th century had to do with her religious conversion. But it is for us to notice how totally real and concrete this desperation is in her every short story and book. It is there in *The Prime of Miss Jean Brodie*, whose proleptic structure causes the book throughout all its merry tales of primeful high jinks, to pivot on final images of waste, frustration and death. There is the image of Miss Brodie herself, no longer in her prime, bent, betrayed, obsessed, soon to die of cancer. There is the image of the girl sent by Miss Brodie to fight for Fascism who dies horribly in an ambush almost before she has set foot in Spain. And there is the image of young Sandy, no longer famous for her vowel sounds and her little piggy eyes, clutching at the bars that enclose her in her Carmelite monastery. Death, waste and frustration are everywhere, too, in *The Girls of Slender Means* (1963), apparently a story about high jinks in a Kensington women's hostel at the end of World War Two, whose droll and lyrical opening passage lyrically and drolly manages to superimpose the image of these 'delightful', 'ingenious', 'movingly lovely, and, as it might happen, more savage' young ladies with the memento mori of a bombed-out building skull. Death, waste and frustration are everywhere in all of Spark's early novels, in which a witty and fond appreciation of the things people get up to in their youth and poverty mingles with a rising stench of what Julia Kristeva calls 'the abject', a desperate disgust with the earthbound fate of flesh. And they are everywhere too in her later novels, in which Spark, as befits her current social position, turns her attention to people of wealth and cosmopolitan circumstances.

Now Muriel Spark is not the only woman and artist in the 20th century to use the mask of glittering lady wit as a way of dealing, head-on but with the necessary protective clothing, with the horror she seems to feel for her biological destiny. Dorothy Parker did this with brilliance and bitterness, and so in her way does Julie Burchill. If you're not grossly fat you're probably too thin, and with a nasty skinny mind to go with it. If you're not irredeemably stupid you're no doubt so sharp you'll end up cutting yourself; and who's ever going to fall in love with a ball-breaking harridan like you? Even if you do manage to escape marriage to some mediocre dolt of a man, you'll probably end up as an embittered old maid instead – and as for being a nun or a lesbian or both, well, unfortunately not all women have a vocation for it, and even if they did, chances are they'd still end up discontented like Sandy, and anyway everybody ends up dying in the long run. Yes, this is all very cynical and nihilistic, and a bit reactionary from the feminist point of view. But that in itself doesn't stop it from being something that most women, even feminists, feel to be the case at some time or another. And it certainly doesn't stop women from loving, and dare I say it, deriving a peculiar sort of strength from, all these women's works. (And men of course love them too, to the point that Dorothy Parker, Julie Burchill and Muriel Spark, with the occasional addition of Susan Sontag, often seem to be the only women writers on whom they seem willing to hang the epithet 'clever'. But that is a different and darker matter.) Feminism alone, in short, doesn't stop Muriel Spark's vision of cursed femininity from being broadly and horribly true. God help us. Life really is unbearable, and particularly for women, and particularly when looked at from the cold and cruel and cynical long-sighted point of view.

But the strange and marvellous thing about Muriel Spark's writing is that, unlike that of Dorothy Parker or Julie Burchill, it never gets brittle or forced or knotted up in its own so-sharp-she'll-cut-herself cleverness. No matter how desperate the things she is writing about get, all Spark's writing has a supple merriment about it, a lightness of touch, a will-ingness to share in fleeting moments of mundane love and pleasure, that cannot come from cleverness alone. It is tempting, amusing and probably fair to assume that Muriel Spark's writing gets its special sort of strength from She That Can Do No Wrong's personal escape-hatch and hotline to God. Many women, after all, in times before the middle of the 20th century, turned to the Church as a way of escaping the dou-ble bind of marriage or a miserable life as a pitied and put-upon spinster aunt. As an intellectual and an artist, Spark is far too worldly, tough and gorgeous to have needed to follow such women all the way to a Carmelite monastery, but it is wonderful nevertheless to watch how she uses the look-but-don't-touch aura of her superior holiness to tease hapless men inside her books and everybody of both sexes reading them outside.

With the exception of *The Only Problem* (1984), in which Spark returns to the subject of Job's afflictions in a significantly more urbane fashion than she was able to manage in the days before her success, Spark seldom bogs her novels down with extended theological discus-sion. But God is there all right, working at the level of form, in the tricks and twists of narrative, in the weird bloom of sublimity that catches on an innocent-looking catch-phrase like 'crème de la crème' or the one about going on one's way rejoicing. Wit, mind, intelligence, spiritedness and spirituality are closely linked qualities in most European languages. And it's because Muriel Spark knows how to turn all of these at once to shape and direct her every utterance that her writing comes to have such beauty and such force. You have only to glance at the work of copyists and pale cousins like the vaguely mischievous Fay Weldon, the clodhopping misanthropic Barbara Vine, to understand that Spark's use of that gorgeously 'cemp' posh-Scottish written voice of hers is really special. Not to mention a host of younger would-be poseuses and charmers who manage the nastiness and the affectation no problem, but come adrift on the matter of making it in the slightest bit compelling.

Now maybe this voice did indeed come straight down the authorial hotline from He Who Must Be Believed In. But it is a tenet of

Catholicism, as of all serious religion, that inspiration comes only to people who are prepared to work their brains with a furious and rigorous discipline in order to be ready to receive it. Hannah Arendt once said of Isak Dinesen that her tales read as if they had been boiled down until they were pure essence of story, and then boiled down again: and much the same could be said of Muriel Spark, albeit from a very different philosophical recipe. It is probably not coincidental that both women came to fiction comparatively late in life with decades of brainwork compressed behind them, stripped of all and any waste, including much that other able writers would think it necessary to keep in. The lightness and slenderness of Muriel Spark's novels may appear to belie the long years of sweated brainwork that had to get finished off before they could even get started. But the years of brainwork can be sensed working somewhere behind them, holding the whole together, just the same.

The happy result of Muriel Spark's method is that she is a writer who writes books against which uninteresting critical categories to do with élitist and populist, highbrow and lowbrow, mean nothing much. She is popular with teenagers, she is popular with oldies, she is popular with highbrow Catholic aristos and she's popular with low-down faithless types like me. And she is popular with all these people in a special and interesting way. Unlike the T.S. Eliot who helped her on the way to her nervous breakdown, Muriel Spark does not write elaborate palimpsests off which you get one thing if you're an initiate and something lesser if you are not. Every creepiness and spite, every structural joke and twist, can be missed by nobody, thanks to the astonishingly willed force of her economy and style. While rereading *The Prime of Miss Jean Brodie* the other day for the first time since I was a teenager, I was amazed to find that I remembered virtually everything about it, chunks of it more or less word for word. And I was struck also by the way that, although I now have many fancy words and theories with which to articulate my responses to that book, every scrap of its wit and peculiarly Catholic sort of dread, I'm pretty sure I, pig-ignorant Presbyterian schoolgirl though I was, picked up on first time around. It's quite a feat, to be able to hold an audience with such intensity and grace, from the cradle to the grave. I can't think of any other novelist who manages it so well, with the no doubt significant exception of Graham Greene.

For many readers, nevertheless, Muriel Spark will probably always be just a light-weight posh-Catholic lady novelist, a crypto-Spectatorite right-wing wit, a snob, a bit of an anti-feminist, and no doubt many things worse short of a wearer of the Sash. And I guess there is nothing in either *Curriculum Vitae* or this present review of it to disabuse them of their opinion – although, it is my duty to point out, there is nothing much to support it either, and it's an opinion which cannot be sustained for long if you read without prejudice a handful of her books. Do Spark's novels take it upon themselves to proselytise for Catholic perversity in the way that other novels proselytise for the life-enhancing properties of an Oxbridge education, a flash job in something trendy, a lot of terribly well-bred, fascinating and sensitive wives and friends with names like Rosalind, Claudia or Toby? (Hint: later novels like *Symposium* (1990) are in fact at their best when taking the rise out of this very genre.) Are they boring, sentimental or intelligence-insulting, full of smarmy little in-jokes and breast-beating vacuities to do with the end of structuralism, the end of history, the end of everything as epitomised by something the author once saw on daytime television about *Alien*[3]? Do they in fact proselytise for the pettifogging interests of any social clique at all, or are they not constructed merely to suggest that for life to be bearable as an artist or a woman in the 20th century, it's probably best if you work that brain of yours, turn yourself out as nice as you can lest death overtake you, and cultivate the independent attitude of a Cat Who Walks By Herself?

6 August 1992

Mallarmé gets a life

Barbara Johnson

Stéphane Mallarmé was the darling of French Symbolism and the demon of Existentialism. Later, in the Sixties and Seventies, he was a central figure for critical movements from psychoanalytic and thematic criticism to structuralism, semiotics and deconstruction. We have had analyses of his work by Charles Mauron, Jean-Pierre Richard, Robert Greer Cohn, Julia Kristeva, Jacques Derrida, Paul de Man, Leo Bersani, Malcolm Bowie and others. It might seem surprising, therefore, not to find a single full-length biography published between Henri Mondor's 1941 *Vie de Mallarmé* and Gordon Millan's *Mallarmé: A Throw of the Dice.** Millan notes in his Introduction that 'the man himself has been all but forgotten, eclipsed and overshadowed by his writings. Anyone reading recent Mallarmé criticism could be forgiven for wondering whether he ever had a life.'

There is a reason for this erasure. The eclipse of the author by the work is not an accident of Mallarmé criticism: it is Mallarmé's principal literary discovery. It was Mallarmé himself who dreamed of 'a Text speaking of and by itself, without the voice of an author'. The affirmative erasure of the poet from the work was a goal for which he never stopped striving: 'The pure work implies the elocutionary disappearance of the poet, who leaves the initiative to words.' And it was Mallarmé himself who created the myth of his lack of biography: writing to Verlaine in 1885 in response to a request for a headnote for his poems, he spoke of his 'life devoid of anecdote'.

Twenty years earlier, Mallarmé had announced to his friend Henri Cazalis, 'I am perfectly dead . . . I am now impersonal and no longer the Stéphane you have known, but an aptitude the spiritual universe has to see and develop itself through what was once me.' But, as Leo Bersani asks in *The Death of Stéphane Mallarmé*, 'what kind of poetry can a dead poet produce?' Similarly, we might ask, what kind of 'life of Mallarmé' can do justice to this poet whose work arose out of the discovery of his own death?

* Secker & Warburg, 1994.

It was largely by learning the lesson of Mallarmé that critics like Roland Barthes came to speak of 'the death of the author' in the making of literature. Rather than seeing the text as the emanation of an individual author's intentions (always a probabilistic and speculative enterprise), structuralists and deconstructors followed the paths and patterns of the signifier, paying new attention to syntax, spacing, intertextuality, sound, semantics, etymology, even individual letters. In each case, Mallarmé had been there before them: calling himself a 'syntaxer' and syntax the 'pivot of intelligibility', writing a book about the meanings of sounds and letters in English words, creating a concrete poem out of typography and position on the page, inventing a style of critical prose as well as poetry in which ellipses, discontinuities and obscurities played an integral part, and criticising romantic subjectivity and bourgeois realism. Freed from conventions of coherence, authority and psychology, texts could be allowed to unfold as infinite signifying systems.

This is not to say that Mallarmé's late, most stylistically radical texts have nothing to do with the desire for coherence. Indeed, one of the paradoxes of Mallarmé is that, along with his fragmentation of all the usual modes of meaning, he also imagined that 'The Book' would put everything back together in a higher synthesis. This impersonal, prismatic, grand oeuvre would also be a key to all mythologies, the 'Orphic explanation of the earth'. Somehow the book would actually *be* the 'musicality of everything', not *mean* it. Another paradox lies in the historical specificity of his most abstract theoretical writings: one of the densest of his discussions of the nature of value, for example, also deals with the failure of the Panama Canal Company. Satanism, an afternoon concert series, an encounter with a construction worker, the authority of the Catholic Church, a vote in the French Academy, a proposal to create a general fund for poets, are all part of the texture of his meditations on what he often capitalised as Literature. And one of his favourite projects was a fashion magazine which, under various pseudonyms, he wrote and edited almost entirely himself.

What, then, might one expect from a Nineties' biography of Mallarmé? The first requirement, I would think, would be some attempt to come to grips with what it might mean to write the life of a post-dead author. For the author was barely cold before the same mourners brought about a resurrection: Barthes and Derrida have written post-autobiographies, Julia Kristeva has written a *roman-à-clef*, and Paul de Man's life has come back into view like a return of the repressed. At the same time, race, class, gender, post-colonial and sexuality studies have suggested that the 'death' of canonical authors is a way of preserving their authority and shielding them from historical and political questioning.

Gordon Millan's biography of Mallarmé is written as though none of these issues, arising from questions Mallarmé himself invented, ever occurred or mattered. Or rather, his attitude toward the past twenty years of Mallarmé criticism is rather like the attitude he describes Mallarmé's grandmother as having towards children: 'She was a woman of quite definite and determined views: children should not be coddled; they must learn to be obedient; they should be seen and not heard, actively discouraged from being too vain or interesting or individual.' The damning epithet invoked on the two or three occasions on which Millan mentions criticism at all is 'exaggerated'.

This, then, is a biography that does not exaggerate. It is not vain or interesting or individual. It is respectful, reasonable, carefully researched and unimaginative. When it quotes a poem, it acts as though, in the context, the poem's meaning is self-evident. After Mondor's lengthy, soft-focus tome, it is rather refreshing to read about Mallarmé's financial and professional incompetence. Instead of idealising the poetic temperament above all else, this biographer occasionally expresses his disapproval of Mallarmé's ingratitude toward his grandmother and stepmother, his unrealistic attitude toward money; and his poor performance as a high-school English teacher. It is rather appalling to learn how often his friends in high places helped him keep his job.

This refreshing everydayness is not, however, matched by any deep historical recontextualisation. The portrait, like those offered by the vast majority of biographies of literary figures, is still mainly that of literary and artistic personalities, narrated from the point of view of the psychological individual, in the context of the family. Mallarmé's many friendships in the world of painters, musicians and writers are concisely and sensibly chronicled, but not reframed against a non-literary backdrop. The Commune, the Franco-Prussian War, the Eiffel Tower, anarchism, the Dreyfus Affair, the golden age of French imperialism – all are given one or two sentences, but Millan fails to defamiliarise the aesthetic focus of all previous work on Mallarmé. It would be interesting to look at the literary and artistic world from the outside as well as from the inside, or to see its intersections with larger political, social, economic and historical events. In Mallarmé's case, such a contextualisation of his deep investment in the aesthetic would have been illuminating. Even some of his own projects are described as though they required no comment. *La Dernière Mode*, the fashion magazine, is treated in two pages, with no discussion of what it meant for a poet with his metaphysical interests to write a fashion magazine, how other poets and writers were involved in similar ventures, where he got the dress patterns, how it linked up with contemporary industrial or commercial enterprises, what was happening in the fashion world etc. The name of Charles Worth is never mentioned. The huge variety of topics covered by Mallarmé's late prose would never be guessed from the ways in which it is described here.

What is good about this biography is its conscientious closeness to primary documents by Mallarmé and his intimates. But it achieves its narrative verisimilitude by never allowing such closeness to go to the point of raising issues of textuality, partiality and readability. These may be omissions that go with the territory of traditional biography, but, in the case of Mallarmé, it seems, at the very least, ironic. Rather than speculating about unconscious signification, discontinuity among documents or textual ambiguity, Millan sticks to facts for which there is evidence that can be construed as coherent. This sometimes leads him to dismiss in one sentence whole schools of secondary literature – particularly psychoanalytic criticism – but it is what enables him to appear to be presenting an uncluttered account of the 'facts' of a life. No life could seem more ordinary: white, male, middle-class heterosexual with wife, two children (and, later, mistress) struggles to make ends meet while seeking to move from the provinces to Paris, from which, when he finally gets there, he escapes more and more often to his summer home. Even the untimely deaths in his family (his mother, his sister and his son) were quite typical of the 19th century. A more ambitious biography, whether literarily or historically, would have ended up being longer. Perhaps someone will undertake one when the correspondence between Mallarmé and Méri Laurent (with whom he enjoyed a friendship both before and after they were lovers) becomes available from the year 2000.

As a short, useful reference work on Mallarmé's life, then, this biography fills a gap in English and provides more details than ever before. Even if it offers no new readings of Mallarmé's work, it describes that work with a certain tact, and weaves a description of the struggle to write into the fabric of a life of ill-health, financial worry, professional irritation and an unusual capacity for friendship. Perhaps it is impossible to engage with what is most challenging about Mallarmé's writing through traditional biography. In an age of grand demystifications, this portrait of an ordinary man may be the most demystifying approach of all.

Nevertheless, everything interesting still remains to be done on Mallarmé's life and times. The late prose cries out for a historicist (new or old) reading that would both research the Panama Canal and the women's fashion industry and come to grips with Mallarmé's textuality. The unfinished notes for 'The Book', in which Mallarmé tries to invent a total performance art (complete with entrance fees, instructions on folding the pages, the layout of chairs and a seasonal schedule) should be studied by theorists of performance. A historical study of group formation could analyse the transferential appeal of a Master who theorised his own absence (at length, every Tuesday in the Rue de Rome). Someone could connect the *Coup de dés* to the history of cyberspace. Someone could analyse Mallarmé's statement that human enterprises are divided between aesthetics and political economy and hold it up to Terry Eagleton's critique of 'the ideology of the aesthetic'. Someone could integrate Mallarmé into the history of Catholicism or mythology. Someone could contextualise the French disapproval of poetry that led parents to threaten to take their children out of the lycée in Tournon when they found out the English teacher had published in *Le Parnasse contemporain*.

But, perhaps more important, the odd fit between this poet's life and this poet's work, and between this biography and everything vital in Mallarmé criticism, only points to the difficulty inherent in any attempt to think about a life and a work as a coherent whole. On the one hand, such a project is immensely seductive. There is a genuine pleasure in mapping out the anamorphoses of biographical detail in poetic texts. On the other hand, such a project usually raises more questions than it answers. The difficulty as well as the appeal of biography as an approach to literature has been reinforced in recent years by debates over sexual and racial identity. How does knowledge of the race, class, religion, nationality, sexuality or gender of an author (or reader) affect the reading of the text? Are these things different from centuries and genres? What does it mean to have 'knowledge' of such things? Yet how could such 'knowledge' fail to affect the reading process? Or is biography only about what is specific to a particular individual? But, as these questions make clear, how can we know what is specific to a particular individual?

In the institutions of literary studies, it is often the authors about whom the least is known (Homer, Shakespeare) that are the most canonical. Was this what Mallarmé understood when he yearned for a text speaking on its own? Why is authority tied to the erasure of particularity? Why are some forms of particularity easier to erase than others? If these are the questions Mallarmé leaves us with, it is clear that they cannot be answered simply with, or simply without, biography.

18 August 1994

Back to the Wall

Nicholas Penny on Picture-Frames*

It is often assumed that easel pictures have always hung on walls, but in fact the backs of many small Renaissance panel paintings, both sacred and secular, were decorated, suggesting that they were designed to be handled as well as hung, and many portraits had lids so that their frames formed the sides of boxes in which the pictures could be safely stored, as well as making handy and attractive borders for the image. The picture-frame began to be an important part of interior decoration in Italy in the second half of the 16th century by which time easel pictures had become increasingly important as wall furniture.

In Venice the 'Sansovino frame', composed of scrolls and masks and swags, was derived from the stucco compartments that architects designed for frescos and reliefs on walls and vaults. It often also matched the carved ornamentation of chairs and tables. Elsewhere in Italy frames were made in which the mouldings nearest the picture were the most prominent and the rest of the structure stepped – and the ornament flowed – back towards the wall. Though inconvenient for many practical purposes, this type of arrangement helped to integrate the picture with its setting. Where numerous pictures were displayed in a single interior, sets of frames were designed which ensured that paintings, however different in size or character, looked well on the wall. The bold and fantastic frames carved for the Medici in Florence – the most famous early examples of this practice – were clearly designed by sculptors or architects.

Meanwhile, the tabernacle frame, which provided a sacred image with an entablature and sometimes a pediment and pilasters or columns, declined in importance. Although architectural, such frames seem to have had no close relationship to the architecture in which they were placed. Intended to isolate a sacred image, often with its own candle, within a domestic space, tabernacle frames had belonged to the picture. Increasingly, frames belonged chiefly to the room.

Painters often designed their own frames in the Renaissance, and they did so again in the 19th century, but the practice was unusual in

---

* Eva Mendgen, ed., *In Perfect Harmony: Picture and Frame 1850–1920* (Reaktion, 1995).

the 17th and 18th centuries. This may seem surprising, because it is striking how well paintings of this period look in frames made at the same date. Meticulous depictions of flowers or sober Dutch wives in crisp white ruffs are happiest bound by hard sharp dark mouldings with a taut skin of silky ebony, rosewood or tortoiseshell in the flat. The convivial portrait *en negligée*, or the broken chain of lovers in a sweetly disordered park, deserve the carved and gilded frames with restlessly curvaceous surface, outline and section that were made in mid-18th-century France.

Yet it could not be plausibly argued that these styles of frame evolved in response to the needs of particular styles of painting. The dark rectilinear frames reveal the same neat machined finish, techniques of veneering and exotic materials found in contemporary cabinets, while the French rococo frames were the work of sculptors who also carved ornamental wall-panelling, and were sometimes created by the leading designers of the luxury furnishings with which they danced in unison.

However well French 18th-century frames matched – or were matched by – contemporary paintings, they simply took the Old Masters over by force. If the prim Dutch matron entered an opulent Parisian hôtel she was divested of her dark suit and dressed for the ball. Poussin's *Worship of the Golden Calf* in the National Gallery, London, is shown in an exceptionally splendid frame that was made for it in Paris more than fifty years after it was painted. Its rolling section, scrolling ornament and contrasted textures and sheens give it a vivacity which upstages that of the dancing Israelites – and the fact that the painting has irrevocably darkened while the gilding is unusually well-preserved (and inevitably overdramatised by electric lighting) makes it all the more evident. Poussin himself is known to have recommended plain mouldings with matt gilding for his paintings.

A frame is often a vestige of the decorative scheme into which a painting was inserted and even if it now seems incongruous it often deserves affectionate regard as a manifestation of the prejudices of previous generations, which cling to all old things we are likely to love. The urge to divorce an old picture from a later frame is often greatest in the very circumstances in which history should be most respected, for it is the interior of the modern museum which exaggerates any incongruity. Were the frame which surrounds the Poussin to retain a cornice above it, consoles beside it and chairs beneath it, all carved and gilt in a style to match, it might, paradoxically, be more easily dissociated from the painting within it. Today, the frame demands attention because it is out of sympathy with both the painting and its setting.

Even more discordant is the sight of an Italian baroque frame with large open-work foliage and scrolls gesticulating against a plain wall. Such frames were often originally designed to blend with the broad patterns of a damask hanging. But Italian frames were not always extravagant. Those in the galleries of Roman palaces, where paintings were tightly packed, tended to be uniform, rectangular, relatively simple and designed to suit paintings that varied in style as well as in size. Eighteenth-century Roman mouldings of this type were so frequently copied by frame-makers in England and used in all sorts of setting that it is easily forgotten that they were designed by architects for a particular style of interior.

After about 1820 the frame still often constituted a part of a scheme of interior decoration, or indeed of architecture, as in the case of those signed by Schinkel for the picture gallery in Berlin, or by Giovanni Montiroli for the Cammuccini collection of Old Masters at Alnwick Castle, or by Stanford White for paintings by Abbot Thayer in the Freer Gallery in Washington. But the involvement of leading architects and sculptors declined: the public exhibition and the art dealer came to assume a dominant position in the art world and specialist frame-makers began to supply products appropriate for both. Frames chosen for exhibitions might be temporary, which encouraged economy, while at the same time a desire to attract attention, or to protect oneself from a near-neighbour's attempts to do so, encouraged the massive and the brash. Off-the-peg frames and standardised mouldings and decorations became commonplace; the kinds of ornament that previously would have been carved were now often imitated in 'composition' or in plaster of Paris, and were sometimes cut out by machine. For the first time, frames were made in imitation of those of previous periods. Some of these were ingenious variants or inspired pastiches, though most were merely crude simplifications, vulgar exaggerations or pedantic replicas. This increase in awareness of past styles eventually led to the collecting of old frames, which in turn made possible the first illustrated studies of frames and their history, published about a hundred years ago.

Recently, the literature on frames has expanded rapidly: the days are long past when the only reliable modern publication on the subject was Claus Grimm's succinct survey of 1977, *Alte Bilderrahmen*. There were major scholarly exhibitions at the Rijksmuseum in 1984 at the Art Institute of Chicago in 1986 and at the Metropolitan Museum, New York in 1990. These were museum initiatives but the stimulus for the revival of interest in the history of frames has often come from frame-makers and dealers – such as Paul Levi to whom the catalogue of the Metropolitan's exhibition of Italian Renaissance frames is dedicated or Timothy Newbery who is one of its co-authors. Dealers have also mounted small scholarly exhibitions in both London and Paris. The most splendid of all recent books on frames *La Cornice italiana: dal Rinascimeno al Neo Classico* (Electa, 1992) which reproduces in excellent colour many of the finest frames in museums in all parts of Italy, and contains illuminating introductory essays and catalogue entries by Enrico Colle and Patrizia Zambrano was edited by one of the leading Italian frame dealers Franco Sabatelli. Wiggins have sponsored learned articles on frames in the *Burlington Magazine* and another London dealer, Paul Mitchell, is the author of the best brief survey of Italian frames in a 1984 volume of *Furniture History* and of an appendix to the catalogue of the Wright of Derby exhibition at the Tate in 1990, which is devoted to that artist's frames (a supplement which all major monographic catalogues should try to emulate).

Few of these exhibitions and publications are concerned with the 19th century. *In Perfect Harmony* is indeed the first book devoted to the investigation of picture-frames of that period. Frame-makers and dealers are not represented in it, and this may explain the lack of information on materials and techniques, as well as the absence of the sectional diagrams which have been so valuable a feature of the recent scholarship. Instead, the book is more concerned with aesthetics and the meaning of the frame. Of the 11 essays it contains, those on Van Gogh, on 'Les XX' (the Belgian avant garde of the Fin de Siècle) and on German and Austrian artists (Lenbach, Böcklin, Stuck, Klimt) are the most valuable – which is appropriate since the book was published in association with an exhibition of the same title shown at the Van Gogh Museum in Amsterdam earlier this year and now at the Kunstforum, Vienna until 19 November. The emphasis is on artists, not on frame-makers, and mostly on artists who were reacting against the norm – who were against routine exhibition mouldings, against the opulence of dealers' frames, against mass-production, even against gilding – and at times we may feel in need of a fuller account of the conventions they opposed. But the scholarship is very impressive, faltering only in the section on the Pre-Raphaelites and other British artists.

In his stimulating preliminary essay Wolfgang Kemp gives special attention to the highly controversial frame that Caspar David Friedrich designed for his *Cross in the Mountains*. It consists of a gothic arch composed of palm fronds, and a predella decorated with wheat, a vine and a diagrammatic eye. In 1808 Friedrich exhibited the painting in this frame in his studio before sending it to Tetschen Castle, where, he claimed, he intended it to serve as the chapel altarpiece (it was in fact hung in a bedroom). The design of the frame did not, however, originate in response to the painting's projected function as an altarpiece, but in the artist's desire to endow landscape with a sacred status. It is an extension of the painting, amplifying its meaning.

Many artists of the later 19th century designed frames with similar additions: symbolic plants, gothic texts, Egyptian ornament and so on. And tabernacle frames were revived, not only for subjects of orthodox devotion but increasingly, in the last decades of the century, to enshrine ideal beauty, the artist's muse, or a terrible vision. The use of such frames made it clear that Rossetti's *Blessed Damozel*, Franz von Stuck's *Die Svende*, Bastien-Lepage's *Sarah Bernhardt* or Leighton's *Bath of Psyche* demanded special attention or at least a central position – indeed Bastien-Lepage's frame is made of steel, which would in itself have encouraged other pictures to keep their distance. Leighton's tabernacle frames are Greek in style (with Ionic capitals of the Bassae type), not in order to match a neo-Greek interior but to suit his Greek heroines. He was unusual not only in implying a comparison between architectural form and statuesque figures, but in making his frames an extension of an architectural space within the picture (reviving, here, a Renaissance idea). Old photographs reproduced in this book give an idea of how such paintings were displayed – Rossetti's narcotic religiosity distinctly ill at ease in Frederick Leyland's genteel drawing-room, or Stuck's *Die Svende* mounted on an altar within the theatrical interior of the artist's villa from which all suggestions of domesticity have been drained away.

Artists in this period may have been obliged to submit to the humiliating competition of the gigantic annual exhibitions, but many of the most successful were able to compensate for this by a special display of their works in their own environment. *In Perfect Harmony* takes us into Franz von Lenbach's villa in the 1870s, where Renaissance bric-à-brac, in suffocating profusion, postured as spiritual heirlooms, and into the eerily empty blue room of Fernand Knopff's villa, where one painting hung – his portrait made in 1887 of his sister wearing an ivory-coloured dress and standing against a pearl grey wall. It was framed in slender silver mouldings, above a shelf on which a fragile porcelain vase and a tennis racket were arranged with sacramental care. In the Renaissance the tabernacle frame had been intended to isolate he sacred image within a room, and it sometimes served that purpose in the 19th century, but on occasion a whole room could be turned into a sacred space, a secular shrine. We catch a whiff here of the high-minded self-indulgence of today's avant-garde 'installations'.

Most of the radical ideas about framing in the last decades of the 19th century which are documented in this book were conceived by artists, and chiefly, often exclusively, with reference to the needs of their own paintings. Whistler also had views about wall colours and hangings; and both in his own house and in special exhibitions, as well as in the home of one indulgent (but eventually exasperated) patron, he designed or modified whole rooms so that, together with the frames, they would complement his paintings. The 'XX' and the Vienna Secession had similar ambitions. As in previous centuries paintings and frames were integrated into schemes of interior decoration, but now the environments were controlled by the painter, rather than created by architects and sculptors.

Many of Whistler's reeded frames have survived, as have a few of Degas's similarly severe mouldings, although gilded as he had not intended. But only one example of a painted moulding remains round a Van Gogh, and the plain white frames favoured by the Impressionists have vanished almost without trace. Of the numerous early Impressionist paintings shown at the Hayward Gallery earlier this year none retained its original frame (although one, a Guillaumin from the Musée Fabre in Montpellier, does have something comparably simple). On the other hand, the majority of the large pictures in the same exhibition which were shown at the Salon in the 1860s and 1870s retained the frames chosen for that occasion (presumably by the artists), almost all of them heavy, with deep, often fluted, hollows and with rich bayleaf or oakleaf ornament on the outer mouldings. This is not difficult to explain: the big Salon pictures were acquired by or for municipal museums which had neither the motive nor the means to reframe them, whereas the Impressionist pictures passed through the hands of dealers and private owners, each one eager to eradicate the traces of his or her predecessor. Moreover, the original extremist white frames can never have been easy to integrate in a drawing-room.

The Impressionists' ideas about frames changed rapidly, and modern commentators, if they were less reverent, would admit that the ideas were inconsistent. Camille Pisarro's opinions are carefully recorded in a chapter of this book. He moved from white frames in 1877, to frames which complemented the colour schemes of his paintings (a green frame for a red sunset and so on) in 1879, but wanted to return to white frames in 1882 when, together with his dealer Durand-Ruel, he devised a new type of white frame which had a gilded outer moulding. In 1887, exhibiting with Georges Petit, he wanted (but didn't get) a broad white border set within an oak outer frame ornamented with gilded laurels. By this date he was no longer averse to gilding, and there is evidence that the standard frame for Monet's paintings of the same period – presumably tolerated and perhaps sanctioned by the artist himself – was the typically lavish dealer's frame, 'éternel cadre doré, à chicorées et à choux', reviled by the avant-garde critics.

The great mystery in the story of Impressionism is which artist or dealer first hit on the solution of using second-hand French frames of the late 17th or early 18th century which were then either partly stripped down to the white gesso or partly overpainted in grey, to stifle the gilding. These old frames were inexpensive and the solution perhaps originated as an economy, but it soon came to be regarded as chic, and was widely adopted. Deplored by some art historians as a compromise with bourgeois taste, these frames can be both subtle and original in character. Their condition and age as well as style may act as a comment on the picture within, at once asserting the place of such paintings within a great French tradition (something especially dear to Renoir) and emphasising their departure from tradition, their matt (originally unvarnished) finish, broken tenure and light palette.

In the 1860s some artists, including Anselm Feuerbach and Dante Gabriel Rossetti, employed imitations of 16th-century Italian frames for paintings made in a 16th-century style and with figures in 16th-century costume. Franz von Lenbach not only found genuine antique frames for his paintings but, we learn in this book, actually made pictures to match such frames. By the end of the century, when the Impressionists were perhaps already adopting second-hand French frames, a few fashionable portrait-painters, especially those who venerated Velasquez, seem occasionally to have adopted 17th-century Spanish and Italian frames – a good example may be found on Sargent's splendid portrait of Mrs Hirsch, currently on loan to the Tate. Meanwhile, inspired by the example of Wilhelm von Bode in Berlin (Bode was in turn influenced by the leading Italian antique dealers), museums began gradually to try to find old frames for old paintings. This became the National Gallery's policy soon after the Great War, and in 1932 fine Italian Renaissance frames collected as furniture in the previous century by the Victoria and Albert Museum were fitted round pictures in Trafalgar Square.

Two or three avant-garde artists also seem to have taken an interest in old frames (Picasso liked old Spanish ones) and to have used them, sometimes in order to achieve an ironic effect. But more of them have been averse to frames of all kinds. It may at first seem that the 20th century's most notable contribution to the history of the picture-frame is the attempt to do away with it altogether, or to rely on minimal, unmoulded borders of bare wood or aluminium. But as the century draws to a close the second-hand frame gains in favour everywhere. Every museum and every wealthy collector now wants period frames for their Old Masters and, if there is none of the right size, a frame is adapted or a copy is made of an authentic model and given a distressed finish. A chapter of *In Perfect Harmony* by Louis van Tilborgh traces the bizarre framing history of the pictures inherited by Van Gogh's sister-in-law, concluding with the Van Gogh Museum's recent unhappy attempt to reconstitute the artist's original ideas. Meanwhile, museums in Britain and the United States have been putting the artist's pictures into rough 17th-century mouldings.

To find the right frame, one which draws attention not to itself but to the painting, one which is acceptable in the company of other frames, one which has the tone of gold that will make a blue sky glow, or sufficient rigidity to contain, and contrast with, any rush or bustle in the composition, or enough depth to make the pictorial space seem deeper, or enough small ornament in low relief to help grand forms to expand, is a fascinating and frustrating task. The right frame for an old painting is indeed likely to be an old one, yet it need not date from the same time and place as the painting. The new curatorial pedantry which insists on authentic period costume is offensive to the poetic mind. It is also ridiculously expensive.

But suppose a patron of determined taste were to commission from an architect or sculptor with sensitivity to mouldings and ornament a uniform frame for his or her collection. This solution still has its attractions, especially if we value a harmonious relationship between paintings and architecture, and want pictures to look truly at home within a room. It was, after all, precisely this concern that conditioned the creation of the great frames of the 16th, 17th and 18th centuries, the very works which have now become the most expensive form of antique furniture on the market. The old frames we strive to match with old paintings were made to fit rooms which have mostly vanished.

21 September 1995

IDEAS

Peacocking

Jerry Fodor on Dawkins and Darwin

'How do you get to Carnegie Hall?' 'Practice, practice.' Here's a different way: start anywhere you like and take a step at random. If it's a step in the right direction, I'll say 'warmer'; in which case repeat the process from your new position. If I say 'colder', go back a step and repeat from there. This is a kind of procedure that they call 'hill climbing' in the computer-learning trade (hence, I suppose, the title of Richard Dawkins's new book★). It's guaranteed to get you where you're going so long as the distance between is finite. (And so long as there are no insurmountable obstacles or 'local maxima' in the way: nothing is perfect.)

Hill climbing is often the theory of choice when a scientist's problem is to explain how something got to somewhere you wouldn't otherwise have expected it to be. That's in part because it's such an abstract and general sort of theory. All it requires is a source of random variation, a filter to select among the variants, and some 'memory' mechanism to ensure that the selected variations accumulate. In all other respects, you're free to adapt it to whatever is worrying you.

For example, the 'here' and 'there' needn't be spatially defined. They might be, respectively, the undifferentiated primal, protoplasmic slime and the vast, intricate proliferation of species of organisms that now obtains. Darwinism (or, anyhow, the adaptationist part of Darwinism) is a hill-climbing account of the phenomenon of speciation: genetic mutation takes the place of your random milling about, the inherited genetic endowments of successive generations of organisms correspond to the succession of positions that you occupy between here and Carnegie; and, instead of my shaping your path with gentle verbal cues, natural selection determines the direction of evolution by killing off mutations that happen to reduce organic fitness.

It all sounds pretty plausible. It might even be true. But the fact that a hill-climbing model could, in mathematical principle, find a way from where you started off to where you ended up, doesn't at all imply that

★ *Climbing Mount Improbable* (Viking, 1996).

you (or your species) actually got there that way. I could just have told you where Carnegie Hall is, and you could have got there by following my instructions ('Directed Evolution'). Or I could have picked you up and carried you there ('Interventionism'). Or you could have started out at Carnegie Hall, in which case the question wouldn't have arisen ('Preformation'). No doubt, other possibilities will occur to you. In the present case, one might reasonably wonder whether we did, after all, get to be us in the way that Darwinian adaptationism says that we did; it's reasonable to want to see the evidence.

Especially so because the scientific success of the hill-climbing style of explanation has often been underwhelming in other areas where it has been tried. Classical economics (by which Darwin was apparently much influenced) wanted to use it to account for the organisation of markets. In a system of exchange where gizmos are produced with randomly differing efficiencies, canny consumers will filter for the gizmos that are best and cheapest. Gizmos that are too expensive to buy, or too cheap to sell at a profit, will be screened out automatically. Eventually an equilibrium will be achieved that comports, as well as can be, with all the interests involved.

That's a nice story, too. But in the event, what often happens is that the big gizmo-makers buy out the little gizmo-makers and suppress their patents. If there's still more than one gizmo-maker left in the field, they compete marginally by painting their gizmos bright colours, or paying some airhead to praise them on television. The evolution of gizmos therefore grinds to a halt. Whichever producer a consumer decides to buy his gizmos from, he finds that they don't work, or don't last, or cost too much.

For another example, consider a version of hill-climbing theory that used to be popular in psychology. How does behaviour get organised? How, for example, do you get from being a babbling baby to being a fluent speaker of English? Here's how, according to B.F. Skinner and the tradition of 'reinforcement theory': babbling is vocal behaviour that's produced at random. When you happen to make a noise that sounds sort of like the local dialect, 'society' reinforces you; and your propensity to make that sort of sound (or better, your propensity to make that sort of sound in those sorts of circumstances) increases correspondingly. Keep it up and soon you'll be able to say 'Carnegie Hall' or 'Jascha Heifetz' or any other of the innumerable things that being able to speak English allows you to. Skinner used to complain, to people who didn't like his story about learning, that he was just doing for the formation of behaviour what Darwin did for the formation of species. There was, I think, some justice in that complaint, but it's an argument that cuts both ways.

In any event, language learning doesn't work by Skinnerian hill climbing: language learners don't make their errors at random in the course of the acquisition process. Rather, as Noam Chomsky famously pointed out, the grammatical and phonological hypotheses about language structure that children think to try out are sharply endogenously constrained. 'Who Mummy love?' is recognisably baby talk, but 'love Mummy who?' is not; it just isn't the kind of thing children say in the course of acquiring English. Ergo, it's not a kind of thing that society is required to filter out in the course of 'shaping' the child's verbal behaviour. But why isn't it if children are hill climbing towards the mastery of English grammar, and making mistakes at random as they go?

So there are at least two cases where, pretty clearly, applications of hill-climbing models tell less than all there is to be told about how a system gets organised. These examples have something strikingly in common. Hill climbing wants a random source of candidates to filter; but, in the market case and the language acquisition case, it appears that there are 'hidden constraints' on what candidates for filtering ever get proposed. The market doesn't produce its gizmos at random, and the child doesn't produce its verbalisations at random either. The market is inhibited by restraint of trade, the child by (quite possibly innate) conditions on the kinds of language that human beings are able to learn and use. No doubt, in both cases, there is some residual random variability, and correspondingly, some filtering which serves to smooth rough edges; so hill climbing gets a sort of vindication. But it's pyrrhic if, as practitioners in economics and psycholinguistics tend to suppose these days, the hidden constraints are doing most of the work.

Clearly the track record of hill-climbing explanations outside biology isn't what you'd call impeccable. What, then, about speciation? Nobody with any sense doubts that adaptation is part of the truth about evolution; but are there, maybe, 'hidden constraints' at work here, too? Or is the environmental filtering of random mutation most of what there is to how creatures evolve? Nobody loses absolutely all of the time. Maybe speciation is where hill climbing wins.

There is, in fact, currently something of a storm over just this issue, the vehemence of which Dawkins's book is too inclined to understate. Palaeontologists, since Darwin's own time, have often complained about what looks, from an anti-adaptationist perspective, like an embarrassing lack of smooth gradations from species to species in the geological record. Maybe evolution gets from place to place by relatively big jumps ('saltations'), the intermediate options being ruled out by hidden constraints on what biological forms are possible. Something like this idea is at the heart of the current enthusiasm for evolution by 'punctate equilibria'. If you want to get to Carnegie, don't bother with exploring the intermediate loci: take a jet.

Dawkins doesn't make much of this sort of option; he's too busy assuring his lay audience that everything is perfectly fine chez classical adaptationism. Issues about evolution have become so politicised that a popularising biologist must be tempted to make a policy of *pas devant les enfants*. Dawkins has succumbed a bit to this temptation. It's a disservice to the reader, who thereby misses much of the fun. For a corrective, try Niles Eldredge's book *Reinventing Darwin*.*

If classical adaptationism is true, then, at a minimum, the route from species A to its successor species B must be composed of viable intermediate forms which are of generally increasing fitness; there must be, in Dawkins's metaphor, smooth gradients leading up the hill that adaptation climbs. Much of his book is devoted to an (admirable) attempt to make the case that there could have been such viable intermediaries in the evolution of vision and of winged flight. Dawkins doesn't (and shouldn't) claim that any of these intermediate creatures are known to have existed. But he is pretty convincing that they might have, for all that biochemistry, physiology, embryology and computer modelling have to tell us. The naive objection to adaptationism is that random mutation couldn't have made anything as intricate as an eye. Dawkins's answer is that, sure it could; there's a physiologically possible path from bare sensitivity to light to the kind of visual system that we've got, and overall fitness would plausibly increase and accumulate as evolution traverses the path. It appears, in fact, that there may be several such paths; eyes have been independently reinvented many times in the course of evolution.

It is, however, one thing to show that evolution might have been mostly adaptation; it is another thing to show that it actually was. Many readers may be disappointed that Dawkins doesn't discuss the evolution of the piece of biology that they are likely to have most at heart: namely, human cognitive capacities. This is, on anybody's story, one of the places where apparent lack of intermediate forms looks most glaring. Cognition is too soft to leave a palaeontological record. And, *pace* sentimental propaganda on behalf of chimpanzees and dolphins, there aren't any types of creature currently around whose cognitive capacities look even remotely similar to ours. Moreover, there is a prima facie

---

*Weidenfeld, 1995.

plausible argument that hidden constraints might play a special role in the evolution of a creature's psychological traits as opposed, say, to the evolution of its bodily form.

It's truistic that natural selection acts to filter genetic variation only insofar as the latter is expressed by corresponding alterations of a creature's relatively large-scale structure (alterations, for example, of the organs that mediate its internal economy or its environmental interactions). The slogan is: genetic variants are selected for their phenotypic fitness. This holds, of course, for the case of nervous systems, too: genetic endowments build neurological structures which natural selection accepts or rejects as it sees fit. Suppose that there is indeed relatively unsystematic variation not only in the genetic determinants of neurological structure, but also in the corresponding neurological phenotypes. Still, brain structures themselves are selected for the fitness of the psychological capacities that they support. They're selected, one might say, not for their form but for their function. And nothing general – I mean *nothing* general – is known about the processes by which neurological alterations can occasion changes of psychological capacities.

Gradually lengthening the giraffe's neck should gradually increase its reach; that seems sufficiently transparent. But it's wide open what tumultuous saltations gradual increase in (as it might be) brain size or the density of neural connections might cause in the evolving cognitive capacities of a species. The upshot is that even if we knew for sure that both genetic endowments and neurological phenotypes vary in a way that is more or less random and incremental, as adaptationism requires, it wouldn't begin to follow that the variation of psychological traits or capacities is random and incremental too. As things now stand, it's perfectly possible that unsystematic genetic variation results in correspondingly unsystematic alteration of neurophysiological phenotypes; but that the consequent psychological effects are neither incremental nor continuous. For all anybody knows, our minds could have got here largely at a leap even if our brains did not. In fact, insofar as there is any evidence at all, it seems to suggest that reading brain structures onto mental capacities must substantially amplify neurological discontinuities. Our brains are, by any gross measure, physiologically quite similar to those of creatures whose minds are nonetheless, by any gross measure, unimaginably less intelligent.

Dawkins likes to 'insist . . . that wherever in nature there is a sufficiently powerful illusion of good design for some purpose, natural selection is the only known mechanism that can account for it.' He's right, I think, but this is another of those two-edged swords. The conclusion might be that adaptation really is most or all of what there is to evolution; or it might be that we don't actually know a lot about the etiology of what appears to be biological good design. Dawkins is inclined to bet on the first horse, but it's not hard to find quite reputable scientists who are inclined to bet on the second. Either way, it's a shame not to tell the reader that what's going on is, in fact, a horse race and not a triumphal procession.

Dawkins is the kind of scientist who disapproves of philosophy but can't stop himself trying to do some. That's quite a familiar syndrome. I should say a few words about what I'm afraid he takes to be the philosophical chapters of his book. They are, in my view, a lot less interesting than the biology. Dawkins says, rightly, that Darwinism teaches us that the biological population of the world wasn't made for our comfort, amusement or edification. 'We need, for purposes of scientific understanding, to find a less human-centred view of the natural world.' Right on. But then he spoils it by asking, in effect, if it's not all for us, who (or what) is it all for? This is a bad question, to which only bad answers are forthcoming.

The bad answer Dawkins offers in the present book follows the same line that he took in *The Selfish Gene*: it's all in aid of the DNA. 'What are living things *really* [*sic*] for . . . The answer is DNA. It is a profound and precise answer and the argument is watertight.' The idea is that, from the gene's point of view, organisms are just 'survival machines' whose purpose is to house and propagate the DNA that shaped them. A creature's only function in life (or in death, for that matter; see Dawkins's adaptationist treatment of the evolution of altruism) is to mediate the proliferation, down through the generations, of the genes that it carries. Likewise for the parts of creatures: 'The peacock's beak, by picking up food that keeps the peacock alive, is a tool for indirectly spreading instructions for making peacock beaks' (i.e. for spreading the peacock's DNA). It is, according to Dawkins, the preservation of the genetic instructions themselves that is the point of the operation.

But that doesn't work, since you could tell the story just as well from the point of view of any other of the creature's heritable traits; there's nothing special, in this respect, about its genetic endowment. For example, here's the Cycle of Generation as it appears from the point of view of the peacock's selfish beak:

> Maybe genes think what beaks are for is to help make more genes, but what do they know about philosophy? Beaks see life steadily and they see it whole, and they think what genes are for is to help make more beaks. The apparatus – a survival machine,

if that amuses you – works like this: beaks help to ensure the proliferation of peacocks, which help to ensure the proliferation of peacock DNA, which helps to ensure
the proliferation of instructions to make more peacocks' beaks, which helps to make
more peacock beaks. The beaks are the point; the beaks are what it's all 'for'. The rest
is just mechanics.

What's wrong with this nonsense is that peacocks' beaks don't have
points of view (or wants, or preferences), selfish or otherwise. And
genes don't either, not even 'unconsciously', though Dawkins is often
confused between denying that evolutionary design is literally conscious and denying that it is literally design. It's the latter that's the
issue. All that happens is this: microscopic variations cause macro-
scopic effects, as an indirect consequence of which sometimes the
variants proliferate and sometimes they don't. That's all there is; there's
a lot of 'because' out there, but there isn't any 'for'.

In a certain sense, none of the teleological fooling around actually
matters (which is, I guess, why Dawkins is prepared to indulge in it so
freely). When you actually start to do the science, the metaphors drop
out and statistics take over. So I wouldn't fuss about it except that, like
Dawkins, I take science philosophically seriously; good science is as
close as we ever get to the literal truth about how things are. I'm dis-
pleased with Dawkins's pop gloss on evolutionary theory because I
think it gets in the way of seeing how science shows the world to be; and
that, I would have thought, is what the populariser of science-as-
philosophy should most seek to convey. Dawkins is rather proud of his
hard-headedness (he writes 'sensitive' in sneer-quotes to show how
tough he is); but in fact his naturalism doesn't go deep enough.
Certainly it doesn't go as deep as Darwin's.

It's very hard to get this right because our penchant for teleology –
for explaining things on the model of agents, with their beliefs, goals
and desires – is inveterate, and probably itself innate. We are forever
wanting to know what things are for, and we don't like having to take
Nothing for an answer. That gives us a wonderful head start on understanding the practical psychology of ourselves and our conspecifics; but
it is one of the (no doubt many) respects in which we aren't kinds of
creatures ideally equipped for doing natural science. Still, I think that
sometimes, out of the corner of an eye, 'at the moment which is not of
action or inaction', one can glimpse the true scientific vision: austere,
tragic, alienated and supremely beautiful. A world that isn't *for*
anything; a world that is just there.

18 April 1996

Demonising Nationalism

Tom Nairn

Two-and-a-half years ago *Time* Magazine published a feature on the future of the world. Being on the cover of *Time* has always been an American honour: the cover of 6 August 1990 carried a portrait of Nationalism.

An elementary tombstone-shaped visage of plasticine, or possibly mud, glowers out from an equally rudimentary map of Central Europe. One primitive, soulless eye is located near Vilnius. Beneath the emergent snout a hideous, gash-like mouth splits the continent open from Munich to Kiev before dribbling its venom down across Yugoslavia and Romania. No semiotic subtlety is needed to decode the image, since a closer look shows the teeth inside the gash read simply 'Nationalism'. But in case anyone failed to register that, the whole image was crowned with a title in 72-point scarlet lettering 'OLD DEMON'.

It wasn't an in-depth retrospect – it hardly could have been at that date – more an early, apprehensive glance during the first round of the ex-Soviet and post-Yugoslav tumult. In fact, it was what most Western or metropolitan opinion really expected, on the basis of these early stirrings. Some time before the Baltic peoples, the Ukrainians or the Georgians had actually established their independence, when virtually all Western diplomacy was still devoted to shoring up Gorbachev and Yugoslavia, a pervasive sense of doom already lurked in the North Atlantic mind. It was summed up in a *Guardian* leader of the same vintage: 'Don't Put Out More Flags!' This editorial did become famous enough to endure mild mockery, but only because it was characteristically over the top, exaggerating what most readers instinctively felt: that if enough new national flags were put out the Old Demon would wreak havoc with the New World Order. The second springtime of nations was, in this glum perspective, already turning to winter, and a bad one at that.

Anyone could see from the outset that there were at least three principal strands in the gigantic upheaval against Communism. There was a popular, democratic rebellion against one-party autocracy and state terror. There was an economic revulsion against the anti-capitalist command economies which for forty years had imposed forced-march development on the East. And thirdly there was the national mould into which these revolts were somehow inevitably flowing – the new salience, in post-Communist society, of the ethnic, or (as in Bosnia) of the ethnic-religious.

The *Time-Guardian* perspective on this triad is that the third element will most likely end by confining, endangering or even aborting the first two. And that perspective is what I am primarily objecting to – the instinctive notion that No 3 in the list is there by unfortunate accident, the bad news which has resurfaced alongside the good, an Old Adam who refuses to let the Angel of Progress get on with it. The conclusion to the *Time* article accompanying the front cover puts this point as well as anything else has, in terms which, since then, have been echoed thousands of times in tones of mounting hysteria: 'Not since Franz Ferdinand's assassination have conditions been so favourable for an enduring new order to replace the empires of the past. With a unified Germany locked in the embrace of democratic Europe, and the Soviet Union re-examining its fundamental values, the way is open for an era of peace and liberty – *but only so long as the old demons do not escape again.*'

But escape they did, notably in what used to be Yugoslavia and especially – as if some truly profound irony of history was working itself out – in and around the very town where Franz Ferdinand perished in 1914. The general view or new received wisdom soon became set in concrete: nationalism is upsetting everything. It has ruined the End of History which has come back like some evil shade, mainly in order to spoil the State Department's victory celebrations.

There were always serious difficulties in store in the East for both democracy and capitalism, of course, and no serious commentator has ignored them. But what has made these insoluble, according to the received wisdom, is the return and dominance of the third force – the atavistic, incalculable force of the ethnic revival, compelling peoples to place blood before reasonable progress and individual rights. Three years ago it already felt as if this might be the story: mysterious unfinished business of Eastern nationality wrecks any 'enduring new order'. And so it has proved. We (in the West) now face a prospect of interminable Balkan and post-Soviet disorder, where forms of demented chauvinism and intolerance risk arresting progress altogether. Putting out many new flags leads only to *etnicko čišćenje*, 'ethnic cleansing'.* Unless

---

* The infamous phrase owes its general currency to José Maria Mendiluce, a senior official of the United Nations refugee agency UNHCR. In April 1992 he accidentally witnessed the expulsion and massacre of the Muslim population of Zvornik, a border town between Serbia and Bosnia,

civilisation intervenes, the newly-liberated nations may end up by replacing nascent democracy with forms of nationalist dictatorship like those prefigured in Gamsakhurdia's Georgia or the Serbia of Slobodan Milosevic. As for economics, the consequences can hardly be anything but intensified backwardness.

This dreary tale is over-familiar: what 'civilised' coverage of Eastern folly perceives is primarily a re-emergence of archaism. It rarely occurs to the editorialists or reporters concerned that this enlightened, liberal perspective on the great change may itself be archaic. Yet I believe it is. Whether or not old demons are returning to haunt anyone in Bosnia and Nagorny-Karabakh, there can be no doubt that old theories – the conventional wisdom of the day before yesterday – have come back to haunt and distort Western interpretations of what is happening. This wisdom is easily dated. One need only head for the nearest available library shelf groaning beneath a set of *Encyclopaedia Britannica*. Turn to 'Socio-Economic Doctrines and Reform Movements'. The signature H.K. stands for Hans Kohn, a prominent writer in the Forties on the political history of nationalism.

The thesis which Kohn argued rested mainly on a distinction between Western and Eastern nationalism. The former was original, institutional, liberal and good. The latter was reactive, envious, ethnic, racist and generally bad. Western-model nation-states like Britain, France and America had invented political nationalism. But, Kohn argued, these societies had also limited and qualified it, linking it to certain broader, more universal ideals. Nationalism may have been a child of Western Enlightenment; but that very fact enabled the original enlightened countries to transcend it at least partially. As time passed, in spite of various imperialist adventures, a measure of tolerance and internationalism came to moderate any remaining crudities of Anglo-French nationalism.

Not so in the East. By the 'East' I think Kohn really meant the rest of the world, typified by Central and Eastern Europe. He was talking about all those other societies which from the 18th century onwards have suffered the impact of the West, and been compelled to react against it. That reaction bred a different kind of national spirit: resentful, backward-looking, detesting the Western bourgeoisie even while trying to imitate it – the sour and vengeful philosophy of the second or third-born. It was this situation (he claimed) which generated genuinely narrow nationalism.

while returning from a meeting with Slobodan Milosevic. Details are given in *The Death of Yugoslavia* (1995) by Laura Silber and Allan Little, pp. 245–7 and 296–8 (on Srebrenica).

Countries were hurled into the developmental race without time to mature the requisite institutions and cadres. Hence they were forced to mobilise in other ways. The intellectuals and soldiers who took charge there needed an adrenalin-rich ideology to realise their goals, and found it in a shorthand version of the Western national spirit. This was blood-based nationality, a heroic and exclusive cult of people and state founded upon custom, speech, faith, colour, cuisine and whatever else was found available for packaging.

Though originally drawn to the West, the Germans had ended by succumbing to an Eastern-style package. It was their blood-cult, developed into a form of eugenic insanity, which threatened to drown the Enlightenment inheritance altogether after 1933. Nazism was mercifully (though only just) defeated in 1945. Out of it, however, came the experience which stamped a lasting impression of nationalism's meaning on both the Western and the Communist mind. Nazism may in truth have been a form of genetic imperialism – in its bizarre, pseudo-scientific fashion universal (or at least would-be universal) in meaning – but its nationalist origins were undeniable, and keenly felt by all its victims. So its sins were inevitably visited upon nationality-politics as such. Since the largest, most important *ethnos* in Europe had gone mad in that particular way, the ethnic as such must remain for ever suspect.

Such is the mentality which the post-'89 events have again brought to the surface. Instead of prompting a search for new theories to account for the extraordinary transformation of the world, these events have by and large resurrected the old ones. On the whole it seems to me that theory has contributed astonishingly little to an understanding of the New World Order, or Disorder, as Ken Jowitt, like nearly everyone else, calls it in the title of his interesting if eccentric 1991 study. The greatest revolution in global affairs since the epoch of world war is currently being explained almost wholly in terms of *Time* Magazine's Old Demons. Somehow a new age seems to have been born without any new ogres.

The creaky old ideological vehicles trundled out to cope with the post-Soviet and Balkan upheavals explain nothing whatever about their subjects. Gore-laden pictures of ethnic anarchy, of the Abyss and the Doom-to-come, start off by obscuring what is, so far, easily the most significant feature of the new world disorder. Since 1988 the post-Communist convulsions have drawn in about forty different nationalities and a population of well over three hundred million in an area comprising about one-fifth of the world. Thanks to the holding operation in Tiananmen Square they did not embrace an actual majority of the world's population, but it's surely reasonable to think that they will end by doing so.

When this scale and those numbers are kept in mind, the most impressive fact is surely not how much the transformation has cost in terms of either life or social and economic destruction. It is how astoundingly, how unbelievably little damage has been done. In one of the few efforts made at countering conventional hysteria the *Economist* did try last September to estimate loss of life in the ex-Soviet empire, and published a map showing that probably about three thousand-plus had perished, mostly in Georgia, Tajikistan and in the course of the war between Armenia and Azerbaijan. 'Fewer than most people think,' it concluded, and far less serious than what was happening in one small part of the Balkans. Social and economic disaster had been brought about by the collapse of the old Soviet-style economies, aggravated – rather than caused – by the political breakaways and national disputes.

This impression will be reinforced if any concrete timescale or historical memory is brought into the picture. The Old Demon mythology is essentially timeless – a dark or counter-millennium of re-emergent sin. In actual time the reflorescence of ethnic nationhood has followed a forty-year period during which humanity cowered in the shadow of imminent extinction. The demonologies of that epoch (anti-capitalism and anti-Communism) at least rested on something real, an array of missiles and other hardware which any serious clash between the empires – or even any sufficiently serious accident – could have activated, with the genuinely apocalyptic results everyone now seems (understandably enough) to have exiled from recollection.

But the old frozen *mentalité* did not vanish with the missiles. Instead it has found the temporary surrogate devil of nationalism. Another End of the World has been located: Armageddon has been replaced by the ethnic Abyss. It is a pretty feeble substitute, in the obvious sense that, even if some worst-possible-case scenario were to unfold – what Misha Glenny calls a 'Third Balkan War' or a Russo-Ukrainian war over the Crimea, or the break-up of the Indian state, or whatever – the consequences would not, by the standards of 1948 to 1988, be all that serious. Nobody would have to worry about taking refuge on another planet.

Almost by definition there is a great deal of anarchy in the new disorder, and no sign of its coming to an end. But there is (I would suggest) no abyss, save the ideological one in metropolitan craniums. As Benedict Anderson says in another of the more critical contributions to the debate (also entitled 'The New World Disorder'), the key misconception is that what's going on is essentially '"fragmentation" and "disintegration" – with all the menacing, pathological connotations these words bring with them. This language makes us forget the decades or centuries of violence out of which Frankensteinian "integrated states" such as the United Kingdom of 1900, which included all of Ireland, were constructed . . . Behind the language of "fragmentation" lies always a Panglossian conservatism that likes to imagine that every status quo is nicely normal.' But as Anderson and anyone else making this kind of objection knows all too well, the immediate response to it is bitter recrimination. One is at once accused of apologising for savagery, or of indifference to the escalating Balkan wars. An appeal to Western Governments and the Secretary-General of the United Nations was published in the *New York Review of Books* last month demanding that the world take action to stop the Yugoslav wars: 'If democracies acquiesce in violations of human rights on such a massive scale they will undermine their ability to protect these rights anywhere in the post-Cold War world. And then, when, as has happened many times before, an armed hoodlum kicks our own doors ajar, there will be no one to lift a finger in our defence or raise a voice.'

In this climate, to suggest that the nationalist course of history after 1989 may on the whole be preferable to what went before, and may not be treatable by any recourse to the old multinational or internationalist recipes, is to risk virtual excommunication. One must be lining up with the armed hoodlums. One is either a dupe of Demons like Tudjman and Karadzic or some sort of narrow nationalist oneself. (I'm not clear which of these is considered worse.)

The point at issue is really a methodological one which, though obvious, usually gets ignored in the new fury of the ideological times. Both anti-nationalism and pro-nationalism are extremely broad attitudes or principles – the kind of important yet very general rules which are needed as signposts or reference-points. But signposts do not map out or explain the journey which they indicate. Attitudes on this plane of historical generality are bound to have – indeed, to demand – hosts of qualifications or exceptions. 'On the whole' inevitably leads to 'but . . .' What these broad attitudes 'mean' in any actual situation isn't, and cannot possibly be, just a deduction or a blanket endorsement or rejection. Exceptions don't exactly prove rules, but they are the lifeblood of useful principles.

This was blatantly true of anti-nationalism. Both in its standard liberal or Western form, and in the socialist or Leninist versions which used to hold court in the East, it was always acknowledged that occasionally, reluctantly, a few more flags had to be run up. This was permitted in cases of hallmarked national oppression. Colonial or imperialist dominance gave legitimacy to nationalism, at least for a time. The existence of 'great-power chauvinism' could morally underwrite small-country national liberation – though only up to the point of independence, when universal values were supposed at once to reassert themselves.

The very least a pro-nationalist can say is that he or she is as entitled to exceptions. Conversely, to say that political and economic nationalism is, very generally, a good thing is not to say that there are no blots, excrescences or failures on the increasingly nationalised map of the world. To recognise that only broadly nationalist solutions will be found for what used to be the Soviet Union, Yugoslavia and Czechoslovakia is not to be an apologist for the bombardment of Dubrovnik or the rape of Bosnian Muslim women. To insist that the small battalions are likely to be 'on the whole' better than the large – particularly the multinational large – is not to imply there can be no pathology of the ethnic, or no cases where nationalists are wrong.

It seems to me that since 1989 the pro-nationalist is also justified in a measure of sarcasm. He or she can observe that, however many pustules and warts there turn out to be in the new world of nations, the small-battalion principle is unlikely to end up consisting of nothing but exceptions. Such has of course been internationalism's fate since 1989. The seamless garment always had to make room for tears and patches: but after 1989 it came to consist of almost nothing except holes, which no amount of lamentation or wish-fulfilment will repair.

For the first time in human history, the globe has been effectively unified into a single economic order under a common democratic-state model – surely the ideal, dreamt-of conditions for liberal or proletarian internationalism. Actually, these conditions have almost immediately caused the world to fold up into a previously unimaginable and still escalating number of different ethno-political units.

Why has the one produced the other? Why has globalisation engendered nationalism, instead of transcending it? This is surely the fundamental problem of theory thrown up by the last three years. It goes far beyond what has become the obsessive question of Yugoslavia, and what should be done there to stop or lessen its crimes and cruelties.

To answer these questions may require some psychic effort of disengagement. I suspect that is necessary, above all, inside the countries of the European Community. Hans Kohn's theorisation of Western liberalism rested on a distinction between West and East (or the West v. the Rest) – a distinction that was not simply resuscitated in 1989 but in a sense fortified.

The reason for that was what seemed to be taking place in the West End of the continent. Innumerable people couldn't help feeling, and repeating with varying degrees of self-satisfaction, 'just look at the difference!' *They* may be breaking up and disintegrating, but we appear to be doing the opposite – to be integrating, getting over at least some features of nationalism, pooling sovereignty, looking rationally outwards, and so on. Extra complacency about the North Atlantic dangerously fortified the old prejudices about the East, and made the search for new explanations appear even less urgent. If Western advance and superiority *was* the explanation, why waste time rethinking history with elaborate theories about comparative conditions of development?

I suppose the worst single incident of that phase was the day Boris Yeltsin turned up at the Strasbourg Parliament in 1991, and found himself (as he put it at the time) being harangued like a backward school-kid by socialist MEPs. Why couldn't he be more like Mikhail Gorbachev, they indignantly demanded, what did he mean by being so nice to all those would-be separatists, could he not see that breaking up the USSR would be a disaster? This outburst of daft parochialism was a symptom of a phase destined rapidly to pass. Maastricht and the Danish and French referenda were not far away, and were soon to produce an abrupt change of climate. The sense of inevitable and uninterruptable progress towards the post-nationalist light gave way to the doubt and uncertainty of the present. It is (at least) not so clear now that never the twain shall meet, and that they represent fundamentally diverging forms of development.

Other important blows to Western confidence have been dealt by events in Canada and Czechoslovakia, especially the latter. This was the central, linking country between East and West, which after its emancipation from Communist rule was generally expected to follow a Western route and act as an example to less fortunate neighbours. The fact that it has chosen the (supposedly) Eastern route of division, civilly and without excessive commotion or animosity, is something whose significance has not been allowed to sink in. Eight weeks ago the birth of two new democratic republics in the heart of Europe was greeted there with a torrent of bile, commiseration and preventive accusations. Every single birthmark was seen as presaging doom. How dare they! Not only out of step but going in the wrong direction! They'll learn, they'll soon be fighting like the rest (and so on).

Liberal-capitalist complacency has been replaced by the mood, darker but also more realistic, which Etienne Balibar conveyed in a 1991 talk about racism and politics in Europe. *Es gibt keinen Staat in Europa* was his title, a remark originally made by Hegel: there is no real state in Europe. 'Before there can be any serious analysis of racism and its relationship to migrations,' Balibar wrote, 'we have to ask ourselves what this word "Europe" means and what it will signify tomorrow . . . In reality we are here discovering the *truth* of the earlier situation, which explodes the representation that we used to have of it. Europe is not something that is "constructed" at a slower or faster pace, with greater or less ease; it is a historical problem without any pre-established solution.' The evaporation of frontiers has not – or not yet – been replaced by the new definitions and boundaries of a European state, one capable of establishing the social and political citizenship so crucial to migrants. In a curious way, Euro-development has led to under-development in this key area. 'All the conditions are present,' Balibar continues, 'for a collective sense of identity *panic* to be produced and maintained. For individuals – particularly the most deprived and the most remote from power – fear the state but they fear still more its disappearance or decomposition.'

I'm not sure about his description 'identity *panic*', but I agree the complacency of 1989 has been overtaken by identity concern, often coloured by anxiety and by a sharp disillusionment with the older European formulae. These features were certainly prominent in both the Danish and the French referenda over Maastricht, and they are also important in the much more smothered, inchoate argument now limping along in the United Kingdom.

Identity alarm can also be read positively, however. It is surely not wholly bad that it has replaced Western (and notably Britannic) identity somnolence. The new sense of dislocation and doubt, created by the new circumstances, may also prompt new initiatives and departures. Ethnic closure and brutal self-defence is one response to a loss of familiar horizons and signposts: but it is not the only one, and not one predestined either to return everywhere, or to triumph easily where it does.

To retain and cultivate a wider, more balanced perspective on the post-'89 transformation must be the task for serious theorists in this new world. Why has the End of History carried us forward into a more nationalist world? Why is a more united globe also (and almost immediately) far more ethnically aware, and more liable to political division?

In the years before 1989 significant advances were made in both the history and the sociology of nationalism. The central weakness of Kohn and liberal theory had been its neglect of economics, its failure to place the rise of ethnic politics within a more substantial framework of development. This failure was remedied by the important work of Ernest Gellner, Anthony Smith and others from the Sixties to the Eighties. They showed, to my mind conclusively, that nationalism was inseparable from the deeper processes of industrialisation and socio-economic modernity. Far from being an irrational obstacle to development, it was for most societies the only feasible way into the developmental race – the only way in which they could compete without being either colonised or annihilated. If they turned to the past (figuratively to 'the blood') in these modernisation struggles, it was essentially in order to stay intact as they levered themselves into the future. Staying intact, or obtaining a new degree of social and cultural cohesion, was made necessary by industrialisation – even (as in so many cases) by the distant hope, the advancing shadow of industrialisation. And *ethnos* offered the only way of ensuring such cohesion and common purpose.

The strategy was high-risk, both because the blood might take over and drown these societies, and because they might never really catch up. However, that risk was unavoidable. It arose from the conditions of generally and chronically uneven development – the only kind which capitalism allows, and the kind which has finally, definitively established itself since 1989 as the sole matrix of further evolution.

In this more rational but insufficiently appreciated perspective nationalism is therefore as much a native of modernity as are democracy and the capitalist motor of development. It is as inseparable from progress as they are. In his earlier work Gellner in particular stressed how vital the function of nationalism was in resisting over-centralised and monolithic development. Without 'fragmentation' and 'disintegration' some type of empire would long ago have appropriated industrialisation to its own political purpose.

I have already mentioned the standard triad of categories used to read the post-'89 changes: democracy, capitalism and nationalism – the third representing some kind of ghost or retreat from reason, an upsurge of atavism interfering with the other two. This view of nationalism is a piece of superstition; a superstition which has unfortunately grown so popular that it has come partly to define (or redefine) the task of nationalist theory. It seems to me that anti-Demonism is the prerequisite of getting anywhere with the debate about ethnic issues and their future.

The fact is that, for all their weight and intellectual superiority to the old commonplaces, studies like Smith's *The Ethnic Origin of Nations* and Gellner's *Nations and Nationalism* have had very little influence on common perceptions of their subject. When the whole world was abruptly compelled to focus on it again, an older common sense took over and explained it all in terms of demons, resurgent fascism or the irrational side of human nature.

There is an interesting reversal at work here. Once upon a time (before 1989) the protagonists of internationalism tended to be over-rational creatures, professorial politicos who occasionally displayed nervous tics. Apologists for nationalism were supposed to be hirsute, romantic souls who took folk-dance too seriously and were liable to get carried away (especially by rogues). I can see little of this pattern in the arguments today. The shocked, semi-hysterical response of the West to the Eastern rebirth has plunged it into the style of unreason once supposed typical of rabid chauvinists and wild-eyed patriot-poets. By contrast, it's now up to the defenders of nationality-politics and *ethnos* to assume a cannier, more balanced point of view on the emergent world. It is they who should assume and develop a perspective based on the enduring theoretical and historical work I have cited. It's they who must look for the broader and more historically informed view, keeping their distance from the metropolitan virtual reality being pumped out in London, Paris and New York. This new perspective ought to find as natural a home in Glasgow as in (say) Kiev, or Ljubljana, or Riga – the newer centres of a more varied, more emphatically nationalist world which, in spite of all those pessimistic titles, and notwithstanding the abscess in Bosnia, will turn out to be more than just disorder and atavism.

Fifteen years ago I wrote something about 'The Modern Janus', likening nationalism to the two-headed Roman deity who couldn't help looking backwards as well as forwards. Since then the whole world has increasingly come to resemble him. But with an important difference. I believe that, on the whole, the forward-gazing side of the strange visage may be more prominent than it was in 1977. Perhaps because today the forward view is that much more open and encouraging than it was then.

25 February 1993

V.G. Kiernan on Treason

Some drooping memories of Cambridge before the war have been revived of late by various writings. One is an autobiography, *Reading from Left to Right*, by a Canadian, Professor H.S. Ferns.* Few socialists of the Marxist persuasion – practically the only sort of people I got to know at college – seem to write memoirs; most of them probably feel that there are always more useful things to be done. Henry Ferns deviated from socialism long ago, but became a distinguished historian. His book, both entertaining and informative, looks back over a lifetime of abrupt, unforeseeable changes of outlook. Then there have been three books concerned with another Canadian of our time, Herbert Norman, a Cambridge Communist who turned into a respected member of his country's diplomatic service, was hunted by the Cold War pack, and ended, a suicide, at Cairo. He has become something of a symbol of Canadian independence from America, but scholars from both countries took part in a conference held a few years ago to assess his life and work: I was invited to speak about his time at Cambridge. The conference papers, edited by Roger Bowen, have been published, and Dr Bowen has also written an appreciative biography. Japanese studies being his subject, he is well qualified to weigh up the writings on modern Japan of Herbert Norman, a missionary's son who grew up there. Very different is a viciously McCarthyite attack on him by an American, J. Barros (who has had the bad taste to thank me for some small assistance I gave him before I discovered what he was up to).† This has stirred up some controversy, and Barros was very effectively dealt with in a long review in the *Canadian Forum* (November 1986) by Reg Whitaker of York University. Henry Ferns, too, had a word to say about him in the same issue of the paper.

And there has lately been another outburst of barking and braying about 'Cambridge traitors'. It has come to be a perennial resort of reaction, when it is left without any fresher topic for claptrap, to indulge in these spasms of virtuous indignation about the wickedness of a small

---

* University of Toronto Press, 1983.
† R.W. Bowen, ed., *E.H. Norman: His Life and Scholarship* (University of Toronto Press, 1984); R.W. Bowen, *Innocence is not enough: The Life and Death of Herbert Norman* (Douglas and McIntyre, 1986); J. Barros, *No Sense of Evil* (Denau, 1986).

number of idealists of years ago. William Empson was stirred to an opposite kind of ire by one of many hack works, *The Traitors* by Alan Moorehead, who 'specifically denounced them for having had the impudence to obey their own consciences', instead of understanding that a citizen's duty is 'to concur with any herd in which he happens to find himself. The old Protestant in me stirred.'

I went to Cambridge, to read history, in 1931, and stayed seven years. My undergraduate time was passed in premises – staircase I, no 2 – on the ground floor of the Whewell's Court annexe of Trinity College. Close by were two incongruous neighbours: A.E. Housman, anchored by misanthropy to this out-of-the-way spot, and James Klugmann, the chief Communist student organiser, and later a life-long Party worker. I.2 was not an ideal residence. When a gust of wind blew, the small fire, over which toast could be made with the help of a long fork and much patience, threw out billowing clouds of smoke, enough sometimes to drive me out into the court gasping for breath. During vacations mice nibbled at the backs of my books. Most of the thoughts of years in that cramped room have vanished, as they no doubt deserved to. Traces of sundry things have survived a half-century, the best of them books. Early in my second year I was reading for the first time Boswell's *Hebrides*, a cherished companion ever since; it was a tea-time luxury, accompanied by one daily cigarette, a limit I was not wise enough to keep to for long, and I can still see the electric blue of the October sky as dusk gathered. Later on I moved to a nobler abode, in Great Court, on the top floor of a staircase beside the main gate. Here I was surrounded by the 'mighty dead', and could listen on summer nights to the fountain's murmur, and on spring days walk out, when work stuck fast, and look at the daffodils by the riverside.

In those days the deportment of senior Cambridge was oppressively genteel and ritualistic. Sciences flourished, as some had always done; history was in a stagnant condition, and at Trinity in particular was heavily overlaid by conservatism and clericalism. There was in general a stifling atmosphere of closed windows, drawn blinds, expiring candles, sleep-walking; outside, a mounting tumult of history in the making, instead of history laid to rest in neat graveyard rows of dusty tomes. With amenities such as the Backs, Wordsworth's *Prelude*, and a second-hand bicycle on which to explore the placid countryside, I was reasonably content, attended lectures as by law obliged, and took their stale fare for granted, like the weather. I became a socialist, then a Communist, before graduating to Marxism, the historical materialism that has been my Ariadne's thread ever since. Slow conversion may last longer than sudden enlightenment; and convictions, as Nietzsche said, are the backbone of life.

We had no time then to assimilate Marxist theory more than very roughly; it was only beginning to take root in England, though it had one remarkable expounder at Cambridge in Maurice Dobb, to whom a section is devoted in Professor H.J. Kaye's recent study of British Marxist historians.* We felt, all the same, that it could lift us to a plane far above the Cambridge academic level. We were quite right, as the rapid advance of Marxist ideas and influence since then has demonstrated. Our main concerns, however, were practical ones, popularising socialism and the USSR, fraternising with hunger-marchers, denouncing fascism and the National Government, warning of the approach of war. We belonged to the era of the Third International, genuinely international at least in spirit, when the Cause stood high above any national or parochial claims. Some of us have lived to see multinational capitalism, instead of international socialism, in control of most of the world: but at the time we had not the shadow of a doubt that capitalism was nearing its end. It was both too abominable, and too inept and suicidally divided, to last much longer. Socialism would take its place, and mankind be transformed not much less quickly.

At such a time, punctilios of 'loyalty' to things of the dying past seemed as archaic as the minutiae of drawing-room manners. And it was about the defenders of the old order that a strong smell of treason hung. We saw pillars of British society trooping to Nuremberg to hobnob with Nazi gangsters; we saw the 'National' government sabotaging the Spanish Republic's struggle, from class prejudice, and to benefit investors like Rio Tinto, blind to the obvious prospect of the Mediterranean being turned into a fascist lake and the lifelines of empire cut. From Spain the vibrations of civil war spread over Europe. The frenzied enthusiasm of the French Right for Franco was the overture to its eager surrender to Hitler in 1940. Amid that tumult the sense of an absolute divide between 'whatsoever things are good' and everything Tory was easy to acquire, and with some of us has remained unshakeable. Our watchword was Voltaire's: *Ecrasez l'infâme*.

Feelings like these were to carry a small number of our generation, from Cambridge and elsewhere, into acts of 'treason', in the lawyer's meaning, not the only or best one. Those acts, amounting in sum to very little, have been sedulously embroidered and exaggerated, and the

---

* *The British Marxist Historians* (Polity Press, 1984).

public has been continually reminded of them. For good measure, politics and sex have been mixed up, as if radicalism went hand in hand with homosexuality. In fact, an innocent could live in left-wing Cambridge without ever suspecting that such a thing existed, outside of Classical literature. The aim of all this pseudo-patriotic hubbub is to distract attention from the distempers of our ancien régime, keep people from thinking about the nuclear war they may well be drifting towards, and make them fancy that without zealous leaders to fend off a legion of spies and subversives, all would be lost. It also helps to nourish the illusion of Britain as a great power, with priceless secrets to be stolen. Writing books about secret-stealers is an easier way than most of earning a living; it benefits from the vogue of spy films and novelettes, symptom of an uneasy society in need of the reassurance of happy endings. 'Truth is sometimes stranger than fiction,' as Mrs Thatcher said when telling the House one of her whoppers. It can certainly be made to look stranger and more fearsome.

I have no doubt that the extent of Herbert Norman's departure from rectitude was to start a small Indian Marxist group at Cambridge, which I inherited from him when he left. Some of its members were closely watched while at Cambridge, and arrested as soon as they went home. Norman had grown up in the Japanese countryside, still half-feudal, and must have been better able than the rest of us to imagine what life was like for Indian peasants under the British rulers who were obstinately denying independence to the country – Churchill most obstinately of all.

Guy Burgess was one of those – James Klugmann and John Cornford were the chief – who helped to induct me into the Party. We belonged to the same college, and hence to the same 'cell'. I remember Burgess as a rather plump, fresh-faced youth, of guileless, almost cherubic expression. I heard him spoken of as the most popular man in the college, but he must have suffered from tensions; he smoked cigarettes all day, and had somehow imbibed a notion that the body expels nicotine very easily. He told me once a story that had evidently made a deep impression on him – of a Hungarian refugee who had been given shelter at his home, a formerly ardent political worker reduced to a wreck by beatings on the soles of the feet. I came on Burgess one day in his room sitting at a small table, a glass of spirits in front of him, glumly trying to put together a talk for a cell meeting that evening; he confessed that when he had to give any sort of formal talk he felt foolish. I never saw him after our exit from Cambridge. He did what he felt it right for him to do; I honour his memory.

Individuals who saw something of the machinations of government from the inside must have seen much to disgust them. If details of whatever secrets they gave away are still being hushed up, it must be because they were secrets discreditable to their superiors. We are always hearing nowadays of 'sensitive papers'. Paper is not sensitive, but those who write on it often have good cause to be, and prefer to blush unread. Anthony Blunt was quoted in his *Times* obituary (28 March 1983) as saying that he acted during the war 'from a conviction that we were not doing enough to help a hard pressed ally'. It is a political if not mathematical certainty that the same men who were adamant against collective security before 1939 were hard at work after 1941 to ensure that the conflict would end with Russia bled nearly to death, as exhausted as Germany. They were treacherously imperilling the whole Allied war effort and the chances of victory. When another Cambridge man, Leo Long, made his public recantation in November 1981, it appeared that what he had taken part in doing was to give Moscow more British information about German troop movements than the British Government chose to give it. Why did he feel obliged to sound so shamefaced? As he said, the information could do no harm to Britain.

If it is the case, as alleged early in 1982, that Maclean was trying at the end to influence Britain away from support of the American intervention in Korea, he was doing something very praiseworthy. It seems that Norman, by that time head of the Canadian mission at Tokyo, fell foul of General MacArthur, whom he had hitherto got on quite well with, by trying to dissuade *him* from intervention. At home, Sir John Pratt, dismissed from the Foreign Office for opposing the Korean War, stumped the country, in spite of his age, and denounced it in fiery terms. I was his chairman at a big meeting in Edinburgh when he referred to his campaign as one of invective against the Government: 'invective', he said very truly, belonged to an old, honourable tradition that ought to be revived. It is indeed a mark of political decadence that there has been so little of it against Mrs Thatcher's regime: none since the war has more deserved it.

Treason has never been easy to define precisely, a fact illustrated by the long series of Tudor laws about it. It is an accusation easy to bandy about, but one that can be levelled in different directions. Antony in Shakespeare's play succeeds by his demagogy in turning popular feeling against the conspirators, and sets the crowd shouting: 'They were traitors!' They had plotted against a usurping dictator; Caesar had plotted against the Republic. In recent years Rome has been canonising batches of Catholics whom Queen Elizabeth's judges sentenced as traitors. Two centuries ago British conservatives were abusing Yankee rebels in the same strain. During the French Revolutionary wars Tory Britain had open arms for all French reactionaries who were plotting against their own country, and welcomed them as allies against it. All the modern empires regarded resistance as treasonable, and employed multitudes of native collaborators, who in the eyes of nationalists were betraying their own people, like black policemen in South Africa today. A Russian who abandons his native land and settles in a hostile country is always credited with the most laudable motives, like the archetypal author of *I chose freedom*.

An honest Soviet dissident like Sakharov is, unquestionably, to be admired. So are the few Englishmen in British India who gave aid to nationalists or Communists. One of them, Michael Carritt, has written a light-hearted account of his brief career in the Indian Civil Service.* At vastly greater risk, a few Frenchmen in Algeria gave aid secretly to the rebels. Admirable too, though unlikely to be admired by Tories or Reaganites, is the young Chinese dissident Wei Jingsheng, jailed for 15 years on charges including the giving of information to foreign journalists about the attack on Vietnam.

Toryism's record shows an elastic conception of loyalty, inspired by fidelity to the interests of class or party much more than of nation. Winston Churchill's father Randolph, when the Tory Party was blocking the way to Home Rule for Ireland, coined the slogan 'Ulster will fight, and Ulster will be right' – a call for insurrection. In 1914 it was repeated by Carson, when a Liberal government was again about to concede Home Rule, or what is nowadays called devolution, and numbers of officers refused, with whole-hearted Tory approval, to take part in any coercion of Ulster. What would they have thought if their men had refused to take part in suppression of a colonial revolt in Africa or Asia? The object of the Army mutiny, as it was very properly called, was to preserve Tory ascendancy in Ireland; the effect was to ensure the loss of most of Ireland to the United Kingdom, and the partition with its legacy of endless trouble. At the time, the Ulster affair may have been one of the factors that induced Germany to gamble on war, and induced the Liberal Government to join in the gamble, as an escape from its embarrassments.

With this precedent in mind, it is easy to understand why it went

---

* *Mole in the Crown* (privately published, 1985).

without saying that British officers would decline to act against white rebels in Rhodesia. Ian Smith and his followers were levying war against the Crown; they received unstinted sympathy from the overwhelming majority of Tories. A speaker at a Tory Conference who ventured to criticise them was howled down. Wilson as prime minister once ventured to remind Parliament that there were penalties for treason, or connivance at it: no Tory took any notice, and no action was taken. Since they own England, Tories naturally feel entitled to do as they like. Their encouragement of Smith was accompanied by wholesale evasion of the embargo imposed on Rhodesian trade: this, too, went unpunished. Tories have continued to cherish fraternal feelings towards the white savages of South Africa, their partners in upholding the natural right of capitalism to exploit its victims: quite indifferent to the moral damage to Britain, but also to the material losses to be expected from an alienation of black Africa and most of the Commonwealth.

It was the end, as Gaitskell said, of a thousand years of history when Britain was hustled by the Tories into the Common Market, and the abandonment of part of its independence. No referendum was held, because everyone knew that the vote would go against it. When Reagan carried out his bombardment of Libya, to please his right-wing voters and warn all other objectors to the American hegemony, Mrs Thatcher deemed it 'unthinkable' that Britain should decline to join in. Would it have been equally unthinkable if Reagan had been bombarding the USSR? Men were tried and hanged at Nuremberg for the kind of crime that this precious pair were committing. It seems clear, moreover, that Britain has taken part in under-cover aid to right-wing insurgents in Nicaragua, in breach of American as well as international law.

Most friendships, said Dr Johnson, are either partnerships in folly or confederacies in vice: the Anglo-American connection is both. Toryism has been selling British independence for a mess of pottage, or of nuclear explosives, and at a time when America's many better qualities are in eclipse, when noisy reaction, political inanity, aggressive jingoism, hold sway, and arms-dealers and the Pentagon, Eisenhower's 'military-industrial complex', are selling mankind's future for thirty trillion pieces of silver. Mrs Thatcher has been happy to play to the American gallery with her long string of anti-Soviet tirades, like the one so loudly applauded at Washington four years ago. How anyone, incidentally, can listen with pleasure to that detestable voice is one of our modern mysteries. Politicians are often given away by their voices, and that proportion of her career which has not been carefully concealed from the public has been one long hiss or scream.

When Franco began his rebellion and brought Moorish mercenaries and foreign troops and bombers into Spain to make it safe for land-lords, capitalists and priests, almost all Tories cheered him to the echo. From their attitude then it may be imagined what it would be in a par-allel situation at home. Human affairs, *res humanae*, are uncertain and obscure, as we learned from our Latin primers: but it is as certain as anything human can be that informal exchanges of views are always under way across the Atlantic, on a variety of confidential levels, to ensure that if ever Britain's 'nationalists' decide that the time has come for action they will not find themselves alone. There will be an open door not only for American forces, but for Germans, Chileans and other champions of free enterprise. The sell-out to America has mas-queraded as a quest for the Holy Grail of a 'special relationship': here is its reality.

By way of a small rehearsal, during the 1983 Election American money was made use of for 'dirty tricks' purposes against opponents. So was information, true or false, from MI5. The secret-service organ-isations, or rather secret societies of the Right, which the public is induced to pay for without asking what they are doing, form a special submarine cable between Toryism and its American congeners. Vastly more serious than the allegation that a handful of their members have been agents of Moscow is the fact that, collectively, they are agents of Washington. It has been belatedly coming to light that they were involved in a plot to 'destabilise' a Labour government – a plot impos-sible for them to have conceived without the approval of high Tory personages and in collusion with American colleagues. If this was not treason, what ever can be? Destabilising foreign governments has been a tactic through the centuries: it has been left to the USA to make it a cornerstone of foreign policy. Labour's leaders were too timid to make any real protest, though the question was one of British independence as well as of their party's fortunes. The people concerned are now bent on preventing any enquiry, and have spent a good deal of the taxpayer's money to that end.

While deafening us with shouts of liberty, our rulers are swathing us in all manner of invigilation, two-footed or electronic. Tory govern-ments in the past, too, were addicted to use of police spies and agents provocateurs against progressives. Police spying was ubiquitous in all Western colonies or semi-colonies, and habits formed there have per-sisted. Kell, the founder of MI5, was in China at the outset of his

career, and then for some time in Tsarist Russia. Like Bulldog
Drummond's Black Gang, it always saw its business as hunting subversives of all sorts, including trade-unionists.

A clique of politicians and generals manoeuvred 'democratic' Britain
into the alliances that landed it in the First World War, and a similar
process is going on underground today. The BBC correspondent
Alistair Cooke once remarked that in Washington ceremonial gatherings
are always being held in honour of foreign visitors to whom nobody has
anything to say, while decisions are taken by small groups, often
through telephone calls. It is hard to see how anyone could be a 'traitor'
to the Washington plotters and their European jackals, any more than
to Nazism. If we want to discover who is really undermining British
welfare and safety, we need look no further than Downing Street.

The Tories came into office determined to sell off a vast stock of
national wealth, at cheap rates, to their party and its financial backers,
and to any voters who could be bribed: in other words, to plunder the
nation they profess so much devotion to. By now an immense sum has
been deftly transferred from the public domain to the pockets of Tories
and, in good measure, their friends abroad. There was a foretaste of
what was to come when Amersham International, the radioactive iso-
topes business, was sold in February 1982 at a price £23 million below
its market value. The Government was accused of making a fool of
itself, but it was the taxpayer it was making a fool of, and what was
politely termed mere ignorance and stupidity, venial faults in any Tory
Administration, ought to have been branded as a swindle. This year two
Tory MPs, caught cheating when other public property was on sale, had
to agree not to stand for re-election: they were given a pat on the back
by their party chairman for making 'honourable' amends for an 'error
of judgment'.

This sort of national asset-stripping is not new, except in scale. Indeed
the history of capitalist property accumulation everywhere has consisted largely of 'privatising' public resources, giving away North
American forests to railway corporations, for example. Plundering the
state has been a besetting temptation to men in power. No sooner was
the breath out of Henry VIII's carcass than the noblemen who surrounded his young son were laying hands on generous acreages out of
the Crown lands, on which the government depended for a good part
of its revenue. During the 18th and early 19th centuries Parliament was
busy voting the village common lands off the map, mostly to be added
to the estates of the landowners who were doing the voting, and the rest

of their species. In old Scotland, where royal minorities were always happening, a king had the right on coming of age to take back lands granted away from the Crown during his nonage. A similar right ought to be vested now in the British public, to be exercised when – if ever – it comes of age.

Human nature being nearly as frail as Tories always tell us, when dismissing socialism as a pipe-dream, it ought to have been insisted on that ministers, MPs, and all others responsible for the privatising – or privateering – operations, should submit to a self-denying ordinance, like Parliament in the Civil War. There ought to have been the fullest guarantees that none of them or their families or hangers-on would benefit personally. No such assurances have been forthcoming. There has always been room in the City for conjuring-tricks of a more or less unsavoury kind, but hitherto a decent reticence has been observed. Now, dizzy with success over the vast hoard of pearls scattered before the swine, it is grunting with indiscreet loudness. We are coming closer to the monstrous regiment of stockbrokers that Marx saw in Bonapartist France in 1853: 'the whole state machinery transformed into one immense swindling and stock-jobbing concern'. And this goes with a further disastrous decline in industrial activity, and its relegation to the background by the sway of speculative finance, the most parasitic, semi-aristocratical, cosmopolitan type of capitalism. From stealing village commons our profiteers went on to rob villagers in Asia and Africa; now they have come back to plundering *us* again.

In 1982 when there were American outcries about information leakage for fifteen years from Cheltenham to the Russians, the *Guardian* made the comment that this flood appeared to have done no perceptible harm. Life seems to jog along just the same whether the Official Secrets mystification is being eavesdropped or not. Much the same can be said of the whole spy scare, kept going for reasons mostly remote from the ostensible one. Searching for spies and traitors to explain why things are as they are is always a search for excuses. 'We are betrayed by what is false within': not Mrs Thatcher's 'enemy within' – miners, for instance, who object to being thrown out of work and have to be ridden down by police storm-troopers with horse and hound – but the falsity engrained in the entire fabric of capitalist society. The real anti-patriots are those who deepen and worsen it, for their own benefit. They are far more of a danger to Britain than any givers-away or sellers of 'sensitive papers', chiefly concealing no more than official trumpery and balderdash.

Morally, the 'treason' of the Thirties cannot for a moment be compared with the morass of crooked dealing, profit-gorging, deception, looting of national resources and indifference to national welfare, that make up the world of Thatcherism. The latest bright Tory idea is to let agriculture follow industry into decay, and turn loose a barbarous horde of 'developers' over what is left of the countryside. One way or another, the country is being drained of vitality, while constantly assured that all is well, because National Security (or Official Secrecy – to Mrs Thatcher the two terms are synonymous) is being vigilantly preserved, and no soldiers with snow on their boots are marching along Whitehall. So far as our unemployed and old people, at any rate, are concerned, they must be feeling like the famished labourer in the Anti-Corn Law cartoon: 'I be protected, and I be starving.'

'If treason prospers, none dare call it treason,' and so far Thatcherism has prospered and been allowed to practise its philosophy. Mrs Thatcher takes it upon herself to lecture the nation on its moral short-comings, and blame its permissiveness for sapping the foundations of law and order. She lectures the Russians on the subject of human rights. On the Anglo-American view, human rights are essential for socialist countries, but can be dispensed with in Latin America, South Korea and elsewhere because there the people enjoy the supreme felicity of free enterprise, alias capitalism, which makes up for every drawback. Mrs Thatcher has had only the kindest words for the Indonesian regime, built on the bones of the hundreds of thousands massacred in 1965, and conspicuous for its conquest of the former Portuguese colony of East Timor, where at least a third of the population is reported to have been killed or driven into exile, with the help of Western arms sales and diplomatic support. Future historians, if any survive to look back on all this, will find our 'civilisation' the hardest of all to comprehend from the language of its statesmen, more indecipherable than any Egyptian hieroglyphics.

If every nation gets the government it deserves, hard though it may be to think of any nation deserving a government like Britain's in recent years, these years speak ill for the British people, or a large section of it. For some years after the war, Tories could claim that they were not as bad as they used to be: with some truth, because they were not allowed to be. Since then, they have been allowed to behave worse than ever, and have flourished accordingly.

Garaudy, the French Marxist and former Communist, wrote of his and my generation, with our eyes on Hitler, Franco, McCarthy: 'We were fighting absolute evil: how, then, could we not feel that our cause was the cause of absolute good?' Painful experience showed that the second of these beliefs was in part illusion. But our ideals and aims were valid, and mean as much now as they did then. If we have not been invariably right, our opponents have been almost infallibly wrong, in anything where public morality or human progress is concerned. After a decade or two of uneasy recovery following the war, economy and society are sinking into another quagmire. None of our fundamental problems have been solved, and on present lines never will be. In Rome, in times of emergency, a 'final decree' of the Senate gave plenary power to the consuls to save the state. In Britain now, a government once elected, even by a minority of the electorate, can feel free to claim plenary power to do whatever it likes, and without telling anyone what it is really doing. It is to Britain's credit that the majority of voters have always been against Thatcherism: but we have been learning that a minority government can do the country immense harm, moral and material, much of it beyond repair. The system of representation that allows this is indefensible, the case for a change has become unanswerable. The alternative is going to be a dictatorship of the rich.

25 June 1987

In Two Minds about Ireland

Colm Tóibín

In 1969, two years after my father died, my mother, my sisters and I went to Wexford for the launch of a new history of the 1798 Rising, *The Year of Liberty* by Thomas Pakenham. The Rising was important for us: from our housing estate we could see Vinegar Hill where 'our side', the rebels, had made their last stand. From early childhood I knew certain things (I hesitate to say 'facts') about the Rising: how the English had muskets whereas we just had pikes, how the English poured boiling tar on the scalps of the Irish and then, when the tar had dried, peeled it off. The names of the towns and villages around us were in all the songs about 1798 – the places where battles had been fought, or atrocities committed. But there was one place that I did not know had a connection with 1798 until I was in my twenties. It was Scullabogue. Even now, as I write the name, it has a strange resonance. In 1798 it was where 'our side' took a large number of Protestant men, women and children, put them in a barn and burned them to death.

It does not come up in the songs, and I have no memory of my father, who was a local historian, talking or writing about it. The landscape of north Wexford, where I was born, is dotted with memorials to 1798, but there is nothing, as far as I know, at Scullabogue. Its memory was erased from what a child could learn about 1798. It was a complication in our glorious past, and it was essential for our past to be glorious if our present, in what Roy Foster in his new book of essays calls 'the disillusioned tranquillity of the Free State', was to have any meaning.* This was what our ancestors fought for; we had it now; it had to be good.

At the launch of his book Thomas Pakenham sat on a podium at the top of the room. A few introductory speeches were made, and then a man whom I recognised, who had been a friend of my father's, stood up to speak. I remember that his voice shook with angry conviction as he spoke. 'The history of 1798 has still to be written.' This book was not the real history, he said. He pointed accusingly at Pakenham. I did not understand.

---

* R.F. Foster, *Paddy and Mr Punch: Connections in Irish and English History* (Allen Lane, 1993).

I understand now because I have been grappling with Pakenham's book for years. In the early drafts of my novel *The Heather Blazing*, the protagonist is working on a history of the rebellion, not from the British side, which is what my father's friend accused Pakenham of having written, but from 'our' side, the Irish side. The following passage from Pakenham's Preface interests my protagonist:

> Today sources are embarrassingly rich on the loyalist [British] side . . . On the rebel side, lack of sources makes it impossible to do justice to the movement. I have found fewer than a hundred revolutionary documents of 1798. For the most part I have had to make do with second-hand (and sometimes second-rate) material; contemporary spy reports, mid-19th-century biographies, folk-songs and hearsay . . . With the volume of written sources weighted so heavily to one side, it is impossible to avoid giving offence.

The rebels left no documents, then, only songs and stories, and the victors got to write history, until Irish nationalists like my father and his friend became the victors in their own state, to find that there were no reliable papers written by the rebels, no letters, few memoirs. Second-hand, second-rate things, as Pakenham so starkly (and perhaps tactlessly) put it. And the hollow nature of the native Irish past was the source of the anger that day at the launch in Wexford of Thomas Pakenham's *The Year of Liberty*. We had founded our state, but outsiders were still coming to write our history.

'I have tried to be fair,' Pakenham wrote in his Preface. 'For the events of 1798, T. Pakenham's *The Year of Liberty* (London, 1969) is unequalled,' Roy Foster wrote in his bibliographical essay at the back of his *Modern Ireland 1600–1972*. But sometimes, despite the fact that I am not an Irish nationalist (or at least I hope I am not), when I read Pakenham's book about the central event in the history of the place where I was brought up, I find the tone and the use of language offensive and hurtful. For a few seconds I become the man at the launch hectoring Pakenham.

For example, Pakenham at one point writes: 'The next three days passed in mounting hysteria for both the inhabitants of Wexford and their prisoners. The mob made some sort of attack on the gaol. By good fortune, two of the dozen or so Catholic priests in Wexford at this time happened to reach the gaol in time to drive off the people. Crowds again gathered outside Lord Kingsborough's lodgings and tried to break in.' 'Mob' suggests mindlessness and lack of civility. 'Some sort' is also dismissive. 'By good fortune' for whom? Hardly for 'the mob'. 'Drive off' as opposed to persuade, or convince, or even warn. 'Drive off' suggests they were animals. And yet all over Wexford there are monuments to them, and songs about them, and the committee to celebrate the 200th anniversary of their rebellion is already in place.

In an essay published in 1986, 'We Are All Revisionists Now', Roy Foster, who is certainly the most brilliant and courageous Irish historian of his generation, wrote that 'the last generation to learn Irish history only from the old nationalist textbooks will soon be middle-aged men and women.' He went on: 'it is occasionally tempting to feel that something has been lost as well as gained; to miss the compelling Manichean logic of the old "Story of Ireland" view, with a beginning, a middle and what appeared (up to about 1968) to be a triumphant end.' There were wholehearted celebrations of the 50th anniversary of the 1916 Rising, which included an exciting drama documentary on television, marches, days off school and, even for this 11-year-old, a feeling of national pride.

As the Irish nation wallowed in its 'liberation', a Jesuit priest called Father Francis Shaw submitted an essay to the Jesuit journal *Studies* which contained what Roy Foster calls a 'swingeing exposé of lacunae in [Patrick] Pearse's ideology'. The piece was not published for six years. The editors felt that Ireland was not ready for a critical examination of Pearse. For those involved in commemorations in Ireland, in 1966 as now, history has no complications or ironies or half-truths; one thing leads to another; there are heroes and traitors and villains. This was not simply the history taught at school in Ireland to those of us 'who will soon be middle-aged men and women': it was everywhere in our culture. But in the universities there had always been dogged individuals working against the national grain, dealing with the complexities rather than the simplicities of Irish history. Now in the Sixties, larger numbers of serious historians (I hesitate to use the words 'trained' or 'professional') began to work on Irish history with louder voices and more confidence and, in some cases, a political agenda; by the end of the decade, as the North blew up, they realised that they had a central role to play in guiding an Irish professional class away from ancient pieties.

They tried it on me. I went to University College Dublin in 1972 to study history and English. If there was a forbidden 'f' word or a forbidden 'c' word while we studied there, they were 'Fenian' and 'colonial'; all the Irish history we studied was parliamentary and constitutional. The 19th century was made up of O'Connell and Parnell, and there was much emphasis on their time at Westminster. Young Ireland, the Fenians, even the poor old Land League were presented as non-constitutional headaches for O'Connell and Parnell. Michael Collins was a Treaty negotiator rather than a warlord.

Outside in the world there were car bombs and hunger strikes, done in the name of our nation, in the name of history. Inside we were cleansing history, concentrating on those aspects of our past which would make us good, worthy citizens who would keep the Irish 26-county state safe from the IRA and IRA fellow travellers.

One day in the library I was reading an essay by Joseph Lee in a book called *The Irish Parliamentary Tradition*. (This title may seem like an elaborate oxymoron, but it was the sort of book published at that time.) The essay was about 1782 and Grattan's Parliament, an important moment in Irish history, according to our school books. Parnell, Roy Foster points out in an essay in *Paddy and Mr Punch*, constantly referred to this parliament, believing, as our school-books did, that it offered Home Rule to Ireland. Joseph Lee made clear that it offered Ireland no such thing, and that it wasn't Grattan's Parliament in any real way, since Grattan had no real power in it. It was all myth, all nonsense.

I remember feeling a huge sense of liberation. I photocopied the piece and made everyone else read it. I was in my late teens and I already knew that what they had told me about God and sexuality wasn't true, but being an atheist or being gay in Ireland at that time seemed easier to deal with as transgressions than the idea that you could cease believing in the Great Events of Irish nationalist history. No Cromwell as cruel monster, say; the executions after 1916 as understandable in the circumstances; 1798 as a small outbreak of rural tribalism; partition as inevitable. Imagine if Irish history were pure fiction, how free and happy we could be! It seemed at that time a most subversive idea, a new way of killing your father, starting from scratch, creating a new self.

I became a revisionist, luckily, just as the word was coming into vogue; it was a term of abuse used about historians who were peddling anti-nationalist views of Irish history. The most seriously revisionist text, however, to appear in those years was John Banville's *Birchwood*, a novel published in 1973, the year of Ireland's entry into the EC. Here, Irish history was an enormous joke, a baroque narrative full of crackpot landlords and roaming peasants and an abiding sense of menace and decay. In 1975, in his book of poems *The Snow Party*, Derek Mahon allowed one of his characters to be 'through with history'. I understood that to be the whole point of revisionism.

'In a country that has come of age, history need no longer be a matter of guarding sacred mysteries,' Roy Foster wrote in his 1986 essay. One of the sacred mysteries remained the 1916 Rising. When in the early Seventies I had imagined a history in which the executions after the 1916 Rising were 'understandable in the circumstances', I meant it as a flight of fancy, much like imagining a future in which the Pope would marry or fish would fly. Now, in 1988, in Roy Foster's *Modern Ireland 1600–1972*, which would be declared a masterwork by most historians who reviewed it, the section on the aftermath of the Rising began: 'The draconian reaction of the authorities to the rebellion should be understood in terms of international war and national security.' When I read the book first I spent some time pondering the 'should' and the 'national'. I wondered, suddenly my father's son once more, what nation Roy Foster could possibly be talking about.

In *Modern Ireland* Lord Mountjoy, who 'successfully commanded the English forces that drove the rebels from the Pale 1601–1603', is described as 'a humane man'. On the other hand, the United Irishman Napper Tandy who, in a biographical note, is said to be 'eulogised in national folklore', is described by Foster as 'the ludicrous Napper Tandy'. I do not know how it is possible to apply such adjectives from the 20th-century perspective to any figure in the 16th century, especially a figure sent by England to Ireland with an army, nor to any figure in the 18th century, even one eulogised in national folklore. The main problem in making such throwaway and offensive (to Irish nationalists past and present) and wrong (Mountjoy was not humane, at least not in Ireland) judgments and using such an arch tone is that it gives the game away. It suggests that underneath the brilliant insights and real originality in Foster's *Modern Ireland* there is an ideology perhaps not as crude as that of any nationalist historian writing school texts in the Twenties, but just as clear.

In *Modern Ireland* Foster is concerned to make Irish history dense and complex. He refuses to take the Whig view of Irish history, which sees the events that led up to 1916 from the perspective of 1916. The style is, by necessity, nervous and jerky; his judgments are qualified by local studies or detailed work. For anyone who wanted to 'use' history, who wanted to claim eight hundred years of misunderstanding between Ireland and England (as, according to Mrs Thatcher's memoirs, Garret FitzGerald did in talking to her), Foster's book would be puzzling and not very helpful. There are continuities in *Modern Ireland* but they are difficult to trace. His book, because of his command of detail, and his ability to construct a narrative, is deeply convincing and valuable.

The problem, perhaps, is not his, but ours. The underlying message in Foster's book, his revisionism, is best defined in an attack on revisionism by Desmond Fennell, an Irish commentator: 'A retelling of

Irish history which seeks to show that British rule of Ireland was not, as
we have believed, a bad thing, but a mixture of necessity, good intentions and bungling; and that Irish resistance to it was not, as we have
believed, a good thing, but a mixture of wrong-headed idealism and
unnecessary, often cruel violence.'

This revisionism is precisely what our state needed once the North
blew up and we joined the EC, in order to isolate Northern Ireland
from us and our history, in order to improve relations with Britain, in
order to make us concentrate on a European future. Foster and his fellow historians' work became useful, not for its purity, or its truth, but
its politics. It can be argued that many of these historians did not
'seek to show' anything, they merely and dispassionately showed it,
and the implications of what they showed happen to coincide with
public policy. But this cannot be argued with much conviction. In
1971, in that same book *The Irish Parliamentary Tradition*, the most
senior and respected Irish historian, F.S.L. Lyons, wrote: 'The theories
of revolution, the theories of nationality, the theories of history which
have brought Ireland to its present pass cry out for re-examination.' As
the historians set out to re-examine Irish history, they did so not in an
ivory tower of disinterest, but in a country of car bombs and warring
factions.

Every night during Easter Week 1966 our family watched the drama-
documentary about Easter 1916 on state television. A friend of the
family who had been in the Rising and had known the leaders came to
watch it with us. The executions were drawn out, each moment drama-
tised – the grieving family, the grim prison, the lone leader in his cell,
writing his last poem or letter. Sometimes the emotion in our house was
unbearable, and when it came to James Connolly's turn to be executed
my mother ran out of the room crying. We had never seen her cry before.

In less than ten years we moved from a time in which the state
sponsored such emotions to a time when the songs we learned at
school were banned on the state radio. Such sudden shifts cannot
occur without consequences, and these were best described in a
pamphlet by the poet Michael O'Loughlin written from his exile in
Amsterdam in 1988:

> For my generation the events of Easter 1966 were crucial, so much so that I think it
> is almost possible to speak of a generation of '66. People from that generation tend
> to share a number of characteristics. An almost total alienation from the state, a cyn-
> icism with regard to national institutions and political life . . . an unspoken
> assumption that everything emanating from official sources is a total lie . . . In my
> school, and in other schools and in the media, republican emotions, if not republic

principles, were openly encouraged . . . What [later came] from Northern Ireland was republicanism with a vengeance. The South's political lies were finally catching up with it. One of these was that 1916 was the culmination of the 700-year struggle for an 'Irish Republic'. This lie . . . eventually became too embarrassing. In an act of astonishing political opportunism, 1916 was revised.

One can hardly blame the historians, however: most of them believed they were going against the grain in the service of truth, believing themselves under attack from Republicans – a belief, as Roy Foster makes clear in his introduction to *Paddy and Mr Punch*, that some of them still hold. They never realised that they were justifying the new state, an Ireland cleansed of its history, which politicians had planned. The received wisdom about the 1916 executions was that they stirred the Irish population into instant and then constant anger. I had always been suspicious of this, especially the constant part, and Foster's analysis in *Modern Ireland* remains judicious: he makes a case for viewing the aftermath of the Rebellion as much in the light of the First World War as in that of the Rebellion itself. If this is revisionism, it is something we badly need to help us think straight about the recent past. But the sudden shift in the state view of the Rising hung heavily on those of us who were watching television in 1966.

Thus we waited for the 75th anniversary of the Rising with considerable interest. This time state television did not re-show the drama documentary and there were no days off school. State television, instead, interviewed various historians and public figures about the Rising: did they think it was right or wrong? Did they think it should be commemorated? Roy Foster said: 'Celebrating 1916, or commemorating it, I think there's a big difficulty there. To celebrate something is, presumably, to say it was wonderful and to, in a sense, re-enact it as a communal ritual. I would think that is undesirable.' This time, if anyone ran out of the room crying, they were crying tears of rage, but most people in Ireland remained reasonably indifferent.

Paddy and Mr Punch contains a brilliantly detailed and lucid essay about the uses to which Irish history has been put. In the essay, Foster talks about 1991: 'When the 75th anniversary of 1916 arrived in 1991, it was treated by the Irish government as a sensitive issue, to be approached in a deliberately restrained way – very different from the unequivocal celebrations of 1966. This caused a small-scale but vociferous old-Republican reaction – featuring not historians but out-of-office politicians, freelance journalists, ex-Sixties activists (including, quaintly, a Pop Art painter) and the members of the Short Strand Martyrs Memorial Flute Band.' There is a sense here that Foster really enjoyed writing the word 'quaintly' and, since this book appeared, there have been earnest letters to the Irish newspapers to point out, among other things, that no one can remember 'the members of the Short Strand Martyrs Memorial Flute Band' being in Dublin for the 1991 commemoration. Even for this over-sensitive, former-nationalist reader, the inclusion of the Flute Band in Foster's list is extremely funny. It must have been even funnier in Oxford, where Foster is Carroll Professor of Irish History.

Things were not as simple in Dublin, however. I had planned to be in Seville for Easter 1991, mainly because I get very depressed in Ireland on Good Friday when the pubs close all day and the sky is low and the churches are full. In the middle of February I received a letter from an organisation called The Flaming Door which, using state money and with state encouragement, sought to commemorate the 75th anniversary of the 1916 Rising by asking Irish writers to join in a marathon reading at the General Post Office in Dublin, where the Rising took place. I thought of attending to read from Beckett's 'First Love': 'What constitutes the charm of our country, apart of course from its scant population, and this without the help of the meanest contraceptive, is that all is derelict, with the sole exception of history's ancient faeces. These are ardently sought after, stuffed and carried in procession. Wherever nauseated time has dropped a nice fat turd you will find our patriots, sniffing it up on all fours, their faces on fire.' But I decided it would be easier to decline. I did not want any work of mine (or any work of anybody else's) being used by the state to replace its own half-heartedness about the past and insecurity about the present. The novelist Anne Enright and I were the only two writers who turned down the invitation.

But others were planning commemorations elsewhere. I met a local politician in Wexford whom I knew and liked. He asked me to join other descendants, mostly grandchildren, of the men who had fought in the Easter Rebellion in the town of Enniscorthy, where I was born and where my grandfather had fought, in a march through the town on Easter Sunday to celebrate the 75th anniversary of the Rising. This was closer to home; there would be no quoting Beckett in Enniscorthy. No one at any of the meetings to plan the march, I was assured, had expressed the slightest doubt about the Rising; no one knew anything about revisionism; it had filtered from the universities to the middle classes in the cities, but not beyond. People in Enniscorthy were simply proud that the town and their forebears had been involved in the Rising. I would love to have marched with them. I wandered around

Seville that Easter wishing things were simpler, wishing that I was not in two minds about everything.

Roy Foster loves two minds, the dual inheritance. Although the essays in *Paddy and Mr Punch* were written for different occasions and contents, there is a single concern running through the book: the way in which the intersection between Ireland and England affects individuals and institutions. He is always deeply aware that this intersection can be dangerous and dark, but in a few essays, he shows that it has also been enriching, and these essays are important and original.

This is a better and more relaxed book than *Modern Ireland* because Foster can choose his ground, write about things which fascinate him, notably individuals such as Parnell and Lord Randolph Churchill (about whom he has already written books) and Yeats (he is writing the authorised biography). Other figures to appear are Trollope and Elizabeth Bowen and Maud Gonne. It is clear that Foster is more interested in posh Protestants than in the members of the Short Strand Martyrs Memorial Flute Band or their like. It is also clear that he does not favour Irish commemorations, even ones which occurred in the past: 'The great Anglophobic outburst of the 1798 centenary celebrations should be seen as therapeutic Anglophobia as much as an endorsement of separatism.'

My grandfather and my grand-uncle took part in those celebrations, as my father and uncle did 50 years later in 1948. They were complex men who had read a great deal of English literature, and they were not much given to Anglophobic outbursts, nor Anglophobia, however therapeutic. It is a pity that Foster is not prepared to offer the same level of nuanced study to the contradictions and complexities in the Irish revolutionary tradition, or to the individuals who took part in it, as he is to, say, Elizabeth Bowen. Thomas Pakenham's 'mob' awaits its historian.

But the descendants of the 'mob' rule Ireland now, on both sides of the border, and do so with the happy conviction that the island is somehow naturally theirs, that history has offered them this birthright, and that outsiders (or indeed minorities) have no natural place on the island. The openness in John Hume's rhetoric, for example, implies that this is his home, and he is ready to make the Unionists welcome here under certain conditions.

Roy Foster has tried to establish what he calls in the final sentence of *Modern Ireland* 'a more relaxed and inclusive definition of Irishness', which has obvious political implications. Elizabeth Bowen, he tells us, 'felt most at home in mid-Irish Sea' . That journey back and forth, the political and spiritual dislocation involved, and how crucial it has been in the Irish experience, concern Foster in most of these essays, especially the last one entitled 'Marginal Men and Micks on the Make: The Uses of Irish Exile *c.*1840–1922'. Marginal Men are 'disaffected British people' using Ireland 'for dreams or ideas or insecurities too uncomfortable for home'. They include Trollope, Lord Randolph Churchill, Maud Gonne. It is perhaps easier to explain Micks on the Make: 'Irish emigrants who went to England and made a good thing out of it.' They are too numerous to mention. There is a real sense in this essay that Foster is writing about these two categories in the present as much as in the past. Enoch Powell, Brigid Rose Dugdale, even John Arden could be included in his list of Marginal Men (and Women); Foster himself and Tom Paulin, to whom the book is dedicated, could easily join the ranks of Micks on the Make. (Paulin, however, also has some Marginal credentials.) Not to speak of Ronan Bennett.

Foster makes the point that Robert Barton, George Gavan Duffy and Erskine Childers, all of whom negotiated the Treaty on the Irish side and all of whom were educated in England, could serve as Marginal Men; just as Michael Collins, who spent nine years working in the English Post Office, could be a Mick on the Make.

W.B. Yeats, who flits in and out of these essays, managed to be both Marginal and Mick as he crossed and re-crossed the Irish Sea. Foster, at his most loftily revisionist, establishes the poet as a Protestant bourgeois, proud to be invited to the Big Houses. Foster writes that skill at fishing – especially trout-fishing – could often be 'taken as an index of gentlemanly status' and then begins a paragraph: 'Yeats would have loved to be able to fish. He posed as a fisherman at Coole . . .' He then goes on to tell anecdotes about Yeats's ineptitude. The next paragraph begins: 'But still he wished he could fish.' The life of Yeats, his creation of a self, is rivalled only by the Story of Ireland, as a narrative in need of thorough re-examination. Foster seems to be proceeding with relish.

He is more respectful about Elizabeth Bowen, as he generally is about people who did not support Irish nationalism. In an essay called 'Protestant Magic' he defines a context for a tradition in Irish fiction – 19th-century Irish supernatural fiction – which includes Sheridan Le Fanu and Bram Stoker and leads to Yeats's interest in the occult. It is a pity that this essay is not placed immediately before the essay on Bowen, because there are interesting connections – some of which Foster makes – between Bowen and the writers of the supernatural.

In his study of Bowen's Irishness Foster is perhaps at his best, prepared to sift through every nuance and examine every shade without ever overstating his case, which is delicate – as delicate and complex as he wants the strands between the varieties of Irishness to remain. Bowen's Irishness is not of mere academic interest to him; there is always the implication that Ireland must take Bowen and her tradition on board if Ireland is to survive. What, then, asks the ghost of my father's friend who tackled Thomas Pakenham in 1969, are we to do about Elizabeth Bowen's activities in Ireland during the war years, when she posed as a journalist or a woman-about-town but was, in fact, spying for the British Ministry of Information? Where was her Irishness then? In any other country, would this not be treachery? 'She was now a kind of spy,' Foster writes, referring to 'the ambiguity of her stance'.

I know that ambiguity is what is needed in Ireland now. No one wants territory, merely a formula of words ambiguous enough to make them feel at home. If we cannot understand Elizabeth Bowen's Irishness, and her British allegiances, then there are other forms of Irishness, and other allegiances, more insistent and closer to us, that we will fail to understand as well. Foster's position is clear: he wants Ireland to become a pluralist, post-nationalist, all-inclusive, non-sectarian place. So do I. But there are other (I hesitate to use the word 'atavistic') forces operating within me too that I must be conscious of. Maybe they come out in odd moments, when I read a book like this, or Thomas Pakenham's *The Year of Liberty*, and know that I am not part of the consensus of which books like these are part. Maybe it would be good if their authors looked again at Catholic Ireland. We, in turn, are learning to talk in whispers. It will take time.

18 November 1993

Paul de Man's Abyss

Frank Kermode

Paul de Man was born in 1919 to a high-bourgeois Antwerp family, Flemish but sympathetic to French language and culture. He studied at the Free University of Brussels, where he wrote some pieces for student magazines. When the Germans occupied Belgium in 1940 he and his wife fled, but were turned back at the Spanish frontier and resumed life in Brussels. The Germans closed the Free University in 1941, so frustrating one possible career; but de Man's uncle, the socialist politician Hendrik de Man, helped him to a job on *Le Soir*, the biggest newspaper in Belgium, which was then under German control. Hendrik de Man had supported the King's decision to surrender, and for a time persuaded himself that the German takeover, though not quite the revolution he had looked forward to, was a revolution none the less, and might bring about what men of good will had wanted so desperately in the pre-war years – an end to decadent pseudo-democratic capitalism and a new era of socialism, even if it had to be national socialism.

Until November 1942, when his contributions abruptly ceased, Paul de Man wrote copiously for *Le Soir*. He later claimed that he left the paper as a protest against German control, though the paper was already under German control when he joined it – it was known as *Le Soir volé*, and its present management say it was 'stolen and controlled by the occupier'. The signs are that at least in the early days de Man did not regard German control as a deterrent; of course the German bosses are quite likely to have turned much nastier in 1942, as they did about many matters. In addition to the hundreds of pages he wrote for *Le Soir* de Man wrote some reviews in Flemish for another German-controlled journal. He also did a lot of translating – including a Flemish version of *Moby-Dick* – which had no connection with war or politics.

After the war he was briefly associated – his opponents suggest feloniously – with an unsuccessful art publishing venture. In 1948 he went to America, where he worked in a New York bookshop and made useful contacts – for example, with Dwight Macdonald and Mary MacCarthy. Soon he was teaching at Bard College. Remarried – his opponents say bigamously – he went to Boston and taught at the Berlitz School. He registered for the PhD at Harvard, became a teaching assistant in Reuben Brower's famous course, Humanities VI, and was recognised as a remarkable teacher, the kind that makes and keeps disciples. In spite of Brower's advocacy he failed to get tenure; in 1960 he moved to Cornell, and thence to Zurich and Johns Hopkins. He ended his career at Yale, where, throughout the Seventies and early Eighties, he was the most celebrated member of the world's most celebrated literature school. He died in 1984.

As academic curricula vitae go, de Man's was certainly unusual, and an account of his publications might seem to make it more so, for his first book, *Blindness and Insight*, appeared only in 1971, when he was 51, and even then, it is said, he published only because Yale drew the line at bookless professors. There were to be only two more essay-collections before his death, but now we have two posthumous volumes, and there may be more to come. Considering the ever-increasing density and strangeness of his work, and its ever-increasing fame, it would take a very tough dean to say de Man had under-produced.*

The corpus is now augmented by a volume he would not himself have wanted to see. This collection of his wartime writings looks like what it is, a heap of ephemera, ill-printed and hard to read in the photocopies. They testify to the exceptional industry and ability of the young literary journalist – he wrote a long succession of literary chronicles and reviewed large numbers of books in various languages – but it is unlikely that any degree of later eminence would have induced anybody to republish them had not their discovery caused such a tremendous bother. The editors, friends of de Man, decided, probably rightly, that in view of all that had been said and written about them on hearsay it would be as well to make them wholly accessible. The editors have not obtruded themselves; they neither justify nor condemn.† And they seem to have been thorough. Here are 170 pieces from *Le Soir*, ten in Flemish from *Het Vlaamsche Land* – these with English translations – plus 100 brief notices written for a book-distributing agency in 1942–3, and a few earlier pieces from student magazines, one of which is here palpably misdated (4 January 1939 for 4 January 1940).

---

* Considered here in particular are Paul de Man, *Wartime Journalism, 1939–1943*, ed. Werner Hamacher, Neil Hertz and Thomas Keenan (University of Nebraska Press, 1988); Paul de Man, *Critical Writings 1953–1978*, ed. Lindsay Waters (University of Minnesota Press, 1989); Christopher Norris, *Paul de Man: Deconstruction and the Critique of Aesthetic Ideology* (Routledge, 1988); Lindsay Waters and Wlad Godzich, eds, *Reading de Man Reading* (University of Minnesota Press, 1989).
† The same editorial team has compiled a volume in which 38 contributors respond to the wartime writings (*Responses*, University of Nebraska Press, 1989).

Keen to extenuate nothing, the editors also include a facsimile of page 10 of *Le Soir* for 4 March 1941, which is headed *Les Juifs et Nous*, and consists of one violently anti-semitic piece on Jews in general, and another claiming that French painting between 1912 and 1932 was *enjuivé* as a result of a plot by Jewish dealers, so that an influx of foreign blood had deflected French art from its natural course, making it morbid and corrupting both to painters and their public. A third essay condemns Freudianism as a further instance of Jewish decadence, and the fourth and last is de Man's now notorious article on the Jews in modern literature. Dissociating himself from vulgar anti-semitism, for which he nevertheless holds the victims themselves partly responsible, he accepts the view that Jews had a lot to do with the disorders of Europe between the wars: but since national literatures evolve according to their own strict laws, they remained largely unaffected by the Semite invasion of other aspects of European life. There were no first-rate Jewish writers anyway; de Man lists some second-rate ones (he doesn't include Proust) and concludes that if the Jewish problem were solved by the creation of a colony isolated from Europe the consequences for 'us' would not be deplorable. It must be added that the page on which this article was printed is decorated with boxes containing comments about Jews from such authors as Ludwig Lewisohn, Hilaire Belloc and Benjamin Franklin, who is said to have wanted Jews, described as 'Asiatics', excluded from the United States by the Constitution. This last citation is spurious.

Some commentators, including Geoffrey Hartman, say that by the standards of the time this was pretty lukewarm anti-semitism. Jacques Derrida – a Jew and a close friend of de Man's – finds it inexcusable, but demands that it be dealt with justly. He repeats that the article deeply wounded him, but discovers in it some redeeming qualities: for example, 'to condemn "vulgar anti-semitism", *especially if one makes no mention of the other kind* [i.e. 'distinguished anti-semitism'], is to condemn anti-semitism itself *inasmuch* as it is vulgar, always and essentially vulgar.' Certainly these interrogations should be carried on justly, but this is all too manifestly a desperate plea. Others have suggested that this article is virtually a unique aberration in de Man's contributions to *Le Soir*; yet others have conjectured that at this stage he was unlikely to have known much about what was already going on in 'colonies' within Europe – the Final Solution wasn't ordained until January 1942. But as even the charitable Geoffrey Hartman feels obliged to remark, and as a reading of this collection makes obvious, neither of these excuses is plausible.

By now these wartime writings have been passionately scanned, especially by Jacques Derrida in the long article quoted above, which was published in *Critical Inquiry* last year.* Here there is room for only a few observations. First, there is certainly more than one anti-semitic piece. An article in Flemish (20 August 1942) about contemporary German fiction deplores the way some Expressionist writers came into conflict with 'the proper traditions of German art which had always before anything else clung to a deep spiritual sincerity. Small wonder, then, that it was mainly non-Germans, and specifically Jews, who went in this direction.' Again, it is surely odd to find in a piece on Péguy (6 May 1941) a short, but not all that short, account of the Dreyfus affair which omits to mention that Dreyfus was a Jew; de Man is seemingly at a loss to understand why the straightforward case of an officer wrongly accused and reinstated by due course of law should have caused such a furor. He admires Péguy, a Dreyfusard, for quarrelling, at the cost of his job, with other liberal-socialist Dreyfusards. Christopher Norris, in a page devoted to this curious essay, remarks that 'any mention of the Dreyfus affair must of course raise the question of anti-semitism,' but fails to add that de Man's mention of it rather pointedly did not; Derrida likewise omits to notice the omission in his *Critical Inquiry* piece, also preferring to emphasise that de Man was here writing admiringly of a Dreyfusard. In fact, the drift of de Man's piece is best expressed in the words *au fond, il ne s'agit pas de grand'chose.*

Even if we recall that the affair lasted over a decade, that the opponents of Dreyfus forged and suppressed evidence, and that the victim spent a long time in prison, it might still be maintained that the level of anti-semitism over all these articles is fairly low. But to confine attention to specific references is misleading, for a survey of the whole collection makes it apparent that anti-semitism was at least not entirely inconsistent with de Man's ideas about the national spirit and the need for cultural development to take place on national (and at any rate in some measure xenophobic) lines. Like his uncle, he was, it appears, ready to believe that the 'revolution' brought on by the *événements* of May 1940 had introduced a new and promising epoch of German hegemony in Europe. Flemish is a Germanic language, and it may have seemed opportune and possibly just, even for a writer of de Man's French formation, to score off France, the dominance of whose

---

* 'Like the Sound of the Sea deep within a Shell: Paul de Man's War', *Critical Inquiry*, Spring 1988. Derrida at the time of writing had seen only 25 of the essays from *Le Soir*.

language and culture was inveterately resented in Flemish Belgium. Yet there is an obvious difference between the French and the Jews. Given a spell of German discipline, the French might yet pull themselves together: but what hope was there for the Jews with their non-European, 'foreign blood'? At the rather abstract level of discourse preferred by the young de Man, there was not much need to be as specific and insistent as some of his fellow contributors, either about Jews or about the flowering of the German spirit demonstrated in the conquests of 1940. Just as he refrains from further overt reflections on the Semite invasion, he silently declines to comment on the continuing progress of German arms, on the Italian alliance (though one article praises the successes of Italian nationalism), on the Russian campaign, the fighting in the Balkans and Africa, the entry of Japan and America into the war. Perhaps he regarded these matters as outside his cultural brief, though the fall of France had not quite been. Yet the military and political developments of 1941 and 1942 must have been of keen and at times disquieting interest to one who had taken the German victories of 1940 as final. For de Man had at first written, understandably, as if in 1940 the war was over, saying more than once that the difference between the two world wars was that the first was long and the second very brief, so that only in the first did people settle down to observable wartime behaviour. Since the Germans had won so completely, any future was going to be a German future, whether one liked the idea or not. But by the time he stopped writing for *Le Soir* the case was somewhat altered, with the Wehrmacht surrounded at Stalingrad, beaten in Egypt, and facing future battles in the west against forces enormously augmented since the American entry into the war. Meanwhile the Final Solution was well under way.

All these events, perhaps along with an increase of supervisory rigour in the office, may have been his inducement to leave *Le Soir*, but there seems to be no evidence for this except de Man's own remark quoted above. And he is said to have offered on occasion rather unreliable versions of his wartime career – for instance, that he worked in England.

In student articles, written during the phoney war or *drôle de guerre* period, de Man argued that the war had been inevitable, and that after the annexation of Czechoslovakia it could no longer be maintained that Hitler merely wished to correct the injustices of Versailles. As an anti-imperialist, he said, one must choose the less objectionable of two imperialisms – namely, the British. But when the war was won we would have to deal with all the problems left over from the Thirties –

unemployment, for example; and that would require a vast reform of European (and imperial) politics generally. May 1940 changed his mind, and a year or so later we find him claiming that the invaders, far from being the barbarians of propaganda and of leaders in the pre-Occupation student paper, are highly civilised. He rejoices at reports that the French are working alongside their victors in a *solidarité purifiante*. Soon he is recommending some German hand-outs explaining National Socialism, and observing that the Germans have made much more generous armistice terms than the French had allowed at the end of the first war.

He sometimes speaks of the irresistible force of a nation's desire for unity, recommending Belgians to study the Italian example and commenting with severity on the record of the French. Ever since Richelieu they had striven to divide Germany. And they had made a bad mistake by refusing to collaborate when they might have done so on equal terms: for they must now choose between doing so on terms much less favourable, and passively submitting to England. He admires the traditional qualities of the French (expressed in the customary terms as clarity of intellect and expression), but rarely loses a chance to compare them unfavourably with the Germans. Under Hitler, he contends, there flourished a pure literature, very different from recent French writing. The Germans would give the French, at this decisive moment in the history of their civilisation, what they now most needed: order and discipline, and presumably purity also. However, in April 1942 he complains that the French do not appear to be responding satisfactorily to 'the reforms at present in progress'.

Opinions of this sort surface from time to time in pieces of which the ostensible purpose is simply literary criticism, and the contention that in the mass these articles are just neutral accounts of books and concerts, leaving only one or two collaborationist obiter dicta to explain away, is simply absurd. Taken as literary criticism, they seem to offer few hints of the writer's future interests, though in saying so I find myself slightly, and unwillingly, at odds with both Lindsay Waters and Jacques Derrida. Some of de Man's judgments are routine – he thought very highly of Charles Morgan, for instance, as the French did in those days. He speaks well of Valéry, and that does remind us of the links between his later thought and his early interest in Symbolism. But his views on history, if he remembered them later, must have seemed embarrassingly undeManian. So with romanticism: an essay from the hand of the scholar of whom it is commonplace to maintain that he changed everybody's attitude to that subject says that romanticism was pretty feeble in France, but strong in Germany because deep in the German national spirit, indeed *la consécration définitive de la nature nationale* (21–22 November 1942) – a version of literary history which he was later to condemn.

Unlike some commentators, both friendly and hostile, I see nothing very reprehensible about his failure to talk about this body of work (as distinct from parts of the work itself). Generally speaking, few writers, of whatever kind, and even if conceited enough to think anybody else would be interested, would volunteer to bring their juvenilia to judgment, even if they didn't contain opinions later seen to be embarrassing or perverted. However, this writer's subsequent fame – and the continuing row between deconstructive admirers and more conservative academics – ensured that people *were* interested, some hoping to use the wartime pieces to discredit de Man and the movement associated with him, the rest needing to defend themselves and their hero. So the significance of these juvenilia is strenuously debated.

Few would deny that at least some of the wartime writing is odious, that of a clever young man corrupted by ideas, and corrupted by war (for in wartime the intellect grows as sordid as the conflict), or merely opportunist, or a mixture of all these. To work for *Le Soir* and *Het Vlaamsche Land* was manifestly to forego any right of dissent. To appear on that anti-semitic page was, as almost everybody would agree, an act amounting to full collaboration. The repeated triumphing over the defeated French, having a possible origin in Belgian domestic conflicts, was presumably not done under direct external compulsion. And it is hard to find indications of concealed dissent in this collection, though some have tried to do so. The simplest explanations may be the least damaging in the end: the young man, on his return from attempted flight, found reasons for thinking it intellectually honest as well as expedient to collaborate with the victors. Others, especially in France, did likewise, until, their reasoning invalidated by events, they saw they must cease to do so; and it could be that de Man gave up his job for similar reasons. One wonders whether, had the Germans occupied Britain at the end of 1940, there would have been no clever young people willing to say in collaborationist newspapers (and wouldn't there have been collaborationist newspapers?) that this was at least not altogether a bad thing.

Lindsay Waters's long and interesting introduction to *Critical Writings 1953–78* amounts to an apologetic intellectual biography of de Man. He dwells on the forces – the failures of democracy, the desire for national redemption, the longing for action – which induced intelligent people in the pre-war period to succumb to 'the fascist temptation'. The comparison with Heidegger is here as elsewhere – and doubtless justly – used in de Man's favour. But the main argument is that in his earliest work de Man embraced an 'aesthetic ideology' – its political manifestation is a rather mystical nationalism – of just the kind he was later to attack with such contemptuous subtlety. This implies that the youthful errors were intellectual rather than ethical, though Waters is in no doubt that anti-semitism, a rather more than merely cerebral blunder, was an essential constituent of German nationalism, and he has no way of excusing de Man's endorsement of it. However; he finds in these 'marginal texts' the seeds or much later work: they display de Man's abiding interest in 'inwardness, interiority', so 'there is a fair degree of continuity'.

This connection seems rather tenuous, but Waters goes on to give a convincing account of the later career, from the early Sartrean phase through the decisive encounter at Harvard with American New Criticism, and the revisionary studies of romantic thought, to the decisive 'turn' to rhetoric and the concord with Derrida, which were the features of de Man's last and most influential phase. His rather exotic academic career in America was a genuine European intellectual adventure, typical of what the writer himself, in a letter of 1955, called 'the long and painful soul-searching of those who, like myself, come from the left and from the happy days of the Front Populaire' – which, though it takes us back to a date before there is any substantial record, is plausible enough, as is the highly metaphysical mode of the soul-search.

In support of his argument for continuity, Waters also supplies what many disciples have been demanding: a selection of uncollected essays from the years before the publication of *Blindness and Insight*, with one uncollected late piece at the end. Many of these items are reviews, some long celebrated, like that of Michael Hamburger's Hölderlin translations. Some – on Montaigne, Goethe and Mallarmé – were originally in French. All have that air of quiet, even tolerant authority which, despite occasional severities and bursts of ill temper, was of the essence of de Man's personality. In an essay called 'The Inward Generation' he remarks of certain 'near-great' writers of the pre-war period – Malraux, Jünger, Pound and Hemingway – that they had all been 'forcefully committed politically, but their convictions proved so frail that they ended up by writing off this part of their lives altogether, as a momentary aberration, a step towards finding themselves.' The whole passage has concealed autobiographical interest. It attributes the course of such careers to the collapse of an aesthetic inherited from Symbolism, and used as a protection from real problems: but the war brought these into menacing actuality, and the political was now a matter of life and death. The political and aesthetic beliefs of such writers make them 'vulnerable targets for today's conservatism – more vulnerable, in fact, than they deserve to be, because their predicament was not an easy one'. Although he distances all this by talking about 'the political and aesthetic beliefs of the Twenties', it seems obvious enough that de Man here had himself in view: and in essence this is the best defence that could be offered. Reviewing books by Erich Heller and Ronald Gray, he remarks that both authors 'too readily call "German" a general feature of the romantic and post-romantic intellect', just as he had done himself.

The most intense of these speculations concern Mallarmé and Hölderlin whose question *wozu Dichter in dürftiger Zeit?* seems to have haunted de Man: he quarrelled over it with the august interpretations of Heidegger. There is a measure of self-absorption about even the least of these pieces. They look forward as well as back, and one of their merits is that they often demonstrate how much can be said in a review or a relatively brief essay: which explains why de Man was so slow to publish a book, and why all his books are collections of essays.

It seems that Christopher Norris had almost finished his book on de Man when the young Belgian scholar Ortwin de Graef uncovered the articles in *Le Soir*, so he comments on them in a postscript. He finds that they contain 'many passages that can be read as endorsing what amounts to a collaborationist line'. It would have been enough to say 'many passages that endorse a collaborationist line', but in general Norris is under no illusions. Before he knew about *Le Soir* he had already noticed National Socialist sympathies in the articles for *Het Vlaamsche Land*, and even in a pre-Occupation piece for the student newspaper. These pieces 'uncritically endorse such mystified ideas as the organic relation between language, culture, and national destiny' – ideas de Man would later 'deconstruct with . . . extreme sceptical rigour'. You can tell how shocked Norris is, for 'mystified', a favourite term of de Man himself, is his usual epithet for ideas he dislikes, and 'rigour' is what deconstructors ought always to use in the necessary business of 'demystifying' them.* So he won't excuse the wartime

---

* Norris has recently published yet another set of rigorously demystificatory exercises in *Deconstruction and the Interests of Theory* (Pinter, 1988). They show, among other things, that

writings as 'youthful aberrations': but de Man is nevertheless a hero and somehow to be excused, if only by a 'totalising' account of his interior life, 'totalising' being a very mystified practice and tolerable only in these very unusual circumstances. Norris outlines the problems of Belgian national politics and the life and opinions of Hendrik de Man, by means of which the young man could, with fatal ease, have got hold of mystified ideas; and argues that the course of his subsequent intellectual travail can be in part explained by the disenchantment that followed their demystifying.

Others, less charitable, have declared that deconstruction is a means of destroying the value of any historical record, or at least blurring a past, as if de Man's work were 'nothing but a series of oblique strategies for pretending it never happened, or at least that there existed no present responsibility for past thoughts and actions'. This is Norris's account of a view that he of course rejects. It has been expressed with much indignation by Stanley Corngold and others – the holocaust, and de Man's own past, they say, conveniently vanish – but it is dismissed, in my view correctly, as founded on a false idea of the relation between deconstruction and history, admittedly a very dark topic. The alternative reading, vigorously expounded by Norris and more or less the same as that proposed by Waters, is that de Man's later life was dedicated to the purging of the false ideology that had once possessed him – in short, an aesthetic ideology, related to an organicism equally responsible for romantic error and for German nationalism with its attendant evils. Looking with 'principled scepticism' at these youthful beliefs, de Man perceived that they must all fall together, as romantic fallacies he had now seen through.

Some may think it strange to regard Nazism and anti-semitism largely as intellectual errors, corrigible by the mere taking of further thought. And although defences of de Man are decently animated by affection for a dead and admired friend, these attempts at biographical exculpation, these rakings through his evolving, exacting, rather melancholy writings, often seem to lack any serious understanding of how even people of high intelligence are sometimes induced to behave,

---

he is not unwilling to be rigorously demystificatory about the very Theory which ought itself to be so, especially when it is put to right-wing or 'irrationalist' purposes, or does its own demystifying with insufficient philosophical rigour. The chapters exhibit a considerable range of interests – from Bloch and Adorno on music, de Man on Kierkegaard, and Rudolf Gasché on de Man, to Pope and Shakespeare post-structurally considered. Norris himself emerges as a demystified left-wing rationalist.

especially when they may be under stress of a kind the exculpators have the good fortune to know nothing about. De Man himself has some tortuous but interesting observations on excuses in an essay on Rousseau's *Confessions* (in *Allegories of Reading*, 1979). For example, he distinguishes between confession and excuse. The former is 'governed by a principle of referential verification', whereas the latter lacks the possibility of verification – 'its purpose is not to state but to convince': thus it is performative whereas confession is constative. He is interested in the curious interaction, in Rousseau, of the two rhetorical modes, but at the same time he is willing to say that Rousseau was clearly dissatis- fied with his performance as judge of himself, and unable to get rid by excuses of a recurrent sense of shame. For the childish theft of a ribbon is only a beginning: it is followed by other faults that likewise call for excuses, such as the abandoning of one's children. (De Man, we are told by some of his accusers, abandoned his own wife and child, but I do not know whether the known facts really permit this inference.) The critic's interest is expressly not in any simple way biographical or eth- ical: it is firmly expressed as devoted to an entirely rhetorical problem. It nevertheless passes belief that anybody could write an essay such as this without reflecting on his or her own life, and it may surely be assumed that de Man did so.

It is true that such considerations are not strictly germane to rhetor- ical theory. Norris quotes an admiring judgment of Minae Mizimura: 'The shift from a concern with human errors to a concern with the problem inherent in language epitomises [de Man's] ultimate choice of language over man,' adding on his own account that it is here – 'at the point of renouncing every tie between language and the will to make sense of language in acceptably human terms – that de Man leaves behind the existential pathos that persists in his early essays'. This apa- thetic purity is what his disciples admire and emulate, though the need to defend the master must sometimes hinder them from quite so scrupulous an avoidance of pathos: the enemy, after all, was repres- enting him as a devious, opportunist, dishonest human being. Furthermore, even if one breathes the air of pure theory, it must some- times seem strained to argue that it is always impossible to say what one means, even if the statement you wish to make is that it is always impos- sible to make such a statement; or to combine this belief with the belief that one can and should intend to say, and say, what will make sense of de Man's life as a whole.

Norris is sometimes critical of his subject – for example, of the way in which his views on undecidability are given what sounds like inappropriately decisive and even authoritarian expression. This is his explanation: de Man's style has 'a rhythm that alternates between claims of an assertive, self-assured, even apodictic character, and moments of ironic reflection when those claims are called into doubt'. This is true: de Man almost always achieves this kind of internal tension, the undecidability of his own writing reflecting the unavoidable undecidability of language itself. He was always looking for the point where necessity encountered impossibility, or intention its fated undoing. He is the great impresario of the rhetorical impasse. The title of his first book, *Blindness and Insight*, reflects its thesis, that in critics the two must exist in inseparable tension. In the late essay 'Resistance to Theory', to be found in the book of the same title, he argues that 'rhetorical readings' are theory and not theory at the same time, the universal theory of the impossibility of theory. It would be easy to extend the list of such paradoxes: de Man's quarrel with the aesthetic is the quarrel of an aesthete, his refusal to accept customary distinctions between literature and philosophy is philosophically-oriented, the denial of any differences between literature and non-literature is highly literary. Some such aporia – another favourite word – is the goal of deManian meditation, a kind of substitute for the obsolete satisfactions of closure, now known to be impossible because of the very nature of texts.

Norris, it must be said, is very clear about de Man's positions. He hasn't enough patience to give a fair hearing to anything that he can dismiss as mystified, but one hardly reads him with any hope of that. Within his own ballpark he is lucidly competent. He makes bold use of digressions. The point of a long one about Hillis Miller is to demonstrate that two colleagues, both deconstructionists, may have, within their sympathy, very different attitudes and styles. There is another on Adorno, registering with approval his view of the negativity of knowledge, in order to confer on de Man the increment of this particular virtue of Adorno. The object is to confute those who accuse de Man of nihilism; they are just as wrong as those who accuse him of quietism. The real problem is to discover in him anything, outside rhetoric, that can be stated unequivocally as a belief; and Norris's book does help one to grasp the nature of that problem.

For a while, given the extraordinary veneration in which he was held, it must have been difficult for admirers to write about de Man without referring first to the man and his death, and then, for it emerged almost before the period of mourning was over, to the wartime writing. One impressive thing about *Reading de Man Reading* is that apart from the fine leading essay by Geoffrey Hartman, mentioned above, the contributors go about their rhetorical deManian business without such allusions. Hartman writes as a Jew, and as one who knows more than most about wartime anti-semitism. He admires the intellectual power of de Man's late work: 'the only peculiar thing is that a philosophical mind of this calibre should turn against the pretensions of philosophy and toward literature.' And now he wonders about the *purity* of these deconstructive essays. 'Hegel or Heidegger or Kant or Proust are not sources but materials only; there is neither piety in this critic for their achievement nor any interest in strengthening their hold on us, consecrating their place in the canon.' He clearly thinks of de Man, the philosophical critic, as having made an extraordinary effort of self-dehumanisation, as if the kind of interest Hartman speaks of were somehow base or inauthentic. Nevertheless he speculates that there may be hidden, in the later essays, 'the fragments of a great confession', and that one might 'link the intellectual strength of the later work to what is excluded by it, and which, in surging back, threatens to diminish its authority'. And when de Man asserts that 'what stands under indictment is language itself and not somebody's philosophical error,' we are to understand that this is a reflection 'by de Man on de Man', for 'the later self acknowledges an error, but does not attribute it to an earlier self – because that would perpetuate its blindness to the linguistic nature of the predicament.' In short, the conscience of the rhetorician is such that it forbids the exercise of conscience in the person.

This gives one a fair notion of the complexity of the problem. Some of de Man's admirers have properly assumed that their business is finally with his mature writings, with the power of his rhetorical procedures; and their ability to continue them is well illustrated in the remainder of this book. Among the most impressive are Neil Hertz's essay on de Man's essay on 'Wordsworth and the Victorians' (in *The Rhetoric of Romanticism*) – a deManian interrogation of de Man, like Carol Jacobs's 'Allegories of Reading Paul de Man' ('*Allegories of Reading* is an elaborate allegory of the impossibility of the fundamental condition of allegory' which 'necessarily relapses into the condition it deconstructs'). Like the master, these critics have become connoisseurs of the symmetry between the impossible and the necessary: as he himself pointed out, 'the impossibility of reading should not be taken too lightly.' Hillis Miller speaks of the 'austere rigour that makes de Man's essays sometimes sound as if they were written by some impersonal intelligence or by language itself, not by somebody to whom the laws of blindness and impossibility also apply, as they do to the rest of us'. On such matters it may, he feels, be best to keep silent, as he says de Man does.

But blindness and impossibilism, a love of the aporetic, seem, among initiates, to promote not silence but an endless linguistic fluency. This is in a way strange, for the prevalent deManian tone might be called depressed; every critical victory, to be recognised as a victory, must be a defeat. You may win the local skirmishes of deconstructive reading, but you have to lose the war. There must, it seems, be a peculiar pleasure in encountering language allegorised as something resembling the great Boyg, with no defence that can be used in that formidable encounter except language itself, now allegorised as a weapon treacherous and very easily broken. In a rare jocular moment de Man himself compared undecidability and aporia to getting stuck in a revolving door, which is perhaps a better figure. Anyway, a definition of reading which claims that hitherto it has never been attempted, and now that it has turns out to be impossible, might well have seemed dispiriting, but it turns out to be positively exhilarating. One might compare these writers to the early Christians, who thought they were the first people ever to read the Jewish Bible properly, were caught in the aporia of an end-time that could not end, and managed to feel pretty exalted about it.

Norris speaks of the essential inhumanity of de Man's views on language, summarised in a neo-Nietzschean manner as 'a wholly impersonal network of tropological drives, substitutions and displacements'. 'To call de Man's position counter-intuitive,' he says, 'is a massive understatement.' Yet it is just this bleakness, this disclaimer of human authority over language, that attracts de Man's luxuriously ascetic followers. They mourn the man but rejoice in his 'inhuman' teachings.

The theory that theory is self-defeating, that it cannot possibly control or comprehend the workings of figural language, is part of the master's charm, but it is also a strange foundation for the ambitious institutional and political programmes now being quite stridently proposed by some – for instance, Jonathan Culler in his recent book *Framing the Sign*.* Norris, no less committed but rather more critical, is less confident of the imperialist possibilities of theory, though he would like some sort of concordat with Marxism. De Man himself, with his 'extreme and principled scepticism', would possibly have thought this out of the question, as it must be if the inevitable terminus is that

* Blackwell, 1988.

revolving door, where language moves in, impossibly, on an understanding of language, and is at once thrown out. The noble course is not to submit to the bewitchments of language, and to recoil from the Acrasian temptations of the aesthetic 'ideology'. But people outside the cult are probably less principled and more prone to mystification. Trilling's students, when he introduced them to the abyss of the Modern, gazed into it politely, said 'how interesting!' and passed by. Others may do the same to de Man's abyss, and carry on thematising and totalising because it is their pleasure to do so, even if it is shamefully human to do so; and they have a long history of resistance to puritanical imperatives. As a rule they will do so without reference to the youthful errors of Paul de Man, and the insiders should now be happy to stop worrying about them and get on with their necessary and impossible projects.

16 March 1989

DIARIES

Pop me under the yucca

Jenny Diski

For some time now, it's been clear to me that consciousness of death is a kindness bestowed on us by the Great Intelligence, so that even if all else succeeded we would always have something to worry about. This, of course, accounts for pussy cats and lions sleeping 18 hours a day and therefore failing to invent the fax machine. Us humans, up and anxious about death, have passed the time thinking up civilisation as a way to distract ourselves, or at least to let others know that we're awake, too. Unfortunately, the fax machine having already been invented, I had to settle simply for being up and anxious all Bank Holiday weekend, brooding darkly and leafing restlessly through the Gazetteer of London Cemeteries.*

It began when my friend Jenny (not me in my Post-Modern mode, but someone else entirely) made me the offer of a lifetime. She'd bought a plot in Highgate Cemetery, she told me, which was a mere snip at £700, especially since it accommodated three ex-people. Would I care to share it with her? Not immediately, of course, but when the time came. Highgate Cemetery is a very nice place, and Jenny is an old and dear friend. I was properly honoured; no one else I've known has ever wanted to spend eternity with me – as a rule the occasional supper is sufficient – and I wished to express my gratitude. But at the same time my heart rate began to speed, and my throat to constrict: classic signs of claustrophobia and panic. I've never been any good at long-term commitment.

'Are you sure?' I asked. 'It's a bit perpetual. What about your children?'

'They can make their own arrangements,' she said darkly.

Jenny is known for going off people – even people who are not her children. She keeps a bottle of Tippex beside her address book to deal with those she's no longer on speaking terms with. I felt that apart from my reservations about making a long-term commitment, we ought to be realistic about the eternal prospects of our friendship.

---

* Hugh Meller, *London Cemeteries: An Illustrated Guide and Gazetteer* (Scolar, third edition, 1994).

'I know we get on well, but we have to think practically. For ever's, well, a very long time to be side by side.'

'Actually, one on top of the other. It's a vertical plot.'

There was a lot to think about here. Assuming that things went according to the Great Chronologist's plan, Jenny-who-isn't-me would be tucked in first, since she's twenty years older. On the other hand, I smoke several packs a day and eat salami like sweeties. There was, therefore, no guarantee that I'd get top bunk.

While I was wondering if this mattered, the Heir Apparent shuffled into the room and announced that she had something to say about all this, since, after all, she'd be in charge of arrangements. We'd already had a prior conversation about the disposal of my remains because she's a sensible girl and doesn't like to leave things to the last minute. I'd suggested cremation (so they could play 'Smoke Gets In Your Eyes' while the casket slid behind the modesty curtain) and that my ashes should be scattered over the threshold of the Hampstead branch of Nicole Farhi.

The only other really appealing possibility was a monomaniacal plan of the Victorian architect, Thomas Willson, who in 1842 designed a brick and granite sepulchral pyramid with a base area the size of Russell Square to be built on Primrose Hill. Its 94 levels (topped by an observatory) would be 'sufficiently capacious to receive five millions of the dead, where they may repose in perfect security'. The scheme foundered, but if anyone feels like reviving it, I'd be happy to make a contribution in return for a guaranteed place somewhere near the pinnacle. Failing that, I thought I would after all settle for the shared accommodation on offer in Highgate Cemetery.

'God, you're always changing your mind,' the Heir Apparent said impatiently. 'If you're buried you'll have to have a headstone. That's more of my inheritance gone, and what's it going to say on it?'

'*Jenny Diski lies here. But tells the truth over there*,' I instructed. 'Also, I'd like a dove, a wing-ed angel, an anchor and an open book, properly carved on a nice piece of granite.'

The Heir's eyes narrowed dangerously.

'You get in for nothing if you've got a relative on site. Otherwise it's a pound a head. So there's a saving,' the other Jenny reassured her. 'And there's much more scope for drama in a proper burial. At the last funeral I went to, the grieving mistress tried to throw herself into the grave. Very satisfactory, and not a thing you can do at a cremation without making a nasty stink.'

It looked like it was decided. I wasn't to go up in smoke, but would instead fatten the worms which feed the birds which keep the London cats sleek, self-satisfied and asleep for 18 hours a day. While the other Jenny went off to spend the holiday weekend in Bradford (which gave more pause for thought about spending eternity in such eccentric company), I hunkered down with my Gazetteer to apprise myself of the interment possibilities.

It was not so much the fact of death as the quantity of it that struck me. In 1906 the Angel of Death dropped in on houses in London at the rate of once every six minutes. Oddly, London's population has resumed to roughly what it was at the beginning of the century, though I suppose that the death rate (Bottomley notwithstanding) must have fallen. I added to my collection of useless but disturbing thoughts the fact that currently the total land used for burial in London is three thousand acres. Anyone with GCSE maths (three thousand acres ÷ six-foot plot × three bodies deep) could work out how many dead are lying around London. I don't have GCSE maths, so I didn't try, but, according to the Gazetteer, Highgate has 51,000 plots containing 166,000 bodies. Do the rest of the arithmetic for yourselves. And if you're very keen, how many people *in total* have died since Homo got to its feet? More than everyone alive today? I only wonder because I like large numbers.

I was troubled by the idea of so many people dying as we wake and sleep and go about our business. It's an astonishing feat of human lack of imagination to be able to ignore all those souls up and down our streets, fluttering off minute by minute, all around us. I remembered an incident in the early Seventies (when else) during a community festival in Camden Square's central patch of railed-off greenery. Perhaps it was midsummer, or Easter, or maybe it was just one of those pseudo-spontaneous street parties that were supposed to weld us all together, before we knew the Eighties were coming. Anyway, we had a great bonfire, a lamb roasting on a spit, rock 'n' roll megawatting through monster speakers and the decidedly mixed inhabitants of the square – the teenage villains, prepubescent truants and lawless toddlers of our Free School plus the recent incoming gentry whose houses they regularly broke into. The robbers and the robbed mingled riotously to celebrate the spirit of their community.

Suddenly, someone was standing out on the street, shouting through the railings. 'There's a woman dying at number 65!' he bellowed at us revellers over and over again, and finally made himself heard. 'Hasn't she got the right to die in peace?'

There was a bit of a lull, long enough for any-man's-death-diminishes-me sort of thoughts to start rolling around in my head, before a bearded and bejeaned community hero spoke up for the collective will. He was sorry about the woman, he told her son or husband or friend, but there were a couple of hundred people out here, also belonging to this square, and we were celebrating life. Man! The very shade of Jeremy Bentham hovered over Camden Square for a second, and then a roar of affirmation went up. The Utilitarians won the day, The Stones were turned up again to ear-splitting level, and John Donne slunk back with the soon-to-be-bereaved protester to get on with private dying behind closed doors. Logical, of course, but for all that, the lamb tasted raw and rotten to me.

It's possible I take death too seriously. It's always seemed a momentous business, coming, as it generally does, after a lifetime's consideration, unlike, for example, birth, which happens (to the new-born, if not the parents) before one has a chance to consider it, so far as I can tell. For a long time I supposed it only happened to very serious and substantial people, but then my father died when I was 17 and I was amazed to discover that something as weighty as death could be done by someone so dedicated to evading life's trickier realities. I confess I was, and still am, impressed that he could have done something so committed as to die.

The Gazetteer, however, kept all such metaphysical thoughts up in the air where they belong, and my feet on the ground. It quotes from the *Builder* in 1879: 'The principles of proportion and of harmony of grace and form which are required by a well-dressed woman in her costume are equally applicable when she comes to choose a tombstone for her husband.' Though not as much fun, I should think, as burying a husband, thoughts about one's own tomb are just as sartorial. What if Armani and Calvin Klein diversified into the undertaking and stone-dressing business? I could fancy an eternity of decomposition under a layered beige, beautifully cut headstone. But could my cheapskate descendant be trusted not to shop around and dump me in the Monsoon cemetery for dead hippies?

Planning the style of one's burial is also a rather cunning way to avoid thinking about its prerequisite, I discovered. The Gazetteer has no mention of people dying or the manner of their death, and in an investigative wander around West Hampstead Cemetery (I thought I'd better wait for Jenny's return from sunny Bradford before visiting my prospective plot) there were very few indications of how the interred got there. I suppose it doesn't matter unless something extra special carried them off. I'm rather partial to the idea of being *translated*, myself, but mostly the dear departed, sorely missed, tended to fall asleep or pass away.

Except for Tony. *Tony* was carved in six-inch lettering on a slab of black marble and under it was inscribed: *I Had a Lover's Quarrel with the World 1947–1987.* I was moved. Forty-year-old Tony. One of my lot. Post-war Tony, agitated by peace and prosperity, his youth a haze of misremembered sex and drugs and rock and roll, as overfull of romantic aspirations as he was of existential despair, threw in his towel after doing the best he could to compose a resonant if pretty yukky farewell to life. Sadly, when I got home, I found it was a quote from Robert Frost. Even so, Tony didn't just pass away and wanted to be remembered for not doing so. Perhaps he died of disappointment at not even being able to think up an epitaph of his own. Mostly, disappointment of one kind or another is what my generation died young of. If it's any consolation to them, those of us who remain find ourselves with the practicalities of not having died young to attend to.

There is, apparently, a cemetery in Buenos Aires which is a veritable city of the dead, with named avenues lined with scaled-down architected homes for the late-lamented. Relatives come and housekeep on Sundays, dusting, polishing and replacing lace doilies while chatting to neighbouring survivors over the fence. This set me brooding about my one-up-one-down resting place in Highgate. What about a mausoleum, I began to wonder. It could be fitted with a wood-burning stove and comfy chairs. I'd leave funds so that a bottle of Scotch and packs of cards would be available in perpetuity, so friends and well-wishers could drop by on gloomy Sundays for a game of poker. The Heir Apparent was not keen on this idea. Quite apart from the drain on her inheritance ('To hell with the expense,' I cried. 'You're so selfish,' she hissed), there was the matter of the earth's resources to consider. She pointed severely to an article on natural death.

'There is some other kind?' I queried.

It turns out there's no legal reason not to bury your dead in the back garden. I was delighted.

'Darling, you can have me around always. Sod Highgate. You can just dig me a nice big hole and pop me under the yucca.'

She explained this wasn't a good idea because it would very likely lower the value of the house when she came to sell it, and she certainly wasn't going to dig me up and take me with her every time she moved.

I called the Natural Death Centre* and a Mr Albery explained that their idea is to use European Union set-aside land to inter bodies and

---

* *Green Burial: The DIY Guide to Law and Practice* can be purchased from the Natural Death Centre, 20 Heber Road, London NW2 6AA (0181-208 2853).

create lovely nature reserves full of you and me, while the farmers get paid for not growing anything useful on it. Instead of gravestones, they'll have trees. I could have a plaque if I wanted it, though he didn't sound enthusiastic. No need for embalming. All those chemicals are just to stop what's going to happen anyway from happening for a while. It seems it's perfectly all right to keep an unembalmed body at home for up to three days, and frankly who wants one around longer? And forget about coffins. Mr Albery advises the use of a simple sheet. By now the Heir was smiling broadly; it was all beginning to look like a pretty thrifty exercise.

However, it turned out that for £85 a specially woven natural woollen shroud can be purchased, which has a plank along the middle (to stop that nasty wobbling corpse effect) and four ropes at each corner for lowering it into the grave. A bargain, I thought, though the Heir muttered that one of our old sheets would do perfectly well. Still, I have a terrible dislike of the cold, especially when it gets into the bones. There was something comforting about the prospect of a woollen shroud, and I think she would have relented if just then I hadn't remembered that I have no desire in this life or after it to conserve resources, that I am and always have been an urban dweller and I didn't see why a detail like death should mean I have to end up in some draughty, disorganised, naturally set-aside bit of rustic. What I fancied was a proper old-fashioned pollution-filled London cemetery to rest my wearied bones, and if I couldn't have it, along with an expensively carved headstone and a very long and elaborate funeral, with hymns and popular hits of the Sixties sung, a certain amount of dancing, and my deeds recounted for the edification of all, then the Heir could whistle for her inheritance and I'd leave everything to the Natural Death Centre including my clothes. That did it. A proper interment at Highgate is assured.

23 June 1994

Heidegger's bad smell

Richard Rorty

Recent attempts to dismiss Heidegger as 'a Nazi philosopher' resemble the Nazis' attempt to dismiss Einstein's theory of relativity as 'Jewish physics'. In both cases, we are urged to test a body of thought not against competing bodies of thought but against something more easily accessible – our moral intuitions. If you know that the very idea of relativity is a product of cultural decadence, you are spared the trouble of labouring through a lot of equations and then deciding whether the phenomena can be explained non-relativistically. If you know that the very idea of 'authentic existence' or of 'harkening to the voice of Being' is inherently fascistic, you are spared the trouble of comparing Heidegger's account of the history of Western philosophical thought with, for example, Hegel's, Dewey's, Popper's or Blumenberg's. You need not labour through Heidegger's fantastic etymologies and idiosyncratic neologisms. What is more, you can brush aside the books of the people influenced by Heidegger – Derrida, de Man, Foucault – as just more of the same discredited claptrap.

Heidegger himself specialised in this sort of quick dismissal. Like Nietzsche, who claimed that his sense of smell told him whether or not a book was worth thinking about, Heidegger claimed to be able to sniff out the 'authentic' or the 'primordial'. Heidegger brushed aside all attempts at increasing human happiness or equality of opportunity as mere symptoms of 'humanism', further indications of our forgetfulness of Being. So when the Nazis came along he felt no obligation to compare their proposals with those of the Social Democrats or the Catholic parties – no need to ask what sort of future Germany might expect under Nazi rule, whether it might be better to live within the terms of the Treaty of Versailles, whether firing Jewish professors might damage German universities. The Nazis smelled right to him. There was something authentic about them.

Thanks to the book by Hugo Ott, reviewed here by J.P. Stern (20 April 1989), and to those by Victor Farias and others, we now know that Heidegger's quest for authenticity was mixed in with a lot of vulgar ambition. We also know that when people tried to call him to account he lied himself blue in the face. But the mistaken political judgment, the ambition and the cowardly hypocrisy – and even, I think, the deep antipathy to democracy – would not bother us much were it not for the fact of Heidegger's silence about the fate of the European Jews. Most of us are prepared to brush aside the vanity, spitefulness and shady dealings of original thinkers and writers (the kind of thing paraded in books like Paul Johnson's *Intellectuals*), and ask: 'But still, what can we learn from these people? What can they do for us? What can we get out of them?' That would by now have become the standard attitude to Heidegger were it not for his postwar silence about the Holocaust – his refusal to acknowledge its existence in any way. That refusal was too much. It was as if we had learned belatedly that certain fabulously original and moving poems had been written by a torturer after finishing work for the day. From then on there would be a bad smell about those poems.

Nevertheless, I think that we should hold our noses, separate the life from the work, and adopt the same attitude to Heidegger's books as we have to other people's. We should test them not against our moral intuitions but against competing books. An original story about the history of Western philosophical thought is not all that easy to come by – no easier than an original story about the movement of the heavens or the structure of matter. Stories of the former sort try to explain why we use the words we do, and thus, among other things, why we have the moral intuitions we have. When a genuinely new story of this sort comes along, we cannot afford to dismiss it. We will do so only if we have the sort of egomaniacal faith in our own noses that Nietzsche and Heidegger had in theirs. Such faith may be a necessary condition for the production of works of genius, but we non-geniuses who think of ourselves as tolerant and open-minded had better try to lose this faith.

We will be willing to separate someone's life from his or her work precisely insofar as we think of moral character – our own and that of others – as varying independently of the possession and deployment of talents. To help ourselves think in this way, we should remind ourselves of a lesson Freud helped us learn: a person's moral character – his or her selective sensitivity to the pain suffered by others – is shaped by chance events in his or her life. Often, perhaps usually, this sensitivity varies independently of the projects of self-creation which the person undertakes in his or her work.

I can clarify what I mean by 'chance events' and by 'independent variation' by sketching a slightly different possible world – a world in which Heidegger joins his fellow anti-egalitarian, Thomas Mann, in preaching resistance to Hitler. To see how this possible world might have been actual, imagine that in the summer of 1930 Heidegger suddenly finds himself deeply in love with a beautiful, intense, adoring philosophy student named Sarah Mandelbaum. Sarah is Jewish, but Heidegger, dizzy with passion, barely notices. After a painful divorce from his first wife, Elfride – a process which costs him the friendship of, among other people, the Husserls – Heidegger marries Sarah in 1932. In January 1933 they have a son, Abraham.

Heidegger jokes that Sarah may think of Abraham as named after the patriarch, but that he will think of him as named after Abraham à Santa Clara, the only other Messkirch boy to make good. Sarah looks up Abraham à Santa Clara's anti-semitic writings in the library stacks, and Heidegger's little joke becomes the occasion of the first serious quarrel between husband and wife. But by the end of 1933, Heidegger is no longer making such jokes. For Sarah makes him notice that the Jewish *Beamten*, including his father-in-law, have been cashiered. Heidegger reads things about himself in the student newspaper which make him realise that his days in the sun may be over. Gradually it dawns on him that his love for Sarah has cost him much of his prestige, and will sooner or later cost him his job.

He still loves her, however, and eventually leaves his native mountains for her sake. In 1935 Heidegger is teaching in Berne, but only as a visitor. Switzerland has by now given away all its philosophy chairs. Suddenly a call comes from the Institute of Advanced Study in Princeton. There Heidegger spends two years slowly and painfully learning English, aching for the chance once again to spellbind seminar rooms full of worshipfully attentive students. He gets a chance to do so in 1937 when some of his fellow émigrés arrange a permanent job for him at the University of Chicago.

There he meets Elizabeth Mann Borgese, who introduces him to her father. Heidegger manages to overcome his initial suspicion of the Hanseatic darling of fortune, and Mann his initial suspicion of the Schwarzwald *Bauernkind*. They find they agree with each other, and with Adorno and Horkheimer, that America is a *reductio ad absurdum* of Enlightenment hopes, a land without culture. But their contempt for America does not prevent them from seeing Hitler as having ruined Germany and being about to ruin Europe. Heidegger's stirring anti-Nazi broadcasts enable him to gratify his need to strike a heroic attitude before large masses of people – the need which he might, under other circumstances, have gratified in a rectoral address.

By the end of World War Two, Heidegger's marriage is on the rocks.

Sarah Heidegger is a committed social democrat, loves America, and is a passionate Zionist. She has come to think of Heidegger as a great man with a cold and impervious heart, a heart which had once opened to her but which now remains closed to her social hopes. She has come to despise the egotist as much as she admires the philosopher and the anti-Nazi polemicist. In 1947 she separates from Heidegger and takes the 14-year-old Abraham with her to Palestine. She is wounded in the civil war but eventually, after the proclamation of independence, becomes a philosophy professor at Tel-Aviv University.

Heidegger himself returns to Freiburg in triumph in 1948. He helps his old friend Gadamer get a job, even though he is acidly contemptuous of Gadamer's acquiescence in the Nazi takeover of the German universities. He eventually takes as his third wife a war widow, a woman who reminds all his old friends of Elfride. When he dies in 1976, his wife lays on his coffin the Presidential Medal of Freedom, the medal of the order *Pour le Mérite*, and the gold medal of the Nobel Prize for Literature. This last had been awarded him in the year after the publication of his brief but poignant elegy for Abraham, who had died on the Golan Heights in 1967.

What books did Heidegger write in this possible world? Almost exactly the same ones as he wrote in the actual one. He tells the same story about a gradual loss of a primordial awareness of Being as we move from Parmenides to Nietzsche. In this other world, however, *Introduction to Metaphysics* contains a contemptuous identification of the National Socialist Movement with the mindless nihilism of modern technology, as well as the remark that Hitler is dragging Germany down to the metaphysical level of Russia and America. The seminars on Nietzsche are much the same as those he gave in the actual world, except for a long digression on Nietzsche's loathing for anti-semites, a digression which contains uncanny parallels with Sartre's contemporaneous but independent 'Portrait of the Anti-Semite'.

In this other world, Heidegger writes most of the same essays he wrote in our world, but also exegeses of passages in Thoreau and in Jefferson, composed for lectures at Harvard and at the University of Virginia respectively. These lectures transfer the pathos of Schwarzwald pastoral on to Mount Monadnock and the Blue Ridge of Virginia. His books in this world are, in short, documents of the same struggle as the one he carried on in the actual world – the struggle to move outside the philosophical tradition and there 'sing a new song'. This private pursuit of purity and originality, this attempt to see the West from a new and utterly different perspective, was the core of his life. That pursuit was incapable of being deflected either by his love for any particular person or by the political events of his time.

In our world, Heidegger said nothing political after the war. In the possible world I am sketching he puts his prestige as an anti-Nazi to work in making the German political Right respectable. He is adored by Franz Joseph Strauss, who pays worshipful visits to Todtnauberg. Social democrats like Habermas regret Heidegger's being consistently on the wrong side in post-war German politics. Sometimes, in private, they voice the suspicion that, in slightly different circumstances, Heidegger would have made a pretty good Nazi. But they never dream of saying such a thing in public about the greatest European thinker of our time.

In our actual world Heidegger was a Nazi, a cowardly hypocrite, and the greatest European thinker of our time. In the possible world I have sketched he happened to have his nose rubbed in the torment of the Jews until he finally noticed what was going on, until his sense of pity and his sense of shame were finally awakened. In that world he had the good luck not to have been able to become a Nazi, and so to have less occasion for cowardice and hypocrisy. In our actual world, he turned his face away, and eventually resorted to hysterical denial. This denial brought on his unforgivable silence. But that denial and that silence do not tell us much about the books he wrote, nor conversely. In both worlds, the only link between Heidegger's politics and his books is the contempt for democracy he shared with, for example, Eliot, Waugh and Paul Claudel – people whom, as Auden predicted, we have long since pardoned for writing well. We could as easily have pardoned Heidegger his contempt for democracy, if that had been all. But in the world without Sarah, the world in which Heidegger had the bad luck to live, it was not all.

8 February 1990

That's Hollywood

Stephen Frears

I had finished my first American film, *The Grifters*, and was looking for another job. I liked a script called *Gloucester Waterfront*, which Columbia owned and didn't want to make. Some friends of mine at Paramount wanted to make it. Columbia changed its mind. I decided to stick by my friends. From a cottage in Somerset I tried to make sense of the transatlantic phone calls. I have on occasion bought a Sunday paper in Crewkerne and had dinner that night on Rodeo Drive.

I was approached to direct a Mafia film called *Donnie Brasco*. The producers were Barry Levinson and his partner, Mark Johnson. We had first met when Levinson, Alan Parker and I had dinner in London. It was a wonderfully smug affair: the last three films we had directed, *Rain Man*, *Mississippi Burning* and *Dangerous Liaisons*, had between them received 23 Oscar nominations. Levinson himself was to have made *Donnie Brasco* but for domestic reasons couldn't leave Los Angeles. When I said I knew nothing of the Mafia, they said nobody did except, possibly, 'your friend Marty'. I had known nothing of the 18th century or indeed of Pakistanis, but Hanif Kureishi had said: 'Don't worry – they're exactly like you.'

Donnie Brasco is about an undercover agent who infiltrated the Mob, became alienated from his family and the Bureau, and came to realise that moral duty involved human betrayal (the same theme, you could say, as *The Third Man*). The spine was the friendship between Donnie, the agent, and a lovable psychopath called Lefty Ruggiero. I asked who they wanted to play Lefty and they named Actor A, but in conversation he had said he would rather play the title role. We joked that the script should have been called 'Waiting for Lefty'. I said A would be perfect as Lefty, and that Actor B would be good as Donnie.

An agent who represented the Producers, the Writer and Actor A rang me (in Somerset) to suggest Actor C, a huge star of the cinema, to play Donnie. I was suspicious, but said I would meet him. I had already planned to be in New York the following week to publicise *The Grifters*, and I agreed to continue my journey to Los Angeles to decide whether I would make the film. The New York bills would be paid by the distributors of *The Grifters*; at the appropriate moment my prospective employers would start to pay.

I flew to New York on Concorde, pausing only to buy new Green Flash sneakers in Hounslow. I had done this when I flew to New York for the *Dangerous Liaisons* interview over lunch at the Carlyle Hotel, and it had brought me luck. I arrived two hours before I left, and half an hour after I got to my Central Park South hotel room, the giant star, Actor C, walked in. He was very nice, wild about the script, talked a lot about the FBI, and began to fill me in about the story. The next day I met Actor A in an empty café. He said if we offered him Donnie, he would accept immediately. I said he was wrong; he would be great as Lefty, and that all he had to do was sit around, make jokes and break people's hearts – what more did he want? He said he would do what he always did; get a group of his actor friends to read the script aloud, with him reading Lefty, the part he didn't want to play and thought he was wrong for.

I flew to Los Angeles on the MGM Grand, and accepted an invitation to stay at the Bel Air Hotel which is, I suppose, as near Paradise as you can get. A friend said I should stay at the Beverly Wilshire because at least there were streets outside, but I can't because of what happened to my former agent, Clive Goodwin, when he was staying there. He had a cerebral haemorrhage on a Saturday night, had asked for a doctor, had been taken for a drunk, and died in the police tank. I met with the Producers and the Studio and we agreed that the film should be made with stars. Levinson said that if we could get Actor A to play Donnie, we should take him, but I asked the studio to offer Lefty to Actor A and Donnie to Actor C. (My participation was always dependent on getting the combination right.) The Studio consulted their computers, worked out that the salary bill for the two actors wouldn't entirely preclude the Studio from getting a return on its money. Meanwhile, Actor A had a hilarious reading of the script, but turned down the part of Lefty.

I had arranged to come back to England on Friday, but Actor C said he could only come to a meeting at four that afternoon. The London planes leave at 5.30 p.m. I resigned myself to another night in the gilded cage, but Virgin Airways turned out to have a late-night flight to Gatwick. (When I turned up to collect my first-class ticket, they gave me as well a voucher – good for a year and transferable – for an economy ticket on the same route.) This second meeting was to discuss the writing of a second draft of the script to accommodate Actor C.

This business of rewriting for the actors takes up a lot of time in America. I am still surprised that John Malkovich agreed to play Valmont without having it written in his contract that he didn't have to die. It would have left him available for *Dangerous Liaisons II*. Diana

Ross, on her way to Paris to make a 'highly personal' (*auteuriste?*) film about Josephine Baker, was asked if she was going to write the script herself: someone else, she trilled, would have to do 'the paperwork'. Meryl Streep spoke glowingly of sticking to the text when they filmed *The French Lieutenant's Woman* from Harold Pinter's script. I first came across the problem in Bangkok when the American actor Fred Forrest would spend the evenings laboriously changing David Hare's dialogue for *Saigon, Year of the Cat*. When I asked him why, he said: 'Can you imagine Marlon sticking to the text?' Forrest had been in *Apocalypse Now*, and had watched Brando climbing palm trees in the Philippines and throwing coconuts at Coppola. When in the heat of filming I asked Forrest what Coppola would do, he would say: 'Go up in a helicopter and think.' In our case, Actor C was younger and less cynical than the character in *Donnie Brasco*, and it made sense to take this into account.

We also talked about *GoodFellas*. 'My friend Marty' is the director Martin Scorsese, who had produced *The Grifters*. His fine film *GoodFellas* had just opened, and *Donnie Brasco* strayed into its territory. We had missed each other in NewYork and Los Angeles, but eventually met at Michael Powell's memorial service. (He said he would probably not have made *GoodFellas,* but Powell had picked up the script and said how good it was.) Scorsese liked *Donnie Brasco* very much, pointed out the differences between the two films, and thought I should make it.

I flew back to London to home and children and to meet the Writer for the first time. He had been on his honeymoon in Europe, but – such is the power of celluloid – we were able to divert the happy couple to London for two days' work. He is a handsome Italian-American (a 'hyphenate') who has the confidence of the good writer who will rewrite anything if the reasons are right. We talked, he went back and produced a second, better draft of the script. It went off to Actor C – and indeed, back to Actor A to see if it wouldn't change his mind. My producers installed a separate phone line in my house (for calls to the US) and a fax machine. Until its installation I was using my friend Leo's machine; she would arrive in her office to find sixty new pages of script scattered over the floor. Prospects looked good, and agents, lawyers and accountants started to negotiate my contract with the Studio. Words like 'bifurcate' and 'good faith' were in the air, and I was to be paid a weekly wage immediately – a 'holding fee' which would take me off the market. I took a job at the National Film School in Beaconsfield.

There was a long, eloquent silence. Actor C's agents liked the script; they liked it more when I said we were making an FBI movie, not a

Mafia movie. In America a spate of (unsuccessful) gangster films had opened hot on the heels of *GoodFellas,* and at Christmas comes *The Godfather III.* The release of *The Grifters* has been put back because of this. Actor C saw some of these films, especially *GoodFellas,* and did a runner. I had been through this crisis myself some weeks back, but had decided that Mafia films were like Westerns used to be, of their own kind and with their own rules. Renoir had said that one year all film-makers should make the same film: then 'you would see the originality, the differences among the films'. I rang the Writer to say how sorry I was. Before this, however, Actor A had asked if, in the event of Actor C turning the title role down, he could be offered it. The Studio did their sums again and agreed. Actor A flew to New York with his agent, acting out the part on the plane. He then organised another read-through, this time with him reading the coveted title-role. Alas, he discovered that the part he was right for was Lefty – and for various reasons he couldn't accept it.

All this time I had been dealing with the question of ethnicity. It was in *The Godfather* and *Mean Streets* that Italian-American actors were first cast to play Mafiosi: before then they were played by Cagney and Bogart, George Raft and Edward G. Robinson. Al Pacino and Robert de Niro changed all that. Now I concentrated on two Actors B and D, who were not Italian-American. I had surreptitiously met Actor B, my original choice, while I was at Fox meeting a producer from Columbia. He was nice but depressed and frustrated, and only for ten seconds, when mocking an Italian accent, had his face lit up as you dream Garbo's must have done. Like everyone else, Actor B thought it was a wonderful script. How could we meet? he kept asking down the phone. I arranged to fly to New York the following week, but on Monday news from London reached me that he wanted massive rewrites or else he would 'pass'. The next night, he listed various things that ought to be in the script. When I pointed out that they already were in the script, and spoke about the ten seconds at Fox, he again wanted to meet: all he wanted, he said, were 'little' changes. By the following night, he was gone, his final complaint being that it was too much a 'Barry Levinson movie': why couldn't it be an 'Actor B movie'?

As for Actor D, his agent, though he, too, thought the script was wonderful, advised us not to get involved. His client was doing four films over the next two years. Although we might be able to find a 'window' (in which he could make our film), the four contracts stipulated that no other films could be released with this actor in the summer or at Christmas in the next two years. If we went an hour over the contracted period, we would be sued. Actor E had heard the script was great but, understandably in his case, didn't want to play a gangster or a cop. The Producers, the Writer, the Studio have been thoughtful and generous. The actors are under enormous pressure, and anyway are the ones who have to do it. We have defended the script but have no stars. I have told the producers to go ahead and cast the film. If the combination makes sense to me, I'll direct it. In the meantime I enjoy teaching, and have written this on the instructions of my therapist.

20 December 1990

I was interested to read my article in the *LRB* (20 December 1990). Not being an academic, I don't have to apologise for the disorderliness of my mind, and the other half of a clearly divided personality had various subsequent thoughts.

In the case of *Donnie Brasco,* the actors were right. Their instincts were better than mine. It was idiotic to try to set up a film about the Mafia half-way between *GoodFellas and Godfather III.* I've always thought that casting a film was 95 per cent of my job, for on a good day an actor can dance through the text like Gascoigne passing to Platt. I was taught to cast by Miriam Brickman in a shed behind the Royal Court. When on a Friday night, we were trying to persuade some poor sod to play Metellus Cimber in *Julius Caesar,* Peter Gill would say: 'He's lucky to be offered it.'

I remember being sent to Hackney on the opening day of rehearsal and being told not to come back without Stephen Moore (I didn't). One day Peter Gill said there was a girl in the *Daily Mirror* who'd just made her first record and would be very good as Nicol Williamson's daughter in *Inadmissible Evidence.* The girl auditioned (for the non-speaking part), got the job, came to the read-through; her name was Marianne Faithfull. That week her record went up seven places in the charts and she disappeared. We went down to the ABC Café in Kingsway (next to the Thames Television studio where she was recording *Ready Steady Go),* and Andrew Loog Oldham, her manager, explained the facts of life. Money was never any help at the Court. Leading actors got £30 a week. Olivier got £50 for Archie Rice.

People like to hear stories which fuel their anti-Americanism: tales of censorship, stupidity, immorality, corruption. But if such things happen in Hollywood, they're kept well away from me. I can see that people there are nervous and work ridiculously hard, that they are more welcoming to foreigners than we are, that you need to be both stoical and crusading to work there. The people I meet are by and large intelligent, grifters, people for whom I naturally have an affection, small con-artists, people like me.

Meanwhile in Paris, Jacques Lacan and Juliette Binoche have holed up in the Hôtel Heidegger on the Rue Noel Annan while outside an old woman in a van . . .

Stephen Frears

24 January 1991

Burying Ronnie

Iain Sinclair

A crisp, clear morning, bright and fresh and cold enough to make the flaunting of black anklelength crombies no burden: the perfect day for a funeral. Walking south towards Bethnal Green, through Haggerston Park and over Hackney Road, I appreciate the unnatural, expectant stillness – dispersed by the fretting traffic that is already beginning to snag up. Outsiders, transients, put it down to road works; an extension of the tarmac hole that is London. But *three* helicopters to the south, somewhere over Vallance Road or Cheshire Street, that is unusual. One chopper, ferrying traumatised meat to the Royal London Hospital, we're used to that. Three choppers, catching the light, remorselessly circling the same patch, are worth remarking; an arrogant display of budget that speaks of royal visitations, the finish of the London Marathon, or John Major on walkabout, prospecting for inner-city blight. But on this unearned, mint morning, the fuss is all about real royalty, indigenous royalty: one of our local princes of darkness, a cashmere colonel, is about to be boxed.

A mob of expectant necrophiles are packing the fringes of Bethnal Green Road, dodging motors, climbing on lamp-posts – and that's just the salaried media. They're here to give an elderly, Romany/Jewish businessman, who has been living out of town for a quarter of a century, a decent send-off. It's a great turn-out for a notorious homosexual predator who Peter Tatchell, somehow, never got around to outing. George Cornell's efforts in this direction (both sexist and weightist) having murderously back-fired: 'fat poof' was an ad lib that was exposed in a dramatically public act of political correction. But say what you like about the doped inertia of the slacker generation, the timidity of the pensioners, give them what they want and they'll make the effort. Give them the biggest gangland funeral since the Albert Dimes do and they know how to show their appreciation. (The Twins set the benchmark in floral tributes with their wreath for Albert: 'To A Fine Gentleman From Reg And Ron.' At £25 a letter.) The point is that no other social group has such a rigorous sense of tradition, such a memory for previous plantings. The East End had its reputation to uphold: sentiment backed by discipline. The salty tear trickling down the butcher's cheek. Senior members of the Firm had been shuttling to Maidstone for days, to go over points of procedure. A discredited era had been put on the spike, there would never be another Ronnie Kray. 'Nothing to touch it since Churchill,' said Carole McQueen, florist to the fraternity.

Splitting the Twins, divorcing Reggie from his 'other half', was like splitting the atom – it had done something to the sky, to our perception of time. Sharp-edged shadows were printed into the asphalt. This special quality of the light teased phallic clusters of lenses; engorged telephotos could be displayed without embarrassment.

The merely curious, the event junkies who read this day as a living newspaper, were out early, packing the pavements of Bethnal Green Road and Vallance Road, covering the route the hearse would take from W. English's funeral parlour to St Matthew's Church. They were tactfully backlit, tired hair scorched into seraphic aureoles. A frieze of witnesses in an El Greco apotheosis. This was one of those rare occasions when the crowd is as important as the central figure. The stature of the dead man has been weighed in the ranks of those who are prepared to stand for hours to collar a few details of the final journey.

Ron had known for some time that his earlier fantasy, retirement, dog breeding, would never happen. He'd died without that consolation. But for the others, the retirement home villains, dog love justifies everything. Reg and Ron never recovered from premature exposure to *Lassie Come Home*. It blighted their emotional development. It helped to formulate the lodge rules for survival in the dance halls, clubs and spielers; never badmouth a Cockney mum and never harm one hair of a dog's head. Even wrong 'uns like Cornell and Jack McVitie didn't go that far. They cheated, popped pills, blasted pub ceilings, did damage for cash, but they loved their families and patted Alsatians for luck. They were cursed for another reason entirely: they cost the Twins their lives. 'It's because of them that we got put away.' A nice piece of sophistry – to blame your victims for making you kill them.

Now the dog days were over. Ronnie Kray had been laid out in the back room of W. English's establishment at 464 Bethnal Green Road; painted, primped, pressed. The coming procession was significant because the journalists, the hearse chasers, said it was. Many of the crowd didn't know, or care, who was being buried. The event was television and that was good enough for them. Messrs English were quietly ecstatic, soberly smashed by the chance to show what they could *really* do. It was like a bucket and spade firm picking up the contract to clear Hyde Park after the VE Day celebrations. Their trade name sympathised with the mood: English as the lettering in a stick of Margate rock.

Bethnal Green was one big street party: high ritual and low comedy, conspicuous expenditure. Newsreel crews, deals made, filmed the principal faces, while secret state technicians panned the crowd. The press lived in the confusion between burns of hyperactivity and intolerable wedges of boredom. Style scribes prepared themselves by thumbing through red pulp memoirs, to be sure they'd recognise Frankie Fraser or Tony Lambrianou when they poodled into the churchyard. Researchers were busy inventing quotes, hammering golden nuggets into the carious mouths of bemused recidivists. Photographers risked everything, setting rickety ladders on traffic islands, dangling from stop signs. The Kray funeral was a major boost to the local economy: paydirt for florists, renters of black horses, firms that stretch limos. Knownothings asked if the dear old Queen Mum had snuffed it.

Even with Ron stiff as a starched dicky, the duckers and divers were taking no chances with their floral tributes. They hadn't been privileged to get a peep inside the coffin. Rumours of death had often been exaggerated. The Krays had long since moved into the realms of mythology; youngsters aping their dress code, their hairstyles, thought they were contemporaneous with Jack the Ripper. The Twins co-existed with Craig and Bentley and the Reservoir Dogs as natural-born killers of the spectral plane.

The funeral cortège would turn into Vallance Road at the Cornwallis pub, where there are two street names: the shabby original and the new Tower Hamlets-approved version. New signs, in my experience, mean trouble. Cleanliness comes with a price. 'Safe' neighbourhoods and restored iron railings have to be paid for with Kray-style tithes. Eco-babble underwritten with brass knuckles. Tony Lambrianou is a spokesman for this new ethic: 'Today, if I see anyone damaging a tree, or drawing graffiti, I go absolutely potty.'

We have grievously misinterpreted the Kray philosophy: the pitch was Green, and the boys were disadvantaged precursors of the Goldsmith Brothers. Free-market capitalists who cared deeply about the environment, channelling excess profits straight back into high-profile charity. Good housekeeping that isn't afraid, when strictly necessary, to rap the odd knuckle. Anthropomorphism so intense that it bleeds into voodoo ritual. It's a shame that the Krays' political careers were aborted so soon: the Twins were active members of the Bethnal Green Conservative Association. Lady Mancroft, president of the Association at that time, recalls 'a frightful row . . . they attacked someone, threw him across the road through a shop window. The police were very close and the hospital managed to sew the chap's ear back on.' Geoffrey Howe, a coming man, was on call to provide free legal advice. This liveliness, unexceptional in the House, was deemed to be over the top in the East End. So the careers of two grassroots Tories took a different turn.

The mortician at English's outlined the day's ceremonies. Six plumed black horses, with 26 top-of-the-range limousines to follow. Poland has been invaded with less. A dark oak coffin with gold handles displayed in a glass-sided hearse, borne on a gun carriage – as befits the deceased's martial status. The dimensions of the gun carriage would test the ingenuity of Carole McQueen and her horticultural engineers: how to fit 'The Colonel' onto such a narrow border, how to heap the roof with such a profusion of blooms. It seemed as if the corpse had flowered; as if the body's gases had exploded into spiral clusters of red and white and blue. A wake of pollen and steaming horse dung trailed behind the procession like the phantom traces of an ocean liner. Some of the cars had to be pressed into service as wreath transporters; there were more than enough floral tributes to replant Nevada. Four pall-bearers – Charles Kray (North), Freddie Foreman (South), Johnny Nash (West), Teddy Dennis (East) – would symbolise the seigneurial homage paid by the four cardinal districts of London. The conceit was Blakean, the Sons of Albion 'dividing the space of love with brazen compasses'.

St Matthew's is one of those typical East London parish churches with its own patch of grass, no particular ambience, sinister or otherwise, and permanently locked doors. The churchyard is a useful shortcut, a toilet for dogs. A moderate crowd, bareheaded, behind crush barriers watched . . . nothing very much. Accredited media paced inside the fence. OB vans. Tripods on the pavement, trainee clipboard-directors letting their cameramen set up in any way that took their fancy. Production assistants plotting their coffee runs. Small groups of near-strangers working together, professionals of ennui. An outbreak of yellow cones and plods in scrambled-egg vests. Bethnal Green is *en fête*, a celebration that cannot quite declare itself. Freakishly stretched limos, like silver cigar torpedoes, barely make it around the tight turn into Wood Close. Some of these villains are so old they think they're being flash by giving two fingers to petrol rationing. Hidden away behind tinted glass, they are instantly recognised by a passing bag lady, a Carpenters Arms familiar. She hoots her derision.

One minor TV mouth, toasted to an unhealthy walnut tan by studio lights, fannies about inside the fenced area, screaming into his mobile:

'Where are we? Can somebody *please* tell me where the fuck we are?' Grey bullet heads in Brick Lane buffalo jackets bunch up on the west side of the street. Down at the far end, beyond the Carpenters Arms, you find the same knot of foot-stamping ghouls that used to wait out-side Pentonville for the posting of an execution notice.

It's easy to forget: somewhere in the middle of all this is a recent corpse. The hard old men are closer to it, arthritic claws knuckled in sovereigns, throats goitred in gold. All those faces last seen making up the numbers in souvenir snapshots from the Kentucky Club: Eric Mason, Frankie Fraser, Terry Spinks (a cortisone cherub). Ruthlessly ironed handkerchiefs peeping from the gash of a breast pocket. This turnout has been a killing for the car rental mobs, the muscle agencies, the barbers. Who says London refuses to oblige major film productions? Roads closed off, police, colourful extras, banks of cameras: the funeral is a one-day epic with a minimalist performance at its centre. There's nothing for the uninvited to witness. One hundred and forty ticketed seats barely cover the worldwide media interest; reporters book in for a taped rendering of Sinatra's 'My Way' and Whitney Houston torching 'I Will Always Love You' – before the reading of the honour role of those who are unable to attend, 'friends from Broadmoor and prison'.

Other business later that day prevented me from following the funeral procession on its 12-mile journey, another Blakean progress, through Old Ford, Stratford, Leyton, Walthamstow, to Chingford Mount. I let it lie for a few weeks and then, on a pleasant Sunday morning, cycled out along the tow path of the Lea to Chingford.

The freshly turned earth, and perhaps forty yards of grass behind the tombstones of Ronnie Kray's father, mother and sister-in-law, were blanketed in dead flowers, the gaudy colours faded to browns and mauves. The look was of the traditional 'wedding cake left out in the rain'. Ribbons and bunting gave the shallow tumulus the appearance of a place of pilgrimage.

Fathers led young children by the hand, so that they would get an authentic taste of it – mortality, the survival of pre-posthumous fame. Hollywood has, since Valentino, lost its vampiric piety. Hereditary roy-alty is an unconvincing soap opera. The Krays have replaced all that. This site is a massive attraction. Young women in long skirts: some of them have brought small bunches of wild flowers, violets, which they drop without show onto the floral carpet.

The effect was both emotive and grotesque, an overblown rhetoric of grief. Self-aggrandising tributes to a man who had been, for years, a chemically palliated zombie; a man whose humanity had died with his victims. In a sense, he couldn't die: he was dead already, estranged from himself. Victim and servant of the voices in his head, the endlessly repeated (and revised) fables of those short months of glory, which left him trapped for ever in a coffin of newsprint.

Dead ground had burst prematurely into bud; the sweet-sick stench of home-brewed perfume, flower heads rotting in water. *Ronnie. The Colonel. The Kray Twins.* Spelled out in pink carnations, with scarlet tulip crowns for emphasis, like lettering on the side of a neon gambling hell. Colour combinations too rich to stomach. Flesh pinks with broken veins. *The Other Half Of Me.* Floral chains linking Ron to Reg, as if they had been buried together. (The crowds outside St Matthew's called for Reggie's release, an end to this unnatural punishment. Which can never happen. That would be like rewriting history, opening the grave to make us see the spectre of our past, touched by time, pinched, crook-backed, shrunken.)

Ronnie iced into a birthday cake of daisies, into a boxing ring. The sacrifice of thousands of carnations, pink and white and sclerotic. Puce roses sweating with shame. Eggy bundles of lilies pinched at the waist by purple ribbon corsets. Wreaths like the wheels of articulated lorries. Hearts the size of Sri Lanka. A plethora of tributes from Birmingham: *Actress & Bishop, Muldoon Auto's* (with grocer's apostrophe). *Freedom At Last, Flanagan.* Showbiz signatures: Barbara Windsor, Roger Daltrey. A giant's body woven from flowers. The East End loves them, heaped on pavements at the site of a killing or a road accident.

A nail-varnish scarlet BMW, engine running, leaking fumes into the still air, cruises the cemetery path. A couple of black T-shirt, leather jacket tearaways slouch across to the grave, primed to pick up the vibes. Blatant herb merchants, mobiles in pocket, stepping forward to make the touch. 'This Ronnie Kray, mate?' The five-foot letters spelling out name, rank, sobriquet, were not enough. They wanted the verbals before making the energy exchange, soliciting the blessing of the dead. An impertinence that would have the colonel spinning through the clay like a drill bit: lowlifers dressed like vagrants, German motor, peddling drugs, no bowwow. The filth he'd wasted his prime keeping off the streets.

The smell of this exterior boudoir, reds, pinks, greens, left me swaying in a state of visually induced nausea. I couldn't wait for the undergrowth to take over, the revenge of the ivy. A child, encouraged by her parents, let a bunch of daffs drop on the mound. The mother balled up the newspaper wrapping and bowled it onto the grave of some faceless unknown.

8 June 1995

Takeover

W.G. Runciman

Readers of my occasional contributions to the *London Review* who have consulted the Notes on Contributors will know that I earn my living as chairman of a public limited company rather than as an academic. But only those who are also readers of the Business Sections of their newspapers will know that the company in question has recently been involved in fighting off a hostile takeover. I meant, when it started, to keep a proper diary day by day. But the intention soon wilted in the *Sturm und Drang* of battle, and I am left only with a few internal company memos, a file of press cuttings, a set of circulars to shareholders, and some clear but no doubt imperfectly reliable recollections of particular episodes. When asked, 'What was it like?' I generally answer: 'bad for the schedule but good for the adrenalin.' But more to the point, it was one of those things like a divorce or a car crash which you think only happen to other people until the day they actually happen to you.

The outline facts are these. The company is a long-established, originally family-controlled, shipping-based mini-conglomerate which diversified some time ago into insurance and security engineering. In the late Seventies and early Eighties, when the shipping industry was being savaged by a horrendous global recession which sent many larger as well as smaller shipowners to the wall, the name of the game was survival; and diversification into engineering was little or no help at a time when UK-based low-tech manufacturing was itself grappling with a painful conjunction of domestic overcapacity, inflated costs and shrinking demand. But we survived all right, and after that the game was to move through recovery to sustained organic growth. During that period, as the share price predictably languished, just under 30 per cent of the shares were accumulated in the market by an investment trust specialising in 'strategic' stakes – which amounts to an open invitation to some would-be predator to have a go. This summer, such a predator duly appeared, in the form of a quoted engineering-based company of similar size which, having bought most of the investment trust's stake, launched a hostile bid for the whole company. We at once denounced it as totally inadequate; they raised it; we denounced it again; and by the closing date they had secured acceptances from shareholders representing 12 per cent of the total equity, so that with the 28 per cent they by then held themselves they were still 10 per cent short of control.

What view you take of any such story will largely depend on the presuppositions you bring to it. Readers for whom the City is a dirty word will no doubt see it as vindicating their distaste for the evil machinations of financial capitalism, while those who think that traditionally-minded British managements need to be kept on their toes by the bracing impact of uninhibited shareholder aggression will no doubt wonder if we hadn't deserved to be despatched to the knacker's yard long before. From where I sit, the function of my fellow directors and myself is to play the hand we've been dealt in the best interests of shareholders, customers and employees as we see them, and we therefore deserved to win if, but only if, we were right to believe, as we do, that we can do more for long-term earnings per share than whoever else might have been installed in our places. But the point of telling you the story is not to solicit your plaudits or otherwise. It is to describe to you just how different the experience was from what I would have expected beforehand.

The first surprise was the extent to which takeover battles are conducted according to ritual. They run for precisely 60 days within a detailed set of laid-down constraints. Our merchant bankers at once produced their booklet written to guide the inexperienced combatant through the thicket of the rules of play according to which this jousting is conducted, and answered with avuncular patience questions to which they simply couldn't believe we didn't know the answers already. Would we really not be allowed to disclose any new information to our shareholders after day 39 even though the predator would then still have until day 46 to increase his bid? Would we really be expected to put out three or even more expensively-printed circulars justifying our policies and prospects to our shareholders? Could we really not tell the journalists exactly how good next year's profits could already be predicted to be? Would we really have to get the consent of an extraordinary general meeting to do things we'd decided to do already simply because we could otherwise be falsely accused of doing them to frustrate the bid? And so on. I quickly learned that you don't argue the loss with your financial, legal and PR advisers any more than you do with the consultant specialist called in by your GP. But it was disconcerting to realise that I was so ignorant not just of the ritual but even of the language. I suppose I should have known already that in Moneyspeak 'ready to help' means 'willing to exploit', 'a commercial view' means 'short-term greed', 'an agreed deal' means 'a surrender' and the epithet 'gentlemanly' is a term of unmitigated contempt. But I didn't.

The second surprise was the extent to which – as, I suppose, in a real war – the outcome depends as much on intelligence in the military sense as on the relative size of the opposing battalions. Of course I knew that what matters is what people believe, not what's true. And of course I wasn't surprised to hear the rumour mills grinding away from day one: it was, I was assured, being said in one place that I had deliberately engineered the bid for my own devious ends, and in another that my family had been panting to unload their holdings for years. But after our hoots of laughter had died down, we had to consider the serious possibility that the predator might have been led to believe that the company would be worth a lot more in his hands than was actually the case. What then? If somebody offers a group of people ten one-pound coins for every five-pound note in their pockets, they are presumably well-advised to take them. But what good does it do anybody if a company which is going to be worth a lot more in a year or two's time is prematurely hijacked at a price which doesn't in fact yield the predator the short-term gain he thought he could extract? We had already, with such a possibility in mind, done what we could to secure our better-than-statutory redundancy terms for our employees, protect our pension fund from being raided or wound up, and guarantee the executives responsible for the company's recovery adequate compensation in the event of dismissal; and in the event, the argument turned on future earnings potential rather than inflated estimates of asset value put about by the rumour factory. But it hadn't seriously occurred to me that we might have to defend ourselves against criticisms based, not on the quality of our investment decisions, but on somebody else's erroneous estimate of what those investments would fetch on a break-up, or that a predator might launch a bid entirely because of a mistaken belief that by putting us 'into play' (as they say in Moneyspeak) he would prompt some other bidder to jump in at a higher price and give him an instant profit for nothing.

Meanwhile, the Stock Market was pricing the company's shares some way above the value of the cash alternative in the predator's offer. When I asked the advisers what this meant, I was told that it meant the market thought the bid would fail. But in that case, I said, wouldn't the price fall *below* the bid? Oh no, I was told, the market only thinks *this* bid will fail – they'll still be hoping for another. So, I said, wouldn't it be a good sign from our point of view if the price *did* fall? Oh no, I was told, that would expose us to the risk that the predator could then buy enough shares in the market to get control that way (the rule being that a predator may not buy in the market at anything above his own bid). But then, I said, what happens if the whole market takes a nose-dive and our shares and the predator's both plunge by 30 per cent? Oh in *that* case, I was told, every one of your shareholders will be advised to accept the cash alternative, because the predator can't withdraw even if he wants to and he will *have* to pay £3.28 for a share which is otherwise worth only £2.28 or less. It's all obvious enough when you think about it. But again, the possibility hadn't seriously occurred to me that another stockmarket crash like the one in October of last year might give the predator a victory which he wouldn't then want and wouldn't otherwise have had. At that point, I began to have an uneasy feeling that we might be walking blindfold straight into Catch 22. But as it turned out, the price hovered nicely round their cash alternative; and the final distribution of the votes was almost exactly what our intelligence had led us to expect.

But votes are, of course, what it's all about. The shareholders are the sovereign electorate, and if there was any chance that victory might not be a foregone conclusion we had to try just as hard as any party politician to gather them in. The rules allow a company to require its nominee shareholders to disclose who they really are, so unless we were up against holders hiding behind nameplate companies in foreign territories where Maggie's writ won't run, we knew who our electorate consisted of. But just how many floating voters might it turn out to contain? Going the rounds of our institutional shareholders, I was struck by the immediately obvious differences in their attitudes to contested bids in general. In one office, we were poured our cups of coffee by a senior director who told us they didn't believe in hostile takeovers and wished us the best of luck, while in another we were received by a team of beady young screen-watchers who might as well have been wearing tee-shirts blazoned with 'I ♥ short-termism'. But we still had to be sure of getting our message across as best and wherever we could. And that brought us face to face once again with the familiar thought that what matters isn't being right but persuading other people that you are.

The advisers were splendidly disdainful of the quality of argument, or lack of argument, in the predator's circulars, which did indeed contain such flights of rhetoric as 'Do you believe in fairy-tales?' But once more, after our hoots of laughter had subsided, we had to contemplate the possibility that there might be some shareholders out there for whom this style of argument held an appeal. And we had to make sure of getting our own case across in the press. Talking to financial journalists is a funny business. They are, I found, both shrewder and fairer-minded than I had feared. But their object is to get good copy, not to uphold the higher scholarship, and I quickly learned that the risk is not that *they* might say something they shouldn't, but that *I* might. They hope, quite rightly, to provoke an intemperate comment, an indiscreet prediction, a hasty agreement or disagreement with something somebody else has said: and you have nobody to blame but yourself if they get it. In the event, we were very fairly treated (and very well advised by our PR consultants). But it was an alarming thought that a single foolish remark (or failure to make a sensible one) might result in a newspaper item which, however unfair we might think it, could have an effect on a section of shareholder opinion which we could not then hope to undo. I remarked, in this connection, to an old friend who is a Member of the House of Commons that I now understood what it must be like to fight an election campaign, to which he replied: 'Yes. But if I lose, I can win my seat back next time. If you lose, you won't ever win back your company.'

Oddly enough, the one episode which rendered me speechless with irritation concerned not something said in the press, but the Takeover Panel's attitude to our use of it. The rules are, very sensibly, strict about selective quotation. You can't tell your shareholders that the company has been described as '. . . a gem . . .', even if, as in our case, that is what the newspaper has actually said. But what you *can* do (or so we thought) is reproduce it in the whole of its relevant context, always provided the board is willing to endorse whatever assertions it contains. So we duly reproduced the article in its entirety, having been advised by our merchant bankers that they had cleared it with the Panel over the telephone. No sooner, however, had it gone out on the inside cover of a circular to shareholders than the Panel decided that we had to make clear in a separate communication that in saying that we seemed to be 'embarking on a prolonged period of profit growth' the author of the newspaper article was expressing his own opinion, and that in quoting him we were not committing ourselves to a profit forecast as the Panel defines it. I was (and am) at a total loss to understand how anyone could possibly have supposed otherwise. But the advisers told us it could only be counterproductive not to do what the Panel said. I asked them whether in these circumstances Rupert Murdoch or Robert Maxwell or one of the other so-called 'big hitters' would pay any attention to the Panel whatever, and was told that they probably would not. But here I was up against Catch 22 with a vengeance. I am a member of the Securities and Investments Board, the body which is responsible for regulating the financial markets in parallel with the Takeover Panel. So if a company of which I am the Chairman were to flout a Panel directive, wouldn't that just look great in tomorrow's edition of the *Financial Times*? The merchant bankers put the Panel on notice that if the predator sought to make capital out of this ruling, they would protest in the strongest possible terms. Predictably, that is exactly what the predator later did, and so the protest was accordingly lodged. But the Panel (or rather a committee of it), having debated the issue for (literally) hours, decided – if you can believe it – to say and do precisely nothing.

Nothing else actually lost me my cool. I kept being asked by mock-solicitous acquaintances whether I was losing sleep or weight, to which the honest answer was that as long as we felt we were going to win it was rather fun. The trouble is, however, that as Yogi Berra of the New York Yankees used to say, the game isn't over till it's over, and by the closing week the nerves did start to wear thin, with the consequent psychological risk of lurching uneasily from complacency to paranoia and back again. Afterwards, a merchant banker friend told me that the late Lord Beeching had once told him that fighting off a hostile takeover was the most stressful episode in his whole business career. But it is, after all, one of the problems that boards of directors are paid to handle. Compared with the sort of thing that one of my fellow directors was decorated for doing in the war it has to be kindergarten stuff. What is more to the point is that from the company's point of view, as opposed to the Board's, it was not only expensive but distracting. Not only did it make our employees understandably worried about their personal futures: it also diverted much too much management attention from running the ship to manning the boarding netting. But the remark which I suspect may stay with me longest was made by one of the fund managers to whom we went to present our case: 'We often find that beating off an unwanted takeover is the best thing that ever happens to a company.'

So what is the conclusion to draw? Was it all an unnecessary waste of resources typical of a market where (unlike either Germany or Japan) the pressure of short-term gain is allowed to outweigh the achievement of long-term investment objectives, and genuine wealth-creation is subordinated to the interests of parasitical financiers and their hangers-on? Or was it a heartening illustration of the workings of healthy competitive capitalism, in which survival is the only test which either can or ought to apply? Unfortunately, these questions cannot now or ever be answered objectively. The difficulty is not the passions and prejudices which they arouse (although of course they do). It is that there is no possible way of ever knowing what would have happened if the outcome had been different, and therefore no possible way of judging whether the company's subsequent performance is better or worse for shareholders, customers, employees, or the nation at large.

I know the moral I'd *like* to draw: that nice guys – dare I say gentlemen? – don't always finish last. But I suspect the more plausible moral is simply that in a market economy everything has its price. The going rate for the acquisition of a well-run plc against the wishes of its board seems currently to be somewhere around 18 times next year's prospective earnings, at which level of price it becomes rather difficult for the directors to tell the shareholders they would be wrong to accept an offer of good negotiable paper underwritten with a cash alternative. In the case of Walter Runciman plc, such a multiple of prospective earnings would (in some kibitzers' estimates) take the shares up to well over twice what they are trading at today. But the only certainty is that anyone who claims to be able to predict a share price twelve months ahead is either a fool or a charlatan. So don't all start reaching for your stockbrokers at once.

8 December 1988

1995 Diary

Alan Bennett

13 January. One of Peter Cook's jokes, several times quoted in his obituaries, is of two men chatting. 'I'm writing a novel,' says one, whereupon the other says: 'Yes, neither am I.' And of course it's funny and has a point, except that Peter, I suspect, felt that this disposed of the matter entirely. That people did write novels or poetry and were heartfelt about it didn't make much difference; literature, music – it was just the stuff of cocktail party chatter, nobody really did it, still less genuinely enjoyed it when it was done. Forget plays, pictures, concerts: newspapers were the only reality – not that one could believe them either.

16 January. Listening to Michael Heseltine justifying the £475,000 of Mr Brown, the chairman of British Gas, I remember Joe Fitton. During the war Dad was a warden in the ARP, his companion on patrol a neighbour, Joe Fitton. Somebody aroused Joe's ire (a persistent failure to draw their blackout curtains perhaps) and one night, having had to ring the bell and remonstrate yet again, Joe burst out: 'I'd like to give them a right kick up the arse.' This wasn't like Joe at all and turned into a family joke, and a useful one too, as Dad never swore, so to give somebody a kick up the arse became known euphemistically as 'Joe Fitton's Remedy'. With Dad it even became a verb: 'I'd like to Joe Fitton him,' he'd say. And that's what I felt like this lunchtime, Joe Fittoning Michael Heseltine, and Mr Brown too.

20 January. Note how much pleasure I get from anemones. I love their Victorian colours, their green ruffs and how, furry as chestnuts, the blooms gradually open and in so doing turn and arrange themselves in the vase, still retaining their beauty even when almost dead, at every stage of their life delightful.

I used to like freesias for their scent (and when I was at Oxford and bought them in the market two or three flowers would scent a room). But florists (and certainly Marks and Spencer) have now bred a strain which has no scent at all except faintly that of pepper. Considering this is a flower which is not much to look at, the whole point of which is its scent, this must be considered a triumph of marketing.

24 January. Somebody writes from the *New Statesman* asking me to contribute to a feature on Englishness, the other contributors, the letter says, 'ranging from Frank Bruno to Calvin [*sic*] MacKenzie'. I wish, as they say.

26 January. The papers are full of the beastliness of Eric Cantona who kicked some loud-mouthed, pop-eyed Crystal Palace supporter and got himself suspended for it . . . for ever, some soccer lovers hope. Currently Walker's Crisps are running a TV advert in which Gary Lineker, returning home from Japan, sits on a park bench beside a little boy and then, saying 'No more Mr Nice Guy,' steals the child's crisps. If Walker's were smart they would make a sequel in which Lineker, making off with the bag of crisps, is stopped in his tracks by Cantona who kicks him and makes him give the crisps back. Then the British Public would be thoroughly confused.

13 February. To Westminster for the last two days of shooting *The Abbey* documentary. Happily they coincide with one of the rare showings of the 13th-century Cosmati pavement in the Sanctuary. Knowing it only from photographs, I'm slightly disappointed when the carpets have been rolled back to see the original. Portions of it, particularly the bits of *opus sectile* in black and white, I'd like to grub up and frame, but some of it seems crude and the colours vulgar and I've no means of knowing whether the parts I like are the original stones and the vulgar bits Victorian renovation or the other way round. Certainly the much later tiles round the altar are more faded and pleasing than the harsh reds and blues of ancient glass in the original work (which probably come from medieval Islam); and the purple and green porphyry, which must of its nature be original, isn't to my taste at all. During the day the pavement is roped off but once the Abbey is closed I am allowed to walk across it in my stockinged feet.

14 February. A courier, a good-looking dark-haired boy, comes this Valentine's Day with a single rose for someone next door. Having rung the bell, he waits with his rose and clipboard: today's Rosenkavalier needs a signature.

Huge crowds at the Abbey for the unveiling of the Oscar Wilde window, both transepts full with people standing (some on chairs) to catch a glimpse of the speakers. The most notable is of course the 90-year-old Gielgud, black overcoat, velvet collar, a half-smile always on his lips as of someone prepared to indulge the world in its fondnesses but with his thoughts already elsewhere. Michael Denison and Judi Dench do the handbag scene from *The Importance*, J.G. reads from *De Profundis* and Seamus Heaney gives the address. The congregation look sober and worthy, Gay Pride not much in evidence with the wreath laid by Thelma Holland, Wilde's daughter-in-law, a link which vaults the century.

After the congregation clears we do cutaway shots of the window, 'the little patch of blue', and that's the end of our filming in the Abbey which has been going on, on and off, since last September. As the crew packs up I go and have another look at the tomb of Henry III's children in the south ambulatory which I've just read incorporates one of the medieval relics of the Abbey, the stone supposedly with the imprint of Christ's foot when he took off for the Ascension. I'm not sure if this is the square stone on the front of the tomb or the roundel on the top but I lay my hand on both as maybe pilgrims did once, though why I'd find it hard to say. It's a beautiful tomb, the arch still with traces of vermilion paint and black and green foliage, the top studded with bits of mosaic. Not expecting any elegiac feelings (I will after all be coming back to record the commentary), I am surprised to find how sad I am the shoot is over and that I shan't be coming here regularly as I have the last five months.

17 February. To Leeds where the decent cupola'd building on Woodhouse Moore that housed both the public library and the police station has been converted into a pub, The Feast and Firkin. The Woodman, the pub opposite St Chad's, has been renamed Woodies Ale Bar, in homage, I suppose, to *Cheers*. The more real community has dwindled in the last twenty years the more cheap marketing versions of it have multiplied.

20 February. In the evening to the National Gallery for a private view of the Spanish Still Life exhibition which I don't expect to like but do, very much, particularly the Cotáns, vivid vegetables of horticultural-show proportions (tight cabbages, huge cardoons) strung up in dark boxes as if for the strappado. There are some ravishing Zurbarán still lives, the most appealing a beaker on a dish with a rose belonging to the Saltwood Bequest and so to Alan Clark who is somewhere about, though I don't see (or hear) him. Then there are lots of terrible flower paintings before some wonderful Goyas in the last room, including a heap of dead fish. The look in the eye of one of the dead bream seems familiar then I realise it's also the look in the eye of the man throwing up his hands before being shot in *The Third of May*. Find no one to hand with whom I can quite share this (probably mistaken) perception so come away.

22 February. Switch on *Newsnight* to find some bright spark from, guess where, the Adam Smith Institute, proposing the privatisation of public libraries. His name is Eamonn Butler and it's to be hoped he's no relation of the 1944 Education Act Butler. Smirking and pleased with himself as they generally are from that stable, he's pitted against a well-meaning but flustered woman who's an authority on children's books. Paxman looks on undissenting as this nylon-underpanted figure dismisses any defence of the tradition of free public libraries as 'the usual bleating of the middle classes'. I go to bed depressed only to wake and find Madsen Pirie, also from the Adam Smith Institute for the Criminally Insane, banging the same drum in the *Independent*. Not long ago John Bird and John Fortune did a sketch about the privatisation of air. These days it scarcely seems unthinkable.

28 February. There have been football riots in Bruges, where Chelsea have been playing, with, responsible for their suppression, the commissioner of police for Bruges, one Roger de Bris. This gives quiet pleasure as it's also the name of the transvestite stage director in Mel Brooks's *The Producers*, who makes his appearance bare-shouldered and in a heavy ball gown.

7 March. Our pillar box is now emptied at 9 a.m. not by the Royal Mail van but by a minibus marked Portobello Car and Van Hire.

10 March. To Bradford for the provincial premiere of *The Madness of King George*. The Lord Mayor is present and R. sees him afterwards in the Gents, mayoral chain round his neck, trying to have a pee. His badge of office dangles just over his flies so that he has to take great care not to piss on it. Eventually he slings it back over his shoulder rather like a games mistress and her whistle.

29 March. Nell Campbell calls from New York to say that Don Palladino, maître d' at the Odeon and Café Luxembourg, died last night. He was very gay in his concerns, even the historical ones. 'Yes,' Nell says, 'we like to think he's with Marie Antoinette now.'

17 April. Easter Monday. On Saturday with T. and R. to Oxford, where we find most places (the University Museum, the Ashmolean) closed. Also all the colleges, and not just not open to visitors, but the gates actually locked. I ring the bell at Exeter but there is no answer so we hang about until an undergraduate goes in (entry now by Swipecard). An expressionless figure in the lodge, looking like a middle-ranking police inspector, says the college is closed. I say I'm a Fellow which produces no change of expression but at least procures us admission, and we go into the garden and look at the grandstand view of Radcliffe Square, now without cars much improved.

The day is redeemed when going back via Dorchester we call in at the Abbey to look at the 13th-century crusader tomb of a knight struggling to draw his sword in death. The naturalism of the pose and the fall of the draperies make it extraordinarily impressive and modern-seeming. I've no notion whether the sculptor was English or French though, as R. says, if it were in a German church he would certainly be known as the Master of the Crusader Tomb. What contributes to its freshness is that whereas a nearby 15th-century tomb is covered in centuries of graffiti, the knight, perhaps because he was originally under a grille, is virtually untouched.

24 April. The Tories are now in a great hurry to mop up any corners of the state that have not been privatised, presumably against probable failure at the next election. Next on the list is the nuclear industry, not a popular project as the de-commissioning of the older nuclear power stations has no commercial attractions and safety considerations are likely to be skimped. But of course it will provide the Government with some election pin-money, which is what it wants. The real driving force, against all common sense and reason, is ideology. When the Germans were withdrawing from Italy in 1944 and were short of trains, troops and every other resource, priority was given when crossing the Po not to military formations but to the transports involved in the last-minute deportation of the Italian Jews. The analogy will be thought offensive but it is exact. Ideology, as I think Galbraith wrote, is the great solvent of reason.

1 May. A drunk clinging onto the railings in Inverness Street gathers himself up to speak.

'Excuse me, squire, but how far has yesterday gone?'

'Sorry?'

'How far has yesterday gone?'

I say helpfully that it's six o'clock.

'Six o'clock? Six o'clock? What sort of fucking answer is that?'

Of course I could have said: What sort of fucking question was it in the first place?

3 May. Invited to Speech Day at Giggleswick, where the Guest of Honour is to be Lord Archer. Write back and say I can't come but I look forward to being invited next year when doubtless the guest will be Bernard Manning. Giggleswick doesn't have many distinguished old boys though one which it never seems to acknowledge was the critic James Agate. This reticence may be on account of Agate's well-known propensity to drink his own piss.

13 June. Three police acquitted in the case of Joy Gardner who died after being gagged with 13 inches of tape, a restraining belt and leg irons. It's not unexpected. I can't offhand recall any serious case in the last ten years in which the police have been found guilty and punished. Or even sacked.

20 June. Three jokes from George Fenton.

1. Man has bad pains in his bum. Friend says it's piles so he applies various creams which do no good. Another friend says: 'No, creams are useless. What you want to do is have a cup of tea then take the tea leaves and put them up your arse. It's like a poultice. Do the trick in no time.' So whenever the man has a cup of tea he puts the tea leaves up his bum. No joy. When at the end of the week he's no better he goes to the doctor. The doctor tells him to take his trousers down, looks up his bum and says: 'Yes. Well, there are two things to say. One is that you're quite right, you do have piles. And the other is, you're going to go on a long journey.'

2. Devout Jewish man is desperately anxious to win the lottery. Goes to the synagogue and prays that he may win. Saturday comes round, but he doesn't win. Goes to the synagogue again and remonstrates with God, pointing out how often he comes to the synagogue, how devout he has been etc etc. Saturday comes round again and again he doesn't win. Back he goes to the synagogue and prays again to God, this time in despair. Suddenly the clouds part and there is a figure with a grey beard leaning down between the clouds: 'OK. So you want to win the lottery. But please, meet me halfway: *buy a ticket.*'

3. Man buys green bottle at car-boot sale. Rubs it. Out pops genie. Offers him one wish. Man asks to be the luckiest man in the world. The wish is granted and the genie disappears. Next week the man wins millions on the football pools and takes his mates out to celebrate. He

explains about his luck but they don't believe him, saying: 'Right, if you're so lucky, try pulling that beautiful Indian bird.' So the man goes over and chats her up and sure enough she's all over him, they go back to her place and have a fantastic time. In the morning he wakes up, and looks down at her beautiful naked body and thinks how lucky he is. She is still fast asleep and as he gazes at her sleeping face, he sees the little red spot she has on her forehead. Gently he scratches it – and wins a Renault 5.

All these come from musicians, George the only one of my friends who still hears jokes or moves in circles that tell them, or make them up.

27 June. Most adverse comments on John Redwood's appearance remark on his resemblance to Mr Spock or someone from outer space. Actually he looks like Kenneth Williams in one of those roles (Chauvelin, for instance) when the eyes suddenly go back and he goes wildly over the top. The smirking crew around Redwood are deeply depressing, Tony Marlow and Edward Leigh both fat and complacent and looking like two cheeks of the same arse. It's all so sixth-form, the prefects in revolt.

4 July. Letter this morning saying the Tokyo production of *Wind in the Willows* is to be revived for two weeks in August, the revival to be super vised by a Nigel Nicholson. Mole and Ratty as Harold and Vita now (and Violet Trefusis as Mr Toad).

29 July, Ménerbes. Stripping some redcurrants this evening reminds me how when I was writing both *Getting On* and *The Old Country* I could never think of something for the wife to do while the husband was talking. In *Getting On* I think I made Polly top and tail gooseberries and in *The Old Country* I even gave Bron some flowers to press (I go hot with shame at the thought). Of course, if I'd had any sense I would have seen that if it was so hard to think what it was the woman should be doing then there was something wrong with the plays or that this was what the plays should have been about, as in a way it was. Neither of the wives had seemingly ever had a job, an omission I had to some extent recti-fied by the time I got to *Kafka's Dick*, when the wife has at least been in employment at some period (she was an ex-nurse). But again the men did the jobs and most of the talking. In *Enjoy*, which is set in Leeds, the women do most of the talking, which is how it always used to be when I was a child. It was only when I got to London that the men started talking and the women fell silent.

8 August. A new strategy for not working: empty the fluff not only from the sieve on the dryer door, which is routine, but from the grilles on the machine itself. This involves prising off the plastic covers and poking about with a skewer to dislodge the fluff that has fallen through. A quarter of an hour can be made to pass in this way.

9 August. Surprised to find from today's *New Yorker* that Madame Chiang Kai-shek is still alive at 97. My surprise is less surprising when I realise I have her inextricably confused with the Duchess of Windsor who I know is dead. Both, in Geoffrey Madan's words, 'part governess, part earwig'.

11 August. In the yard at the back of Camden Social Services in Bayham Street a mound of tangled Zimmer frames.

14 August. Toothache, and I make an appointment for the dentist. The trouble is almost inevitably deep under one of my many caps and bridges. It will be like having to go through the dome of St Paul's in order to repair the floor of the crypt.

16 August. Life in Camden Town. As I come in this afternoon two young men are sitting by the garden wall drinking cans of beer. One looks like a Hong Kong Chinese, the other is Australian, fair, brown and not unlike the actor Jack Thompson who used to figure in sheep-shearing films. I sit and work at my table, where I can hear the murmur of their talk. Then the Australian, slightly reluctantly but egged on by the Chinese, goes over and has a piss in the gateway of number 61. Before they go the Chinese does the same; had they not seen me come in mine would doubtless have been the gateway they would have patronised. I groan inwardly at the loutishness of it all (the beer cans just left on the pavement), but a couple of hours later I am coming up Inverness Street when a large Mercedes draws up outside the Good Mixer and the two pavement drinkers get out. I suppose they're from the fashionable music fraternity which now heavily patronises the pub, the crowd at weekends spilling right across the road which means the street is seldom effectively cleaned, and always littered with cans and broken glass first thing in the morning when I go down for my paper. The pleasures of drinking here must be diminished (or who knows, heightened) by the squalor of the setting, the recycling bins opposite, every doorway a urinal, the pavements caked in the market's grease and muck. Such squalor is these days about average for Camden Town, the end of Inverness Street now a haunt for drug dealers.

17 August. 'Grounded' meaning a withdrawal of privileges is a word I dislike. It's off the television (*Roseanne* notably) but now in common use. (I just heard it on *Emmerdale Farm*, where they probably think it's dialect.) I would almost prefer 'gated', deriving from Forties public school stories in *Hotspur* and *Wizard*.

Other current dislikes: 'Brits'; 'for starters'; 'sorted'; and (when used intransitively) 'hurting'.

9 September. Drive into Oxfordshire, stopping first at Ewelme to look at the church. The village is too manicured for my liking, though the mown lawns and neat gardens don't quite eliminate an air of rural brutishness I often sense in Oxfordshire. Note features in the church I'd forgotten – the gilded angel with outstretched wings which acts as part of the counterweight for the font cover and the angels that spread their wings to support the aisle roof. Then on through terrible Didcot to Faringdon and Buscot Park which belongs to the National Trust. The house is well set with beautiful long vistas down alleys of trees to water gardens and a lake and from the terrace at the back vast views over Oxfordshire. Inside, though, it's disappointing with a Rembrandt that I'm sure isn't, a nice Ravilious of the house but none of the rooms informed by vision or individual taste and like a rather dull country house hotel. As we're going out a scholarly man, whom I'd seen carefully studying the catalogue, pauses by the desk.

'Could you tell me,' he asks of the lady on duty, 'how the first Lord Faringdon made his money?'

She gives him a vinegary look as if the question were in very bad taste: 'I've no idea.'

11 September. Nick Leeson, the errant young man from the Singapore Stock Exchange, is interviewed in his Frankfurt prison by David Frost, the interview, made by Frost's production company, broadcast by the BBC at ten this evening. The papers, which have had a preview, are full of Leeson's self-justifications, but nobody seems to question the propriety of broadcasting such an interview in the first place; and like so many of the interviews Frost is involved with it's a pretty seedy affair. Not that Frost isn't highly respectable but his rise as a political commentator is in direct proportion to the decline of respect for politicians. Major, Blair and Ashdown meekly trot along to be lightly grilled by the heavily made-up Frost, and indeed use the occasion for statements of policy and matters of national importance. It's as if Jesus were to undertake the feeding of the Five Thousand as a contribution to *Challenge Anneka*.

[Much is explained when in October the filming of the Leeson story is announced, starring Hugh Grant and produced by D. Frost.]

14 September. The house next door is empty and I have got their mice. Having watched a mouse last night gambolling away among the poison pellets behind the gas oven, I find this morning that it (or a colleague) is in one of the humane traps. I have been told mice have a good homing instinct so I take the trap up to the railway bridge, give the box a shaking to disorientate the occupant (and teach it a lesson) then empty it onto the railway line. I find I am a little cheered by this.

19 September. A young man walks up the street dressed with casual care in blue T shirt and narrow jeans and with the loose bouncing walk I associate with an (albeit humble) assumption of moral superiority. Say this to K. 'Yes. He walks like a vegetarian flautist.'

28 September. Pass a gown shop off Manchester Square called Ghost and Foale. Mention this to Mary-Kay as seeming an unusual name. Not at all, apparently, as both names are famous and fashionable in the world of frocks. More amusing to her was my calling it a gown shop.

19 October. To Accord near Poughkeepsie in New York State where Don Palladino had a house which Lynn has been clearing out before the new owner takes over next week. It's a little clapboard cottage, idyllically situated on the bank of a broad shallow river backed by woods and looking across meadows to the distant Catskills. A huge catalpa shades the house and beyond it a derelict canal. We roll up matting and put it on top of the van along with two bikes, then pack the inside with bedding and books and lampshades. When it's done I sit on the brick terrace in the warm sunshine looking across the river and watching the dozens of birds, most of them strange to me, even the pheasants looking more like turkeys, as they peck about among the sweetcorn.

Emptied, the little house still manages to be a temple to Marie Antoinette. Her bust is on the mantelpiece, books about her line the stairs and there is French wallpaper incongruously on the walls and a few damp tapestried chairs marooned in the dining-room. Most of this is to be left for the new owner, though a garrulous handyman hangs about hoping to pick up what he can. 'Of course he loved it here, only I gather he got sick.' We walk along the dried-up canal for a bit, before driving to Rhinebeck for some tea, then back along the Taconic

Parkway through the famed autumn tints to a huge red sun setting over New York.

21 October. Lynn has some firewood delivered, around thirty neat boxes, panniers almost, which, stacked in the hall, look so tidy and pleasing they might be an installation or an art object. These thirty or so boxes apparently constitute a *cord* of wood (128 cubic feet), which is how wood is still ordered in this old-fashioned city. I doubt if it is in London and certainly not in rural Yorkshire.

Language: Disabled Toilet in America becomes Handicapped Bathroom.

22 October. We pick up a cab at Lincoln Center tonight and drive down to 19th Street. The cab-driver says into a small microphone: 'The fare is five dollars fifty. Would you please pay the cashier?', whereupon a white rabbit, presumably a glove-puppet, appears in the interconnecting hatch and makes a bow. Lynn pays the rabbit, the rabbit bows again, the cab-driver says, 'Have a good evening,' and off he goes.

31 October. At the bottom of the moving walkway in the local Marks and Spencer's there often lurks a security man. He will be squinting under the plastic partition at the upper floor, keeping an eye on putative shoplifters (or, at any rate, their ankles). This particular corner of the store is where they sell underwear, the theft of which is, I suppose, more common and more of a thrill than nicking the broccoli, say. The security men wear beige uniforms, short-sleeved shirts and peaked caps with that steep neb which I still associate with redcaps, the military policemen who, when I was in the Army, were one of the hazards of mainline stations, always lying in wait for timid and slipshod soldiers like me. The other paramilitary force in Camden are the parking wardens who are also kitted out in peaked caps, theirs having scarlet ribbons. Though inoffensive-looking there's something not quite right about them either; they remind me of the forces of the wicked Regent in films like *The Prisoner of Zenda*, decent enough but misled.

12 November. The judicial murder of Ken Saro-Wiwa and his colleagues in Nigeria properly outrages world opinion. Quite apart from the merits of his case the death of this writer has more readily caught the public imagination for a very simple reason – the euphonious nature of his name. Ken is a good ordinary start but with Saro-Wiwa the name takes flight and, unlike many African names, is both easy to say and brings with it an almost incantatory pleasure. So in the last few days many people have been enjoying saying his name. Not, of course, that this did him any good.

28 November. Cycling down to the West End, I'll often cut out the boring windswept stretch of Albany Street by going the back way along Stanhope Street, through the council estate that was built in the Fifties over what was once Cumberland Market. The tower blocks are named after beauty spots: Derwentwater, Dentdale, all of them (I see the connection now) places in what was Cumberland. Between two of the blocks is a grass plot and in the far corner of it a curved concrete screen about ten foot high with a doorway opening on either side, this screen, and the slightly raised platform on which it stands, converting the unkempt patch into a kind of auditorium. There's no sign that it's ever used as such but I imagine that this is what it was intended for, part of some vision for this estate back in those still-hopeful days after the war. Did the architect, I wonder, in his presentation to the planners, sell this podium as a place where pageants could be held, bonny babies paraded or even Shakespeare performed? Probably, as architects fleshing out their bleak vision are ever sanguine and never modest. Nowadays this little Epidaurus off the Hampstead Road looks a touch forlorn; the scrubby grass is strewn with litter and matted with dogdirt, the shops opposite operate behind steel shutters, the estate is riven with racial conflict and nobody takes the stage.

8 December. Trying to find someone a Meccano set for Christmas, I'm reminded of a couple, friends of Russell H., who had a son of twelve or so who they were worried might be growing up gay. However, they were greatly heartened when the boy said that what he wanted for Christmas was a Meccano set. Delighted by what they saw as an access of butchness, they bought him the biggest set they could find; it was a huge success and he took it to his room and played with it for hours. The day came when the boy asked to show them what he had been making and they were made to wait with their backs turned while he manoeuvred it carefully into the room. When they turned round the boy stood there shyly peeping at them from behind a vast Meccano fan.

4 January 1996

Notes on Contributors

Perry Anderson teaches history at UCLA. His books include *Lineages of the Absolutist State* and *A Zone of Engagement* (Verso).

Neal Ascherson, for many years a foreign correspondent, writes a column for the *Independent on Sunday*. He has written books about Africa and about Eastern Europe. *Black Sea* was published by Cape in 1995.

Alan Bennett's collection of his pieces from the *London Review of Books*, *Writing Home*, was published by Faber in October 1994. It sold over 200,000 copies in hardback, and was top of the bestseller list for three months. The film of his play, *The Madness of King George*, won several awards.

Terry Castle's *The Female Thermometer: 18th-Century Culture and the Invention of the Uncanny* came out from Oxford University Press in 1995. She teaches at Stanford.

Stanley Cavell teaches philosophy at Harvard. His works include *Pursuits of Happiness*, about Hollywood films; *A Pitch of Philosophy: Autobiographical Exercises* appeared from Harvard in 1994. *In Quest of the Ordinary* came out in the US the same year.

Amit Chaudhuri's prize-winning first novel, *A Strange and Sublime Address*, was published in paperback in 1992. His second novel, *Afternoon Raag*, won the 1994 Encore Award and the Southern Arts Literature Prize.

Linda Colley is Richard M. Colgate Professor of History at Yale. She is the author of *In Defiance of Oligarchy: The Tory Party 1714–1760*, *Namier* and *Britons: Forging the Nation*, which was published in paperback by Pimlico in 1994.

Jenny Diski's new novel, *The Dream Mistress*, was published in 1996. She is the *Mail on Sunday*'s radio critic.

Jerry Fodor's *The Elm and the Expert* was published by MIT in 1993. He is a professor of philosophy at Rutgers and at the City University of New York Graduate Center.

Paul Foot writes for *Private Eye* and the *Guardian*. He is the author of *Murder at the Farm*, about the Carl Bridgewater affair, *Who Killed Hanratty?*, *Who Framed Colin Wallace?* and several other books about British justice and its miscarriages. A collection of his essays, *Words as Weapons*, many of which appeared originally in the *London Review of Books*, was published by Verso in 1992.

Stephen Frears's films include *My Beautiful Laundrette*, *The Grifters*, *Dangerous Liaisons*, *The Snapper* and, most recently, *The Van*.

Ian Hamilton has written biographies of J.D. Salinger and Robert Lowell and his *Keepers of the Flame: Literary Estates and the Rise of Biography* is available in paperback from Pimlico. A collection of his essays, *Walking Possession*, came out in 1995 and he edited *The Oxford Companion to 20th-Century Poetry in English*. He has written a book about Paul Gascoigne, *Gazza Italia*, and edited *The Faber Book of Soccer*. He is currently writing a book about Matthew Arnold.

Christopher Hitchens writes the Cultural Elite column for *Vanity Fair*. His books include a collection of journalism, *For the Sake of Argument*; *Blood, Class and Nostalgia: Anglo-American Ironies*; *International Territory: The United Nations 1945–1995*, featuring the photographs of Adam Bartos; and a book about Mother Teresa, *The Missionary Position*.

Fredric Jameson directs the Literature Programme at Duke University. His most recent books include *Postmodernism, Or, the Cultural Logic of Late Capitalism*; *The Geopolitical Aesthetic*; *Late Marxism*; *The Seeds of Time*.

Barbara Johnson is Fredric Wertham Professor in the departments of English and Comparative Literature at Harvard University. She is author of *The Critical Difference*, *A World of Difference* and *The Wake of Deconstruction*.

R.W. Johnson is the director of the Helen Suzman Foundation in Johannesburg. He is the author of, among other books, *The Long March of the French Left, The Politics of Recession* and a collection of essays, *Heroes and Villains. Launching Democracy in South Africa*, which he edited with Lawrence Schlemmer, was published by Yale in 1995.

Frank Kermode's books include *Romantic Image, The Sense of an Ending, An Appetite for Poetry* and *The Uses of Error. Not Entitled: A Memoir* was published by HarperCollins in 1996.

V.G. Kiernan, an emeritus professor of history at Edinburgh University, is the author of many works on history and literature, most recently *Imperialism and its Contradictions*, essays edited by Prof. H.J. Kaye (Routledge, 1995), and *Eight Tragedies of Shakespeare: A Marxist Study* (Verso, 1996).

Edward Luttwak is director of geo-economics at the Center for Strategic and International Studies in Washington. His book, *Strategy: The Logic of War and Peace*, appeared in 1988 and *The Endangered American Dream: How to Stop the Third-Worldisation of America* was published by Simon and Schuster in 1993.

Ross McKibbin, a fellow of St John's College, Oxford, is the author of *The Ideologies of Class*. His *Cultures of Democracy* will be published by Oxford University Press in 1997.

Tom Nairn is the author of *The Enchanted Glass: Britain and its Monarchy* and *The Break-Up of Britain*. He teaches sociology at Edinburgh University and the University of Northumbria.

Nicholas Penny is Clore Curator of Renaissance Painting at the National Gallery. His *The Materials of Sculpture* was published by Yale in 1993.

Adam Phillips's books include *On Flirtation, On Tickling, Kissing and Being Bored* and *Terrors and Experts*. His latest book, *Monogamy*, was published by Faber in 1996.

Richard Rorty, Kenan Professor of Humanities at the University of Virginia, is the author of *Philosophy and the Mirror of Nature* and of *Contingency, Irony and Solidarity*.

W.G. Runciman is a senior research fellow of Trinity College, Cambridge, Chairman of Andrew Weir & Co Ltd, Joint Deputy Chairman of the Securities and Investments Board and Treasurer of the Child Poverty Action Group. The third and final volume of his *Treatise on Social Theory* will be published by the Cambridge University Press in 1997.

Edward Said's books include *Blaming the Victims: Spurious Scholarship and the Palestine Question, Musical Elaborations* and *Culture and Imperialism. Peace and its Discontents: Gaza–Jericho 1993–95*, which contains some articles written for the *LRB*, was published by Vintage in 1992. He is Parr Professor of English at Columbia.

Iain Sinclair's third novel, *Radon Daughters*, came out in 1995. *Lights out for the Territory*, a book of London essays, many of which were first published in the *LRB*, is expected from Granta in 1997. He has edited an anthology of contemporary poetry, *Conductors of Chaos*, which was published in June 1996. His other books include *Downriver*, which won the James Tait Black Memorial Prize and the Encore Award in 1991, *White Chappell, Scarlet Tracings* and *Flesh Eggs & Scalp Metal*.

Nicholas Spice works as publisher at the *London Review of Books*.

Colm Tóibín is a novelist living in Dublin. His books include *Bad Blood – I Walk Along the Irish Border, Homage to Barcelona* and *The Story of the Night*.

Jenny Turner writes for the *Guardian*.

Michael Wood teaches at Princeton. He is the author of *Stendhal, America at the Movies* and *The Magician's Doubts*, about Nabokov.

Index

Printed in Great Britain
by Amazon

38744136R00192